AN INSTITUTIONAL INVESTOR PUBLICATION

THE HANDBOOK OF
DERIVATIVE
INSTRUMENTS

INVESTMENT RESEARCH, ANALYSIS AND PORTFOLIO APPLICATIONS

ATSUO KONISHI
RAVI E. DATTATREYA

EDITORS

PROBUS PUBLISHING COMPANY
Chicago, Illinois

Library of Congress Cataloging-in-Publication Available

ISBN 1-55738-154-2

Printed in the United States of America

BC

2   3   4   5   6   7   8   9   0

DEDICATION

To my wife, Mitsuyo

Atsuo Konishi

To my wife, Goda

Ravi E. Dattatreya

Contents

Chapter 1

Introduction

Atsuo Konishi
S.B.C.M.(UK) Limited

Ravi E. Dattatreya
Sumitomo Bank Capital Markets, Inc

A derivative is commonly defined as a security whose value depends in some way upon the values of other more basic underlying securities. Examples are futures on the long Treasury Bond and the call option on IBM stock. Not too long ago, these derivatives played a secondary role in finance. They were used mainly for hedging, e.g., the short sale of a future or purchase of a put option to hedge a long position in the underlying security. Derivatives were also used by some investment managers to enhance returns, perhaps by selling covered call options on an existing portfolio. With such a limited application, many participants had the choice of learning about these derivatives or totally ignoring them. Needless to say the latter choice was the more popular one.

Today, the situation is dramatically different. Derivative products dominate the financial markets. The number of derivatives has increased several fold. Numerous futures and options are available in almost every market. In most cases, the size of the derivative market is much larger than the size of the underlying or "cash" market itself. The influence of the derivatives on the basic market is so great that the latter now follows the former. For example, many bond traders look to the Treasury futures markets in order to price Treasury bonds. The large size of the futures market and the corresponding superior liquidity and higher frequency of trading means that a trader has greater confidence in the futures price as a representation of the current market level rather than the price indication for a cash bond. As far as pricing is concerned, therefore, the roles of the derivative and the underlying seem to have been reversed: The price of the underlying security now responds to the price changes in the derivative.

There are many reasons for the success of derivatives. In a world of advanced communications, speed is everything. Market players constantly receive new information. In order to act on this information, they automatically gyrate toward the derivative market as it offers speed of execution along with an acceptable transaction cost, in addition to other advantages such as anonymity. It is simply cheaper and faster by dealing with derivatives. Liquidity is a property of a market that feeds on itself because a liquid market naturally attracts greater participation and thus achieves greater liquidity.

Another important reason for the success is the ability of a large portion of the market to quickly and reliably price the derivatives. The rapid advances in modeling and mathematical techniques and their general availability have brought an unprecedented level of comfort and confidence to the valuation of derivatives. The valuation technology will continue to play a major role in the further development of these markets in the future. A major goal of this book is to introduce several of these techniques to the reader.

Derivative products are not limited to exchange traded instruments, nor are they conceptually new. Options have always been an integral part of the financial markets in the form of loan commitments, prepayment rights and insurance contracts. Where exchange traded instruments do not exist or have been slow to develop, other types of markets have sprung up instead. The stripped zero coupon market is an excellent example. Another is the interest rate swap market, which began modestly to arbitrage the credit spreads in different markets, and which is today one of the most dynamic derivative markets in the world, with its size approaching $2 trillion. In line with this phenomenon, this book covers the usual exchange traded products, such as futures and options, as well as others such as convertible bonds and interest rate swaps.

In the current environment dominated by derivatives, therefore, the market participants do not have any alternative but to gain a good understanding of how derivative products work. Derivatives, fortunately, are not necessarily always more complex than cash securities. For example, bond futures and options on bond futures are more easy to model and value than many cash instruments such as callable bonds and mortgage-backed securities. In several cases, we can look at a derivative, such as a bond option, as representing the simpler building blocks of a cash security, such as a callable bond. This interpretation of derivatives becomes more clear if we view any security as a collection of parameters or properties such as duration and convexity. Often, a derivative highlights or embodies a single property with all other properties playing minor roles. Thus, we can use derivatives to change the character of a portfolio without adding excess bulk. For example, we can increase the duration of a portfolio by purchasing bond futures without increasing the current market value of the portfolio or without any need for additional investment. The bond future thus represents the *essence* of a bond's price volatility or duration. Similarly, an option on a bond or on the bond future can add a great amount of convexity to a portfolio, but for a much smaller a cash investment than is possible with a cash bond. Also, the option, not the bond, can add convexity without significantly increasing the duration of the portfolio at the same time. In this context, we can think of derivatives as condiments which can be used to prepare a portfolio to our taste.

Generally speaking, a derivative, to be successful, must represent the broad market. By so doing, it will appeal to most participants in that market. Secondly, it must closely follow an existing security without duplicating its function exactly. Thirdly, the underlying securities must be reasonably liquid themselves. Finally, there should not be too much drag due to regulatory, accounting, legal and tax issues. The long bond future is an excellent example of a successful derivative. They are attractive to a large number of participants as they broadly represent the long term interest rates, represented by the large and liquid long Treasury bond market. They are not an exact duplicate of a position in any one long bond. Yet they are close enough to such a position that they naturally attract arbitrageurs. The arbitrageurs can use futures positions to trade against bond positions and thus will provide the other side for those who use futures for hedging.

In financial activities, a methodology for the valuation of the different securities is an essential requirement. Invariably, this methodology includes a set of assumptions, implicit or explicit, about the market. We call the methodology along with the assumptions a *framework*. A framework should satisfy many different requirements including tractability, computational ease, etc., but there are two fundamental requirements in a framework. The first is that the assumptions in the framework should not be self-contradictory. That is, the framework should have *internal consistency*. Second, the framework should agree with the market realities. We call this property *external consistency*. The ideal situation, of course, is one in which a single, consistent, universal framework can be used to value all securities including the various derivatives. In the study of derivative products, one should look for the building blocks and the insight necessary to construct a suitable framework. The insight gained in such a study is far more valuable than the detailed knowledge of contractual particulars, numerical procedures and arcane techniques. Often, application to derivatives can highlight and expose weaknesses in commonly used thumb-rules and ad hoc procedures. For example, the still-popular use of yield as a measure of value fails totally when applied to futures and options as there are no well defined fixed cash flows in the case of these derivatives. Derivative products are an excellent touchstone for analytical frameworks.

Figure 1 shows the Capital Market Concept Chart. It starts at the bottom with simple securities in the equity, fixed income, money-market and foreign exchange areas. It ends at the top with portfolio management. The implication is that every single activity in finance can be viewed as a portfolio management activity. The conceptual network between the goal (portfolio management) and the starting point (basic securities) is spanned essentially by derivative securities. Thus, we believe that the basic securities are only just the starting point on the financial landscape, and that the derivative products are an integral part of the portfolio management process.

Derivative products began their reign of the financial markets with the introduction of financial futures and options in the early Seventies, and their dominance is expected to continue for a long time into the future.

A ROAD MAP

The chapters in this book are broadly divided into three parts. The first part covers interest rate derivatives.

We start with a descriptive discussion of the interest rate futures and options contracts traded on the Chicago Mercantile Exchange. Even though the main thrust of this book is concept and framework oriented, the contractual details cannot be ignored, and this discussion provides a flavor of these details. It is also a very good introduction to interest rate futures and options for the beginning reader. The chapter includes a discussion the Eurodollar futures contract which is among the most successful.

Bruce Peterson then provides a simple approach to modeling of fixed income futures contracts. As we stated earlier, we believe that the proper valuation of the derivative products plays a major role in the further development and broadened application in this market.

One of the most successful futures contracts has been the Treasury long bond contract, traded on the Chicago Board of

Figure 1   Capital Markets Concept Chart

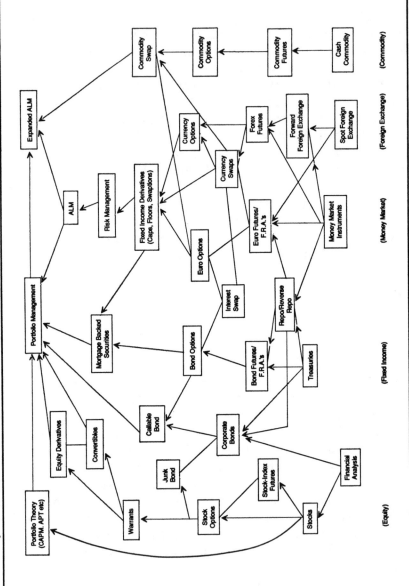

Trade. This contract has some complexity in that it allows a number of Treasury bonds to be delivered and provides some flexibility in the timing of the delivery as well. These optional characteristics are collectively called delivery options. This feature, though was largely ignored in the initial days of futures modeling, has recently gained popularity among researchers mainly because of advances in computer and modeling technology. Steve Koomer discuses these optional qualities of the futures contract in detail.

Fischer Black, Emanuelle Derman and William Toy then present a simple model to value interest rate options. To model debt options, we have to assume how interest rates behave. A reasonable and relatively simple approach assumes that the yield curve at any point in time can be fully determined by knowing one independent variable.[1] In many such models, known in literature as one-factor models, the independent variable can be interpreted as the short term rate. The model discussed in this chapter is such a one-factor model. The main input data for this model is the current yield curve. But it has an innovation: it also uses the volatilities at various maturities as input, and generates an interest rate process consistent with these volatilities. It uses the binomial approach for numerical computation which was first used in the options area by the recent Nobel Laureate William Sharpe and was later popularized by John Cox and Mark Rubinstein. The model satisfies the internal and external consistency conditions reviewed above. The internal consistency condition places several restrictions on the relative movements of rates at different maturities and their corresponding volatilities. Therefore, it is sometimes possible that a consistent binomial tree cannot be generated with a given set of data representing the yield levels at various maturities (i.e., the discount function) and the corresponding volatilities.[2]

The philosophy apparent in this chapter is to eschew complexity for its own sake; the authors demonstrate that the simple

---

1   See, for example, Ravi E. Dattatreya and Frank Fabozzi, *Active Total Return Management of Fixed Income Portfolios*, Probus Publishing, Chicago, 1989.

2   This is because the number of degrees of freedom available in a binomial model is not sufficient to handle an arbitrary set of input data. Perhaps a multinomial, but still one-factor, model can provide more flexibility.

one-factor model can be extended to include a variety of details, such as a volatility structure.[3] Thus there is no need nor is there any obvious justification for the computational and data-gathering complexity associated with multi-factor models. The one-factor model is complicated enough.

Basically, options mainly price volatility. Therefore, obtaining a good handle on volatility is arguably the most important factor in option modeling. With this in view, Ken Leong discusses the role of volatility in option pricing. Note that interest rate volatility is not only important in the modeling of options, but also in the modeling of futures of all types because of the optional features in some and the daily margin requirements in all contracts.

The interest rate swap is a fascinating derivative product that developed into a multi-billion dollar global market without any help or hindrance from the established exchanges. Raj E. S. Venkatesh, Vijaya E. Venkatesh and Ravi E. Dattatreya develop for the beginning reader an excellent introduction to this captivating market. This chapter includes discussion of swap pricing techniques and of the many varieties of swaps and associated products such as swaptions and caps.

Part I of the book concludes with a chapter by Ira Kawaller who brings together two different derivative products: interest rate swaps and the Eurodollar futures contract. The introduction of the Eurodollar contract provided significant boost to the volume and liquidity of the short term interest rate swap market by providing an effective hedging vehicle for swap providers. Yet, there are sufficient differences between a straight swap and a synthetic swap created by a strip of Eurodollar futures so that the future, rather than killing the swap market, increases participation by providing arbitrage opportunities.[4]

---

3 Though not discussed in this chapter, this model is not just for the valuation of fixed income options. It can also be used to determine the value of securities whose cash flow is not fixed, e.g., inverse floaters. It can also determine horizon returns under various scenarios as well as the probability of those scenarios. See reference cited above.

4 As we said earlier, a successful derivative closely but *not exactly* mimics another successful product. The similarity between the old product and the new creates hedging and arbitrage positions and the difference between the two products ensures that participants are available to take *both* sides of these positions by allowing for differences of opinion.

Part II deals with equity derivatives. It has been said that the 1990s will be the decade of equity and equity derivatives just as the 80s were dominated by debt and interest rate derivative products. We expect significant amount of innovation as well as modelling attention to come to the equity market in the next few years.

This part begins with a descriptive presentation of the stock index futures and options traded on the Chicago Mercantile Exchange. The stock index future discussed here joins the Eurodollar future and the long bond future as one of the most successful futures contracts.

Bruce Collins then shows how to value stock index futures and use them in a variety of applications including hedging and arbitrage. As more participants understand the valuation procedures and become comfortable with them, the size of this market as well as its breadth should increase significantly.

The key difference between forward contracts and futures contracts is that the latter are settled daily, resulting in variation margin flows. This feature affects hedge ratios and in general introduces some uncertainty in all futures transactions and is usually addressed by a technique called tailing. Ira Kawaller and Tim Koch examine this issue as it relates to the application of stock index futures and show how to manage the associated cash flow risk.

To most practitioners, the derivative products market really started in the early Seventies with the introduction of exchange traded stock options and the contemporaneous development of the Black-Scholes-Merton option model. The original arbitrage argument used in this model will continue to be a major concept driving all modeling activity in finance. Richard Bookstaber examines the modern approaches to modeling stock options and their applications. This is a very useful introduction for the beginning reader.

Equity warrants, and the more recent Americus Trust Scores, though much like stock options, appear as though they are elusive to accurate theoretical modeling. Therefore, Sidney Fried applies his considerable practical experience and knowledge on these important equity derivatives and sheds light on their valuation. In the chapter on warrants, he derives a simple empirical valuation 'formula' based on market knowledge. In the chapter on the Americus Trust scores, he discusses their key characteristics and many factors to consider in investing in them.

Perhaps the most neglected security in the area of modeling has been the convertible bond. The complexity of two independent variables—the stock price and interest rates—has no doubt been an important reason for this lack of attention. We believe, however, that the convertible is an under-utilized capital rising tool. This is especially so in the United States as the convertible has some very attractive tax benefits associated with it. As new structures such as the zero-coupon convertible are introduced that highlight these benefits, this market should grow significantly. Also, the convertible provides a smooth transition from the debt-laden Eighties to the Nineties where, we believe, equity will be king. In concluding the part on equity derivatives, Tom Ho develops an elegant approach to pricing this elusive instrument.

Part III covers the investment, hedging and trading strategies using the derivative products. By no means is this coverage exhaustive. The collection of chapters in this part is intended to provide the reader with a flavor of the types of applications that are possible with derivatives.

This part starts with a discussion of the currency futures and options traded on the Chicago Mercantile Exchange. These currency products have not yet fully realized their full potential in the portfolio management arena. However, as the financial businesses become more global in nature, as the participants become more comfortable with currency risk and as the regulating entities wake-up to the fast developing world of derivatives, the use of currency products should increase in depth and breadth.

The next chapter covers the emerging commodities swap market. David Apsel, Jack Cogen and Mike Rabin provide a very interesting approach to an are which is already well established in the futures exchanges. The swap is a natural next step for commodities.

The next two chapters deal with trading applications in fixed income futures. In the first, Eileen Baecher reviews spread trading in interest rate futures. In the second, Ira Kawaller and Tim Koch examine the trading opportunities of the cash-and-carry kind.

The recent trend toward globalization of the capital markets has increased interest in international equity portfolios. Fischer Black derives some interesting results in the area of optimizing currency risk and reward in such portfolios.

Option replication, that is, synthesizing an option with other instruments, was originally a way to price options. Simply stated, the price of an option should be equal to the cost of replicating it. The obvious second step for replication was to use it not just as a modeling technique, but as a way to create options that did not exit in the market. Portfolio insurance is such a replication strategy that synthesizes a put option on a portfolio. Richard Bookstaber looks at the subtle details of the still arcane replication technology.

There are two types of volatilities in the options markets. The first is the actual market volatility of the price of the underlying security. The second is implied volatility, that is, the volatility derived from the price of an option on the underlying. How these two numbers must be empirically related is a question debated eternally by option strategists. Stan Jonas, with a delicate touch of humor, provides an insight into this problem. Remember, however, that the definition of volatility itself is quite elusive, and implied volatility is more complex by an order of magnitude because of its dependence on an option model.

In developing the option model, Black and Scholes made several simplifying assumptions which are known not to hold strictly. Yet, the market prices of stock options exhibit remarkable agreement with the Black-Scholes model. Fischer Black provides tips on how to use the holes in Black-Scholes to trading advantage.

Interest rate swaps have traditionally been used mainly for hedging purposes. Analytically, swaps behave like interest rate futures or forwards. Therefore, they can also be used in portfolio management applications. In the concluding chapter, George Eliopoulos provides numerous examples in this innovative use for swaps.

PART I

INTEREST RATE DERIVATIVES

Chapter 2

Using Short-Term Interest Rate Futures & Options

Chicago Mercantile Exchange

INTRODUCTION

The International Monetary Market (IMM), a division of the Chicago Mercantile Exchange, introduced the trading of financial futures in 1972. Since then, the value of futures in transferring financial risk has been widely recognized and financial futures trading has experienced explosive growth.

The first financial futures were currency contracts. In 1976, the IMM introduced the three-month Treasury bill futures contract, the first interest rate futures contract based on a money-market instrument. Its success indicated the need to transfer short-term interest rate risk. In 1981, the IMM initiated trading in two other futures contracts also based on three-month money-market instruments: domestic bank Certificates of Deposit and Eurodollar deposits.

In 1984, Eurodollar futures contracts identical to those traded on the CME began trading at the Singapore International Monetary Exchange (SIMEX). Under a linked clearing program called the Mutual Offset System, Eurodollar futures can be traded on one exchange and held or liquidated at the other. Because SIMEX is open when the CME is closed, traders have access to an extended trading day.

Options on Eurodollar futures were introduced on the Index and Options Market (IOM) division of the CME in 1985, and options on Treasury bill futures were opened in 1986. Options, used separately or in combination with the futures, offer additional trading flexibilities and positioning choices.

What Are Interest Rate Futures?

The 91-day U.S. Treasury bill futures contract is an agreement to buy or sell, at a given time in the future, a U.S. Treasury bill with 91 days to maturity and a face value of $1,000,000. The three-month Eurodollar Time Deposit futures contract is an agreement to place a deposit (lend) or to take a deposit (borrow) at a given time in the future of $1,000,000 for three months in the London Interbank Market. The contracts are traded using a price index, which is derived by subtracting the interest rate from 100.00. For instance, an interest rate of 10.00 percent translates to an index price of 90.00. If interest rates move higher, the price of the contract falls; if rates move lower, the contract price rises.

What Are Options on Interest Rate Futures?

A futures option contract confers the right from seller to buyer to take a futures position at a stated price. Two types of options are traded on the CME's Index and Option Market: calls and puts. Calls are the right to buy the futures at a predetermined "exercise" price. If the futures price rises above the exercise price, the calls give the holder the right to buy the futures at a below market price. Puts are the right to sell at that fixed price. If the futures price falls below the fixed exercise price, the puts give the holder the opportunity to sell the futures at an above-market price.

Who Should Consider Interest Rate Contracts?

Banks, security dealers and other financial firms were the early users of financial futures and options for managing their interest rate exposures. Interest rate contracts are an obvious and effective risk management tool where uncertain interest income and expense are integral parts of a business.

Interest expense is, in fact, an important expense component in nearly any type of business because interest rate volatility can have a major impact on earnings and cash flows. Any firm with a substantial interest rate exposure—temporary or permanent—should investigate the risk-minimizing benefits that financial futures and options can provide. The money market comprises the markets for short-term, heavily-traded credit instruments with maturities of less than one year. Money market instruments include Treasury bills, commercial paper, bankers' acceptances, negotiable certificates of deposit (CDs), Federal funds and short-term loans collateralized by such securities ("repos"). The markets for these instruments are distinct, but interdependent. Their respective interest rates reflect general credit conditions with adjustments for differences in credit risk and liquidity.

The money market has expanded rapidly in recent years because of changing economic conditions. Volatile interest rates have advanced the rate of financial innovation. With the development of money market funds, small investors no longer were locked out of the money market by large minimum transaction barriers.

As both corporate and individual funds sought higher money market returns, negotiable CDs and Eurodollar time deposits (both developed in the 1960s) became key funding sources for banks. Floating rate deposits, a response to the growth of money market funds, further reduced a bank's core of stable-rate funds. As the banks found it necessary to pay money market rates for lendable funds, they became reluctant to make fixed-rate loans of longer maturities. So, through bank loans based on floating rates, even

Figure 1   3-Month T-Bill Rates: Annual Averages

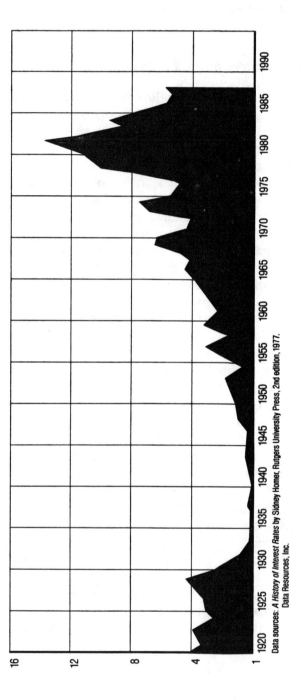

Data sources: *A History of Interest Rates* by Sidney Homer, Rutgers University Press, 2nd edition, 1977.
Data Resources, Inc.

companies too small to participate in the commercial paper or Eurodollar market became indirect money market borrowers.

Corporations today are making more aggressive use of cash management techniques. No longer willing to leave balances as unproductive, non-interest-earning demand deposits, the corporate cash manager places funds in short-term or overnight securities that have little or no credit risk. As these markets have become more liquid, corporate debt managers borrow in the commercial paper or Eurodollar markets when they offer a price advantage.

T-Bills: The Primary Money Market Instrument

U.S. Treasury bills are the foundation of the money markets because of their unique safety and liquidity. As direct obligations of the U.S. Treasury, they are considered risk-free debt instruments. So, changes in the yields on T-bills reflect "pure" interest rate movements, free of credit concerns which may dominate price movement in riskier securities. The most common maturity, 91-day (or 13-week) T-bills, are auctioned weekly by the U.S. Treasury.

The aggregate volume of T-bills outstanding has more than tripled in 10 years due to government deficits. As a consequence, a large and active dealer network has developed. Dealers—who transact their business over the telephone—buy and sell securities for their own accounts, arrange transactions with customers and other dealers, and buy debt directly from the Treasury for resale to investors. There are fewer than 40 primary dealers in T-bills, about a third of which represent commercial banks. Dealers, whose chief assets are inventories of T-bills, tend to be highly leveraged because they so easily can borrow against those inventories.

Eurodollar Time Deposits: Tapping the International Market

The volume of Eurodollars—U.S. dollars on deposit outside the United States—has grown tremendously over the past 40 years as the dollar has become the major currency used in greatly ex-

Figure 2   Growth in Money Market Funds

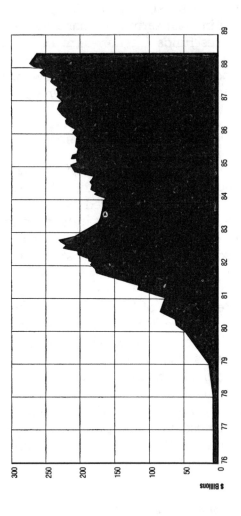

Figure 3 Growth of T-Bills Outstanding

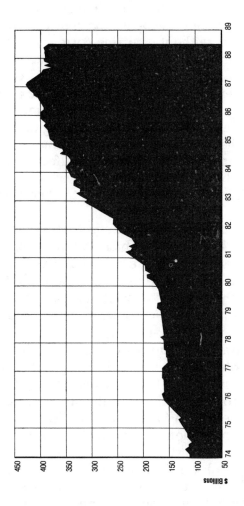

panded international trade. Eurodollar deposits in foreign branches of U.S. banks and in major foreign banks provide the base for an important international capital market. The interbank market for immediate and forward delivery of offshore dollars is deep and liquid, giving these banks the ability to fund dollar loans to foreign importers without incurring currency exchange risks.

Eurodollar time deposits are money market securities with a distinction. The deposit is not transferable, and cannot be posted as physical collateral. However, Eurodollars are a very important part of the money markets because any short-range maturity date is always available either for taking or placing deposits. A bank or corporation that has deposited Eurodollar funds can, at any point, borrow for the same maturity date. The effect is the same as the sale of a security because the funds are available again; the difference is that both transactions remain on the books until the maturity date.

Being more risky, Eurodollar deposits typically have a higher interest rate than U.S. Treasury bills. As direct obligations of the U.S. Treasury, Treasury bills are considered risk-free debt instruments. Eurodollar deposits are direct obligations of the commercial banks accepting the deposits and are not guaranteed by any government. Although they are considered low-risk investments, Eurodollar deposits are not risk-free.

Since the Eurodollar futures contract was introduced by the Chicago Mercantile Exchange in 1981 along with the Treasury bill futures contract, spreading between these two (the simultaneous purchase of one contract and sale of the other) has become increasingly popular. The reason for trading the "TED" spread is to take action based on an opinion of what will happen to the rate differential between the two instruments.

The TED spread is a "quality play." One takes action on an opinion that, all else being equal, the gap between rates required for U.S. Treasury bills and rates required for Eurodollar time deposits will widen or narrow. As the gap in rates moves, so does the gap in the prices of the respective futures instruments. If the gap in rates widens, then the gap in prices widens, and vice versa.

THE MECHANICS OF FUTURES TRADING

Although trading in the money markets takes place over the telephone between dealers, interest rate futures trading occurs in an open outcry auction market in which all traders have equal access to the best price at the time of the trade. If interest rates move higher, the price of the contract falls; if rates move lower, the contract price rises. To protect against a rising interest rate, sell the futures contract (go short). If rates rise and the futures price falls, buy back the contract at a lower price to produce a profit on the transaction. Also, to protect against falling rates, buy the futures contract (go long). If rates fall and the futures price rises, sell the contract at a higher price to produce a profit on the transaction.

Discount vs. Add-On Yield and the IMM Index

U.S. Treasury bills are sold on a discount basis and mature at face value. The smallest face value amount available is $10,000; the most actively traded unit is a face value of $1,000,000. For the right to obtain the face value some time in the future, the buyer pays less than the face amount today. The difference between the face (or maturity) value and the purchase price is the discount on the issue. T-bill yields are quoted as a 360-day discount rate based on the discount from the face amount:

$$\text{Discount Rate} = \frac{\text{Discount}}{\text{Face Value}} \times \frac{360}{\text{Days to Maturity}}$$

To trade T-bill futures, a simple index equal to 100 minus the discount rate was created. T-bill futures are traded on the basis of the discount rate traditional in the marketplace, but the price movements conform more closely to traditional commodity prices. (When the price of a T-bill rises, the IMM index price rises.)

Eurodollar futures also are traded by index price. 100 percent minus the add-on (or interest-bearing) yield determines the index price. Eurodollars are quoted on the basis of this add-on yield over a 360-day year. The add-on yield is the interest to be earned divided by the purchase price, rather than by the maturity value used with T-bills.

To convert a T-bill to an add-on yield equivalent, simply base the interest (discount) on the purchase price:

$$\text{Add–on Yield Equivalent} = \frac{\text{Discount}}{\text{Purchase Price}} \times \frac{360}{\text{Days to Maturity}}$$

Longs and Shorts

Before buying or selling a futures contract, a manager opens a trading account, depositing "initial margin" with a broker—either a cash deposit or another form of collateral. This margin serves as a good-faith deposit, guaranteeing performance. The price at which a buy or sell order is executed becomes the "entry" price; at the end of trading on that day, the contract value is "marked-to-market." The account balance is adjusted, reflecting the profit or loss based on the difference between the entry price and the "settlement" (or closing) price. This process continues for each day the position is open.

Because each futures contract covers $1 million face amount of three-month securities, each "basis point" (0.01) of price change is worth $25 (.01% × $1,000,000 × 1/4 year = $25). So in a long position, buying the contract at 91.05 and settling at 91.20, the manager is credited with a profit of 15 basis points × $25 per point, or $375. If the price falls on the next day by 10 basis points from 91.20 to 91.10, the account is then debited with a loss of $250 for that day's trading. In other words, each day the contract position is marked to the new settlement price until he sells the same contract to close the position. At that time the position is marked to the sale price.

If he sells a contract to open a short position, it works the same way in reverse. If he shorts the contract at 91.05 and it settles at 91.20, the position is debited with a loss of 15 basis points, or $375. The position is "marked to market" daily until it is closed by buying an identical contract.

Profits that bring the brokerage account above the initial margin requirement can be withdrawn while a contract position is still open; but if daily losses cause the trading account to fall below a certain level (the "maintenance margin" level), further funds are required to bring this account back to the initial margin level.

Futures Pricing

Although the cash and futures prices of a three-month security generally move in tandem, the price relationship between them, called the "basis," is affected by changes in the shape of the yield curve.

The futures price is related directly to the cash price of the deliverable security (for example, an already-issued one-year or six-month T-bill that will mature 91 days after the T-bill futures' first delivery day).[1] On the futures' delivery date the futures contract becomes a cash position so that the two prices are the same at that point. Prior to contract delivery, the futures price (yield) reflects the market price (yield) of the deliverable security, as well as the financing rate associated with holding the deliverable security until the contract delivery date.

If the short date financing rate is higher than the yield on the deliverable security, there is a cost of carrying the deliverable; and the yield implied by the futures price tends to be lower than the deliverable's yield. Conversely if the financing rate is lower than the deliverable's yield, there is a profit from carrying the deliverable and the futures yield has to be higher.

As the futures' delivery date approaches, the effects of yield curve changes on the futures price become smaller until the futures, the deliverable and the current three-month security all become identical and thus assume the same price on the futures' expiration day.

---

1   Although Eurodollar Time Deposits are not transferable, market participants can generally place or take deposits for any date, so that the same pricing mechanism is in place.

Delivery

Although relatively few contract position holders ever take or make actual delivery of securities, the integrity of the contracts rests heavily on the exchange's ability to provide an accurate, timely transfer when called upon to do so.

The two interest rate contracts have distinct delivery procedures:

- Treasury bills—the futures settlement price on the last contract trading day determines the purchase price paid by the long to the short for the delivery of new 91-day or aged six-month or one-year bills with 91 days left to maturity.

- Eurodollar Time Deposits—Because time deposits are not transferable, "delivery" is actually a cash settlement. The full contract value is not exchanged; rather, the long and short positions simply are marked to a price dictated by the cash market. More precisely, the settlement price of the futures is determined by an authoritative exchange poll on the final contract trading day. The cash market offered rate for three-month Eurodollar Time Deposits (the London Interbank Offered Rate, or LIBOR) is deducted from 100 to determine the final contract settlement price.

THE MECHANICS OF OPTIONS TRADING

Taking a position on a T-bill or Eurodollar rate by buying a call or a put option requires no margin. The price paid for the option is the absolute limit of the buyer's risk; margin security is, therefore, unnecessary.

An option buyer has the right, but not the obligation, to take a position in the underlying futures contract.[2] The decision whether to enter the futures market is entirely up to the manager as the option holder. Rather than "exercising" the option, he may re-sell it in the market, or simply let the option expire if it has no value.

---

2   Upon taking a futures position, a margin deposit will be required.

Buying a call option gives the right to take a long position in the underlying (same contract month as the option) futures at a specific price—the strike or exercise price. If the futures price rises (interest rate falls), the price of the call tends to rise. The call's likelihood of profit increases, and therefore its price rises.

Buying a put option gives the right to take a short futures position at a specific strike price. If the futures price falls (the interest rate rises), the price of the put tends to rise. As the futures price falls, the probability increases that the put will bring a short futures position at a profit.

The option "writer," who sells the option to open a position, assumes the obligation of taking a futures position opposite to the option holder if the option is exercised. The call writer stands ready to take a short futures position. The put writer stands ready to take a long futures position.[3]

The option writer sells the right to exercise in order to earn the option price with the passage of time and no movement or adverse movement in the futures price. This position carries unlimited risk, but it can be liquidated at any time before expiration by buying the same option. Many option writers limit their risks by writing the option against an opposite futures, cash or option position. This enables any loss on the written option to be offset by profit from the other position.

Strike Prices

The strike price of an interest rate option is the price at which a manager takes a futures position upon exercise. The strike prices that currently are listed for trading are at every 25 basis points.

As is the case with the futures contracts, trading for option contracts is on the March-June-September-December cycle. On the first day of trading for options in a new contract month, exercise

---

3 The writer of an option is required to post a margin deposit when the position is opened. The amount of margin required is recalculated daily until the option position is closed. The writer of an option must post margin because it is the writer who must stand ready to take a futures position at an unfavorable price at any time before the position is closed.

prices for puts and calls are listed above and below the settlement price of the underlying futures contract.

Each strike price and month represents a distinct option contract, just as puts and calls are distinct. For example, to offset a long March T-bill 93.00 call position, only the sale of that same call will do. After the first day of trading, new exercise prices for puts and calls are created based on the upward and downward movement of the underlying futures contract.

Option Prices

To simplify trading, option prices (or premiums) are quoted in terms of index points rather than a dollar value. Because the futures price, the option price and the strike price are quoted in the same terms, the price relationships are very evident. The dollar value of a T-bill or Eurodollar option price is equal to the quoted index price times $2,500. One option covers one futures contract, and like the futures contract has a minimum price change of .01 index points, equal to $25.

The price of an interest rate option is directly related to the underlying futures price, rather than to the current cash market interest rate. The option price is shaped by the following three factors.

1. **Relationship of the strike price of the option to the current underlying futures price.** If the current futures price is higher than a call's strike price, the call is said to be "in-the-money." If the call holder exercises it today, he takes a long futures position at the strike price. The difference between the futures price and the strike price is the amount he is credited, and is termed the option's "intrinsic value." Also, if the futures price is lower than the strike price of a put, that put is "in-the-money." The exercise of an in-the-money put results in a sale of the futures at an above-market price.

In general, the greater an option's intrinsic value the higher that option's price. If the option is "out-of-the-money" (currently has no intrinsic value because the futures price is lower than the call's strike or higher than the put's strike), the more out-of-the-money it is the lower the option price.

2. **Time.** The more time that remains until an option's expiration, the higher the premium tends to be. The longer time period provides more opportunity for the underlying futures price to move to a point where the purchase or sale of the futures at the strike price becomes profitable. Therefore, an option with six months remaining until expiration has a higher price than an option with the same strike price/futures price relationship and with only three months until expiration. The time component of an option's value tends to be largest when the underlying futures contract is trading near the exercise price of the option—that is, when an option is "at-the-money."

   An option is a wasting asset. As the option approaches maturity, the time value declines to zero. At expiration, the option's value is only its in-the-money amount.

3. **Volatility.** The more the futures price fluctuates, the higher the potential profit on the option. Volatility is a measure of the degree of fluctuation in the futures price. If volatility increases and all else remains the same, the option price rises; if it declines, the option price falls.

   There are a number of different measures of volatility. The following exhibit, for instance, illustrates the two most common measures: historical volatility is based on the futures contracts' price movements over a specific time period in the past. In contrast, the implied volatility is a measure of variability "implied" by a given option's price. It is the volatility underlying each of the options prices determined by the marketplace.

**Figure 4   Eurodollars: Implied Volatility vs.
            30-Day Historic Volatility**

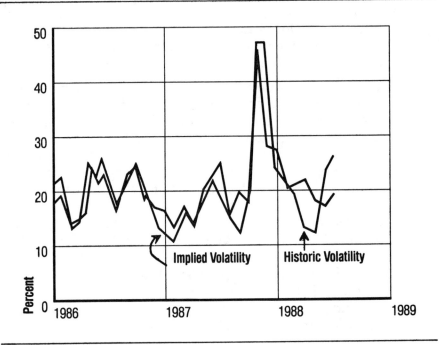

The "Delta Factor"

How will the changing price of an option relate to changes in the price of the underlying futures contract? The relationship is usually not one-for-one. A price change in the futures usually results in a smaller change in the option's price. The option's potential is related to the time remaining and to the futures' volatility, as well as to the futures price.

The option's price consists of intrinsic value, if any, and time value. The greater the intrinsic value portion of the option price, the more responsive it is to a changing futures price. On the other hand, the more time value makes up the option price, the less responsive it is to a changing futures price. The price-change relationship between the option and the underlying futures is summarized in what option theorists call the "delta factor."

The delta factor is a measurement drawn from the mathematical option pricing formula and serves several purposes. Basically, it can be used to gauge the change in the option price for a given change in the futures price. For instance, if a call's delta is 50 percent and the futures price rises quickly by 25 basis points, the call's price should rise by 12 or 13 basis points. If the futures fall, the delta predicts the loss in option value of similar magnitude.

The table below lists hypothetical deltas for some calls with the futures price at 91.50 and with various lengths of time remaining until expiration. Notice the symmetry represented. Put deltas have a very similar distribution when the strike prices across the top are reversed in order.

The deltas also can be considered ratings of the probability that the option will expire in-the-money. If the 92.50-strike call is far out-of-the-money with the futures price at 91.50, it makes sense that as the time to expiration diminishes, so does the delta. With only a week to expiration, a small futures price move does not attract many buyers to the call, so that the call's price does not react. On the other hand, the 90.50-strike call is very likely to fin-

Table 1   Hypothetical Call Deltas (with the futures price at 91.50)

Call Strikes:	90.50 (%)	91.25 (%)	91.50 (%)	91.75 (%)	92.50 (%)
Time Remaining:					
1 day	100	96	50	4	–
1 week	100	75	50	25	–
1 month	90	62	50	38	10
3 months	77	57	50	43	23
6 months	70	55	50	45	30
1 year	64	54	51	47	36

ish in-the-money with only a week to expiration. Even a small futures price change reflects a change in the potential in-the-money amount at expiration, and thus, the call's price varies nearly one-to-one with the futures.

The table illustrates that deltas vary with both changing futures prices and the passage of time. Deltas also are affected by changes in volatility. An increase in the futures' volatility drive up the time value of the options, and consequently their prices. Higher time value tends to drives up the out-of-the-money option deltas and diminish the in-the-money deltas, leaving the at-the-money deltas nearly unaffected. A decrease in volatility decreases the out-of-the-money deltas and increases the in-the-money deltas. The longer the time until expiration, the more effect a volatility change has on the option prices and deltas.

Exercising the Options

A manager may exercise an option on any business day the option is open for trading, including the day on which it is purchased. Exercise of a call results in a long futures contract at the call's exercise price, effective on the next trading day. Exercise of a put option results in a short futures contract at the put's exercise price. The account is credited the difference between the exercise price and the closing futures price, and it is required to post futures margin. The investor can hold the futures position, or liquidate it immediately with an offsetting transaction.

He would exercise the call only if the current futures price is higher than the call's exercise price, and exercise the put only if the current futures price is lower than the put's exercise price. Further, he normally would exercise an option prior to the expiration day only if it is very deep in-the-money. If the option carries any time value in addition to its intrinsic value, he profits more by selling the option and directly entering a futures position.

At expiration, an option has no remaining time value, so he would probably exercise any open in-the-money option contracts. Exercise of a T-bill option on expiration day results in a futures position that has two to four weeks of trading life remaining. On the other hand, Eurodollar option exercise on expiration day results in a cash settlement instead of a futures position. Because the Eurodollar options and futures expire on the same day and the futures are settled in cash, exercise of expiring in-the-money options results in a cash payment to the option holder of the final in-the-money amount. The CME clearing house automatically exercises expiring in-the-money Eurodollar options. However, the T-bill option is not automatically exercised because it involves depositing margin and taking a futures position.

When an option is exercised, a writer of that same option is chosen randomly and assigned for exercise. The assigned option writer's position is transferred into the futures contract on the next trading day. A written call results in a short futures position; a written put results in a long futures position. The futures position can, of course, be offset or held. If offset on the assignment day, the writer's position account is marked from the exercise price to the exit price. If held, the futures position is marked from the exercise price to the daily settlement and futures margin is required.

Expiration day exercise of T-bill options results in the assignment of futures positions to the option writers. Exercise of Eurodollar options on the expiration day, including automatic exercises, results in cash debits charged to the option writers. The relationship of the Eurodollar futures final settlement price (because the futures contract expires simultaneously) to the exercise price determines the debit amount.

HEDGING WITH INTEREST RATE FUTURES

The idea behind hedging with interest rate futures is to offset an existing interest rate risk. This offset is accomplished by maintaining an appropriate futures position that generates profits to cover the losses associated with an adverse interest rate move. Note that a properly constructed futures hedge also generates losses that offset the effects of a beneficial interest rate move. Consider these hedge examples:

Hedging a Forward Borrowing Rate

In late September, a corporate treasurer projects that cash flows will require a $1 million bank loan on December 15. The contractual loan rate is one percent over the three-month Eurodollar rate (LIBOR) on that date. LIBOR is currently 9.25 percent. The December Eurodollar futures, which can be used to lock in the forward borrowing rate, are trading at 90.45, implying a forward Eurodollar rate of 9.55 percent (100.00 − 90.45). By selling one December Eurodollar futures contract, the corporate treasurer hopes to ensure a borrowing rate of 10.55 percent for the three-month period beginning December 15. This rate reflects the bank's one percent spread above the rate implied by the futures contract.

By December 15, the existing Eurodollar rate rises to 11.10 percent, and the December futures price declines to 89.00 (reflecting an 11 percent rate). As a result, the treasurer's interest payment to the bank is $30,250 for the quarter ($1,000,000 × 12.10 percent × 1/4 year). However, the decline in the futures price produces a profit on the short futures of $3,625 (that is, 90.45 − 89.00 × $2,500 or, more simply, 145 × $25). So the net interest expense for this quarter is $26,625 for an effective annual rate of 10.65 percent.

This example illustrates that the realized cost of funds may differ somewhat from the cost of funds anticipated at the time the hedge is initiated. The difference can be accounted for by the difference between the spot market LIBOR rate and the rate implied by the futures contract at the time the hedge is liquidated. The LIBOR rate was 10 basis points higher than the rate implied by the December futures contract on December 15, accounting for the 10 basis point differential between the anticipated and realized cost of funds. In this case, the difference worked against the hedger; but in other situations the difference may prove beneficial. In general, this hedging inaccuracy, called "basis risk," is minimized the closer the loan-pricing date is to the delivery date of the futures contract.

Modifying Maturities

Asset managers can lengthen the effective maturity of short-term investment assets by buying futures contracts, and shorten the effective maturity of those assets by selling futures contracts. Liability managers can achieve the same effects by doing the opposite, i.e., selling futures to lengthen their liabilities and buying futures to shorten them.

For either assets or liabilities, hedging serves as an alternative to restructuring the portfolio in the cash markets. The use of futures may be attractive when physical restructuring is not possible (e.g., term deposits cannot be bought back prior to their maturity dates). It also may be cheaper to use futures because (a) transaction costs in the futures market may be lower than those in cash markets, or (b) liquidity conditions in the cash market would result in substantial market penalties.

Figure 5 demonstrates the use of futures to shorten the effective maturity of a Treasury bill from 174 days to 83 days so that the 83-day yield is locked in. Figure 6 shows how to extend the maturity of an 83-day Treasury bill and fix a rate of return over a longer period. (All rates and prices shown are hypothetical, and the two examples are independent. Also note that daily marking-to-market is ignored.)

Both of these examples show the purchase of the asset on the day the maturity-altering futures transaction takes place. The analysis is identical if the investment or liability is already in the portfolio. The manager merely determines the market price of the instrument on that day.

By phrasing the examples in terms of buying the T-bills, the examples show that managers also can use futures to improve performance without changing the basic maturity structure of their portfolios. Referring again to Figure 5, if on April 1 the manager held the June 23 bill with 83 days to maturity and if that bill provided a yield of less than 10.25 percent, he improves performance

Figure 5   Shortening a Treasury Bill's Maturity

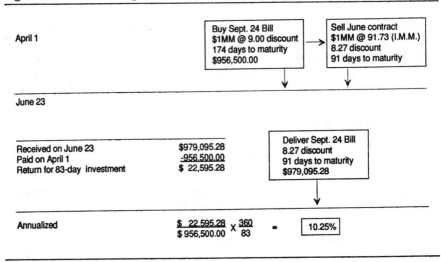

April 1	Buy Sept. 24 Bill $1MM @ 9.00 discount 174 days to maturity $956,500.00	Sell June contract $1MM @ 91.73 (I.M.M.) 8.27 discount 91 days to maturity

June 23

Received on June 23	$979,095.28	Deliver Sept. 24 Bill 8.27 discount 91 days to maturity $979,095.28
Paid on April 1	-956,500.00	
Return for 83-day investment	$ 22,595.28	

Annualized $$\frac{\$\ 22,595.28}{\$\ 956,500.00} \times \frac{360}{83} = \boxed{10.25\%}$$

Figure 6   Extending a Treasury Bill's Maturity

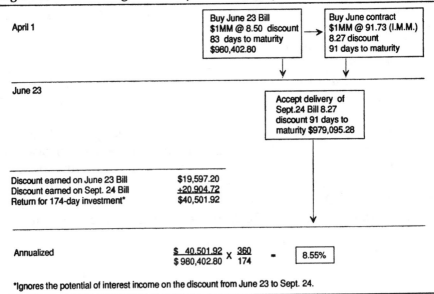

April 1	Buy June 23 Bill $1MM @ 8.50 discount 83 days to maturity $980,402.80	Buy June contract $1MM @ 91.73 (I.M.M.) 8.27 discount 91 days to maturity

June 23

Accept delivery of
Sept.24 Bill 8.27
discount 91 days to
maturity $979,095.28

Discount earned on June 23 Bill	$19,597.20
Discount earned on Sept. 24 Bill	+20,904.72
Return for 174-day investment*	$40,501.92

Annualized $$\frac{\$\ 40,501.92}{\$\ 980,402.80} \times \frac{360}{174} = \boxed{8.55\%}$$

*Ignores the potential of interest income on the discount from June 23 to Sept. 24.

by selling that bill and entering the cash/futures combination shown in that figure. Analogously, in Figure 6, any manager who held a September 24 bill earning less than 8.55 percent is better served by the cash/futures combination that results in that same maturity.

Cross Hedging to Establish Yields on Forthcoming Asset Acquisitions or Liability Issuances

The asset manager who knows that funds will be available for investment beginning on some forward date may buy futures to establish a rate of return for this investment. Also, the liability manager who plans for a forthcoming debt issuance can prearrange funding costs by selling interest rate futures. In either case, the manager may hedge even if his risk does not involve precisely the same instrument that underlies a futures contract. For example, although short-term interest rate futures contracts are traded only for 91-day Treasury bills and Eurodollars, a manager with a portfolio of, say, commercial paper could still benefit by employing a "cross hedge." In such cases, the hedge manager must allow for less-than-perfect hedge performance.

Consider the case of a corporation that plans to issue $30 million one-month commercial paper at some date in the future. Recently, interest rates have undergone major declines; but evidence of renewed upward pressure seems to be developing. The decision is made to hedge the issuance of commercial paper. The choice of which short-term interest rate contract to use is based on the comparison of historical rate changes: the instrument underlying the futures compared to the cash instrument being hedged. Following this analysis, the analyst finds that the Eurodollar contract proves to be the most desirable choice due to a consistently closer relationship to commercial paper rates than shown by Treasury bills.[4]

The number of contracts used for the hedge reflects two considerations: (a) the difference between the dollar value of a basis

---

4 The choice also should reflect a judgment that liquidity conditions are sufficient to support the trading activity.

point change on the instrument being hedged (that is a change of 0.01 percent in the interest rate) and the dollar value of a basis point change in the futures contract price; and (b) the difference between the ways the two interest rates are expected to move—a function of the differing credit risks and the different maturities of the two debt instruments.

The value of a basis point for a three-month instrument of $1 million face value equals $25 (= $1,000,000 × .0001 × 90/360) while the value of the basis point of a one-month instrument with the same face value is only $8.33 (= $1,000,000 × .0001 × 30/360) or one-third as much.

From charting the historical movement of these two rates (as shown on the facing page), it can be seen that they move together. A closer analysis reveals that one-month commercial paper rates likely will move about 75 basis points for every 100 basis point change in the three-month Eurodollar rate.[5]

The number of contracts needed to hedge each $30 million issuance is estimated:

	principal amount	$30 million
×	basis point value ratio	× 8.33 ÷ 25.00
×	correlation ratio	× 75 ÷ 1.00
	number of contracts needed	8 contracts

Therefore, the liability issuer sells eight contracts. Had the example dealt with locking in an investment yield in commercial paper, the hedger buys these contracts.

The performance of this cross hedge is largely a function of how well the rate movement relationship estimate performs. In theory, if the credit risk and maturity differences cause the rate on one-month commercial paper to move 75 percent as far as the rate changes on three-month Eurodollars, any higher costs due to an

---

5 Varying degrees of rigor can be employed in determining this ratio, from the visual approach to a more exacting statistical analysis.

Figure 7   Month Commercial Paper Rate vs. 3-Month Eurodollar Rate (LIBOR)

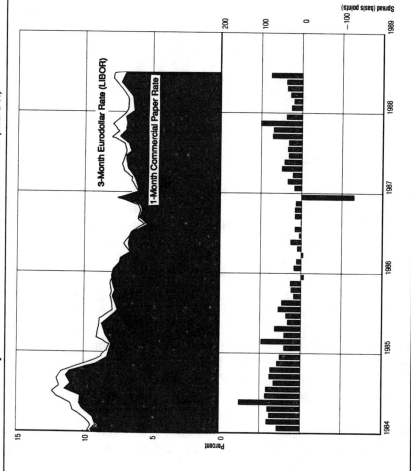

increase in the commercial paper rate is offset by profit on the futures contracts. Conversely, any lower costs due to a decline in the commercial paper rate is offset by losses on the futures contracts. In essence then, the futures hedge "locks in" a commercial paper issuing rate.

In practice, however, the credit risk/maturity relationship is rarely stable, and this introduces hedging inaccuracy. The degree to which these relationships change determines the degree to which the actual outcome differs from the expected outcome, either positively or negatively.

Locking in a Funding Rate

Consider the case of a bank that funds itself with three-month Eurodollar Time Deposits at the London Interbank Offered Rate (LIBOR). This bank has a customer who wants a one-year fixed-rate loan of $10 million, with interest paid quarterly. At the time of the loan disbursement, the banker raises three-month funds at 12.55 percent; but he has to roll over this funding in three successive quarters. If he does not lock in a funding rate and interest rates rise, the loan could prove to be unprofitable.

The three quarterly refunding dates fall shortly before the next three Eurodollar futures contract expirations in March, June and September. At the time the loan is taken down, the prices of these contracts are 86.81, 86.45 and 86.20, respectively. These prices correspond to yields of 13.19 percent, 13.55 percent and 13.80 percent. Coupled with the initial funding rate of 12.55 percent, the banker locks in a cost of funds for the year equal to the average of these four rates (13.27 percent). He sells 10 contracts for each expiration, reflecting the funding need of $10 million per quarter. Then on the refinancing dates, the banker takes in three-month Eurodeposits and simultaneously liquidates the appropriate hedging contracts by buying them back. With the March refunding, the March contracts are liquidated; June contracts are liquidated in June and September contracts are liquidated in September.

As it turns out, the banker is able to re-fund at 14.55 percent, 14.30 percent and 11.30 percent for the respective quarters. The

Table 2

Quarterly Eurodeposit costs	
Qtr. 1: $10 million × .1255 × 1/4 = $313,750	
Qtr. 2: $10 million × .1455 × 1/4 = $363,750	
Qtr. 3: $10 million × .1430 × 1/4 = $357,500	
Qtr. 4: $10 million × .1130 × 1/4 = $282,500	$1,317,500
Less the futures profits	
Mar: 10 contracts × (8681–8542) × $25 = $34,750	
June: 10 contracts × (8645–8573) × $25 = $18,000	
Sep: 10 contracts × (8620–8892) × $25 = –$68,000	– $ 15,250
Net Interest Expense	$1,332,750
Effective Rate	13.33%

corresponding futures are liquidated at 85.42 (14.58 percent), 85.73 (14.27 percent) and 88.92 (11.08 percent). The overall results are presented in Table 2.

The unhedged interest expense over the four quarters would have been 13.18 percent—lower, in fact, than the hedged expense. However, the funding rate was quite volatile over the period and easily could have resulted in a loss on the loan program. It should be recognized that effective futures hedges materially lock in an interest rate, precluding both advantage and loss from rate movement.

Recall that the banker had expected to lock up funding at 13.27 percent. In fact, funds actually were acquired at 13.33 percent, or six basis points higher. This discrepancy occurred because of less-than-perfect convergence between the cash refunding rates and the futures liquidation rates. If the bank had funded at exactly the same rate as the futures liquidation rate, the target would have been achieved. In this case, however, the actual funding over the term of the loan was, on average, six basis points higher than the futures liquidation rates. Put another way, these basis adjustments adversely affected performance.

The minimal difference between the target rate and the effective funding rate can be attributed to the fact that the refunding dates were quite close to the futures expiration dates. If the respective dates were further apart, the funding rates and the futures rates would not necessarily converge so closely.

This example of a one-year loan funded with three-month deposits is an example of a negative interest rate "gap"—that is, where shorter-term liabilities are funding a longer-term asset and rising interest rates have an adverse impact. The same basic hedging approach can be followed to remedy an overall balance sheet maturity mismatch.

HEDGING WITH OPTIONS ON INTEREST RATE FUTURES

Whenever T-bill or Eurodollar futures can be used to lock-in a rate, options on futures can be substituted to guarantee a rate floor or ceiling. As an alternative to a long futures position, which predetermines a forward investment return for an asset, a long call can be substituted. The call gives the right to buy the futures contract at a stated price. This provides a floor for the asset return while preserving the opportunity for better performance. On the other hand, instead of taking a short futures position to predetermine a liability rate, a long put option can provide protection. The put gives the right to sell the futures at a stated price, providing a ceiling for the liability rate while preserving the opportunity for a lower cost of funds.

The floor or ceiling rate provided by the option is determined by its strike price and the premium paid. The "strike yield" (100 minus the option strike price) is adjusted to reflect the cost of the option. For example, suppose the following prices are used:

Sep Eurodollar futures	91.74
Sep 91.50-strike call	.43
Sep 92.00-strike call	.18
Sep 91.50-strike call	.18
Sep 92.00-strike call	.42

Under these conditions, the user of the futures contract locks in a target LIBOR of 8.26 percent (100.00 − 91.74)—an asset return if long or a liability cost if short. Subject to basis risk, this yield is locked up regardless of whether market rates rise or fall over the hedge period.

Using the 91.50-strike call to hedge a floating-rate investment, a hedger guarantees a minimum LIBOR return of 8.50 percent for a cost of 43 basis points. In other words, the realized minimum LIBOR return is 8.07 percent as a worst case (8.50 − .43).

If the rate falls below 8.50 percent, futures prices rise and the call option increases in value. The fallen investment rate on the asset is supplemented by the profit on the call to ensure a minimum net return of 8.07 percent. On the other hand, if the rate rises above 8.50 percent, the option is worthless at expiration, and the investor simply loses the cost of the option and receives the higher market rate on the asset.

Using the 92.00-strike call, the investment hedger establishes a minimum LIBOR return of 7.82 percent (100.00 − 92.00 − .18). Why use the 92.00-strike call rather than the 91.50 strike call when the 91.50-strike call offers a higher minimum return? The question goes to an important tradeoff consideration.

While it is true that the 91.50-strike call provides a more attractive worst-case scenario, it does so for a larger up-front cost. The purchase of the 91.50-strike call pays $1,075 for this protection ($25 × 43 basis points), while the cost of the 92.00-strike call is only $450 ($25 × 18 basis points).

To hedge floating rate liabilities, put options present an analogous set of choices. A short futures contract establishes a forward

LIBOR of 8.26 percent; the 91.50-strike put provides a ceiling rate of 8.68 percent (100.00 − 91.50 + .18) for the risk of $450 ($25 × 18 basis points); and the 92.00-strike put provides an 8.42 percent (100.00 − 92.00 + .42) ceiling rate for the risk of $1,050 ($25 × 42 basis points).

Options offer a special advantage for hedging contingent liabilities or investments. If it is not certain whether funds are needed or available, interest rate options can secure a rate at the least risk. If the contingency eventually is not realized, forward or futures hedging commitments present sizable losses. The potential loss on long puts or calls, on the other hand, is limited to their purchase price, which is known in advance.

Creating a Cap-Rate Loan

Suppose a financial manager has access to funding at three-month LIBOR plus 1/4 percent, and he wants to put a limit on how high this rate rises by the time he borrows in September. In effect, he wants insurance that pays off if rates increase, but does not generate losses if rates fall. A Eurodollar put serves this purpose.

At the time of the decision (July 1), three-month LIBOR is 8 3/4 percent, the September Eurodollar futures are trading at 90.60 (9.40 percent) and the 91.00-strike put is trading at .72. At these prices, this put provides a maximum cost of funds equal to 9.97 percent (100.00 − 91.00 + .72 + .25—where .25 reflects the 1/4 percent spread above LIBOR).

When the put is purchased in July, the manager knows what he can expect in September. If LIBOR at that time is less than nine percent, the put expires worthless, and the manager simply borrows at LIBOR plus 1/4 percent. Of course, he has to add the initial .72 cost of the put option to his total cost, but even with that expense it is never higher than 9.97 percent (9.00 + .25 + .72).

In the event that LIBOR rises above nine percent, the price of the futures contract declines, and the put has intrinsic value at its expiration equal to LIBOR minus 9.00 percent. Suppose, for example, LIBOR rises to 11.50 percent at the expiration of this option contract. In this case, the cost of funds from the bank is 11.75 percent (reflecting the 1/4 percent spread) for an interest cost of $29,375 per million for the quarter ($1,000,000 × .1175 × 1/4 year). The final value of the 91.00-strike put is $6,250 (91.00 − 88.50) × $25). The profit on the put, $6,250 less its initial cost (72 bps. × $25 = $1,800), is deducted from the interest expense. Net interest expense thus is $24,925 per million for the quarter (29,375 − 6,250 + 1,800). On an annualized basis, the effective rate is calculated:

$$\frac{24,925}{1,000,000} \times \frac{360}{90} = 9.97\%$$

It is important to note that this same rate results regardless of how high market rates rise.

Insuring Against a Falling Re-investment Rate

Just as the financial manager in the prior example used puts to cap liability rates, so could he purchase calls to provide a floor rate for his short-term investment portfolio.
Consider these market prices:

Current 3-month T-bill discount	7.65%
Sep T-bill futures	92.50
Sep T-bill calls	Sep T-bill puts
92.50-strike .28	92.50-strike .28
92.75-strike .15	92.25-strike .15
93.00-strike .10	92.00-strike .10
93.25-strike .05	91.75-strike .06

If the investment manager expects falling rates, he can buy at-the-money 92.50-strike calls, which gain value quickly as rates fall. The profit on these calls serves to offset lower interest income (again, subject to basis risk) due to the lower rate available for portfolio re-investment. The 92.50-strike calls establish a floor return of the strike yield (100.00 − 92.50) less the calls' price (.28), or

7.22 percent. If the rates rise unexpectedly, the portfolio benefits, less the .28 percent cost of the calls (if they are held to expiration).

Suppose the manager expects rising rates, and desires to pay for only a calamity-type insurance at a lesser out-of-pocket expense. He buys out-of-the-money 93.00-strike calls to protect against a sharp fall in his re-investment rate. The floor return is lower (100.00 − 93.00 − .10 = 6.90 percent), but the up-front cost of protection is less.

If the expectation is for a steady rate environment, the manager secures a higher level of protection at low cost by selling puts as well as buying calls. He gives up the potential benefit from a sharp rise in rates to establish a higher floor at low cost. For example, he buys the 92.75-strike calls for .15 and sells the 92.00-strike puts for .10. His net cost is .05, and he establishes a re-investment range of 7.20 percent to 7.95 percent.

The combination of calls and puts can take any form to suit any set of expectations and hedging goals. The choice of strike prices for calls and puts allows the manager to tighten or expand the re-investment range, or to tilt it in one direction or the other.

The two preceding examples are based on the simplest buy-and-hold strategy in order to keep the exposition simple. Delta and other option-pricing parameters can be used to weight option positions and manage them. Further study yields several other option combinations that can be useful to the sophisticated trader.

CONCLUSION

Determining which hedging strategy is best—using futures or options—depends on the goals of the hedger. A futures contract essentially locks in a rate, making the holder indifferent to the way interest rates move. On the other hand, the hedger who buys an option is purchasing one-way protection with upside potential. In return for the price of the option, he receives compensation if adverse conditions evolve; but if good news develops, he is able to reap the benefits.

The choice of which instrument to use is really a judgment call, reflecting the probability of an adverse interest rate change, the potential damage of such a rate adjustment and the cost of protection. In all likelihood, different choices are made at different times, as conditions change. For that reason, an understanding of both futures and options provides managers with the greatest opportunity for effective risk management.

APPENDIX I: GLOSSARY

Add-On Yield   Standard yield calculation for Eurodollars; relates annualized interest to original principal.

Asset-Liability Management   The process by which a bank or institution monitors its portfolio of assets and liabilities to control company-wide interest rate exposure. There are three standard measures: *gap* analysis, which measures the mismatch in discrete time intervals; *ratio* analysis, typically rate-sensitive assets divided by rate-sensitive liabilities; and *profit sensitivity*, a measure of predicted changes in profit from a six-month or one-year interest rate increase of 100 basis points.

Basis   The price or yield difference between a futures contract and the underlying cash instrument; the primary risk in a hedge is a basis shift.

Call Option   An option that gives the holder the right to enter a long futures position at a specific price, and obligates the seller to enter a short futures position at a specific price, if he is assigned for exercise.

Clearing House   An adjunct to a futures exchange through which transactions executed on the floor of the exchange are settled using a process of matching purchases and sales. A clearing organization also is charged with the proper conduct of delivery procedures and the adequate financing of the entire operation.

Convergence   The movement of a futures price toward the price of the underlying cash instrument as the delivery date approaches (the basis with the deliverable instrument approaches zero). Until the settlement date draws near, there is a natural difference between the cash and futures price because of the cost of carry.

Cost of Carry   The cost of holding a commodity, including financing cost, storgage and security. In the case of interest-paying securities, a negative cost of carry (benefit of carry) exists when the security yields in excess of the short-term financing cost.

Cross Hedge   Hedging a cash market position with a futures contract for a different, but price-related commodity. Example: hedging commercial paper with Eurodollar futures.

Daily Settlement   The cash adjustment required by futures participants who are charged for losses or credited for gains at the end of each trading day.

Discount Yield   Some money market instruments, principally T-bills and commercial paper, are priced on the basis of a discount from the par value. The ratio of the annualized discount to the par value is the discount yield.

Exercise (or Strike) Price   The price at which the futures transaction takes place if the option holder exercises the option.

Forward Contract   A contractual agreement *between two parties* to exchange a commodity at a set price on a future date; differs from a futures contract because most forward commitments are not actively traded or standardized, are not market to market, and carry a risk from the creditworthiness of the other side of the transaction.

Futures Contract   A standardized contract, traded on an organized exchange, to buy or sell a fixed quantity of a defined commodity at a set price in the future. Positions easily can be closed or offset by taking the other side in the open outcry auction.

Gap Analysis   A technique to measure interest rate sensitivity. Assets and liabilities of a defined interest-sensitivity maturity are netted to produce the exposure in established time intervals. Rate sensitivity liabilities are subtracted from assets. A positive (negative) result denotes a positive (negative) gap. With an overall positive (negative) gap, an institution is exposed to falling (rising) interest rates.

Hedge   An attempt to reduce risk by either: (1) taking a futures or option position opposite to an existing or anticipated cash position; or (2) shorting a security similar to the cash position.

Hedge Management   Monitoring a hedge for basis risk and the changing sensitivity of the cash position.

Hedge Ratio   The number of futures or options contracts used in a given hedge.

Intrinsic Value   The value of the option if it were exercised immediately. It is the amount the futures price is higher than a call's exercise price; or the amount the futures price is below a put's exercise price.

LIBOR   London Interbank Offered Rate on Eurodollar deposits traded between banks. The IMM's Eurodollar deposit contract is based on the three-month LIBOR.

Long Hedge   A hedge in which the futures contract is bought (a long position). Long hedges can be used to protect the investment of future cash flows (anticipatory) and to shorten the interest sensitivity duration of a liability.

Money Market   The market in which short-term instruments are issued and traded. Money market instruments have a maturity of one year or less and include T-bills, commercial paper, CDs, bankers' acceptances and repurchase agreements.

Put Option   An option that gives the holder the right to enter a short futures position, and obligates the seller to enter a long futures position at a specific price if he is assigned for exercise.

Short Hedge   A hedge that involves the selling (shorting) of a futures contract. A short hedge guards against a price decrease in the underlying commodity; a short position in interest rate futures protects the hedger from rising rates.

Time Value   The part of the option price that is not intrinsic value. It is the risk premium demanded by the option seller, and depends on the relationship of the futures price to the exercise price, the volatility of the futures price and the amount of time remaining until expiration.

Volatility   The degree of price fluctuation in the futures contract. Volatility is commonly defined as one standard deviation of price moves over a one-year period, expressed as a percentage of the current price. One standard deviation added to and subtracted from the current futures price describes the range which encompasses two thirds of all price moves in the sample.

APPENDIX II: FOLLOWING CME PRICES

Trading activity can be monitored daily in the business pages c most major newspapers. The following are illustrations of the wa these prices are shown.

Futures

1   Contract delivery months that currently are traded.

2   Prices represent the open, high, low and settlement (or closing) price for the previous day.

3   One day's change in the settlement price.

4   The interest rate implied by the settlement price.

5   One day's change in the futures' interest rate-equal and opposite to change in the settlement price.

6   Number of contracts traded in the previous two trading sessions.

7   The number of contracts still in effect at the end of the previous day's trading session. Each unit represents a buyer and a seller who still have a contract position.

8   The total of the right column and the change from the prior trading day.

Eurodollar (IMM)—$1 million; pts of 100%

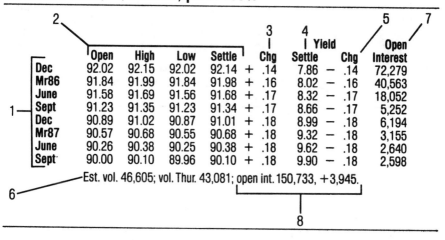

	Open	High	Low	Settle	Chg	Yield Settle	Chg	Open Interest
Dec	92.02	92.15	92.02	92.14 +	.14	7.86 −	.14	72,279
Mr86	91.84	91.99	91.84	91.98 +	.16	8.02 −	.16	40,563
June	91.58	91.69	91.56	91.68 +	.17	8.32 −	.17	18,052
Sept	91.23	91.35	91.23	91.34 +	.17	8.66 −	.17	5,252
Dec	90.89	91.02	90.87	91.01 +	.18	8.99 −	.18	6,194
Mr87	90.57	90.68	90.55	90.68 +	.18	9.32 −	.18	3,155
June	90.26	90.38	90.25	90.38 +	.18	9.62 −	.18	2,640
Sept	90.00	90.10	89.96	90.10 +	.18	9.90 −	.18	2,598

Est. vol. 46,605; vol. Thur. 43,081; open int. 150,733, +3,945.

Options

1 Most active strike prices*

2 Expiration months*

3 Closing prices for calls and puts.

4 Volume of options transacted in the previous two trading sessions. Each unit represents both the buyer and the seller.

5 The number of option contracts (each unit represents both a long and a short) that were still open at the end of the previous day's trading session.

Eurodollar (CME)—$1 million; pts of 100%

EURODOLLAR (CME) — $1 million; pts of 100%

Strike Price	Calls — Settle			Puts — Settle		
	Dec-C	Mar-C	Jun-C	Dec-P	Mar-P	Jun-P
9050	1.64	1.48	1.26	. . .	0.03	0.14
9100	1.14	1.04	0.91	. . .	0.09	0.27
9125	0.89	0.84	0.76	. . .	0.13	0.35
9150	0.65	0.67	0.62	0.01	0.20	0.45
9175	0.43	0.51	0.50	0.05	0.29	0.56
9200	0.25	0.38	0.39	0.11	0.40	0.69
9225	0.13	0.28	0.30	0.24	0.54	0.84
9250	0.05	0.19	0.23	0.41	0.70	1.01

Est. vol. 11,866, Thur.; vol. 5,059 calls, 5,394 puts.
Open interest Thur.; 27,319 calls, 43,420 puts.

* Note that further option expirations and strike prices usually will be available. Check with a broker for quotations.

APPENDIX III: CONTRACT SPECIFICATIONS

	Three-Month U.S. Treasury Bill	Options on Treasury Bill Futures	Three-Month Eurodollar Time Deposits	Options on Eurodollar Futures
Ticker Symbol	TB	Calls: CQ Puts: PQ	ED	Calls: CE Puts: PE
Contract Size	$1,000,000	1 TB futures contract	$1,000,000	1 ED futures contract
Contract Months	Mar., Jun., Sep., Dec.	Mar., Jun., Sep., Dec.	Mar., Jun., Sep., Dec.	Mar., Jun., Sep., Dec.
Strike Price Intervals	N.A.	Below 91.00: .50 points Above 91.00: .25 points	N/A	Below 88.00: .50 points Above 88.00: .25 points
Minimum Price Change	.01 = $25	.01 = $25[2]	.01 = $25	.01 = $25[2]
Price Limit	None	None	None	None
Trading Hours[3] (Chicago Time)	7:20 a.m.-2:00 p.m. (last day-10:00 a.m.)	7:20 a.m.-2:00 p.m.	7:20 a.m.-2:00 p.m. (last day-9:30 a.m.)	7:20 a.m.-2:00 p.m. (last day-9:30 a.m.)
Last Day of Trading	The business day immediately preceding the first delivery day	The last business day of the week, preceding by at least 6 business days the first business day of the underlying futures contract	2nd London business day prior to the 3rd Wednesday of the delivery month	2nd London business day prior to the 3rd Wednesday of the delivery month
Delivery	Three successive business days, beginning the day after the last day of trading	Exercisable on any trading day until expiration on the last day of trading	No delivery for ED futures. Final cash settlement on last day of trading.	Exercisable on any trading day until expiration on the last day of trading

Chapter 3

Introduction to Futures Pricing

Bruce Peterson
Goldman, Sachs & Co.

PRICING FUTURES

The traditional definition of a financial futures contract is an agreement which obligates the buyer to purchase and the seller to deliver a specified quantity of a particular security (long-term U.S. Treasury Bonds, for example) on a specified date. The price of this transaction is established via open auction on organized exchanges at some point in advance of the settlement date, hence the term "futures."

While this definition is not incorrect, it is somewhat misleading and, in the case of several contracts, not applicable. Futures generally are used as a price-fixing mechanism for anticipated transactions, or as a method of gaining or reducing market exposure without buying or selling physical securities. In most instances actual transferral of securities does not take place.

Perhaps a more accurate definition of a futures contract is an agreement between a user (either buyer or seller) and a broker to maintain a mark-to-market account with the broker to meet margin calls or receive margin as movements in the price of the underlying security or index dictate.

For the purpose of introducing futures, however, it is helpful to describe them as though delivery was the normal method for settling transactions. This renders many of the features of the contract less alien. In addition, the delivery or settlement process is important in price determination of the various contracts, regardless of the actual frequency or quantity of deliveries taking place.

Typically financial futures are available for settlement in the months of March, June, September and December, spanning a period of two or three years. As with any investment in fixed income securities, prices of financial futures vary inversely with the level of interest rates for comparable securities. A rise in Eurodollar time deposit rates, for example, results in a fall in the price of Eurodollar futures.

Futures contracts are defined by their prices, delivery dates and delivery specifications. Table 1 is the descriptive information concerning one day's trading in the long-term U.S. Treasury Bond Contract, as it would appear in a typical newspaper. Note that on this particular day, bond futures fell 2/32 of one percentage point in price in each delivery month, indicating a slight rise in long-term Treasury Bond rates.

Futures are available for a wide variety of financial instruments. Table 2 outlines the principal futures contracts and the major exchanges on which they trade including the Chicago Board of Trade (CBT); the International Monetary Market, a part of the Chicago Mercantile Exchange (IMM); the London International Financial Futures Exchange (LIFFE); the Marche A Terme d'Instruments Financiers (MATIF) and the Tokyo Stock Exchange (TSE).

Market Participants

Financial futures markets support and are supported by the activities of two major groups: hedgers and speculators. A hedger, broadly defined, takes a position in the futures market as a substitute or proxy for taking a comparable position in the cash market. For example, an owner of U.S. Treasury notes might not want to, or be able to, sell the notes for several weeks and is afraid of a fall

Table 1 8% Long Term U.S. Treasury Bond Futures[1] (CBT)[2], $100,000[3], Points and 32nds of 100%[4]

Month[5]	Open[6]	High[6]	Low[6]	Close[6]	Change[6]	Yield[7]	Change[7]	Volume[8]	Open Interest[8]
Sep	88-25	88-30	88-20	88-23	-2	9.248	+.010	88,134	129,478
Dec	87-24	87-28	87-17	87-20	-2	9.382	+.010	10,747	59,657
Mar 89	86-22	86-24	86-16	86-19	-2	9.511	+.010	684	15,259
Jun	85-23	85-26	85-18	85-20	-2	9.634	+.010	41	7,336
Sep	84-26	84-29	84-23	84-24	-2	9.747	+.011	102	11,631
Dec	83-30	83-00	83-28	83-30	-2	9.853	+.010	12	3,374
Mar 90	83-05	83-08	83-05	83-06	-2	9.953	+.010	11	1,354
Jun	82-14	82-17	82-14	82-16	-2	10.046	+.011	10	1,318
Sep	81-29	81-29	81-26	81-27	-2	10.136	+.010	1	1,352
Dec	81-08	81-08	81-08	81-08	-2	10.218	+.011	2	22
Mar 91	80-27	80-27	80-23	80-25	-2	10.284	+.011	1	6
Total								99,745	230,787

1 Contract type.
2 Exchange (in this case, the Chicago Board of Trade).
3 Contract size.
4 How the price is quoted (in this case, percent of par, and 32nds of percent of par).
5 The delivery month.
6 The opening price, the high price, the low price, the settle price (or closing price) and change in price from the settle price of the prior day.
7 The yield and the change in yield from the prior day produced by buying the underlying security at the settle price (in this case assuming an 8%, 20-year U.S. Treasury bond is delivered).
8 The trading volume for the day, and the open interest (the total number of open contracts) as of settlement.

Note that on this particular day, bond futures fell 2/32 of one percentage point in price in each delivery month, indicating a slight rise in long-term Treasury bond rates.

Table 2

Contract	Size	Price Quotation[1]	Value of a Tic[2]	Exchange
20 Year 8% US T-Bond Futures	$ 100,000	Pts/32nds	$31.25	CBT
20 Year 8% US T-Bond Futures	$ 100,000	Pts/32nds	$31.25	LIFFE
10 Year 8% US T-Note Futures	$ 100,000	Pts/32nds	$31.25	CBT
3 Month US T-Bill Futures	$1,000,000	Pts/100ths	$25.00	IMM
3 Month Eurodollar Futures	$1,000,000	Pts/100ths	$25.00	IMM
3 Month Eurodollar Futures	$1,000,000	Pts/100ths	$25.00	LIFFE
3 Month Eurodollar Futures	$1,000,000	Pts/100ths	$25.00	SIMEX
Muni Bond Index Futures	$ 1,000 × Bond Buyer MBI	Pts/32nds	$31.25	CBT
U.K. Government Long Gilt	L 50,000	Pts/32nds	L 15.625	LIFFE
3 Month Sterling Futures	L 500,000	Pts/100ths	L 12.50	LIFFE
Japanese 10 Year Bond	Y 100,000,000	Pts/100ths	Y 10000	TSE
French 10 Year Bond	FF 500,000	Pts/100ths	FF 250	MATIF
13 Week French Treasury Bill	FF 5,000,000	Pts/100ths	FF 125	MATIF

[1] For example, Treasury bond futures are quoted in terms of percentage points and 32nds of percentage points of par. A bond futures price of 88-04 equals 88.125 of par, or $88,125 per $100,000 bond. Short-term instruments generally are quoted in points or 100ths of points. A price of 93.25 for a Treasury bill equals 93.25% of par.

[2] A tie is the smallest unit of price for a particular contract. For bonds and notes for example, it is 1/32nds of 1%. The value of a tic is equal to the dollar (or pound) change in value of one contract associated with a one-tie price move.

in their market value. Taking a short position in Treasury note futures allows the investor to accomplish the same effect as the sale, by establishing a sale price at the time the futures are sold.

If rates rise, losses in the value of the Treasury notes are offset by gains from the short position in Treasury note futures and vice-versa. It is important to note that any hedge other than actually selling the securities is subject to some risk. That is to say, gains and losses of the Treasury notes, in this example, may not be offset fully by changes in the value of the Treasury note futures.

Speculators who use the futures markets to create market exposure do so for a variety of reasons. One motivation may be that they do not want, or are unable, to commit the capital resources necessary to conduct such transactions in the cash markets.

The combined activities of hedgers and speculators have created several highly liquid markets, in which large amounts of business can be transacted quickly. This volume is, in itself, a reason the futures markets are used. Before describing further uses of the futures markets, several features of the contracts should be outlined.

Standardization

Because futures contracts are available on broad categories of financial instruments, such as long-term U.S. Treasury bonds or Eurodollar time deposits, the contract must specify what is to be delivered in order that buyers and sellers can arrive at a price. The contract specifications define an amount, a coupon and a maturity. The contract does not, however, require that only bonds meeting these exact specifications be delivered. It allows for an equivalent position in bonds of other coupons.

For example, the U.S. Treasury bond contract allows for the delivery of any Treasury with 15 or more years until its maturity or call date. Any bond delivered is adjusted by a factor in order to account for different coupons and maturities. The factors are equal to the price of the particular bond required to produce a yield to maturity of 8 percent as of the first delivery date of the futures contract.[1]

For example, an 11.25 percent bond with a maturity of 21.5 years has a factor of 1.3310, while a 7 percent bond with 25 years to maturity has a factor of .8926. The factor determines the invoice or delivery price of the contract. If the futures contract is trading at a price of 78, the delivery price of the 11.25% bond equals:

Contract Size	$ 100,000
Price	× .78
	$ 78,000
Factor	× 1.3310
	$103,818.00 ,plus accrued interest

The invoice price for the 7% bond equals:

Contract Size	$ 100,000
Price	× .78
	$ 78,000
Factor	× .8926
	$69,622.80 ,plus accrued interest

The factor-adjusted prices do not produce equivalent yields among the various Treasury bonds in all interest rate environments. If yields differ from 8 percent, certain invoice prices produce higher yields tan others. A more complete description of this phenomenon, and how it affects the price of futures, follows.

Forward Settlement

The forward nature of futures transactions is of particular importance. Futures trades do not settle until the delivery date of the

---

1 In fact a slight adjustment is made to this factor, rounding its maturity down to the nearest whole quarter. For example, a bond with a maturity of 23 years, 5 months has a maturity of 23 years 3 months for purposes of calculating a factor.

contract. That is, cash and bonds[2] do not change hands until the delivery date. At any time between the transaction date and the delivery date, the contract can be offset with an opposite position at whatever price is prevailing in the market at that time. A long and a short position in the same contract are paired off by the clearinghouse and the position is closed. The profit (loss) is the difference between the sale price and the purcnase price.

So futures provide the market exposure of a position in bonds without requiring the actual cash or securities for that position. A buyer of a March bond contract, for example, could sell the contract before the March delivery, closing it. Similarly, a seller of the June bond contract could buy back the June contract at some time before June. An example of each of these transactions follows:

Example 1:

May 10: buy 1 March bond contract ($100,000) at a price of 78-0/32	$(78,000)
Nov 17: sell 1 March bond contract at a price of 80-0/32	+ 80,000
Profit (loss)	$ 2,000

Example 2:

Jan 13: sell 1 June bond at a price of 79-0/32	$ 79,000
Apr 4: buy 1 June bond contract at a price of 80-0/32	+ (80,000)
Profit (loss)	$ (1,000)

This is, in fact, how the majority of futures trades are settled. This chapter has described "delivery," but as noted at the outset, futures contracts generally are not used as a method of acquiring or liquidating securities through the delivery process. More often,

---

2   The term "bond" is used as a generic term referring to the cash instrument underlying the futures contract.

they are used to fix the price of an anticipated transaction or to increase or reduce market exposure.

For example, an investor can buy futures and resell those futures when the cash bonds are acquired. Changes in the price of the cash bonds before the purchase date are reflected in the futures price. If changes in interest rates cause the bond price to rise during this period, the higher price is offset by a futures profit. Similarly if the price falls, the reduced cost is offset by a loss on the futures.

The price-fixing role of futures is more apparent in the design of several contracts which do not require delivery. For these, the settlement price on the final trading day is based on an index of some cash market security or securities, with profits and losses computed by comparing the purchase price or sale price with that index.

Leverage

The forward nature of the settlement of contracts is not entirely a distinguishing feature of the futures markets. Forward markets exist for several sectors of the cash market. In addition, even in areas lacking forward markets, transactions may be undertaken which look very much like futures trades. For example buying a Treasury Bond contract, in terms of cash flow and market exposure, is like buying bonds and financing them n the repo market. Selling futures is like selling bonds short and borrowing them in the repo market. It is true that certain speculators in the futures market are unable to finance their positions in the cash market; but it is a mistake to refer to the "leverage" associated with futures as being a distinguishing characteristic.

Margin

The profits and losses produced by the two hypothetical transactions (Examples 1 and 2) do not tell the complete story of the mechanics of these transactions. Futures contracts require margin deposits. A customer buying or selling futures must place with the broker a minimum deposit of an amount specified by the exchange. This "initial margin" is a performance bond to assure settlement of the contract. It is typically of a magnitude slightly larger than the maximum movement in price allowed for a single day by the particular exchange.

The initial margin requirements are small relative to the size of the contract. For bond futures as of this writing, initial margin is $2,000 per $100,000 contract. Initial margin can be in the form of cash or Treasury bills. A second type of margin associated with a futures contract is variation margin. These funds are sent to or received from the broker to cover the daily change in value of the contract. These changes in value are calculated based on the settlement price of the contract at the end of each day. As with initial margin, the broker, in turn, must settle variation margin with the exchange before trading begins each day. In the case of variation margin, cash is the only form of payment. Example 3 illustrates the basic mechanics of a "round trip" in the futures market.

The profit from this transaction equals $750, which is equal to the sale price (.7875) minus the purchase price (.7800) multiplied by the contract size ($100,000). The results from this example are consistent with those from Examples 1 and 2 (i.e., the profit is simply a function of the purchase price and the sale price). The difference is that Example 3 shows the path by which this profit was reached. During the course of this position, there were instances of greater profits, lesser profits and losses. What ultimately mattered, however, were the purchase and sale prices.

Example 3:

	Cumulative Send	Receive	Net Flow
August 1			
Buy 1 Dec bond contract at a price of 78	—	—	—
Settlement Price: 79-00			

	Cumulative Send	Receive	Net Flow
August 2			
Deposit initial margin (cash or T-bills)	($2,000)		
Receive variation margin due price rise (.79–.78) × 100,000		$1,000	($1,000)
Settlement Price: 77-24			
August 3			
Send variation margin due to price fall (.7775–.79) × 100,000		($1,250)	($2,250)
Settlement Price: 78-08			
August 4			
Receive variation margin due to price rise (.7825–.7775) × 100,000		$500	($1,750)
Sell 1 Dec bond contract at a price of 78-24			
Settlement price: 78-00			
August 5			
Receive difference between sale price and prior days settle price (.7875–.7825) × 100,000		$500	
Receive return of initial margin		$2,000	$750

Reasons for Futures Market Use

Hedgers and speculators use the financial futures markets for a number of reasons, many of which have been described:

Liquidity For a hedger wanting to take the market risk out of a cash market investment quickly, or to create market exposure quickly, futures often can be the most liquid market for their transactions. An investor wishing to liquidate a large portfolio of bonds, for example, might use futures to hedge the value of the bonds and sell them gradually (concurrent with lifting a portion of the hedge) in order to reduce the transaction costs of a major liquidation. This is particularly important during periods of significant volatility.

Confidentiality Transactions may be conducted in the futures markets with total anonymity. This may be important, for example, when the markets are used as a hedge of an anticipated cash market transaction such as the liquidation of a large portfolio of corporate bonds, or a sizable debt issuance.

Relative value At certain points in time, futures contracts may be cheap or rich relative to comparable cash market securities, making them attractive purchases or sales.

Flexibility Timing may create imbalances between cash inflows and desired investment strategies. For example, financial futures can be a temporary investment vehicle while waiting for cash flows to fund investment in actual securities.

Accounting and Regulatory Considerations Often a desired strategy may be prevented due to accounting constraints. For example, a financial institution may wish to sell its long-term asset portfolio and invest the proceeds short-term to reduce its exposure to rising interest rates. If the book value of assets is above market value and the contemplated sale is large enough, the book losses may prohibit the sale. Selling futures is an alternative that does not require booking the losses and creates a similar portfolio (or market) exposure.

Futures Pricing

As in the purchase of sale or cash securities, use of the futures markets requires a thorough understanding of the factors which influence their prices. Two primary factors influence the price of a financial futures contract: current prices (yields) of comparable cash market instruments and the forward rate structure implied by the yield curve. The first means that futures prices in large part reflect price levels of related cash securities, and that change in these cash market prices are reflected in changes in the price of the futures contract.

Interest Rates

Because both futures and the instrument underlying the futures contract are a function of interest rates, the price of the futures contract should be correlated to the price of the underlying instrument. Certainly in September the price of a September bond future should be very close to the price of deliverable bonds in the cash market. Any differences would be minimized by arbitrate activity. This price correlation allows market participants to use futures as an alternative to or substitute for a cash market transaction. From the perspective of market exposure, a long position in bond futures is comparable to buying bonds in the cash market. A rally in the bond market results in comparable gains for an investor long futures and an investor long comparable cash bonds. The same correlation applies to short positions in cash and futures as well.

An example of the comparability of cash and futures is shown in Figure 1. Note the apparent correlation of prices between the 7.25 percent Treasury bonds of 5/15/16, and the June bond future (adjusted by the delivery factor for this bond) in Figure 1. It is clear that as bond prices rise and fall, the futures follow (or vice-versa). However, the bottom graph in Figure 1 shows that the price of the bond future across this time period rises relative to the cash price. On the final day of trading for the bond future, the spread is negligible, as expected. In April, the spread is close to 1.10 percent, or 35/32's. What causes this differential?

Contract Term

Based on the relative rise in the futures price shown in Figure 1, the fact that contract prices are increasingly lower as the delivery dates are further in the future is not unexpected. The data suggest that a second factor, aside from the price for comparable cash mar-

Figure 1

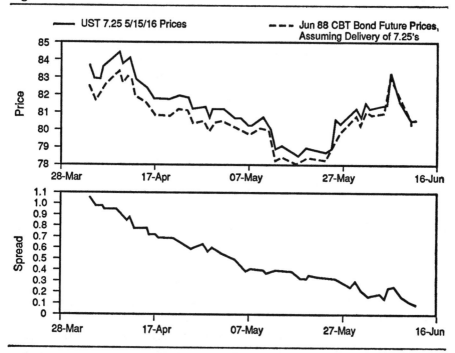

ket securities, influences the price of the futures, and that this second factor is a function of the time until settlement. More specifically, the prices of futures contracts relative to cash prices for comparable securities reflect the structure of interest rates for comparable maturities, or the shape of the yield curve. This also applies to the relative prices of the futures contracts from delivery month to delivery month (also known as intramarket spreads). The Treasury bond futures prices in Table 3 illustrate the forward pricing drops required by an upward sloping yield curve.

Implied Forward Rates

In order to understand this concept fully, it is important to review the yield curve and all the information it provides. Note the hypo-

Table 3

Contract Month	Price
Jun 88	87-22
Sep	86-24
Dec	85-29
Mar	85-04
Jun 89	84-12
Sep	83-22
Dec	83-01
Mar	82-10

thetical yield curve shown in Figure 2, which reflects interest rates for the period spanning one to six years. Table 4 lists the data graphed in Figure 2.

Note that a one-year investment produces a return of 10 percent, while a two-year investment produces a return of 10.75 percent. If $100 is invested for one year at 10 percent, at the end of the year the value of the portfolio is $110. If $100 is invested for two years at 10.75% per year, the final value of the portfolio equals $122.66. If the investor has a two-year time horizon, the funds could be invested for two years at 10.75 percent or for one year at 10 percent, with reinvestment for another one-year term at the end of the first year. In the latter case, the interest rate in the second year is unknown, making the total return also unknown. The two would produce an equal return, however, if the interest rate in the second period equaled:

$$\frac{122.66}{110.00} - 1 = 11.51\%.$$

Figure 2   Cash Yield Curve

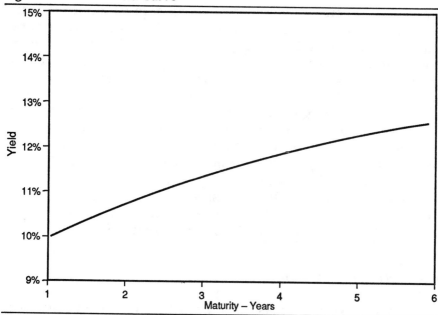

Table 4

Term of Investment	Rate (%)
1	10.000
2	10.750
3	11.375
4	11.875
5	12.250
6	12.600

So the yield curve implies that a one-year yield one year forward is 11.54 percent.[3, 4] Similarly, the curve implies rates for various terms at all forward points on the curve. Table 5 outlines the actual and implied rates for this hypothetical yield curve, with the data graphed in Figure 3. These data imply, for example, that a three-year investment, three years forward, produces a return of 13.839 percent. It also suggests that a buyer or seller of a five-year security would be indifferent between a five-year security yielding 12.25 percent and a "forward-forward" agreement to a series of five one-year investments with rates locked in today at 10.000 percent, 11.505 percent, 12.636 percent, 13.389 percent and 13.763 percent respectively. Each would produce the same total return to the investor or cost to the seller. The seller would not accept a higher interest rate (lower price) during any period, while the buyer would not accept a lower rate (higher price) during any period.

Forward Prices and Futures

A futures transaction looks very much like this hypothetical forward-forward transaction. The security, price, quantity and date all are specified in advance. In fact, the differences between this transaction and a futures market transaction (exchanges, standardized contracts, margin flows, brokers, liquidity) largely are mechanical. The buyer and seller in this case have entered into the equivalent of a futures agreement. This is, in fact, how an equilibrium price is established for the various futures contracts. As in the forward-forward example where the buyer and seller agreed to a price for each rollover of the one-year investment based on the yield curve, buyers and sellers in the futures markets arrive at an equilibrium which reflects the rates (and prices) implied by the yield curve.

---

3   The relationship between implied rates and rates on the yield curve is $Rn = ((1+r1) \times (1+r2) \times \ldots \times (1+rn))^{1/n} - 1$, where Rn equals the rate from the yield curve for a period of n years and r1, r1, etc. are interim rates, either real or implied for individual years. Rn, and r1, r2 etc. are expressed in decimal form.

4   Because: $((1.100) \times (1.1100) \times (1.1201) \times (1.1301) \times (1.1402))1/5 - 1 = .12250$ or 12.250%

Table 5

Term	Spot Rates	Implied Rates				
	t = 0	t = 1	t = 2	t = 3	t = 4	t = 5
1	10.00%	11.51%	12.64%	13.39%	13.76%	14.37%
2	10.75	12.07	13.01	13.57	14.06	
3	11.37	12.51	13.26	13.84		
4	11.87	12.82	13.54			
5	12.25	13.13				
6	12.60					

Figure 3   Actual and Implied Yields

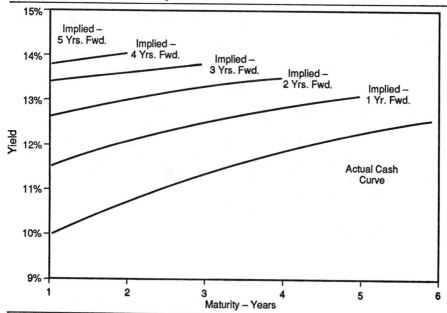

When the yield curve is positively sloped, implied forward rates are higher than spot rates for comparable maturities. Because futures reflect forward rates, their prices are lower than comparable maturity cash securities. As time passes and the delivery date approaches, however, futures yields necessarily and increasingly reflect spot yields for comparable securities. This means that when the yield curve is positively sloped, the price of a futures contract rises relative to the price of the underlying cash security as delivery approaches. This convergence of futures to cash (as shown in Figure 1) translates the yield curve effect on futures prices into dollars. A long position benefits from convergence, while a short realizes it as an expense.[5] Two illustrations of its effect on investment returns follow.

Assume that an investor wants to own long-term U.S. Treasury bonds. They either can be purchased today in the cash market or through the futures market, with the cash invested in short-term investments either as a "permanent" substitute or while waiting for delivery (or closeout of the futures position in conjunction with a cash market purchase as discussed earlier). In both cases the bonds have been purchased as of a price settled today.

Because the risks of ownership are comparable, so should be the rewards. With the cash purchase of bonds, the investor receives long-term yields immediately in the cash market. With the purchase of bonds through the futures market, the investor earns a short-term return on the cash investments.

How are these results comparable? With the futures purchase the investor also benefits from the convergence of the lower futures price to the cash price. When the yield curve is positively sloped, this convergence causes the futures price to rise to the cash price, resulting in income for the long position. This income brings the total return of the transaction into line with the long-term return earned by the purchase of bonds in the cash market. Conversely, when the yield curve is inverted, the convergence reduces

---

5   If the yield curve is inverted, the log position will realize an expense form convergence, while the short will receive income from convergence.

the return of the short-term investment/long futures combination, bringing it into line with long-term rates.

Suppose, instead, an investor wishes to have a short-term investment. The investor either could buy Treasury bills, or buy Treasury bonds and sell them in the futures market. Once again, the risks and rewards are comparable. The convergence of futures to cash, causing the contract to rise in price, reduces the return from the bonds and produces a short-term yield comparable to the bill yield.[6]

Delivery Specifications

A third, more subtle, influence on the price of a futures contract is the influence of the delivery factors and specifications. As noted above, many contracts allow for the delivery of a number of similar instruments, with an adjustment (factor) made for the various coupons in an attempt to standardize them. The delivery factors are imperfect; as market conditions change, they do not result in equality of delivered yield between one bond and another.

This imperfection, combined with cash market differences in yields between bonds, causes the futures market to establish an equilibrium price based on the bond which is most advantageous for the seller to deliver (the specific bond to be delivered is at the option of the seller). So the futures price does not reflect an average or generic price of deliverable securities, but rather the price of a specific "cheapest-to-deliver" bond. The cheapest-to-deliver is not something that is continuously in a state of flux; as market conditions move, a new cheapest-to-deliver may result and cause a change in the contract price.[7]

---

6 Several simplifying assumptions are included in this description. There are differences in risks and, therefore, rewards between the cash investment and the cash/futures alternative. For example, the short futures position has certain options allowed for in the delivery process for which the market assesses a charge, causing the yield on such transactions to be lower than Treasury bill yields.

7 For further data on these concepts, refer to the article "The Bond Basis Report," Bruce Petersen, Futures Services.

Impact of Pricing Considerations

The fact that futures markets reflect the level of interest rates (and, therefore, cash prices) allows investors and liability managers to use futures to hedge cash positions. As noted, futures can be an attractive alternative to cash for a number of reasons, including: relative value to cash, flexibility, liquidity, lower transaction costs, and certain accounting and regulatory constraints. These features, combined with correlation to the cash market, allow hedgers to use futures either temporarily or permanently as substitutes for cash market positions. The fact that futures prices reflect the shape of the yield curve also has a significant impact. A long-term asset sold in the futures market no longer will return a yield comparable to a long-term asset. When both the impact of the hedge (due to convergence) and the interest income from the security are considered, the asset produces a yield comparable to that of an investment with a maturity equal to the contract month.

Similarly an issuer of such short-term liabilities as commercial paper who wants protection from rising liability costs by selling futures, will produce a synthetic liability that reflects longer term interest rates. As in the cash market when the yield curve has a positive slope, synthetically reducing asset duration and increasing liability duration using futures has a cost attached (the difference between long-term and short-term rates).

Without recognition of this fact, a hedger will feel that a hedge has failed when, for example, rates do not move and yet there are losses associated with the futures position. These losses are merely the result of moving along the yield curve. Conversely, the yield generated by a hedge of along term bond purchase, for example, using a short term cash investment and a purchase of bond futures is comparable to higher long-term yields.

Futures may be the only available strategy at times due to liquidity, accounting or regulatory considerations. At other times, futures may be used because of perceived value relative to the cash market. Obviously, all factors influencing the pricing of futures including spot and forward rates, transaction costs as well as those factors related to the delivery process must be given full consideration when attempting to evaluate this relative value of futures and comparable cash market transactions. Any hedging strategy should be considered in this context and compared with available cash market strategies which produce the same risk position.

Conclusion

This chapter was devoted in large part to defining the distinguishing characteristics of futures contracts such as margin, forward settlement and exchanges. The characteristics which draw financial futures within the universe of fixed income securities, however, are of greater importance to the majority of financial market participants. Of these, the pricing of futures as a function of interest rates is most important. Rather than viewing futures as something separate or distinct, they should be thought of as elements in the set of securities available for achieving desired levels of risk and return. They exist alongside cash market securities and should be evaluated based on their relative cost effectiveness in achieving financial goals.

Chapter 4

Delivery Options for Bond Futures Contracts

Steve Koomar
Goldman, Sachs & Co.

A bond futures contract, in simple terms, is a financed position in the cheapest-to-deliver bond when the long grants the short a number of options for bond delivery. The short pays a "premium" for purchasing the delivery options by selling the futures contract at a price that is less than the theoretical forward price for the cheapest-to-deliver bond. Because it is relatively easy to identify the cheap-to-deliver bond, knowledge of the delivery options that are embedded in the futures contract is an important ingredient in analyzing the relative value of the futures contract.

This chapter outlines all of the bond futures contract delivery options. The emphasis is not on valuation, but rather on how the delivery options are executed and when it is profitable to execute them. The options that are given to the short in the contract specifications are first identified. The specific strategies that the short can use to realize value from these options are described, as strategies to profit from "wild card plays" are outlined. Then, strategies to profit from a change in the cheap-to-deliver bond (including one option that can be "exercised" only after trading in the futures contract has ended) are described. It concludes with a schedule of dates relevant to the delivery plays that can be made in the December 1987 contract.

DELIVERY OPTIONS

According to contract specifications, the delivery options granted to the short are:

1. **Wild Card Option** The wild card option results from the ability of the short to give notice of intent to deliver for up to six hours after the close of futures trading each day (2 p.m. to 8 p.m., Chicago time) and still deliver against that day's closing futures price. This time frame is known as the "wild card" period.

2. **Timing Option** The timing option results from the ability of the short to make delivery on any business day during the delivery month. Delivery occurs two business days after notice of intent to deliver is given formally to the exchange.

3. **Bond Selection Option** This is a result of the ability of the short to determine which of the bonds that meet contract specifications will be delivered. Notification of which bond will be delivered is made the day after notice of intent to deliver is given by the short.

These options can be translated into a number of different delivery plays from which the short can profit.

Wild Card Options

The Chicago Board of Trade 8 percent conversion factor method for delivery, which equates all eligible bonds to an 8 percent coupon, creates the opportunity for wild card plays by establishing a "tail" on hedged trades. The tail is the amount that the hedge ratio differs from 1.0. Because the hedge ratio for the cheap-to-deliver bond is equal to the conversion factor, the tail for the cheap-to-deliver bond is equal to the conversion factor minus 1.0.[1]

Hedge ratios are appropriate only until the short tenders notice of intent to make delivery. The short must deliver a par amount of bonds that is equal to the par amount of futures sold. Therefore, the short should "cover" the tail when making delivery by either buying or selling the bonds required for the par amount of bonds held to be equal to the par amount of futures. For example, assume that a trader holds $10 million in bonds and has sold $15 million in futures to hedge his position. When the trader gives notice of intent to deliver, another $5 million of bonds must be purchased. Wild-card play opportunities arise because of the need to cover the tail when making delivery.

The option works in the following manner. The short can make delivery on any business day during the delivery month. Notice of intent to deliver can be made at the 2 p.m. settlement price until 8 p.m. Assuming that the short has a tail of 5 million futures, an additional $5 million of bonds must be purchased for the delivery. If the market price for the bond falls during the 2 p.m. to 8 p.m. wild card period, the short profits. The short simultaneously purchases the bonds at the lower evening price and delivers them at the higher 2 p.m. settlement price.

This example illustrates that when the hedge ratio is greater than 1.0, a futures tail is established and the short holds an implicit put option on the futures tail. In contrast, when the hedge ratio is less than 1.0, a bond tail is established and the short holds an implicit call option on the bond tail. Depending on which bonds are cheap or nearly cheap-to-deliver, the short may have an implicit call, an implicit put or both. These options are outlined in detail below.

---

1 In most instances, the cheap-to-deliver bond also is the cheapest bond for a wild card delivery. In these situations, the conversion factor is the appropriate hedge ratio. However, other eligible bonds also may become viable for wild card delivery; and in those cases, the correct tail cannot be derived from the conversion factor alone. A duration-based hedge ratio must be used.

THE WILD CARD PUT OPTION

If the hedge ratio is greater than 1.0, the short holds an implicit out-of-the-money put option on that bond during the wild card period. The short has a tail of futures contracts that must be covered for delivery. The short can earn a profit if bond prices fall dramatically during the 2 p.m. to 8 p.m. wild card period by purchasing the bonds necessary to cover the tail at the lower evening prices and simultaneously delivering the entire bond position at the higher 2 p.m. futures settlement price. The break-even bond price for delivery during the wild card period is the price at which the short earns back the carry[2] remaining on the bond held through contract expiration plus the value of any remaining delivery options.

The decision of whether to exercise the delivery option should be made relative to the alternative of selling the remaining delivery options and the remaining carry (to contract expiration) by reversing the basis trade. So assuming that the value of carry and the value of the delivery options to contract expiration do not change significantly between 2:00 p.m. and the start of the next futures trading session, the short must earn back the entire bond basis[3] (as of 2:00 p.m.) for the wild card delivery to be more profitable than reversing the basis trade.

The formula for determining the break-even price is:

---

2   Carry is the amount earned by holding the bond, as determined by the difference between the yield on the bond and the cost of financing the bond through the short-term financing rate or repo rate.

3   The basis is defined as the absolute value of: (futures price × conversion factor)-cash bond price. For the cheapest-to-deliver bond, it is equal to the value of positive carry on the bond through contract expiration, plus the market value of delivery options. If the bond has negative carry, it is equal to the value of carry minus the value of the delivery options. A "basis trade" is a position in cash hedged with an opposite futures position.

$$BE_{put} = P - \frac{[B \times h]}{T}$$

when BE = Break even bond price on wild card put[4]
        P = Bond price at 3 p.m. close
        B = Basis, in absolute value
        h = Hedge ratio for the bond to be delivered
        T = Tail = hedge ratio –1.0, in absolute value

Table 1   **June 15, 1987**

Bond	Price	Factor	Futures Settlement Price	Basis	Modified Price Duration
12% of 2013	131.8438	1.4037	93.5313	0.5539	9.10

Using June 15, 1987 prices shown in Table 1 and assuming that the 12 percent bond of 2013 is really cheap-to-deliver[5], the June 15 break-even price is:

$$BE_{put} = 131.8438 - \frac{0.5539 \times 1.4037}{0.4037}$$

$$= 131.8438 - 1.926 = 129.918 \text{ (or 129 29/32)}$$

---

4 This price assumes skip-day settlement. In the formula "(B × h)" represents what must be earned to break even on early delivery, and "T" represents the portion of the total futures position from which the short can earn a profit from delivery.

5 Based on a $100 million par amount, the position held by the short at 2:00 p.m. would have been: Long $100 million 12% of 2013, short $140.4 million June futures (or 1,404 contracts).

This means that the short profits by delivering the 12 percent of 2013 only if the price falls below 129 29/32 during the wild card period.[6] Essentially, the strike price of the put option is nearly two full points out-of-the-money. Because price levels normally fluctuate, the break even price changes accordingly every day.

Also, because futures and cash prices tend to converge, the price-change necessary to break even tends to decline as contract expiration nears. Therefore, the wild card put option generally becomes less out-of-the-money as contract expiration draws closer.

With the recent introduction of night trading at the Chicago Board of Trade, the short now has an alternative of covering the tail for the wild card put by purchasing futures contracts (if prices drop before 8 p.m.), rather than by purchasing the bonds for delivering on the tail. The break-even futures price for the execution of the wild card put in this fashion is:

$$FBE_{put} = F - \frac{B}{T}$$

when   FBE = Futures break even purchase price
          F   = Futures 2 p.m. settlement price

Again using the prices shown in Table 1, the night session futures price needed to break-even on a wild card delivery on June 15 are:[7]

$$FBE_{put} = 93.5313 - \frac{0.5513}{0.4037}$$

$$= 93.5313 - 1.3656$$

$$= 92.1657 \text{ (or } 92\ 5/32)$$

---

6 To exercise, the short would buy $40.4 million of the 12% of 2013 at a price below 129 30/32 and simultaneously give notice of intent to deliver on $140.4 million in June contracts at the 2 p.m. settlement price.

7 The transaction needed to exercise the delivery option, assuming $100 million par and the 12% bond being held at 2 p.m., is to buy $40.4 million June contracts at a price below 92 5/32 and give notice of intent to deliver on $100 million in June futures.

If the futures price falls by 1 12/32, to a price of 92 5/32, during the wild card period, the short is indifferent to purchasing futures to cover the tail during the evening of June 15 for a wild card delivery and reversing the basis trade on the following day.

THE WILD CARD CALL OPTION

In contrast to the implicit put option described above, an implicit call option is held by the short if the hedge ratio on a bond is less than 1.0. Hedged (basis) traders hold a bond tail which must be covered for delivery by either selling bonds or selling futures. The analysis of this out-of-the money call option is analogous to the put option analysis described previously. The break-even price for this call option, when exercised by selling bonds to cover the tail, is:

$$BE_{call} = P + \frac{[B \times h]}{T}$$

Table 2   June 15, 1987

Bond	Price	Factor	Futures Settlement Price	Basis	Modified Price Duration
7 1/4% of 2016	86.4375	0.9159	93.5313	0.7722	10.95

In order to show an example of the wild-card call from the price data for June 15, as shown in Table 2, make two assumptions. First, assume that the cheap-to-deliver bond is the 7 1/4 percent of 2016, making the hedge ratio equal to its conversion factor. Second, assume that the basis on the 7 1/4 percent of 2016 is 4/32 (or 0.125).

Given these assumptions, the break-even price on the cheap-to-deliver bond is:[8]

$$BE_{call} = 86.4375 + \frac{0.125 \times 0.9159}{0.0841}$$

$$= 86.4375 + 1.3613 = 87.7988 \text{ (or } 87\ 26/32)$$

Given the above assumptions, the strike of the wild card call option is 1 12/32 out-of-the-money on June 15. As with the put option, the call option can be exercised by selling futures. When the tail is covered on the wild card play by selling futures, the break-even futures price is:[9]

$$FBE_{call} = F + \frac{B}{T}$$

FACTORS THAT PROMOTE WILD CARD VALUE

The previous examples allude to a number of factors that affect wild card value. These factors are summarized below.[10]

1. If the conversion factor on the cheap-to-deliver bonds is significantly different from 1.0, a large tail is created on basis trades, making the option less out-of-the-money. A large tail dictates that a larger number of bonds be purchased (or sold) to cover the tail and earn back the carry forfeited from early delivery. The larger the bond purchase

8 On a $100 million par amount, the position held is: Long $100 million 7 1/4% of 11/96, short $91.6 million June futures (or 916 contracts). To exercise the wild card call, the short sells $8.4 million of the 7 1/4% of 2016 and makes delivery.

9 To exercise the wild card call with futures, sell $7.7 million in June futures and make delivery of $91.6 million. A position of long $8.4 million 7 1/4% of 2016 and short $76.7 million in June futures remains after the delivery.

10 Each factor is analyzed as if all other factors are held constant. Some factors may in fact, be correlated.

(or sale), the smaller the price change per bond required after the futures close to break even on a wild card delivery. So a larger tail causes the wild card option to be less out-of-the-money, giving the option more value.

2. If positive carry remaining in the contract is small, the option is less out-of-the-money and therefore, is more valuable. When the short delivers prior to contract expiration, the carry that can be earned on the bond (to contract expiration) is sacrificed. If carry (and the basis) are small, the short sacrifices less by delivery early; so the price move required to cover the carry lost on early delivery is small. This implies that the wild card option is less out-of-the money when the yield curve is flat, or when the contract is very close to expiration. Also, each day during the delivery month carry remaining to contract expiration decreases and the option becomes less out-of-the-money. So holding volatility constant, it is expected that more wild card deliveries should occur toward the end of the delivery month when the basis is small.

   If the yield curve is inverted to reflect negative carry, shorts are encouraged to deliver on the first delivery day to avoid paying out carry. It is theoretically possible for negative carry to be great enough to nearly eliminate wild card option value.

3. If general market volatility is high during the wild card period, the chances of the option going "in-the-money" are greater, and so the option is more valuable. Additionally, the release of economic announcements and news of significant world developments during the daily wild card period contribute to higher option value.

4. If the bond market is liquid during the delivery window, execution of the trades necessary to make delivery are less costly, making the option more valuable. However because futures may be substituted for bond purchases or sales, a liquid futures market should provide enough liquidity to

execute wild card plays even if the cash market is not adequately liquid.

5. When bonds with hedge ratios of more than 1.0 and less than 1.0 are both nearly cheap-to-deliver, the short has both an implicit call and an implicit put, enhancing the value of the wild card play.

Bond Selection Option

The wild card option is largely dependent on the size of the tail (dictated by the hedge ratio) and the basis on the cheap-to-deliver bond. Unlike the wild card, the bond selection options are dependent on differences in modified duration and dollar duration[11] between bonds that are cheap-to-deliver or nearly cheap-to-deliver. Two separate options fit into this category, as described below.

OPTION ON YIELD SPREADS AND FACTOR BIAS

This bond selection option exists for a period encompassing all trading days for the futures contracts. It should be noted that the short can deliver any eligible bond. If another bond should become cheap at any time prior to delivery, the short can sell the bond held and buy the new cheap bond for delivery, earning a profit by selling the old bond after it becomes expensive relative to the contract. Two factors can lead to a different bond becoming cheap: conversion factor bias and changing yield spreads between bonds.

Factor bias, a result of the CBT 8 percent bond conversion factor method for bond delivery, relates to changes in bond yield levels. Assuming that the yield curve is flat, whenever yields rise above 8 percent, the bond with the longest modified duration becomes cheap-to-deliver. When yield levels fall below 8 percent,

---

11 Dollar duration is equal to modified price duration × bond price. It is approximately equal to the change in bond price for 100 basis point change in yield. Modified price duration is the percentage change in bond price for a given change in yield.

bonds with the shortest modified duration become cheap-to-deliver. Assuming that the short holds the cheap-to-deliver bond, whenever yield levels change dramatically, the short may benefit by exchanging the old cheap-to-deliver bond for the new cheap-to-deliver bond. Depending on which bond is already cheap-to-deliver, the short may hold an implicit call option, an implicit put option or both.

Changes in yield spreads between bonds also can cause a change in the cheap-to-deliver bond. If the short holds the cheap-to-deliver bond for delivery and that bond's yield declines relative to other bonds, making another bond cheap-to-deliver, the short can realize a gain by exchanging the old cheap bond for the new cheap bond.

Therefore if either yield levels or yield spreads change enough to make another bond cheap to deliver, the short can profit by swapping for the new cheap bond and adjusting the futures hedge for the new cheap bond.

OPTION ON YIELD LEVELS AFTER THE LAST DAY OF TRADING

At the close of the final day of trading, the short must cover the tail to remain hedged for delivery. During the period between the last day of trading and the final day to give notice of which bond will be delivered, the short has an option on yield levels in addition to the option on yield spreads. If the cheap bond on the last day of trading is a high coupon bond, the short holds an out-of-the-money call option on the dollar duration spread between the price of the high coupon and low coupon bonds. If yield levels fall significantly, the high coupon bond held for delivery rises by a much larger amount than the price of low coupon bonds with similar modified durations.

This occurs because the higher price of a high coupon bond causes it to have a larger dollar duration than a low coupon bond. In the event that yields fall during the period after trading has ended yet before final delivery, the low coupon bond price rises by a smaller amount than the high coupon bond. The short can sell the high coupon bond and purchase the same par amount of a low coupon bond for delivery into the contract, earning more on the sale of the high coupon bond than is lost on delivery of the low coupon bond.[12]

Assuming a parallel yield shift, the following formula shows the yield shift necessary for this delivery play:

$$P_L + (i \times D_L) - (F \times f_L) = P_H + (i \times D_H) - F \times f_H$$

Solving for parallel yield shift, this can be simplified to:

$$i = \frac{P_H - P_L + F(f_L - f_H)}{D_H - D_L}$$

which is equivalent to:

$$i = \frac{B_H - B_L}{D_H - D_L}$$

when
i = Parallel yield shift to break even

P_H, P_L = Bond price at close of trading for High Coupon and Low Coupon Bond, respectively

D_H, D_L = Dollar duration of High Coupon and Low Coupon Bond

F = Final futures settlement price

f_H, f_L = Conversion factors for High Coupon Low Coupon Bond

B_H, B_L = Basis for High Coupon and Low Coupon Bond

For example, assuming the short holds the 12 percent bond for delivery, and using June 15 prices and the duration statistics shown in Table 1 and Table 2, the break even yield shift for this option is:

---

12 The option on yield levels after the last day of trading is more valuable when several bonds that are nearly cheap-to-deliver have a large difference in dollar duration.

$$i = \frac{.5539 - .7722}{11.998 - 9.465}$$

$$= -.09$$

This means that if the yield curve had shifted downward by more than nine basis points after the last day of trading, the short profits by selling the 12 percent bond and buying the 7 1/4 percent bond for delivery.[13]

The short also holds a put option after the final day of trading if lower coupon bonds are cheap-to-deliver. The break-even yield shift for this option is determined from the same formula described above.

SUMMARY

A large number of delivery options are available to the short futures positions. The wild card option is often discussed, but options on a change in cheap-to-deliver also are valuable. In order to better understand the potential risks and rewards of holding a futures position during the delivery month, both short and long positions should quantify the prices at which delivery plays can be made.

A calendar of important delivery period dates for the December 1987 contract is given below:

November 27   First day to give notice of intent to deliver. It is the first day that a wild card play can be made.

December 18   Last day the wild card play can be made.

December 21   Last day of trading. All shorts must cover the tail either in the cash or futures market at the close of trading. This is the first day that the play for a

---

13 The short earns even more if the yield spread between these two bonds narrows since changes in relative yields influence which bond becomes cheap-to-deliver.

change in the cheap-to-deliver bond resulting from changes in yield levels (or factor bias) can be made.

December 29   Last day to give notice of intent to deliver. Notice of intent is assumed for all remaining shorts.

December 30   Last day to give notice of which bond will be delivered. Last day to play change on the cheap-to-deliver due to changes in yield levels and yield spreads.

December 31   Last day for delivery versus futures contracts.

APPENDIX I: CALCULATING PRINCIPAL AND INTEREST FOR T-BOND AND T-NOTE DELIVERY

The example is a client taking delivery of 7 1/4% Bonds due 5/15/16 at a futures settlement price of 93 8/32 for 5 June, 1987 Bond contracts. Note that the rounding of decimals is very important to the calculation:

Principal

Delivery Price   =   (futures price × factor) × contract par
      =   (.9325 × .9159) × $100,000
      =   .85407675 (round to 7 places) × $100,000
      = $85,407.68

Interest

Interest   =   semiannual coupon × days from last coupon date to delivery
    =   ($7250/2/184) × 42
    = $19.7010869565 (round to 7 decimals) × 42
    = $19,7010870 × 42
    = $827.45

Total Delivered Price

Principal + Interest = $86,235.13 per contract

To find the total delivered price for five contracts simply multiply the per contract delivered price by five.

$86,235.13 × 5 = $431,175.65

APPENDIX II: DELIVERY DATES FOR BOND FUTURES CONTRACTS

Contract	First Intent Day	First Notice Day	First Delivery Day	Last Trading Day	Last Delivery Day
Mar 88	Feb 26	Feb 29	Mar 01	Mar 22	Mar 31
Jun 88	May 27	May 31	Jun 01	Jun 21	Jun 30
Sep 88	Aug 30	Aug 31	Sep 04	Sep 21	Sep 30
Dec 88	Nov 27	Nov 30	Dec 04	Dec 20	Dec 30
Mar 89	Feb 27	Feb 28	Mar 01	Mar 21	Mar 31
Jun 89	May 30	May 31	Jun 01	Jun 21	Jun 31
Sep 89	Aug 30	Aug 31	Sep 01	Sep 20	Sep 29
Dec 89	Nov 29	Nov 30	Dec 01	Dec 19	Dec 29

Chapter 5

A One-Factor Model of Interest Rates and Its Application to Treasury Bond Options [*]

Fischer Black
Goldman, Sachs & Co.

Emanuel Derman
Goldman, Sachs & Co.

William Toy
Goldman, Sachs & Co.

This chapter describes a model of interest rates that can be used to value any interest-rate sensitive security. To explain how it works, we concentrate on valuing options on Treasury bonds.

The model has three key features:

1. Its fundamental variable is the short rate—the annualized one-period interest rate r. The short rate is the one factor of the model; its changes drive all security prices.

[*] This article appeared in *Financial Analysts Journal* 46 (January/February, 1990).

2. It takes as inputs an array of long rates (yields on zero-coupon Treasury bonds) for various maturities and an array of yield volatilities for the same bonds. We call the first array the *yield curve* and the second array, the *volatility curve*. Together these curves form the *term structure*.

3. It varies an array of means and an array of volatilities for the future short rate to match the inputs. As the future volatility changes, the future mean reversion changes.

We examine how the model works in an imaginary world in which changes in all bond yields are perfectly correlated; expected returns on all securities over one period are equal; short rates at any time are lognormally distributed; and there are no taxes or trading costs.

VALUING SECURITIES

Suppose we own an interest-rate-sensitive security worth S today. We assume that its price can move up to S_u or down to S_d with equal probability over the next time period. Figure 1 shows the possible changes in S for a one-year time step, starting from a state where the short rate is r.

The expected price of S one year from now is $1/2\ (S_u + S_d)$. The expected return is $1/2\ (S_u + S_d)/S$. Because we assume that all expected returns are equal, and because we can lend money at r, we deduce:

(1)
$$S = \frac{\frac{1}{2}S_u + \frac{1}{2}S_d}{1 + r}$$

where r is today's short rate.

Figure 1   A One-Step Tree

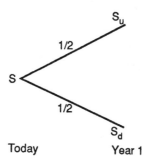

Getting Today's Prices from Future Prices

We can use the one-step tree to relate today's price to the prices one step away. Similarly, we can derive prices one step in the future from prices two steps in the future. In this way, we can relate today's prices to prices two steps away.

Figure 2 shows two-step trees for rates and prices. The short rate starts out at 10 percent. We expect it to rise to 11 percent or drop to 9 percent with equal probability.

The second tree shows prices for a two-year, zero-coupon Treasury. In two years, the zero's price will be $100. Its price one year from now may be $91.74 ($100 discounted by 9 percent) or $90.09 ($100 discounted by 11 percent). The expected price one year from now is the average of $90.09 and $91.74, or $90.92. Our valuation formula, Equation (1), finds today's price by discounting this average by 10 percent to give $82.65.

Figure 2   Two-Step Trees of Short Rates and Prices

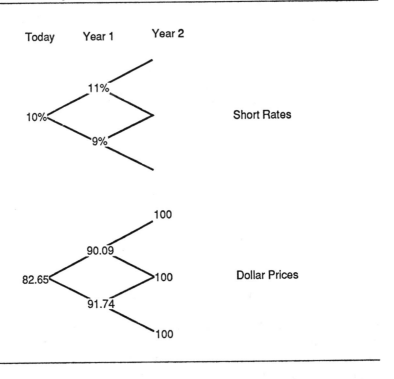

We can in this way value a zero of any maturity, provided our tree of future short rates goes out far enough. We simply start with the security's face value at maturity and find the price at each earlier node by discounting future prices using the valuation formula and the short rate at that node. Eventually we work back to the root of the tree and find the price today.

FINDING SHORT RATES FROM THE TERM STRUCTURE

The term structure of interest rates is quoted in yields, rather than prices. Today's annual yield, y, of the N-year zero in terms of its price, S, is given by finding the y that satisfies:

$$S = \frac{100}{(1 + y)^N}$$
(2)

Similarly, the yields y_u and y_d one year from now corresponding to prices S_u and S_d are given by:

$$S_{u,d} = \frac{100}{(1 + y_{u,d})^{N-1}}$$
(3)

We want to find the short rates that assure that the model's term structure matches today's market term structure. Table 1 gives the assumed market term structure.

The price of a zero today is the expected price one period in the future discounted to today using the short rate. The short rate, r, is 10 percent. Using the price tree of Figure 3, we see that $S_u = S_d = 100$, and $S = 90.91$:

$$90.91 = \frac{\frac{1}{2}100 + \frac{1}{2}100}{1 + r} = \frac{100}{1 + r}$$

Table 1   A Sample Term Structure

Maturity (in years)	Yield (in %)	Yield Volatility (in %)
1	10	20
2	11	19
3	12	18
4	12.5	17
5	13	16

Short Rates One Period in the Future

We can now find the short rates one year from now by looking at the yield and volatility for a two-year zero using the term structure of Table 1.

Look at the two-year short rate tree in Figure 4. Let's call the unknown future short rates r_u and r_d. We want their values to be such that the price and volatility of the two-year zero match the price and volatility in Table 1.

We know today's short rate is 10 percent. Suppose we guess that r_u = 14.32 percent and r_d = 9.79 percent.

Now look at the price and yield trees in Figure 4. A two-year zero has a price of $100 at all nodes at the end of the second period, no matter what short rate prevails. Using the valuation formula—(Equation 1)—we can find the one-year prices by discounting the expected two-year prices by r_u and r_d; we get prices of $87.47 and $91.08. Using Equation (3), we find that yields of 14.32 percent and 9.79 percent correspond to these prices. These are shown on the yield tree in Figure 4.

Now that we have the two-year prices and yields one year out, we can use the valuation formula to get today's price and yield for the two-year zero. Today's price is given by Equation (1)

Figure 3   Finding the Initial Short Rate Using a One-Year Zero

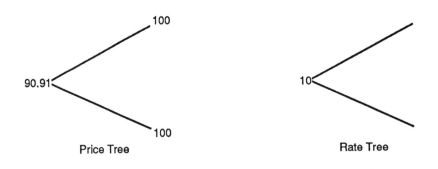

Figure 4   Finding the One-Year Short Rates Using a Two-Year Zero

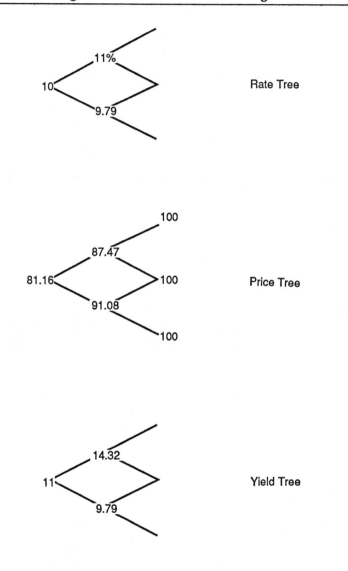

Rate Tree

Price Tree

Yield Tree

by discounting the expected one-year-out price by today's short rate:

$$\frac{\frac{1}{2}(87.47) + \frac{1}{2}(91.08)}{1.1} = 81.16$$

We can get today's yield for the two-year zero, y_2, by using Equation (2) with today's price as S. As the yield tree in Figure 4 shows, y_2 is 11 percent.

The volatility of this two-year yield is defined as the natural logarithm of the ratio of the one-year yields:

$$\sigma_2 = \frac{\ln\frac{14.33}{9.79}}{2} = 19\%$$

With the one-year short rates we have chosen, the two-year zero's yield and yield volatility match those in the term structure of Table 1. This means that our guesses for r_u and r_d were right. Had they been wrong, we would have found the correct ones by trial and error.

So an initial short rate of 10 percent followed by equally probable one-year short rates of 14.32 percent and 9.79 percent guarantee that our the model matches the first two years of the term structure.

More Distant Short Rates

We found today's single short rate by matching the one-year yield. We found the two one-year short rates by matching the two-year yield and volatility. Now we find the short rates two years out.

Figure 5 shows the short rates out to two years. We already know the short rates out to one year. The three unknown short rates at the end of the second year are r_{uu}, r_{ud} and r_{dd}.

The values for these three short rates should let our model match the yield and yield volatility of a three-year zero. We must therefore match two quantities by guessing at three short rates. This contrasts with finding the one-year short rates, where we had to match two quantities with two short rates. As a rule, matching two quantities with two short rates is unique; there is only one set of values for the short rates that produces the right match. Matching two quantities with three short rates is not unique; many sets of three short rates produce the correct yield and volatility.

Remember, however, that our model assumes that the short rate is lognormal with a volatility (of the log of the short rate) that depends only on time. One year in the future, when the short rate is 14.32 percent, the volatility is $1/2 \ln(r_{uu}/r_{ud})$; when the short rate is 9.79 percent, the volatility is $1/2 \ln(r_{ud}/r_{dd})$. Because these volatilities must be the same, we know that $r_{uu}/r_{ud} = r_{ud}/r_{dd}$, or $r^2_{ud} = r_{uu}r_{dd}$.

So we don't really make three independent guesses for the rates; the middle one, r_{ud}, can be found from the other two. This means we have to match only two short rates—r_{uu} and r_{dd}—with two quantities—the three-year yield and volatility in the model. This typically has a unique solution.

Figure 5   Finding the Two-Year Short Rates

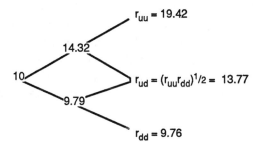

In this case, Figure 5 shows that values for r_{uu}, r_{dd} and r_{ud} of 19.42, 9.76, and 13.77 percent, respectively, produce a three-year yield of 12 percent and volatility of 18 percent, as Table 1 calls for.

We now know the short rates for one and two years in the future. Using a similar process, we can find the short rates on tree nodes farther in the future. Figure 6 displays the full tree of short rates at one-year intervals that matches the term structure of Table 1.

VALUING OPTIONS ON TREASURY BONDS

Given the term structure of Table 1 and the resulting tree of short rates shown in Figure 6, we can use the model to value a bond option.

Coupon Bonds as Collections of Zeroes

Before we can value Treasury bond options, we need to find the future prices of a Treasury bond at various nodes on the tree.

Consider a Treasury with a 10 percent coupon, a face value of $100, and three years left to maturity. For convenience, consider this 10 percent Treasury as a portfolio of three zero-coupon bonds—a one-year zero with a $10 face value; a two-year zero with a $10 face value; and a three-year zero with a $110 face value.

This portfolio has exactly the same annual payoffs as the 10 percent Treasury with three years to maturity. So the portfolio and the Treasury should have the same value. The tree in Figure 6 was built to value all zeroes according to today's yield curve, hence we can use it to value the three zeroes in the portfolio above.

Panel (e) of Figure 7 shows the price of the 10 percent Treasury as the sum of the present values of the zeroes—$95.51. The tree in panel (f) gives the three-year Treasury prices obtained after subtracting $10 of accrued interest on each coupon date.

Figure 6 **Short Rates that Match the Term Structure of Table 1**

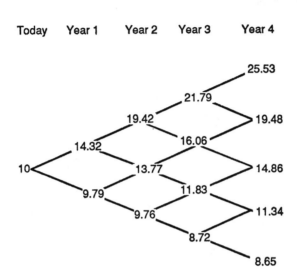

Today   Year 1   Year 2   Year 3   Year 4

25.53
21.79
19.42   19.48
14.32   16.06
10   13.77   14.86
9.79   11.83
9.76   11.34
8.72
8.65

Puts and Calls on Treasuries

We found a price of $95.51 for a three-year, 10 percent Treasury. The security is below par today; it has a 10 percent coupon and yields in today's yield curve are generally higher than 10 percent.

We want to value options on this security—a two-year European call and a two-year European put, both struck at $95. From Figure 7 (e) we see that in two years the three-year Treasury bond may have one of three prices—$110.22, $106.69 or $102.11. The corresponding prices without accrued interest are $100.22, $96.69 and $92.11.

At expiration, the $95 call is in the money if the bond is worth either $100.22 or $96.69. The call's value will be the difference between the bond's price and the strike price. The $95 call will be

Figure 7   Three-Year Treasury Values Obtained by Valuing an Equivalent Portfolio of Zeroes

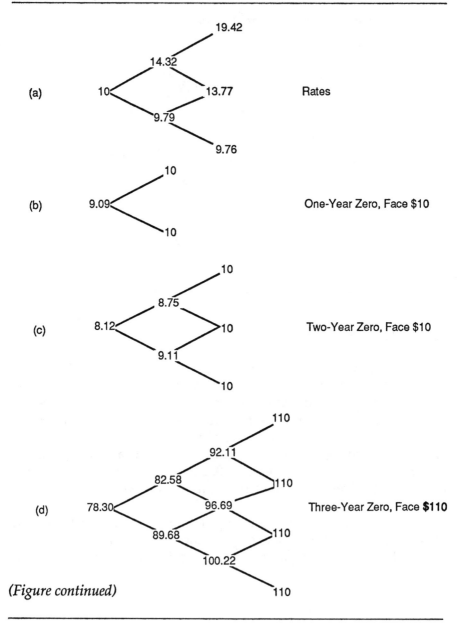

(a)   Rates

(b)   One-Year Zero, Face $10

(c)   Two-Year Zero, Face $10

(d)   Three-Year Zero, Face **$110**

(Figure continued)

Figure 7   (Continued)

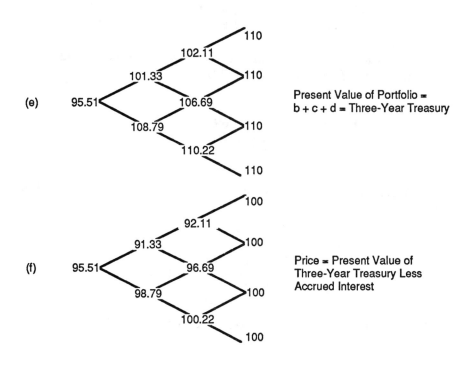

worth $5.22 if the bond is trading at $100.22 at expiration and $1.69 if the bond is trading at $96.69. The call is out of the money, and therefore worth zero, if the bond is trading at $92.11 at expiration. Figure 8 is the short-rate tree over two years, as well as possible call values at expiration of the option in two years.

At expiration the put is in the money if the bond is worth $92.11 (without accrued interest). The put's value will be the difference between $92.11 and the $95 strike price—$2.89. The put is worthless if the bond's price is one of the two higher values, $100.22 or $96.69. Figure 8 gives the put values.

Knowing the call values at expiration we can find the possible values of the call one year before expiration, using the valuation formula given by Equation (1).

If the short rate is 14.32 percent one year from today, the call's value one year before expiration will be:

$$\frac{\frac{1}{2}(0.00) + \frac{1}{2}(1.69)}{1.1432} = 0.74$$

If the short rate is 9.79 percent one year from today, the call's value will be:

$$\frac{\frac{1}{2}(1.69) + \frac{1}{2}(5.22)}{1.0979} = 3.15$$

Given the call values one year out, we can find the value of the call today when the short rate is 10 percent:

$$\frac{\frac{1}{2}(0.74) + \frac{1}{2}(3.15)}{1.1} = 1.77$$

Put values are derived in a similar manner Figure 8 shows the full trees of call and put values.

We have priced European-style options by finding their values at any node as the discounted expected value one step in the future. American-style options can be valued with little extra effort. Because an American option may be exercised at any time, its value at any node is the greater of its value if held or its value if exercised. We obtain its value if held by using the valuation for-

Figure 8   Two-Year Options on a Three-Year Treasury

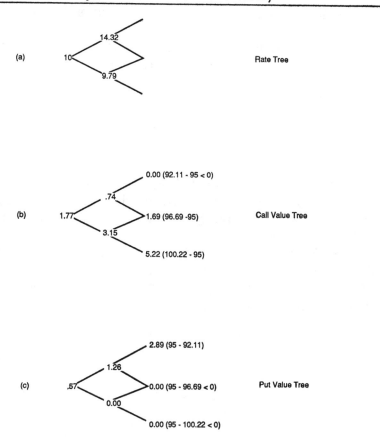

(a)   Rate Tree

(b)   Call Value Tree

(c)   Put Value Tree

mula to get any node's value in terms of values one step in the future. Its value if exercised is the difference between the bond price at the node and the strike price.

Option Hedge Ratios

When interest rates change, so do the prices of bonds and bond options. Bond option investors are naturally interested in how much option prices change in response to changes in the price of the underlying bond. We measure this relation by the hedge ratio (or delta).

Figure 9 shows one-step trees for a Treasury, a call, and a put. For a call worth C on a Treasury with price T, the hedge ratio is:

(4)
$$\Delta_{call} = \frac{C_u - C_d}{T_u - T_d}$$

where C_u and C_d are the values of the call one period from today in the tree corresponding to possible short rates r_u and r_d. A similar formula holds for a put, P, on a Treasury; we simply replace C with P in Equation 4.

For the two-year put and call on the three-year Treasury considered above, start by finding the differences between possible prices one year from today. Given the Treasury prices shown in Figure 7 and the option prices from Figure 8:

$$
\begin{aligned}
T_u - T_d &= 91.33 - 98.79 \\
&= -7.46 \\[6pt]
C_u - C_d &= 0.74 - 3.15 \\
&= -2.41 \\[6pt]
P_u - P_d &= 1.26 - 0.00 \\
&= 1.26
\end{aligned}
$$

We can now derive the hedge ratios, using Equation (4):

$$
\begin{aligned}
\Delta_{call} &= \frac{(-2.41)}{(-7.46)} \\[6pt]
&= 0.32
\end{aligned}
$$

Figure 9   Hedge Ratios for a Call and a Put on a Treasury

$$\Delta_{call} = \frac{C_u - C_d}{T_u - T_d}$$

$$\Delta_{put} = \frac{P_u - P_d}{T_u - T_d}$$

$$\Delta_{put} = \frac{(1.26)}{(-7.46)}$$

$$= -0.17$$

These hedge ratios give us the sensitivity of the option to changes in the underlying Treasury price by describing the change in the option's price per dollar change in the Treasury's price. They therefore tell us how to hedge the Treasury with the option, and vice versa. The call hedge ratio is positive because the call prices increase when the Treasury price increases. In contrast, the put hedge ratio is negative because put prices decrease as the Treasury price increases.

We compute these ratios much more accurately by using finely-spaced trees.

Reducing the Interval Size

In the previous examples, the short-rate tree had coarse one-year steps, Treasuries paid annual coupons and options could only be exercised once a year.

To get accurate solutions for option values, we need a tree with finely spaced steps between today and the option's expiration. Ideally we would like a tree with one-day steps and a 30-year horizon, so that coupon payments and option exercise dates would always fall exactly on a node. We would also like to have many steps to expiration, even for options on the verge of expiring.

In practice, our computer doesn't have enough memory to build a 30-year tree with daily steps. And even if it did, it would take us hours to value a security. Instead, we can build a sequence of short-rate trees, each with the same number of steps but compressed into shorter and shorter horizons. Thus each tree has finer spacing than the one before it. For example, we might use today's term structure to build short-rate trees that extend over 30 years, 15 years, 7 1/2 years, and so on. In this way, no matter when the option expires, we will always have one tree with enough steps to value the option accurately.

To value an option on any Treasury, we use two trees—a coarse one with enough steps to value the Treasury accurately from its maturity back to today, and a fine one with enough steps to value the option accurately from its expiration until today. We find the Treasury values on the coarse tree by using the model's valuation formula from maturity to today. Then we interpolate these Treasury values onto the fine tree, which may often have as many as 60 periods. Maturity, expiration and coupon dates that fall between nodes are carefully interpolated to the nearest node in time. In this way, the option can be accurately valued.

Interpolating across trees gives us accurate, yet rapid, results. Once model values have been found to match the term structure, we can value options in a few seconds.

IMPROVING THE MODEL

We considered more complex models that use more than one factor to describe shifts in the yield curve. Increasing the number of factors improves the model's results. The more factors we use, the better the model. But a multi-factor model is much harder to think about and work with than a single-factor model. It also takes much more computer time. We therefore think it pays to work with different single-factor models before moving on to a multi-factor model.

Along these lines, we examined the effects on our model of letting forward mean reversion and forward short-rate volatility vary independently. (They are tied together in the current model only by the geometry of a tree with equal time spacing throughout.) We found that varying forward mean reversion and varying forward short rate volatility give very different results. We can use one or the other alone, or a mixture of both, in matching the term structure.

Chapter 6

Volatility and Option Pricing

Kenneth S. Leong
Bank of Tokyo

The valuation of an option instrument is very sensitive to the volatility assumption. The pricing volatility in the Black-Scholes model should be the average volatility that is expected to prevail during the lifetime of the option priced. Unfortunately, expected volatility is an unobservable variable and the market's estimate of forward volatility seems to be constantly changing. So the uncertainty in volatility estimation leads to a wide margin of error in option pricing and hedging.

Several major simplifying assumptions made in the Black-Scholes pricing model, which represent abstrations from reality, also increase the potential for mispricing. Practitioners need to be aware of these hidden assumptions whenever a Black-Scholes type of option pricing model is applied. Non-discriminant use of the Black-Scholes model, without constantly checking the suitability of its underlying assumptions, potentially can lead to very costly mistakes. This is particularly true in pricing very short-dated or long-dated options.

Hidden assumptions in the Black-Scholes model also account for some non-market related anomalies observed in the implied volatility over weekends and during days of important economic statistics release.

This chapter describes the ramifications of several simplifying assumptions made in the Black-Scholes model and some market anomalies associated with them. Also discussed are the problems with using historical volatility as a proxy for expected future volatility. Finally, the meaning of volatility in a Black-Scholes context is investigated.

VOLATILITY AND THE BLACK-SCHOLES MODEL

The term "volatility" has many alternative definitions and meanings. Here, "volatility" is used in the Black-Scholes sense because the Black-Scholes model is the most commonly used model for the purpose of option pricing. Intuitively, volatility refers to the propensity for change and variation. In their classical paper, "The Pricing of Options and Corporate Liabilities," Black and Scholes make reference to the "variance rate of the return on the stock." The term "volatility" is never used in the original Black-Scholes paper. Later, academics generalized the concept and coined the term "volatility." It is used generically to mean the variance of the "price relative" of the instrument underlying the option that needs to be priced. "Price relative" here refers to the ratio of the underlying instrument's prices at two different dates.

The Black-Scholes model focuses on the price relatives because of the behavorial assumption it has made regarding the underlying variable. It is assumed that the price of the underlying instrument follows a "stochastic process" (i.e., behavioral pattern) called "Geometric Brownian Motion." This assumption has several important implications:

1. **Price movements happening in non-overlapping time intervals are independent of each other.** More specifically:

(1)
$$
\begin{aligned}
\text{Let} \quad E(i) &= \ln P(i) - \ln P(i-1) = \ln [P(i) / P(i-1)] \\
E(j) &= \ln P(j) - \ln P(j-1) = \ln [P(j) / P(j-1)]
\end{aligned}
$$

where $i \neq j$

Then, E(i) and E(j) are assumed to be statistically independent random variables.

2. **The natural logarithm of price relatives is normally distributed with a variance directly *proportional* to the time interval between the two prices.**

(2) $\text{Var} [\ln P(t + \Delta t) - \ln P(t)] = \sigma^2 \Delta t$

A more rigorous presentation of these mathematical relationships can be found in Appendix I.

Three abstractions that Black and Scholes undertake when modelling the underlying variable's behavior lead to serious problems in estimating volatility. They are described as follows.

Time

The model does not offer any operational definition of time. There are at least three alternative ways of defining and measuring the time element that goes into the pricing model:

Calendar time   actual number of days elapsed

Trading time   the number of days on which the underlying instrument can trade

Economic time   days on which significant economic events take place

Depending on the operational definition chosen, there is a specific measurement of time. Refer to equation (2). The variance of price relatives is expressed as a product of two variables, σ^2 and Δt, where σ^2 is the variance rate per unit of time and Δt is the time elapsed. So, henceforth, refer to $\sigma^2 \Delta t$ as the "effective volatility" and σ^2 as the "standardized volatility." Given the same σ^2, a different measurement of Δt leads to a different effective volatility. For example, an option with a year to expiration has 365 (or 366) calendar days, but only about 250 trading days.

The decision of which definition to use should, perhaps, be determined by empirical evidence. Trading markets, however, move mostly in response to economic events such as the announcement of economic statistics. Because of this consideration, it seems that time measurements based on the economic time concept are more appropriate. Most practitioners who use the Black-Scholes model regularly, however, take time measurements based on calendar days. In the section discussing "market anomalies," it is seen that this practice causes strange behavior in the implied volatilities of traded options.

Constant Volatility

Black and Scholes assume a world of constant and homogenous volatility in deriving the pricing model. This is certainly a simplifying assumption, hence the following observations:

The *empirical* market volatility is different at different times. The magnitude of market volatility tends to fluctutate just like commodity prices.

The market *expects* different volatilities at different times. Traders expect more volatility on days when there are releases of major economic statistics.

Independence Assumption

As stated before, the Black-Scholes model assumes that price movements happening in non-overlapping time intervals are independent of each other. This assumption leads to the result that the underlying security price has a variance rate which is proportional to the time elapsed. To the extent that this independence assumption does not hold in reality, the variance is misestimated. Emprical data analysis has shown that commodity prices demonstrate rather significant serial correlations.

IMPLIED VOLATILITY AND TERM STRUCTURE

The correct volatility to go into the Black-Scholes equation should be the expected volatility for the period covering the remaining life of the option to be priced. Because volatility varies over time, the pricing volatility has to be some sort of average of the daily volatilities which are supposed to prevail on each of the days within the lifetime of the option considered. We will assume here that this average is the simple arithmatic average.

As an illustration, suppose an option has three days to expiration. The change in pricing volatility under no change in market expectation is presented in Appendix II. A volatility of 2.25% for both Day 1 and Day 3 is expected. The expected volatility for Day 2 is 4%, much higher than the other two days because there are GNP statistics to be released on that day. The volatility for entering the Black-Scholes equation is, therefore, computed as (1/3) (2.25 + 4 +2.25) = 2.83%. If the market expectation regarding volatility stays unchanged, after one day, the new pricing volatility becomes (1/2) (4 +2.25) = 3.12%. After the GNP is released, only one day remains to expiration. The new pricing volatility becomes 2.25%. Thus, the pricing volatility changes continuously as time passes even if the market estimate of the daily volatilities stays the same.

Herein lies the problem with "implied volatilities." Because expected volatility is not an observable variable, practitioners calculate the volatilities implied in the prices of traded options as a gauge of volatility expectation. But, as explained above, because the volatility used in the Black-Scholes formula represents a moving average, a change in the implied volatility can be caused by either a change in market expectation or just time passage, or both. Implied volatility has rather limited analytical value because it is not always possible to segregate the moving average effect from the effects of change in market expectation.

Note that the problems encountered here lie in the fact that there are different volatility anticipations on different days. The Black-Scholes pricing volatility, being a summary statistic, smooths over the day-to-day irregularities. Important information is lost in this smoothing process. The situation is analogous to the distinction between the yield-to-maturity approach and the spot rate approach in modeling interest rates. So the "term structure" concept for volatilities is introduced to take care of the period-to-period difference in volatility expectations. This has to be done, however, at the expense of increasing considerably the complexity of the modeling. Appendix III shows how implied forward volatilities can be derived from spot volatilities. The analogy to implied forward rate should be noted.

SEVERAL MARKET ANOMALIES

Researchers and market practitioners have found two market anomalies associated with the simplifying assumptions made in the Black-Scholes model. They are the "weekend effect" and the "economic number effect."

For example, Richard Robb of the Chicago Corporation has observed that the implied volatility of at-the-money T-bond future calls tends to rise from before to after the weekend. This does not mean, however, that money can be made buying calls on Fridays and liquidating the position on the following Mondays. This is because the time decay over the weekend offsets the effect of volatility change so that, on the net, the price change is not significant. It should be noted that calendar time was used as a basis of time measurement in a study of this phenomenon. Given that, in general, there are few economic events happening over weekends, a time measurement using calendar days overstates the time decay. Therefore, the market is rational in keeping options prices rather stable as weekends pass. To counteract the overstated time decay, the implied volatility has to increase.

As a related phenomenon, it is observed that implied volatility tends to fall after an important economic statistic is released. Announcement of economic statistics represents the passage of economic time but not calendar time. These announcements generate effective "time decays" which are not recognized by the Black-Scholes model. Therefore, implied volatility has to decline to simulate the desired price change due to effective time decay.

THE PRICING OF SHORT-DATED OPTIONS

The pricing of very short-dated options is tricky for three reasons:

1. Some theoretical issues regarding the quantification of time to expiration were described above. Henceforth, this is referred to as the "time basis" problem. Obviously, the time basis problem magnifies as the option draws closer and closer to expiration because the discrepancy between calendar time and economic time can lead to a difference in option pricing which is large in proportion to the option price itself.

2. There is some evidence that the market switches its basis of option valuation as the option approaches expiration, referred to here as "basis switch." For longer-term options, say options with over one year to expiration, the volatility estimate tends to be more approximate in nature and does not focus on the day-to-day irregularities. As the expiration date draws close, the market seems to price the option more and more on an economic time basis and the number of economic statistics releases over the remaining life of the option gains importance in determining option value. As an extreme example, a trader is asked to guarantee the price of an interest rate cap for several hours. The trader essentially is asked to write a very short-dated option. The Black-Scholes model is virtually useless in determining the value of such an option.

3. Some practitioners believe that OTC options are, in general, overpriced. More specifically, they believe that the market tends to overestimate forward volatility. If this is true, as the expiration date approaches, the error made in

the initial pricing will become more and more obvious; then a significant drop in implied volatility which is unrelated to the current market condition should be expected, referred to as the "day-of-reckoning effect."

For these reasons, the pricing of very short-dated options has to be done with extra care. In some cases, the classical Black-Scholes approach is not valid. Therefore, occasional mispricings and hence, arbitrage opportunities, can be found.

VOLATILITY ESTIMATION

The most common volatility estimate is the historical variance of the price of the underlying instrument. This estimation method can be biased due to the following reasons:

Change in Market Condition A change in market condition can increase or decrease the market's estimate of where volatility will be. This historical variance method makes the implicit assumption that volatility is a constant number consistent with the Black-Scholes model but inconsistent with market reality. Empirical analysis shows that the daily variance of the underlying price can fluctuate widely from day to day.

Term Structure Even if volatilities could be estimated perfectly without uncertainty, the market can expect different volatilities for different time periods into the future. The historical variance method does not allow for this kind of variation in the volatility estimate. In other words, it does not allow for the term structure effect.

Mean Reversion Some people believe that economic time series such as interest rates have a tendency to revert to some mean level. Depending on the time horizon over which the historical variance is computed, it may or may not capture the mean-reversion effect. "Mean reversion" is a particularly acute problem for long-dated options because it is more probable for mean reversal to happen over a long time horizon.

Unfortunately, there are very few alternatives to the historical approach to volatility estimation. Some option traders use other approaches such as technical analysis or the Box-Jenkin's Method for forecasting future volatility. It is probably difficult to demonstrate that one method is better than another. In any case, the important point is that the pricing volatility should be the volatility that is believed to prevail in the time period covered by the option being priced, which may have very little resemblance to the current empirical volatility.

WHAT CONSTITUTES VOLATILITY

With the understanding that volatility is the key determinant of option value, it is natural to ask what exactly constitutes volatility. According to the Black-Scholes model, higher volatility means higher option value and vice versa. Certainly, not all forms of price variation lead to volatility. Practitioners tend to use the term "volatility" very loosely to mean possibly two things—propensity for big price movements and price uncertainty.

It should be noted that because of the way volatility is defined by the Black-Scholes model, a big price movement per se will not necessarily translate into big volatility. Uncertain price fluctuations (i.e., wave-like movements representing possibilities for both ups and downs), however, always translate into volatility. This is true because Black-Scholes volatility is based on the statistical concept of variance, which measures price uncertainty. One-way price movements, because they do not involve both ups and downs, do not demonstrate price uncertainty and hence do not increase option value.

This concept of volatility is illustrated in Appendix IV which illustrates an extreme example of price variation through time but no price uncertainty. The price of the underlying instrument is assumed to follow exactly a known trend-line. In this case, the evolution of price through time is known with complete certainty. It is proved that the Black-Scholes volatility is zero. Note that an option on an instrument without price uncertainty (i.e., no volatility) is not necessarily worthless. Because the terminal payoff of that option is known, the value of the option should be the expected payoff discounted back to the present at the appropriate "riskless rate." In this case, therefore, the "option" is really a zero-coupon bond.

After determining that the essence of volatility is uncertainty, it is necessary to ask what kind of condition will induce big volatility. For this purpose, a simple example is constructed to assume that the logarithm of the underlying instrument's price follows a Browian motion. The model is presented in Appendix V.

In this model, the logarithm of the underlying's price has only two alternative movements: it can move either up or down by the same amount c. The probability of an up move (a) does not have to equal the probability of a down move $(1 - a)$. Given this specification, it is derived that the volatility is given by $c^2 [1 - (2a - 1)^2]$. The variance is maximized when a is equal to 1/2. In addition, it increases as c increases. These conditions for maximizing variance are met in a market where prices make non-directional choppy movements of large magnitude.

On the other hand, the variance is minimized when a equals either I or O. In either case, the asset price will follow a trend line (either trending up or trending down). This confirms our observation in Appendix IV.

APPENDIX I: VOLATILITY COMPUTATION

Let P_i = price of the underlying instrument on date i
X_i = the natural logarithm of P_i.
N = number of days in the remaining life of the option
V = effective volatility

Then, the effective volatility is given by:

$$V = \text{Var} [\ln (P_N / P_O)]$$

$$= \text{Var} (\ln P_N - \ln P_O)$$

$$= \quad \text{Var}\,(X_N - X_O)$$

$$= \quad \text{Var}\,[(X_N - X_{N-1}) + (X_{N-1} - X_{N-2}) + \ldots + (X_1 - X_O)]$$

Define $E_i \quad = \quad X_i - X_{i-1}$ for $i = 1, 2, \ldots, N$

If the E_i's are uncorrelated with each other, then:

$$V \quad = \quad \sum_{i=1}^{N} \text{Var}\,E_i$$

$$\text{Define} = \sigma^2 = (1/N) \sum_{i=1}^{N} \text{Var}\,E_i$$

Then, $V = N\sigma^2$

Notes

1. $V = \text{Var}\,(\ln P_n - \ln P_O)$

    Because P_O is a known constant, $\text{Var}\,(\ln P_O)$ is zero. Therefore:

    $$V = \quad \text{Var}\,(\ln P_N) = \text{Var}\,X_N$$

2. σ^2 can be represented as an arithmetic average of the daily volatilities expected over the lifetime of the option because the day-to-day price changes are assumed to be independent of each other.

3. Because $V = N\sigma^2$ and σ^2 is a constant, the effective volatility is directly propotional to the time to expiration.

APPENDIX II: PRICING VOLATILITY AS MOVING AVERAGE

	Expected Daily Volatility
Day 1	2.25%
Day 2	4.00%
Day 3	2.25%

Days to Expiration	*Pricing Volatility*
3	(1/3) (2.25 + 4 + 2.25) = 2.83%
2	(1/2) (4 + 2.25) = 3.12%
1	2.25%

APPENDIX III: FORWARD VOLATILITY

Assume an option with N days to expiration. This period of N days can be divided into two sub-periods, referred to as subperiods 1 and 2. Assume that subperiod 2 has considerably more expected volatility than subperiod 1. Refer to the average volatility for the two subperiods as σ_1^2 and σ_2^2 respectively. Refer to the average volatility for the N-day period as σ^2.

Recall from Appendix A that:

$$V = \sum_{i=1}^{N} \text{Var } E_i$$

$$= \sum_{i=1}^{k} \text{Var } E_i + \sum_{i=k+1}^{N} \text{Var } E_i$$
$$= k\,\sigma_1^2 + (N-k)\,\sigma_2^2$$

Because $V = N\sigma^2$, therefore

$$\sigma^2 = (1/N)\,[k\sigma_1^2 + (N-k)\,\sigma_2^2]$$

The volatility for the second period then can be expressed as a function of σ^2 and σ_1^2:

$$\sigma_2^2 = (N\sigma^2 - k\sigma_1^2)/(N-k)$$

APPENDIX IV: VOLATILITY IN A STRICTLY TRENDING MARKET

For a strictly linearly-trending market,

$$P_t = a + bt$$

where a and b are constants

The volatility of the underlying instrument is defined in the Black-Scholes model as:

$$V = \text{Var } [\ln (P_{t+1}/P_t)]$$
$$P_{t+1} = a + b\,(t+1)$$

$$P_t = a + bt$$

Therefore, $P_{t+1}/P_t = \dfrac{a + b(t+1)}{a + bt} = \text{constant}$

and $\ln(P_{t+1}/P_t) = \text{constant}$

Therefore, $V = \text{Var}\,[\ln(P_{t+1}/P_t)] = 0$

APPENDIX V: VOLATILITY IN A CHOPPY MARKET

Let P_t = price of the underlying instrument at time t
X_t = the natural logarithm of P_t

Let the price movement be a Brownian motion process as characterized as:

$$X_{t+1} = X_t + Z_t$$

$$\text{where } Z_t = \begin{cases} c \text{ with probability } a \\ -c \text{ with probability } 1-a \end{cases}$$

We deduce:

$$E(Z_t) = ac - (1-a)c = c(2a-1)$$

$$E(Z_t)^2 = c^2 a + c^2(1-a) = c^2$$

Let V = volatility measure = $\text{Var}(X_{t+1} - X_t)$

Then, $V = \text{Var } Z_t = $ $E(Z_t^2) - [E(Z_t)]^2$

$\qquad\qquad\quad = \quad c^2 - c^2(2a-1)^2$

$\qquad\qquad\quad = \quad c^2[1-(2a-1)^2]$

Chapter 7

Introduction to Interest Rate Swaps

Raj E. S. Venkatesh
Chase Manhattan Bank, N.A.

Vijaya E. Venkatesh
Credit Lyonnais

Ravi E. Dattatreya
Sumitomo Bank Capital Markets

INTRODUCTION

An interest rate swap is a contractual agreement between two parties to exchange a series of payments for a stated period of time. The nomenclature arises from the fact that typically the payments in a swap are similar to interest payments on a borrowing. When combined with an asset or a liability, a swap can change its nature i.e., risk characteristics, by changing the net cash flow. For example, a fixed rate liability can be converted to a floating rate liability using an interest rate swap.

Since its beginnings in the late 1970s, the interest rate swap has grown into an indispensable product and has proved to be a major advancement in the evolution of the world of financial markets. The annual size of the swap business is nearly $2 trillion of notional amount, as shown in Figure 1. The swap market has increased the interconnection between financial resources globally. It has changed, in a fundamental way, the manner in which institutions analyze funding decisions. This is a natural result of the fact that swaps provide new and efficient ways to manage assets and liabilities. The use of swaps is also broad: it is no longer a specialized gadget limited to a selected few. It is now an accepted financing technique of financiers worldwide to the extent that it has become a routine requirement to consider swap financing along with traditional alternatives. In parallel with the increased use of swaps, several innovations have also been developed such as swap

Figure 1   Interest Rate Swaps—Total Market Volume

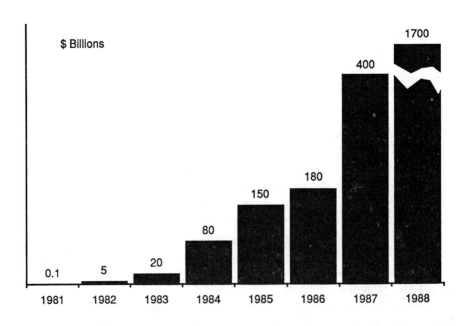

structures with option-like features and derivatives such as caps and floors. The popularity of the swap has also brought several advantages to the users such as increased liquidity and standard documentation. There is the International Swap Dealers' Association (ISDA) which has nearly one hundred members. New players, notably insurance companies, have emerged. Many dealers run matched books, i.e., they offset or hedge one swap against another identical swap; Others use the portfolio approach applying advanced techniques for hedging purposes. The portfolio approach provides maximum flexibility in providing swap products to clients. The general availability of these valuation methodologies and the high level of confidence placed in them by the swap dealers has in no small way fueled the growth of the swap market.

The phenomenal success of the swap market justifies the prevailing sentiment that it is perhaps the single most important development in recent years. The success itself arises from the fact that the swap fills a need no other existing product can efficiently satisfy. It is qualitatively different from other innovations. The swap is not a specific response to a unique market condition. It is an outgrowth of a long unsatisfied demand.

The capital markets have recently been characterized by unprecedented volatility. Institutional expectations naturally change in response to shifting market conditions. The swap provides an effective way for institutions to act on these changed expectations: they can lock-in any gains, or minimize higher potential losses. Available alternatives are either too expensive or have balance sheet implications, e.g., early retirement of debt. While hedging with the usual derivatives such as futures and options requires frequent monitoring and rebalancing, swap hedging requires no such constant attention and activity for long periods of time. The swap simply has no equal as a financing and risk management tool.

Given that swaps pervade the financial markets world wide, it is essential for every participant in the markets to obtain a thorough understanding of swaps. This is especially so because the swap market, due to its enormous size, has begun to exert significant influence in many other markets.

A SIMPLE INTEREST RATE SWAP TRANSACTION

To understand how a swap works, let us look at Figure 2 which presents a simple, so called 'plain vanilla' swap. Recall that a swap is an agreement between two parties, each called a *counterparty*.

Example (A Simple Swap). SM is a swap market maker. SM serves its clients by offering to enter into swap transactions of various kinds. RB is a regional bank. RB has just issued $100mm of fixed rate Eurobonds of 5 year maturity at a spread of 40 basis points over the 5 year Treasury. The Treasury yield is at 8.20% and therefore the coupon on the bond is 8.60%. RB is using the proceeds from the bond issue to fund a $100mm floating rate loan. The loan is of 5 year maturity and has a rate of six-month LIBOR plus 50 basis points.

In this case, RB has a floating rate asset, the loan, but a fixed rate liability, the bond. This situation is known as an asset/liability *gap*. The gap is much more than an intellectual curiosity. It can have significant financial implications on RB in the following way. If rates fall, the cash flow from the loan will decrease but the cash flow due on the liability remains constant, resulting in a loss of the spread earned. Similarly, if the rates rise, the spread increases due to the higher level of cash flow from the asset. The spread that RB earns is thus subject to rate risk.

Example (*continued*). RB can bridge the asset/liability gap and lock-in the spread by using an interest rate swap. Assuming that the swap spreads are at 65 basis points, it can contract with SM to pay, for a period of 5 years, six-month LIBOR on a notional principal amount of $100mm in return for fixed annual cash receipts from SM of 8.85% (8.20% Treasury rate plus the 65 basis point swap spread) on the same notional amount. RB pays LIBOR to SM out of the cash flow received from the loan, retaining the 50 basis point spread. The 8.60% interest payments due on the bond issue is covered by the 8.85% swap payments from SM. Even here, RB retains the 25 basis point spread. Thus, RB earns a total of 75 basis points (50 basis point spread over LIBOR from the loan, 25 basis

Figure 2   A Simple Swap Transaction

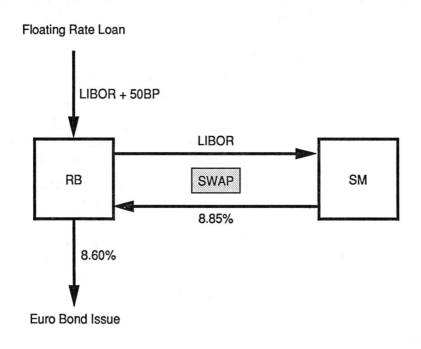

point spread over the bond coupon from the swap) from the combined transaction.

More importantly, this spread is virtually locked-in. The earned spread is immune to interest rate changes. As the interest receipts from the loan change, the payments due on the swap change in lock-steps, effectively insulating RB from rate volatility.

REVIEW OF THE SIMPLE SWAP TRANSACTION

Several important characteristics of a swap can be illustrated using the simple transaction above.

1. In an interest rate swap transaction, only payments resembling or corresponding to the interest payments on a notional (loan) amount are exchanged, the principal amount itself is not. This fact has important implications on the amount of credit risk in a swap transaction.

2. One party pays a floating rate, the other party pays a fixed rate. This is typical of most interest rate swap transactions even though both parties could pay floating (or fixed). typical floating rate indexes used are LIBOR, commercial paper, Fed funds rate, prime rate and T-Bill rate. Most (about 75%) of the swaps in dollars are based on LIBOR.

3. The swap has a specific notional amount and maturity. The floating side has a specified index, e.g., six-month LIBOR.

4. The swap rate, i.e., the fixed rate, is quoted as a spread over the appropriate maturity current coupon Treasury. The payments on the floating side are usually made flat, i.e., at the selected index rate without any spread.

TERMINOLOGY

Interest Rate Swap.   Refers to the contractual agreement to exchange specified cash flows between the two parties.

Counterparties.   The two principal parties involved in a swap transaction.

Floating-Rate Payer.   This is the party that pays floating rate in a swap. This party also receives fixed rate cash flows and is said to be long the swap.

Fixed Rate Payer.   This is the party that pays fixed rate in a swap transaction. This party also receives floating rate flows and is short the swap.

Notional Principal Amount. This is the amount that is used to determine the actual cash flows paid or received by applying the corresponding interest rates for the appropriate calendar periods.

Coupon. The swap coupon refers to the fixed rate of interest in a swap. This is also known as swap price, swap rate and swap strike.

Term. This refers to the period commencing from the first day of coupon accrual and ending on the maturity date.

Trade Date. This is the date on which the counterparties enter into a swap transaction. The swap rate is also agreed upon on this date.

Settlement Date or Effective Date. This is the date on which the coupon starts accruing. This is the first day of the swap term, and is usually two business days after the Trade Date.

Reset Date. The date on which the floating rate is set. The rate set on this date is generally applicable for the subsequent period until next reset date. In an arrears swap (discussed later), reset date is at the end of the payment period to which the rate is applicable.

Reset Frequency. Number of times reset dates occur in a year. Generally, reset frequency reflects the floating rate index. This frequency is not necessarily the same as the number of payment dates in a year.

Maturity Date. Interest stops accruing on this date. Generally, there is an exchange of principal amount also on this date in case of a currency swap (defined later). This date is also referred to as the Termination Date.

Intermediary. A third party that stands between two principal parties in a swap transaction.

At-Market or At-the-Money Swap. An interest rate swap in which no up-front payments by either party is necessary, that is, the value of the swap is zero. The corresponding swap rate is the at-market or at-the-money swap rate.

Off-market Swap. (a) Above-market. The swap is above-market if the rate is greater than the at-the-money swap rate. The value of the swap is positive. In this case, the fixed payer will receive an adjustment, e.g., up-front premium. **(b) Below-market.** In a below-market swap, the fixed rate is less than the at-the-money swap rate. The swap value is negative. In this swap, the fixed receiver will receive an adjustment or premium.

SWAP APPLICATION EXAMPLES

There are countless ways of using interest rate swaps to manage cash flows. The actual objectives sought by swap users are also numerous. Generally, swaps are used by institutions as a tool to render fund raising more efficient.

The attraction of swaps in financing applications is based on the concept of comparative advantage. That is, two institutions can achieve mutual economic benefits by exchanging funds that are available to them at relatively cheaper costs. It is commonly observed in the fixed income markets that the credit spread between higher and lower rated institutions for fixed rate borrowings is wider than the corresponding spread for floating rate borrowings. Obviously, the higher rated borrower pays a lower rate in either market. Yet, the lower rated borrower pays a lesser credit spread in the floating rate market. In other words, the lower rated borrower has a *relative* or *comparative* advantage over the higher rated borrower in the floating rate market. Conversely, the higher rated borrower has the relative advantage in the fixed rate market.

Now, if each borrower raised funds in the market in which it has the greater relative advantage, then the corresponding interest payments can be swapped to achieve cheaper funding rates for both. This concept can be illustrated with a simple example.

Example 1 (Comparative Advantage). HR, a high rated borrower can raise funds at 8.60% fixed or at LIBOR flat. LR, a low rated institution, can borrow at 9.60% fixed or at LIBOR+0.50%. That is, the credit spread in the fixed rate market is 100 basis points whereas for floating rate borrowings, it is just 50 basis points. Suppose, as in Figure 3, HR borrows fixed at 8.60% and LR borrows floating at LIBOR+0.50%. HR and LR can then enter into a fixed/floating swap where HR pays LIBOR and receives 8.85%. The net interest payments are LIBOR-0.25% for HR and 9.35% fixed for LR. Thus, each borrower has achieved a savings on its own borrowing: HR saves 25 basis points relative to a straight floating rate borrowing (LIBOR-0.25% vs. LIBOR flat); LR also saves 25 basis points compared to a straight fixed rate borrowing (9.35% vs. 9.60%).

In practice, in addition to achieving cheaper funding, effective interest rate risk management is also a common objective. Unlike other derivative products such as futures and options, swaps can be used for interest rate hedging over long periods of time without any need for frequent monitoring and rebalancing.

The following additional examples should provide a flavor of the variety in swap usage.

Example 2 (Reduce Fixed Rate Cost). A midwestern manufacturing company, MM, seeks fixed rate funding for 5 years. It can borrow fixed for 5 years at 9.30% or floating at LIBOR+1/8. Suppose that swap rates are at 8.85%. The company can borrow floating, and execute a swap transaction on which it would pay 8.85% and receive LIBOR. The net cost of funding using swaps is 8.975% (8.85% payment on the swap plus the 1/8 spread over LIBOR paid on the loan), a 32.5 basis point saving relative to the straight 9.30% financing.

Example 3 (Obtain Fixed Rate Funds). A Japanese trading company, JT, needs fixed rate borrowing. It normally raises funds through a CP program. By using a swap transaction, JT can achieve its goal of fixing its interest cost while continuing to raise funds in the traditional manner in the commercial paper market. It can enter into a 5-year fixed/CP swap, paying 8.80% in return for monthly payments close to its CP funding cost. The cost of swap related financing is 8.80%.

Example 4 (Reduce Floating Rate Cost). A California retailer, CR, has traditionally borrowed at LIBOR+1/8 from its banks. It discovers that 5-year funding can be obtained from the public markets at 8.55% or 0.35% above Treasuries. Swap rates are at 8.85%. The retailer can issue the fixed rate public bond and enter into a swap paying LIBOR and receiving 8.85%. The combination of the bond and the swap results in a net funding cost of LIBOR-0.30% (LIBOR payment on the swap plus the 8.55% coupon on the bond less the 8.85% receipt on the swap), at a savings of 42.5 basis points over traditional borrowing.

Example 5 (Guarantee Liquidity). A Boston technology company, TC, has an active CP program, but would like to reduce its dependency on the commercial paper market for liquidity reasons. Yet, it prefers to fund at CP from risk management point of view. TC can borrow fixed at 8.70% (.50% over Treasuries) and enter into a swap whereby it receives 8.70% and pays CP index less 10 basis points. This rate is competitive with its own CP issue, and TC now has liquidity cushion.

Example 6 (Convert to Floating). A European automotive company, AC, borrowed fixed for seven years at 11.25% three years ago. Now, with the four-year Treasuries at 8.15% and swap spreads at 55 basis points, the treasurer feels that the average short rates will be considerably less than 11.25% for the remaining life of the debt. He therefore swaps into floating, receiving 8.70% and paying LIBOR. With 6-month LIBOR at 8.06%, his net cost for the first six months is 10.61% (8.06% plus 11.25% on the bond issue less 8.70% received on the swap), a savings of 64 basis points (11.25% old coupon less 10.61% new initial coupon). He has potential for further savings in the future if his forecast of a lower level of interest rates hold good.

Figure 3   Using a Swap to Exploit Comparative Advantage

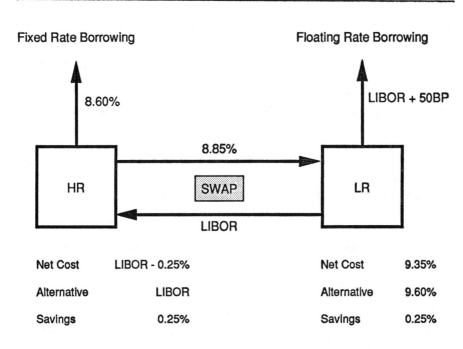

Fixed Rate Borrowing   Floating Rate Borrowing

8.60%   LIBOR + 50BP

8.85%

HR   SWAP   LR

LIBOR

Net Cost	LIBOR - 0.25%		Net Cost	9.35%
Alternative	LIBOR		Alternative	9.60%
Savings	0.25%		Savings	0.25%

Example 7 (Lock-in Low Fixed Rate).   Four years ago an oil company, OC, executed an 8-year, 13% fixed rate new issue swapped
into floating at LIBOR-0.30%. Today, the treasurer feels that the US
rates are at a low point. He wishes to execute another interest rate
swap to lock-in today's rates for the remainder of the issue. He
pays 8.70% for a new swap, receiving LIBOR. His net cost is 8.40%
(8.70% payment on the new swap less LIBOR receipt on the new
swap plus (LIBOR-0.30%) net cost of previous financing) for the
remaining life of the bond.

Example 8 (Obtain Desired Structure).   A start-up company, SC,
has access to floating rate funds from its traditional banker, TB.

SC, however, would like fixed rate funding. In addition, it would like to keep its interest costs low in the initial years and is willing to pay a compensating higher rate in the later years. In this case, the bank (TB) can make what is known as a step-up coupon loan to SC. This loan starts with a small interest rate, and after a few years, the interest rate will step-up. TB can then enter into a swap where it receives floating and pays fixed cash flows closely reflecting the step-up cash flow from the loan. In effect, the bank will have a floating rate loan, and SC will have a fixed rate, step-up borrowing. Note in this case that achieving the desired structure is perhaps more important to SC than squeezing the last basis point out of the market.

The swap participants in the above examples will have different objectives. The swaps executed to meet these objectives are also different in overall structure. Yet, the attentive reader can observe that the needs of each party seem to mirror that of another, and can be fulfilled by combining them in swap transactions appropriately. MM and CR can enter into a 5-year fixed/LIBOR swap, where MM will pay fixed and CR will pay floating. JT and TC can execute a 5-year fixed/CP swap with TC paying the CP index and JT paying fixed. Finally, AC can enter into a 4-year fixed/LIBOR swap with OC with OC paying fixed, and AC paying floating.

However, in the real world, the selection of counterparties is not as obvious, nor is their ready availability as easy, as is implied by these illustrative cases. The swap required by SC's bank, TB, is a good example. It is unlikely that TB would quickly find an appropriate counterparty wishing to pay floating and receive fixed on a step-up structure. In general, the situation is complicated by several factors such as:

a. the swapping needs of one party are not generally known to the other party.

b. parties have very limited ability to evaluate and accept credit risk of the counterparty.

c. the payment date and maturity requirements of one party may not match those of the other

d. some parties may not be able to meet the cash buy-out requirements of their counterparties.

e. the timing requirement of one party might differ from that of the counterparty.

f. there might be differences in the funding sizes of the different parties.

Many of these problems can be solved by the intervention of a swap dealer. The dealer may perform a purely intermediary function, or hold one of the swaps in inventory until another closely matching swap is available. The dealer typically will hedge each swap using liquid market securities, such as Treasuries and futures contracts, during the inventory period as well as to adjust any residual mismatches after the offsetting swap has been executed.

SWAP PLAYERS

As in all financial markets, various types of players participate in the swap business and serve different functions.

End-users are the ultimate consumers of swaps. They usually have some assets or liabilities that they wish to hedge using swaps. There are also speculators that enter into swap transactions seeking trading profits. A popular trade is to match a short term swap against a position in Eurodollar futures.

Market Makers, as the name implies, provide liquidity by making two-way markets in swaps. In general, market makers are the major source for swaps. They usually hedge their swap positions with the more liquid instruments such as Treasuries and futures. They also actively seek offsetting swaps so as to limit the size of their hedge positions and limit any risk not hedgeable with liquid market instruments.

An *intermediary* stands between two swap parties, shielding each from the other's credit risk. The major risk to the intermediary itself is the credit exposure to the two parties. Intermediation is used when one party cannot take the credit risk of the other party or when other considerations, e.g., those related to tax and accounting issues, apply.

These three types of players are principals in swap transactions, that is, they are actually the counterparties. On the other hand, *brokers* or *agents* do not enter into swaps themselves. They simply find parties that can execute swap transactions. Among these are many investment banks who do not have their own swap operations and brokers who provide information on available swaps through data screens.

SWAP PRICING

The maturity of the dollar interest rate swap market is indicated by the widely available bid and offer quotations in maturities from 2 to 10 years. Rates are quoted as a spread over the bond yield of the on-the-run Treasury of appropriate maturity. For maturities of up to 3 years, the rates are commonly quoted using the money market practice, i.e., as an absolute level on an annual, actual/360 day basis.

Usually, simultaneous execution of offsetting swaps by a swap dealer is uncommon. Therefore, it is likely that one or both parties to a swap will execute a Treasury trade to hedge the swap position. Swaps up to 3 years maturity can also be hedged in the Eurodollar futures market.

In general, the fixed rate payer will base the rate on the offered price of the Treasury, and the receiver will base it on the bid side. The bid-offered difference can be overcome by the payer of the fixed rate actually purchasing the Treasury from the receiver.

Several practical considerations enter into the pricing of a swap by a swap dealer. Among them are:

1. prevailing market conditions, e.g., the term structure of interest rates

2. structure of the swap, e.g., maturity, floating index, size

3. the current position of the firm

4. ready availability of offsetting swaps

5. credit quality of the counterparty

6. regulatory constraints, e.g., capital requirements

It is insightful to look at swap pricing on a more conceptual level. Given that a swap is simply a stream of cash flows, it stands to reason that the value of a swap can be easily computed by discounting these cash flows. There are a few complications that need to be addressed before we can apply the discounting rules. First, we need an appropriate discounting function, that is, a set of discount rates corresponding to the timing of each cash flow. The discounting function is popularly known as the zero-coupon curve. In practice, it is generated using a variety of market data such as the current Treasury yield levels and Eurodollar futures prices. The goal in using all this data is to derive a curve that represents the rates for the appropriate credit as represented by swaps. Second, unlike bonds or other investments, the swap has two-way cash flows. This problem can be handled simply either by computing the value algebraically (i.e., by including the sign) or by splitting the incoming and outgoing cash flows and valuing them separately.

Third, the cash flows on the floating side are unknown, except perhaps for the first payment which is set at the outset. The solution to this problem is to replace each of the unknown floating rate flows by the corresponding forward rate computed from the discount function.[1] That is, as far as valuation is concerned, we are indifferent between the unknown floating rate cash flows or the known cash flows represented by forward rates.[2] Once the floating

---

1 Note that the zero curve or the discount function is being used to serve two functions: (1) to determine the implied forward rates which in turn fix the future (floating) cash flows, and, (2) to determine the appropriate discounting rate to use for cash flows occurring at various times. Normally, the discount function derived represents LIBOR, given that the data used to generate it includes LIBOR rates and Eurodollar futures prices. Therefore, if the floating rate index used is not LIBOR, then we need two zero curves: one to generate forward rates corresponding to the actual index and another (based on LIBOR) to discount all cash flows.

2 Note however, that there is no assumption, implicit or explicit, that the interest rate in the future will actually be equal to the forward rate. We are willing to substitute known forward rates for unknown future rates for valuation purposes because we can, if we so desire, effectively lock-in or fix the future cash flow at a level implied by the forward rates by using appropriate hedging techniques.

side has been so 'fixed,' its present value is first computed simply by discounting each flow to the present.[3] The swap rate can then be easily computed by determining that fixed rate which will have the same discounted present value as the floating side. This procedure seems logical, because, in a swap, the two cash flows exchanged, floating and fixed, should have identical discounted present values. The swap is therefore said to have zero (net) value. Of course, bid-offered spreads are used to appropriately modify the swap rates derived where needed.

If market rates have moved since the pricing of a swap, then the swap will be off-market. That is, the present values of the floating side and the fixed side will not be equal. The swap value will not be zero; it can be positive or negative with respect to a counterparty depending upon whether the receive or the pay side of the cash flow has greater value. This swap value is determined simply by

(1) fixing the floating side using the currently prevailing forward rates

(2) computing the present values of each side by discounting using the current discount function, and,

(3) finding the difference between the two present values.

The confidence and comfort in this simple and logical procedure has enabled swap dealers to price virtually arbitrary sets of cash flows, and has resulted in greater liquidity, availability of larger sizes, narrowing of bid/offered spreads as well as the variety in swap structures.

Figure 4 presents a simple example which shows input rates required to obtain the zero curve, the zero curve obtained, and the

---

3 Care must be taken to ensure that appropriate day count conventions are used in computing the interest payments as well as in discounting. Payments on the fixed side are usually quoted on a 30/360 day basis. Floating payments are generally computed on an actual/365 day basis. In addition, if there is any compounding involved, the correct forward rates based on the compounding calendar have to be used to compute the cash flows. Compounding usually is required when the reset frequency is greater than the payment frequency, e.g., LIBOR set monthly, paid semi-annually.

Figure 4   Swap Pricing

A: INPUT

LIBOR Rates Term (days)	Rate	Eurodollar Futures Contract	Price	Treasuries Term (years)	Rates	Swap Spread (basis points)
1	8.250%	MAR	91.65	2	8.267%	61
7	8.250%	JUN	91.60	3	8.338%	62
28	8.313%	SEPT	91.50	4	8.365%	73
59	8.375%	DEC	91.27	5	8.341%	80
89	8.375%	MAR	91.19	7	8.399%	83
181	8.438%	JUN	91.08	10	8.428%	89
		SEPT	91.03			
		DEC	90.96			
		MAR	91.00			
		JUN	90.96			
		SEPT	90.91			
		DEC	90.81			

Notional Amount $10,000,000

Pay   Fixed (30/360) Semi-annual payment

Receive   6-Month LIBOR (Actual/360) Semi-annual payment Semi-Annual reset

B: CALCULATIONS

Payment Period	Floating Rate Forward	Floating	Fixed	Zero Rate	NPV Floating	NPV Fixed
1	8.438%					
2	8.597%	$424,224	$447,886	8.556%	$406,727	$429,413
3	8.914%	$444,194	$452,862	8.636%	$408,251	$416,218
4	9.100%	$443,224	$442,909	8.770%	$391,191	$390,913
6	8.981%	$467,639	$450,374	8.554%	$398,433	$383,724
7	9.029%	$454,019	$447,886	8.929%	$370,189	$365,188
		$458,974	$445,398	8.967%	$360,549	$349,884
				Total:	$2,335,340	$2,335,340

C: RESULTS

Swap Price: 8.958%

calculation of the fixed rate which makes the net present value of the two sides equal.

INTEREST RATE RISK CHARACTERISTICS

The risk characteristics[4] of a swap are quite interesting. The popular risk measure, *duration*,[5] can be roughly defined as the change in value for a unit change in interest rates. Floating rate bonds usually have very small interest rate sensitivity, i.e., low duration. It is therefore tempting to look at the duration of the swap as equal to the duration of the fixed side only, ignoring the floating side as having zero or low duration.

However, it turns out that the floating side of a swap does not have a small duration. In fact, it has a (large) negative duration.[6] This fact can be easily demonstrated. A little reflection reveals that the floating side resembles the coupon stream from a floating rate bond. In other words, we can synthesize a floating rate bond by combining the floating side with a zero coupon bond representing the principal payment. Viewing this another way, the floating side is equivalent to a portfolio of a long position in a floating rate bond and a short position in the zero coupon bond representing the principal payment.

Floating Rate Bond = Floating Side of Swap + Zero Coupon Bond

Floating Side of Swap = Floating Rate Bond − Zero Coupon Bond

---

4 For a discussion of the popular interest rate risk measures, their computation, usage and limitations, please see, Ravi E. Dattatreya and Frank J. Fabozzi, *Active Total Return Management of Fixed Income Portfolios*, Probus Publishing, Chicago, 1989.

5 Duration is traditionally defined as the percentage change in value for a unit change in rates. Since (at-market) swaps have zero value, the percentage change is undefined. Therefore, it is more useful to deal with dollar duration which is the actual dollar change in value for a unit change in rates. In this discussion, we use the term duration to mean dollar duration.

6 The floating side of a swap in some situations is known as the *VIRA*, Variable Interest Rate Asset. It is an asset with the negative duration property of a liability.

The equality holds not only for value, but also for *change* in value, i.e., for interest rate risk or duration. Therefore, the duration of the floating side should be equal to the duration of this portfolio. Now the long position in the floating rate bond has a very low duration. Therefore, the portfolio duration is roughly equal to that of the short position in the zero coupon bond. That is, it has negative duration in the sense that, unlike most fixed income instruments, its value increases if rates increase and decreases if rates fall.

From the point of view of the fixed rate receiver, the fixed receipts have the same duration as that of the coupon stream on a fixed coupon bond. The floating payments have the negative of the duration of a zero coupon bond.[7] Combining these two durations algebraically, i.e., changing the sign of the duration of the payment side, we conclude that the duration of a swap is equal to the sum of the durations of the coupon stream on a fixed coupon bond and the duration of a zero coupon bond representing the principal. That is, the duration of a swap is equal to the duration of an equal maturity bond with the coupon equal to the fixed rate.

We can arrive at the same conclusion in a different way. A swap position is essentially similar to the leveraged holding of a bond. That is, we can synthesize the cash flows of a swap by borrowing cash at a floating rate and investing in a bond. Therefore, the interest rate sensitivity of the swap should be equal to that of the leveraged position. In other words, swap duration is equal to bond duration.

There is another way to determine the risk characteristics of a swap. Since the swap is valued based on market rates such as Treasury yields, it is possible to determine the change in the value of the swap as a result of a small change in one of the market rates, say the 5-year Treasury yield. This number, called the *risk point*,[8] represents the interest rate sensitivity of the swap *relative* to

---

7 Floating *receipts* have negative duration. Floating *payments* have negative of the negative duration, that is, positive duration equal to that of a zero coupon bond.

8 For a discussion of the risk point method of measuring interest rate sensitivity, please see, Ravi E. Dattatreya, "A Practical Approach to Asset/Liability Management," in *Asset/Liability Management*, Atsuo Konishi and Frank Fabozzi, eds, Probus Publishing, Chicago 1990.

the particular Treasury bond. To completely represent a swap's risk profile, we have to compute the risk point of the swap relative to each market rate used in its valuation. The risk point vector is not as compact a summary measure as traditional duration, but is very useful in many hedging situations.

SWAP STRUCTURES

One of the most striking features of such a liquid instrument as the swap is the fact that it is a privately negotiated contract. As such, the terms and conditions of the swap contract can be customized to meet the needs at hand. As end users of swaps have aggressively used this flexibility, new swap structures with descriptive names have developed. The advances in swap pricing, such as the portfolio pricing methodology, have facilitated the increase in the variety of available swaps.

The *Bullet Swap* or the *'Plain Vanilla'* interest rate swap is one in which the notional amount does not vary.

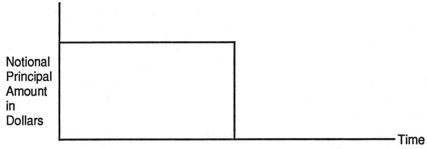

An *Amortizing Swap* has the property that the notional principal on which interest is calculated decreases in regular or irregular increments over the life of the swap.

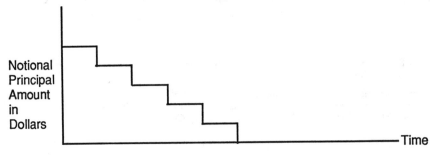

In an *Accreting Swap* or *Appreciating Swap*, the notional princi-pal increases in regular or irregular increments over the life of the swap.

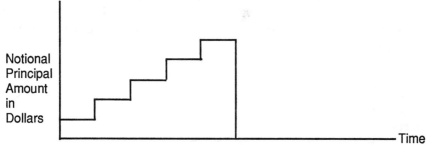

The *Roller Coaster Swap* combines the amortizing and the ac-creting swaps, with the notional principal amount fluctuating in arbitrary increments.

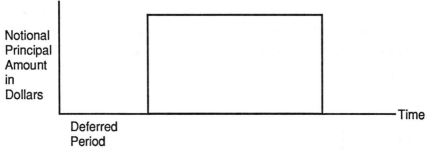

A *Forward Swap* is one in which the Start Date of the swap is delayed anywhere from a few days to several years. Clearly, we can have combinations such as forward amortizing swaps.

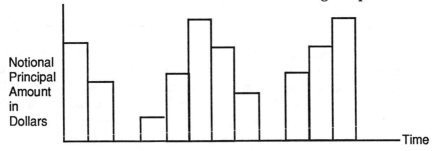

A popular swap variation is the *Zero Coupon Swap*. Here, one counterparty will make the floating-rate payments at regular intervals, while the other counterparty makes a lump sum payment usually on the Maturity Date. The credit risk associated with this type of transaction can be large if the weaker credit counterparty is paying the zero. In a *Reverse Zero Coupon Swap*, the lump sum payment is made up front.

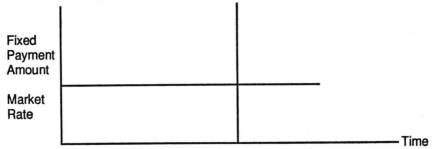

In *Off-Market Swaps*, the swap rate is set above or below the normal market rate. In return, the party paying a lower rate or the party receiving a higher rate will make a lump sum payment, usually up front, to the other party.

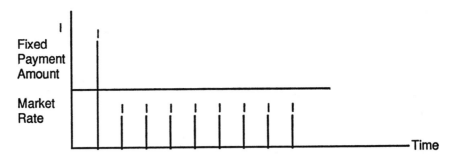

Swap-in-Arrears (SIA) is an interesting recent innovation. Normally, the floating rate, say LIBOR, is set at the beginning of a period and the actual payment is made at the end of the reset period. In SIA swaps, the floating rate is set at the *end* of the period and the corresponding amount is paid immediately. Swaps of this type have lower quoted fixed rates in a market environment where the yield curve is upward sloping. This is because the rate includes the effect of the higher forward rates implied by the positively sloped yield curve.

BASIS SWAPS AND ASSET SWAPS

In an interest rate swap, it is not necessary that one of the payments be based on a fixed rate of interest. The two payment streams may be based on two different floating rate indexes. Such transactions are termed *basis swaps*. Typical examples are commercial paper versus LIBOR or 1-month LIBOR versus 6-month LIBOR.

Example (Basis Swap). NEB, a New England bank, owns a floating-rate asset tied to LIBOR, but it has been funded via a commercial paper program. The spread realized by NEB therefore is exposed to the spread variation between LIBOR and commercial paper. to eliminate the 'basis gap' between the asset and the associated liability, NEB enters into a swap in which it pays LIBOR and receives CP. Now, the spread earned on NEB's asset is more stable and predictable.

Conceptually, a basis swap locks-in the spread existing at the time of the agreement between the two indexes. Basis swaps are quoted as a spread over the more frequently reset index versus the other index quoted flat.

An *asset swap* is used by an investor to modify the cash flow of an asset in his portfolio.

Example (Asset Swap). FI is an investor in fixed income securities. He owns a fixed rate bond that he considers a very attractive asset. However, he believes that interest rates might rise. He can sell the fixed rate bond and convert his holding to floating. Alternatively, he can continue to hold the attractive asset, but at the same time hedge his interest rate risk by entering into an asset swap. On the swap he will pay fixed and receive floating. The payments made on the swap are offset by the coupon received on the bond. the receipts on the swap effectively convert the fixed rate bond into a floating rate asset.

SWAP SPREADS

Basically, swap spread can be viewed as a measure of credit risk. the LIBOR rate represents on the aggregate an A to AA rated financial institutional credit. Therefore, intuitively, we can say that the swap spread should be related to the spread over Treasuries commanded by institutions of this credit quality on their intermediate term borrowings.

Typically, fixed rate bond markets have tended to require a wider credit quality spread between higher and lower rated parties than in the floating rate markets. Although the higher rated issuer borrows more cheaply than does the other in either market, the former enjoys a greater advantage in bond markets. Conversely, the lower rated issuer faces less of a quality differential in the floating rate market. If each borrower raises funds in the market in which it has relative advantage, the resulting interest rate payments can be swapped to achieve cheaper funding for both.

To date, the leading driving force in the swap market has been such an arbitrage. Thus, swap spreads have followed closely the yield levels of investment grade corporates over Treasuries in the public debt markets in the US and in Europe. They basically have remained in an approximately 30 basis point range straddled by AA and A spreads. This relationship can be explained in the context of the credit arbitrage mentioned above. The fixed rate available through the swap market must be lower than that in the bond market for the fixed payer—usually the lower rated party. Thus, the A bond rate forms an upper bound for swap spreads. Similarly, the synthetic floating rate obtained through a swap must be lower than that of a straight floating borrowing for a higher rated party. Thus, the lower bound for swap spreads is the spread over Treasuries paid by AA rated issuers plus the spread under LIBOR commanded by them for floating rate borrowing. Due to various market factors, these upper and lower bounds are not strict.

Swap spreads in the short maturities are strongly tied to the Eurodollar futures market. A borrower wishing to fix the exposure on short term liability indexed to LIBOR could either enter into a swap, or could sell a series of Eurodollar contracts matching payments on the underlying liability. Either technique locks-in a fixed rate. If LIBOR rises, the corresponding higher financing costs are offset either by matching swap payments or by gains realized on the futures contracts. Even in the shorter end, the spreads are related to perceived corporate credit through the Eurodollar futures which are tied to LIBOR.

Historically, higher swap spreads (and corporate spreads) have been associated with lower absolute Treasury levels and lower spreads with higher levels. To the extent that lower Treasury levels reflect 'fight to quality,' the corresponding higher swap spreads can be explained based on the corporate credit represented by the swap market.

TYPES OF RISKS IN SWAPS

Swaps are unlike most other financial instruments in that they involve two-way payments and, correspondingly, two-way exposure to risk. That is, each party is exposed to the other in terms of credit risk. Usually, some type of offset is agreed upon such that if one party defaults, the other party is not obligated to continue to make the payments. It is useful to review the types of exposure in the swap markets.

Interest rate risk or *market risk* is clearly the leading concern of swap players. We have seen above that the interest rate sensitivity or duration of a swap is similar to that of a bond. Therefore, when interest rates move, the value of the swap moves as well. To the extent that the swap is being used to match the gap between assets and liabilities, the variation in the value of the swap in response to market changes is not a concern. Swap dealers with unmatched swaps in their inventory are exposed to market risk, and hedge appropriately.

Credit Risk is an integral part of a swap transaction. However, in a generic interest rate swap, the perceived credit risk is small compared to that in an outright loan of the notional amount due to two reasons. First, only the interest payments are involved, not the principal amount. Since the principal amount represents a larger proportion of the value of a shorter maturity loan, the shorter the maturity of the swap, the smaller is its credit risk relative to an outright loan. Second, there is usually an offset arrangement such that in the event of the default by one party, the other is no longer required to continue to make payments on the swap. Note that in general the effective termination of a swap due to a default can suddenly increase the interest rate risk in a hedged position.

However, in some special swap structures, the credit risk can be significant, e.g., zero coupon swaps, where one party makes all payments before the other makes any. In such cases, it is best to examine the credit risk of the swap as if it were a loan. The credit spread charged should also reflect this view.

Another type of risk is *mismatch risk*. Normally, mismatch refers to the position of a swap dealer who has two offsetting swaps that hedge each other, but are not exactly matched. They may differ in the timing and frequency of payments, maturity, floating rate index used, etc. End-users of swaps are also exposed to mismatch in certain circumstances.

Example (Mismatch Risk).   Consider a situation in which an industrial corporation, IC seeking fixed rate funding, uses the commercial paper market to raise funds, and swaps into fixed. In this case, several mismatches are possible. The floating payments on the CP/fixed swap are set to the A1/P1 commercial paper composite index. In addition, the maturity and timing of the commercial paper actually issued may differ from the payment frequency and timing of the swap cash flows. The mechanism by which the index is set may be different from the way the borrowing rate is determined.

In general, however, as far as the end-user is concerned, the credit risk of the counterparty is the main concern. Since the swap market does not seem to differentiate finely between high and low quality credits, it is in the best interest of the end-user to always deal with the highest rated counterparty available at the desired rate.

SWAP TERMINATION

A swap normally matures with the last scheduled payment. Mechanisms are in place to make available a level of liquidity, however, and a swap can be terminated before its maturity date by mutual agreement between the counterparties. Usually, a swap terminated before maturity is off-market, that is, it has some residual value. Therefore, an appropriate payment from one party to the other is necessary at termination. To determine this adjustment, the swap is revalued at the market conditions prevailing at the time of termination.

A swap can be terminated by a *buy-out* where an up-front payment that reflects the adjustment for the prevailing market conditions is made. In a *reversal*, a new swap transaction that exactly offsets the original is executed. This new swap is obviously off-market, and requires an up-front payment from one party to another. As an alternative, the up-front payment can be amortized over the remaining life of the swap by adjusting the fixed payment rate. Another form of termination is by *assignment* where the swap is assumed by a third party in the secondary market. This happens when one of the parties in the original swap does not wish to complete termination. The party that is willing to terminate will receive from or pay to the third party a fee reflecting the value of the swap. The party that terminates the swap is free from all obligations on the original swap. The rights and responsibilities are completely transferred to the third party.

CURRENCY SWAPS

In the same way an interest rate swap can effectively change the nature of a cash flow from fixed to floating, it is also possible to change the underlying currency itself via the swap mechanism. Such a transaction is called a *currency swap*. Normally, currency swaps are used to convert a liability (or an asset) from one currency to another. The cash flows at maturity corresponding to the principal amounts in the two liabilities (or assets) may not be equal in value.[9] Therefore, unlike an interest rate swap, the currency swap includes the exchange, at maturity, of the principal amounts as well. In this sense, the currency swap closely resembles a back-to-back loan. It is also possible to have coupon-only currency swaps with no exchange of principal. Such swaps are useful in hedging dual-currency liabilities where the interest is paid in one currency and the principal in another. Depending upon whether the two sides of a currency swap pay a fixed or floating rate of interest, the transaction is classified as a fixed/fixed, fixed/floating, or floating/floating currency swap. As can be expected, the final exchange of principal imparts additional complexity to non-standard structures and to terminations.

SWAP DERIVATIVES

Whenever a product gains popularity, it is only natural that other derivative products also emerge to claim their rightful share of the market. The interest rate swap is no exception, and a cluster of its own derivatives with option-like characteristics has developed.

In a *callable swap*, the fixed payer has the right, at his option, to terminate the swap on or before a scheduled maturity date.[10] The floating payer is compensated for this option either by an up-front premium or by an increase in the fixed rate received. A typical user for a callable swap is a fixed payer who expects the interest rates to fall. By terminating the swap at an opportune time, he can enter into another one at a lower fixed rate.

A *putable swap* mirrors the callable swap. Here, the floating payer has the termination right. The payment for this privilege is made either by reducing the fixed rate received or by making an

---

9 In a simple interest rate swap, the cash flows at maturity corresponding to the principal payments are equal in value since they are equal in size, timing and currency. Therefore, this payment can be eliminated entirely from the swap. This is not the case in a currency swap.

10 When the swap is terminated under this optional right, no adjusting payment is required from either party. Therefore, the holder of the right will exercise it only when it is in his advantage to do so.

up-front fee. A corporation that has issued a fixed rate callable bond and that wishes to have floating rate funding can use the putable swap. At the time the corporation calls the bond, it will also simultaneously exercise its right to terminate the swap.

Extendible Swaps are similar to callable and putable swaps. Here, one of the counterparties has the right to extend the swap beyond its stated maturity date as per an agreed upon schedule.

A *capped swap* is one in which a ceiling rate is set on the floating side. If the index rises above this ceiling, the floating rate payer simply pays the ceiling rate. The floating rate payer either pays an up-front premium or receives a fixed rate lower than the market in return for the protection provided by the ceiling or cap. Typical users of capped swaps are borrowers wishing to limit exposure to high short term interest rate levels. Another example is an asset swap where the cash flow from a portfolio of capped adjustable-rate mortgages is converted to fixed.

Other variations such as the *floored swap* with a lower limit for the floating rate or the *collared swap* with both a cap and a floor are also available.

Swaptions are options on swaps. That is, they represent the right to enter into an underlying swap, that is, the swap as described in the swaption agreement. For example, a *call swaption*[11] gives the owner the right to enter into a swap where he receives fixed and pays floating. A *put swaption*, on the other hand, represents the right to enter into a swap, receiving floating and paying fixed. Callable and putable swaps can be viewed as combinations of regular swaps and swaptions. Swaptions have been used by corporations to monetize the call option owned by them in a callable bond issue.

Example (Swaption Arbitrage).   A corporation, C, wishes to obtain 7-year fixed rate debt. It issues a 7-year bond callable at par after 4 years. By doing so, C has implicitly purchased a call option from the bond holder, and paid for it in terms of the higher cou-

---

11 The swaption terminology is designed to closely resemble option terminology in fixed income. Thus, a call swaption is roughly equivalent to a call option on a bond in terms of its response to interest rate movements. Correspondingly, a put swaption is similar to a put option on a bond.

pon on the bond relative to a non-call coupon. To monetize the call option it owns, C simultaneously sells a swaption giving the buyer the right to enter into a swap where C pays fixed. If the swaption is exercised, then C, in turn, will call its bond. Thus, it will pay a fixed rate for the full 7-year initial term of the bond issue: to the bond holder until the bond is called, and to the swap counterparty (swaption holder) after the swaption is exercised and the bond is called.

The reason C prefers to enter into this type of financing rather than the more straightforward 7-year non-callable bond issue is arbitrage. The cost of the option embedded in the callable bond issue that it purchases from the bond holder is lower than the swaption that it sells. The profit thus generated effectively reduces C's funding cost on the fixed rate financing.

A *cap* is a contract that has a contingent periodic cash flow. Whenever the prevailing floating rate index is greater than an agreed-upon rate called the *cap rate*, the cash flow is equal to the difference between the cap rate and the prevailing interest rate applied to the notional amount. If the prevailing rate is lower than the cap rate, there is no cash flow. The lower the cap rate, the higher the price of a cap. A floating rate borrower can cap or limit the interest expense in any period by purchasing a cap. A capped swap is simply a combination of cap and swap.

Suppose a floating rate lender would like to be assured of a guaranteed minimum amount of interest income. Then, he can purchase a *floor*. The cash flow from a floor is equal to the difference between the *floor rate* and the prevailing rate applied to the notional amount. This payment is made only when interest rates are below the floor rate. Clearly, the higher the floor rate, the higher the price of the floor. A floored swap is a combination of a floor and a swap.

Often, floating rate borrowers wish to limit the interest rate exposure by purchasing a cap and financing the purchase by simultaneously selling a floor. The effect of such a combination of a long position in a CP and a short position in a floor, called a *collar*, is that the interest expense to the borrower is always between the floor rate and the cap rate. Often, the floor rate and the cap rate are chosen such that the cost of the cap is equal to the price to the floor. Such a combination is also called a *zero-cost collar*.

The cap and the floor are also related to the swap another way. If the cap rate and the floor rate are both set equal to the swap rate, then the corresponding collar is just an interest rate swap. This relationship is similar to the put-call parity condition in options analysis.

CONCLUSION

Since its inception several years ago, the swap market has grown into a multi-billion dollar, global market. The swap market is so large that its influence can be seen in other areas such as corporate debt issuance and interest rate futures. It therefore behooves us to obtain a basic understanding of how the market works and how swaps and swap products are evaluated.

The success of the swap as a product stems clearly from the fact that it serves a much needed function that cannot be satisfied by other existing derivative products. As a privately negotiated contract, it can be customized to fit the requirements of the situation at hand. Swap derivatives such as swaptions, caps and floors, are also beginning to make their presence felt in a significant way as legitimate financial products of today's capital market. For most end-users, the swap has no equal in efficient interest rate risk management.

Chapter 8

Interest Rate Swaps versus Eurodollar Strips

Ira G. Kawaller
Chicago Mercantile Exchange

INTRODUCTION

An interest rate swap is a contract between two parties, A and B. A calculates his interest obligation on the basis of a floating rate benchmark such as LIBOR. B calculates his obligation based on a known fixed rate. A periodic adjustment is made between the two parties, commensurate with the difference between the two obligations. A swap allows A to convert from a floating rate sensitivity to a fixed rate; it does the opposite for B. In practice, such swaps often are designed to offset, or "hedge," existing rate exposures.

The Eurodollar futures contract sets rates on Eurodollar time deposits, beginning on a specific forthcoming date. As interest rates rise, futures prices fall, and vice versa. The futures market participant can maintain either a long position (which benefits if yields fall) or a short position (which benefits if yields rise). The participant has to mark the contract to market on a daily basis and make daily cash settlements for changes in value.

Strips of Eurodollar futures are simply the coordinated purchase or sale of a series of contracts with successive expiration dates, the objective being to "lock in" a rate of return for a given term. The construction of the strip depends on the prices of the contracts, the amount of principal plus interest paid or received in each quarter, and the number of days in each quarter. Actual returns from a correctly-constructed hedge should come very close to the expected return.

Both interest rate swaps and strips of Eurodollar futures contracts allow a manager to decrease (or increase) exposure to interest rate changes by converting a floating rate exposure to a fixed rate (or vice versa). With swaps, however, the precise fixed rate is readily identifiable. The ultimate outcome with interest rate strips is somewhat uncertain. This article provides a framework for making direct comparisons between Eurodollar strips and interest rate swaps. This eases the task of identifying the more attractively priced instrument considerably.

SWAPS

Figure 1 summarizes the standard, "plain vanilla" swap agreement. Here two counterparties enter into a contract in which A calculates an interest rate expense obligation based on a floating interest rate benchmark and B calculates an obligation based on a known, fixed rate.

The amount of the interest expense for which A is responsible clearly rises in a rising rate environment and falls with declining rates. In contrast, B's obligation is constant, based on the stated, notional amount specified by the swap agreement and the contractually determined fixed interest rate. The swap requires periodic interest payments in which the difference between the two interest obligations (the net) is passed from the party with the greater obligation to the party with the lesser obligation.

Consider the case in which A agrees to pay B based on the London Interbank Offered Rate (LIBOR) on three-month Eurodollar deposits, and B agrees to pay A based on a fixed, money mar-

Figure 1   Plain Vanilla Swap

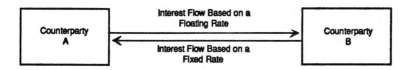

ket rate of 10 per cent.[1] Assume a notional amount of $100 million for the swap and quarterly interest payments. With each fixing of LIBOR, A establishes its forthcoming interest obligation.

If LIBOR is equal to 10 per cent at the first rate setting, for example, no cash adjustment is made by either party. If LIBOR is 11 per cent, counterparty A pays B $250,000 ($100 million × 0.11 × 1/4 – $100 million × 0.10 × 1/4). If LIBOR is 9 per cent, counterparty B pays A $250,000 ($100 million × 0.09 × 1/4 – $100 million × 0.10 × 1/4). This process continues for the term of the contract, following each reset of LIBOR.

If both A and B have no exposure to interest rates prior to executing the swap contract, the swap exposes A to the risk of higher short-term rates and the opportunity of lower rates; B's exposure is the opposite. Often, however, counterparties use swaps to offset existing exposures. In the first case, the swap is being used as a trading vehicle; in the second, it is being used as a hedge.

---

1   The terms of the swap often relate the fixed rate to some benchmark (e.g., 300 basis points above five-year U.S. Treasuries). This allows a general swap agreement to be worked out so that the pricing details reflect market conditions at the time the deal is signed.

EURODOLLAR STRIPS

The Eurodollar futures contract sets rates on Eurodollar time deposits, commencing on a specific forthcoming date—the third Wednesday of March, June, September or December, depending on the contract expiration month. Operationally, futures prices are derived by subtracting an interest rate (in percentage points, carried to two decimal places) from 100. As interest rates rise, futures prices fall, and vice versa.

The face amount of the Eurodollar futures contract is one million dollars, and its maturity is three months. Every basis-point move in the futures price (yield) translates to a value of $25 (= $1,000,000 × 0.0001 × 90/360). In general, movements in the Eurodollar futures market are closely correlated with yield movements in the underlying Eurodollar time deposit market, although changes are not precisely equal over any given period.

The futures market participant can maintain either a long position (hoping the market will rise in price and decline in yield) or a short position (hoping the market will decline in price and rise in yield). In either case, the participant is obligated to mark the contract to market on a daily basis and make a daily cash settlement for any change in value. This obligation can be terminated at any time by simply "trading out" of the position (i.e., making the opposite transaction to the initial trade).

Upon expiration of the contract, any participant still maintaining contracts makes a final marked-to-market adjustment, with the final settlement price based on an average derived from a survey of London bankers who report their perceptions of the cash market three-month LIBOR to the Chicago Mercantile Exchange at the time of the survey.

Strips of Eurodollar futures are simply the coordinated purchase or sale of a series of futures contracts with successive expiration dates. The objective is to "lock in" a rate of return for a term equal to the length of the strip. For example, a strip consisting of contracts with four successive expirations locks up a one-year term rate; eight successive contracts lock up a two-year rate, and so on. As is the case with swaps, futures strips may be used to take on additional interest rate risk in the hope of making trading profits, or as an offset or hedge to an existing exposure.

CALCULATING STRIP YIELDS

What is the term rate that can be expected to result from employing a strip of Eurodollar futures? And how should the hedge be constructed to achieve this rate?

The answers depend on the objectives of the strip creator with respect to the accruing interest. That is, creation of a synthetic zero-coupon fixed income security requires one particular hedge construction, while creation of a synthetic coupon-bearing security requires another.

The Zero-Coupon Strip

Consider the problem of creating a one-year, zero-coupon strip with four successive contract expirations. Assume the prices for these contracts are 92.79, 92.51, 92.27 and 92.05, respectively. Under these conditions, the hedger has four hedgeable events designed to lock up rates of 7.21 per cent (100 – 92.79) in the first quarter, 7.49 per cent (100 – 92.51) in the second quarter, 7.73 per cent (100 – 92.27) in the third quarter and 7.95 per cent (100 – 92.05) in the fourth quarter.

To arrive at the number of contracts required for the hedge, the hedger first determines the amount of principal plus interest at the end of each quarter. Assume the number of days in each of the quarters are 91, 91, 91 and 92, respectively. At the end of the first quarter, the principal plus interest is calculated as the starting principal plus that principal multiplied by the first futures' interest rate (7.21 per cent) multiplied by 91/360.[2]

---

2 The denominator, 360, reflects the convention that LIBOR is quoted as a money market rate, counting the actual number of days during the period in the numerator

Table 1   Strip Hedge Objectives

Quarter	Amount to be Hedged (millions)	Quarterly Futures Interest Rate (%)	Days Per Quarter	Principal Plus Interest (end of quarter)
1	$100.00	7.21	91	$101.82
2	101.82	7.49	91	103.75
3	103.75	7.73	91	105.78
4	105.78	7.95	92	107.93

This end-of-quarter value serves as the amount to be hedged in the second quarter. Table 1 illustrates the process over the four quarters, assuming an initial value of $100 million.

The number of contracts required is found by dividing the value per basis point of each quarter's amount to be hedged (the prior quarter's ending principal plus interest) by $25, which is the value of the basis point per futures contract. The actual hedge ratio has to be rounded to a whole number, of course, as futures cannot be bought or sold in fractional units. Table 2 gives the calculations.

Bond-Equivalent Yields

Incorporating the concept of the bond-equivalent yield allows a generalization from this specific example. The bond-equivalent yield for a strip of virtually any length (up to the maximum number of quarterly expirations available) can be derived from the following formula:

(1) $\left(1 + RF1\frac{DQ1}{360}\right) \times \left(1 + RF2\frac{DQ2}{360}\right) \times \left(1 + RF3\frac{DQ3}{360}\right) \times \left(1 + RFN\frac{DQN}{360}\right) = (1 + Reff_{/P})^{(N \times P_{/t})}$

Here RF1, RF2, RF3 and RFN are the respective annual futures rates (100 minus the appropriate futures prices, expressed as deci-

Table 2   Hedge Ratio Calculations*

Quarter

1	($100.0 million × (0.001) × 91/360)/$25 = 101 contracts
2	($101.82 million × (0.001) × 91/360)/$25 = 103 contracts
3	($103.75 million × (0.001) × 91/360)/$25 = 105 contracts
4	($105.78 million × (0.001) × 92/360)/$25 = 108 contracts

* This hedge construction implicitly assumes that the rate on the Euordollar strip will move point-for-point with the rate on the exposed instrument. Clearly this assumption may be modified by simply adjusting the hedge ratios by a factor designed to take into account the expected relative rate change.

mals). DQ1, DQ2, DQ3 and DQN are the days in each three-month period beginning with the third Wednesday of the respective futures' expiration months.[3] N is the number of quarters in the strip. Reff is the effective annual bond-equivalent yield for the strip. P is the number of periods per year for which compounding is assumed.

The left-hand side of Equation (1) shows the effect of borrowing (or lending) for each quarter at the interest rate designated by the appropriate futures contract. The right-hand side incorporates the effective yield required to generate the same principal plus interest by the end of the term. In all cases, effective yields are approximations, as the periods covered by the futures contracts may either overlap or have gaps.

Despite the fact that futures expire quarterly, an effective term rate can be calculated assuming any compounding frequency. Most likely, the choice of P reflects the compounding assumptions implicit in the fixed rate quotation of an instrument to which the strip yield may be compared.

If, as in the above example, a one-year strip is arranged with contracts priced at 92.79, 92.51, 92.27 and 92.05, respectively, the

3 The number of days in the quarter should be measured by counting from the calendar day of the third Wednesday of the expiration month to that same calendar day three months later (e.g., March 17 to June 17, which measures 92 days).

Table 3 Interest Rates Rise to 15 Per Cent

*Futures Results**

Quarter

1	101 contracts × (85.00 − 92.79) × \$2500 = −\$1.97 million
2	103 contracts × (85.00 − 92.51) × \$2500 = −\$1.93 million
3	105 contracts × (85.00 − 92.27) × \$2500 = −\$1.91 million
4	108 contracts × (85.00 − 92.05) × \$2500 = −\$1.90 million

End-of-Quarter Balances

Quarter

1	100.0 million (1 + 0.15 × 91/360) − 1.97 million = \$101.82 million
2	101.82 million (1 + 0.15 × 91/360) − 1.93 million = \$103.75 million
3	103.75 million (1 + 0.15 × 91/360) − 1.91 million = \$105.78 million
4	105.78 million (1 + 0.15 × 92/360) − 1.90 million = \$107.93 million

* As prices are reflective of percentage points, rather than basis points, the multiplier becomes \$25 × 100, or \$2500.

target return is 7.93 per cent.[4] Tables 3 and 4 illustrate two extreme cases that demonstrate the robustness of this hedge.

For both tables, end-of-quarter balances are found by investing the initial \$100 million at the spot LIBOR and adjusting the ending principal plus interest by the gains or losses on that quarter's hedge. This adjusted figure becomes the principal amount to be rolled over and reinvested. Such practice is consistent with the accounting tradition of allocating hedge results to the quarter for which the hedge is designed. (On a cash flow basis, hedge gains and losses for all contracts are generated daily, and variation margin adjustments are called for. Returns calculated from actual cash flows, therefore, differ from the calculations shown.)

4 This result follows from an ending principal plus interest of \$107.93 million one year after an initial principal of \$100 million. It assumes that P equals one.

Table 4   Interest Rates Decline to 2 Per Cent

Futures Results

Quarter	
1	101 contracts × (98.00 − 92.79) × \$2500 = \$1.32 million
2	103 contracts × (98.00 − 92.51) × \$2500 = \$1.41 million
3	105 contracts × (98.00 − 92.27) × \$2500 = \$1.50 million
4	108 contracts × (98.00 − 92.05) × \$2500 = \$1.61 million

End-of-Quarter Balances

Quarter	
1	100.0 million (1 + 0.02 × 91/360) + 1.32 million = \$101.82 million
2	101.82 million (1 + 0.02 × 91/360) + 1.41 million = \$103.75 million
3	103.75 million (1 + 0.02 × 91/360) + 1.50 million = \$105.78 million
4	105.78 million (1 + 0.02 × 92/360) + 1.61 million = \$107.93 million

Table 3 assumes that LIBOR immediately skyrockets to 15 per cent following the initiation of the hedge and remains there; so all futures are liquidated at 85.00. Table 4 assumes that LIBOR drops to two per cent and remains there; so all futures are liquidated at 98.00. That both cases result in identical ending balances demonstrates the robustness of the hedge.

Real-World Considerations

It should be noted that the analysis above assumes perfect convergence between LIBOR and the Eurodollar futures rate each time a futures contract expires or is liquidated. A non-zero basis at the time of hedge liquidations can alter the results. The size of the alteration depends on the magnitudes and directions of the basis at liquidation.

For the long strip (when the futures contracts are purchased originally), a LIBOR at liquidation higher than the rate implied by the futures contract is desirable. A LIBOR below the futures rate is undesirable. For the short strip, the opposite applies.

It is worthwhile to look at some possible adverse market conditions that might apply when futures contracts are liquidated.[5] Assume, for example, that a long strip is created, as in the examples above. With LIBOR at 15 per cent, assume the worst case of futures liquidation at 84.75, or a rate of 15.25 per cent for each futures contract. The worst-case projected results differ from the results in Table III because of the somewhat greater futures losses in each quarter.

The differences equal the number of contracts for that quarter's hedge times 25 basis points times $25 per basis point, as Table 5 shows. Because of the greater futures losses, a return of 7.65 per cent results, rather than a bond-equivalent yield of 7.93 per cent, as initially targeted.

The above calculation demonstrates that an adverse basis of 25 basis points at each hedge liquidation lowers the perfect convergence target by 28 basis points (7.93 − 7.65)—just about one-for-one. But this represents the results for what is judged to be a worst-case scenario.

In many cases, the actual shortfall is substantially smaller. It can be virtually negligible in the case where hedges are scheduled for liquidation at or near futures expiration dates. Furthermore, the basis conditions of hedge liquidation can be favorable, in which case the hedge performance is better than that indicated by the perfect convergence calculation.

EXTENSIONS AND REFINEMENTS

When considering a strip as an alternative to another fixed income security, the user should try to arrange the strip so that it mirrors the cash flow properties of the competing instrument as closely as

---

5 The existence of gaps or overlaps because of the futures expiration cycle can be considered a special case contributing to this risk.

Table 5   Worst-Case Scenario

Futures Results

Quarter

1	101 contracts × (84.75 − 92.79) × $2500 = −$2.03 million
2	103 contracts × (84.75 − 92.51) × $2500 = −$2.00 million
3	105 contracts × (84.75 − 92.27) × $2500 = −$1.97 million
4	108 contracts × (84.75 − 92.05) × $2500 = −$1.97 million

End-of-Quarter Balances

Quarter

1	100.0 million (1 + 0.15 × 91/360) − 2.03 million = $101.76 million
2	101.76 million (1 + 0.15 × 91/360) − 2.00 million = $103.62 million
3	103.62 million (1 + 0.15 × 91/360) − 1.97 million = $105.58 million
4	105.58 million (1 + 0.15 × 92/360) − 1.97 million = $107.65 million

possible. For example, if the alternative to the strip is a two-year swap and the fixed payments are scheduled semiannually, the strip should be formulated to replicate semiannual cash disbursements.

Think about the two-year fixed income obligation as if it were a series of four six-month, zero-coupon strips and the bond-equivalent yield of each six-month strip is calculated and implemented as explained above. The effective rate for the whole two-year period reflects compounding of all substrip segments. The appropriate general formula is:

(2) $$(1 + BEY1/P)^t \times (1 + BEY2/P)^t \times \ldots \times (1 + BEYK/P)^t = (1 + R/P)^{Kt}$$

when:

   BEYi =   the bond-equivalent yield of the ith substrip

   P   =   the assumed number of compounding periods per
             year

   t   =   the length of each substrip, in compounding
             periods

   K   =   the number of substrips.

Table 6 gives the characteristics relevant to the above synthetic two-year, semiannual-coupon, fixed-income construction. Days per quarter are counted rigorously, from the third Wednesday of the expiration month to that calendar day three months later, and the two-quarter strip yields are calculated using the methodology of Equation (1).[6] Given the bond-equivalent yields from Table 6 and Equation (2), the annualized yield to maturity, r, is 9.18 per cent.

Because this synthetic construction is designed to mimic a security with semiannual coupons, the amount to be hedged, in the first, third, fifth or seventh quarter is the notional amount of the deal. For a $100 million deal given the respective days in each of these quarters, the hedge ratios are 100, 100, 102 and 100 contracts, respectively (see Table 7). For the remaining quarters (two, four, six and eight), the calculation takes the original notional amount plus the interest income from the prior quarter, based on that quarter's futures rate. That is, the hedge ratio for the second quarter depends on the futures rate locked up in the first quarter; the hedge ratio for the fourth quarter depends on the third quarter's futures rate; and so on. These calculations are shown in Table 7.

Like the case with the zero-coupon strip construction, the actual outcomes may differ somewhat from the calculated target because of rounding errors and the prospect of imperfect convergence. So appropriate allowance for some deviation from

---

6   P in Equation (1) is assumed here to be two, reflecting semiannual compounding.

Table 6   Two-Year, Semiannual-Coupon Synthetic

Contract Expirations	Futures Price	Days Per Quarter	Bond-Equivalent Yield (two-quarter strips)
1	91.22	90	
2	91.34	92	8.91
3	91.21	90	
4	91.04	92	9.08
5	90.87	92	
6	90.90	91	9.37
7	90.82	90	
8	90.75	91	9.37

Table 7   Hedge Construction for $100 Million in Semiannual-Coupon, Two-Year-Maturity Fixed Income Obligation

Quarter		Hedge Ratio
1	$100 million × 0.0001 × (90/360)/25 =	100
2	$100 million × (1 + 0.0878 × 90/360) × 0.0001 × (92/360)/25 =	104
3	$100 million × 0.0001 × (90/360)/25 =	100
4	$100 million × (1 + 0.0879 × 90/360) × 0.0001 × (92/360)/25 =	104
5	$100 million × 0.0001 × (92/360)/25 =	102
6	$100 million × (1 + 0.0913 × 92/360) × 0.0001 × (91/360)/25 =	103
7	$100 million × 0.0001 × (90/360)/25 =	100
8	$100 million × (1 + 0.0918 × 90/360) × 0.0001 × (91/360)/25 =	103

these calculations should be given when determining whether or not to choose a strip as the preferred transaction vehicle. With these considerations in mind, failure to choose the alternative with the more (most) attractive yield necessarily leaves money on the table and so reflects a suboptimal market decision.

CONCLUSION

Constructing Eurodollar strip trades requires a certain amount of care. In particular, a strip should match as closely as possible the cash flow provisions of the competing alternative instrument. The payoff for making the correct calculation and implementing it properly is an incrementally superior return. There can be no question that choosing the more attractively-priced alternative necessarily enhances performance.

PART II

EQUITY DERIVATIVES

Chapter 9

Using Stock Index Futures and Options

Chicago Mercantile Exchange

INTRODUCTION

What are S&P 500 futures and options on futures? Where do they come from? What can they do for you, creative investor? These are some of the questions this chapter will help you answer.

Stock price index futures and options are contracts that allow the creative investor to effectively buy or sell an extremely well-diversified portfolio of stocks. They are also opportunities to make investment decisions based on the investor's opinion of the overall stock market. The center of trading in these contracts is the Chicago Mercantile Exchange. In 1982, the CME introduced the S&P 500 stock index futures contract, which now represents 80 percent of all stock index futures trading. The exchange subsequently established trading in options on S&P 500 futures (1983).

Stock index futures and options are powerful and versatile instruments, whether the intention is to risk personal capital for investment reward, or to insulate an investment capital from risk. They afford unique advantages by allowing investors to:

- Participate in broad market moves with one trading decision, without having to select individual issues (and with no up-tick requirement for selling short)
- Protect the value of a portfolio during bear markets without incurring high transaction fees and without adding to downward selling pressure on individual issues
- Speculate on short-term market moves
- Benefit from a bull market move even before funds become available to purchase stocks

The pages that follow give a fuller explanation of these contracts and the beneficial role they can play in an investment program. S&P 500 futures and options at the Chicago Mercantile Exchange have shown tremendous growth in trading volume, strong evidence of their wide acceptance in a relatively short time.

THE INDEX: A PROXY FOR THE MARKET

The S&P 500 composite stock price index is designed to be an accurate proxy for a diversified portfolio of highly capitalized, blue chip stocks. It is based on the stock prices of 500 companies—about 400 industrials, 40 utilities, 20 transportation companies and 40 financial institutions. The market value of the 500 firms is equal to approximately 80 percent of the value of all stocks traded on the New York Stock Exchange.

The four broad industry groupings are maintained in order to monitor the index's continued diversification, and the number of companies in each grouping changes from time to time to allow S&P more flexibility in choosing new companies for the index when openings occur.

The S&P 500 is a capitalization-weighted index reflecting the market value of the 500 listed firms.

Each component stock's price is multiplied by the number of common shares outstanding for that company and the resulting market values are totaled. The total market value of all the 500

Figure 1   S&P 500 Index

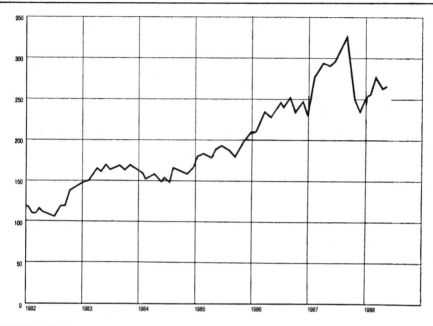

firms is compared to the base period (1941–1943 = 10) to derive the index value.

Because the index is weighted in this manner, a price change in any one stock influences the index in proportion to the stock's relative market value. The index thus shows the relative importance of each stock price change, gauging dollar-value market forces.

Adjustments to the Index

The S&P 500 index is widely recognized as a benchmark by investment professionals because of Standard & Poor's years of experience in index construction and maintenance. Standard & Poor's is not involved in the trading of securities, and acts independently of the exchange in decisions regarding the maintenance of the index.

S&P adjusts the index to avoid distortion when there are stock splits or dividends, other distributions or purchases of shares by the component company itself, mergers, acquisitions or divisional spin-offs. In each case, S&P modifies the index (through the divisor used to compare current to base value) between trading sessions. The index then remains at the same value on the opening of trading as it was at the prior close; any performance difference is insignificant.

S&P 500 FUTURES

An investor can use stock index futures and options to shift the risk of stock market changes. Or, if the investor attempts to forecast the market's direction and wants to position himself to profit from such a move, these contracts hold other opportunities.

What Is Traded?

A futures contract is an agreement between seller and buyer to deliver and take delivery of respectively a specific commodity at a specified future date. In the case of S&P 500 futures, the "commodity" is a portfolio of stocks represented by a stock price index. The delivery is actually a cash settlement of the difference between the original transaction price and the final price of the index at the termination of the contract. More accurately, the cash settlement occurs in increments daily until the termination of the contract, as the contract trading price changes.

THE "VALUE" OF FUTURES

The value of the S&P 500 futures contract can be calculated by multiplying the futures price by $500. For example, with a price of 300.50, the value would be $500 × 300.50, or $150,250. The minimum trading price change ("tick") for the contract is .05, so a tick up or down in the

> futures price, say from 300.50 to 300.55 has a value of $25
> a contract ($500 × .05).

The futures contract price responds to changes in the underlying index, with the index recalculated as the component stock prices change. The price of the futures contract looks very much like the index price itself; however, the futures price may be higher or lower than the index, depending on other factors described further in the chapter. While the futures price does not move point-for-point with the index, it tracks closely enough to act as an effective proxy.

The "Long" and the "Short" of Futures

A "long" futures position holder, one who buys a contract, profits from a rising futures price and contract value. A "short" futures position holder, one who sells a contract, profits from a price decline, because he then buys in at a lower price to "offset" or liquidate the position. The long and the short sides of the original transaction are separated so that each can trade with any other party to liquidate his position at any point.

Both the buyer and the seller of a futures contract establish margin accounts with their brokers. Margin, a small fraction of contract value, serves as a security deposit guaranteeing performance. This account is debited or credited for the position's daily gains or losses.

Positions are re-valued or "marked-to-market" every night. If he buys (goes long) the futures contract at 293.65 and the price rises to 293.75, he has $50 in cash added to the account ($500 × .10 = $50). If the price falls to 293.55, $50 is deducted. If the account falls below the designated maintenance level determined by the brokerage firm, he has to meet a margin call to continue holding that position.

Futures positions can be held until a particular contract expires, or closed out at any time by an equal and opposite transaction. For example, assume the long September contract is marked to the close yesterday at 293.55, and he decides to liquidate today.

If he sells a September contract at 293.10, the account is charged for the difference, 45 points or $225, and he has no open position.

If he holds a position until the contract expires, the entire value of the contract does not change hands. There is a cash settlement instead of a delivery of securities. This takes the form of a final debit or credit to the trading account, marking the contract position from the futures settlement price on the last day of trading (Thursday) to the Special Opening Quotation of the index the next morning (the third Friday of the contract delivery month). This index quotation is calculated to the nearest .01, and it is "special" because it is determined by the official opening values of the 500 stocks, even if there are delayed openings in some stocks. The normal opening index quotation uses "last sale" prices for stocks until they open trading.

As an example of this final marking to the cash index, if he is short the expiring futures contract, which settles on Thursday at 293.45, and the Special Opening Quotation is 292.97, the .48 difference (.48 × $500, or $240) is credited to the account as a final settlement. The short position is closed, and no further obligation exists.

Theoretical "Fair Value"

S&P 500 futures prices generally move with changes in the underlying index value, but the futures price is usually different than the current index value. There is a definite relationship between the current (or cash) index value and the futures price of that index. Supply and demand—sellers and buyers—determine the current futures price; but, through arbitrage, market expectations are reined in as a futures pricing force.

Essentially, the futures contract serves as a substitute for owning the actual portfolio of stocks that forms the index. With either the futures or the "cash" portfolio, there is a capital interest in the stock prices. The index price difference arises from the fact that the actual stock holder receives dividends, but must pay full value for the stocks or pay interest on the margined amount. The futures contract holder receives no dividends, but deposits only a small fraction of the contract value as security. He can invest the remainder in other earning assets, such as Treasury bills.

The chief difference between these alternatives, then, is the difference between the dividend return and the available return on other earning assets. In recent history, the average dividend yield on S&P 500 stocks has ranged between three and five percent.[1] If money market yields are much higher, then the futures represent a better yielding alternative, and the futures price will be higher than the cash portfolio price (the current index value). Because these yields are time-related, the yield differential becomes less important as the contract maturity approaches, until the futures price and the cash index converage at expiration.

In considering the purchase of a futures contract, an investor might not like to pay a premium over the current index, but he should realize that he is paying for real advantages. Aside from the yield differential, assembling a well-diversified stock portfolio is far more difficult and expensive than a futures purchase; and the portfolio is far less liquid than a futures position.

The sale of index futures, on the other hand, brings these transactional advantages as well as the usual ability to sell the futures at a premium. While this may seem an unfair advantage, the alternative—selling stocks instead of the futures—brings a cash inflow that the outright futures sale does not.

Arbitrage

If the futures price does not reflect accurately the yield differential, then a wise investor buys the relatively cheap alternative, and sells the relatively expensive one. Because both alternatives have the same value on the futures delivery date, the investor can liquidate both stocks and futures positions at a guaranteed profit. This is the process of arbitrage that enforces the "fair value" pricing relationship. Arbitrage transactions performed to take advantage of any

---

1 Dividend payments are not smoothly distributed over time.

Figure 2   Typical Distribution of Divident Payouts

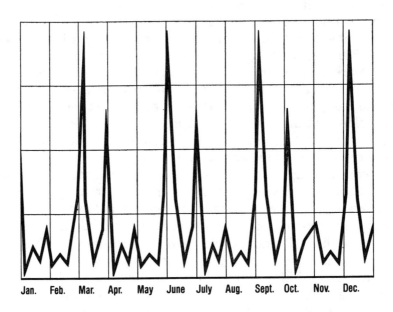

Source: Salomon Brothers Inc.

Over short periods of time, the dividend yield/other earnings assets yield relationship can vary, causing the "fair value" futures price to change in relationship to the cash index. Arbitrage activity serves to smooth this relationship.

disparity result in the cheaper alternative being bid up and the expensive being sold until the prices are in line.

The relative transaction cost and liquidity of the cash and futures positions enter into the arbitrageur's decision-making and, thereby, affect the pricing relationship. A pure arbitrage requires the purchase or sale of each of the index component stocks in shares-outstanding proportions to replicate the S&P 500.

Large investment funds and dealers maintain index-matching inventories of stocks to arbitrage. But for most investors the com-

Figure 3   Cash versus Futures Price Relationship

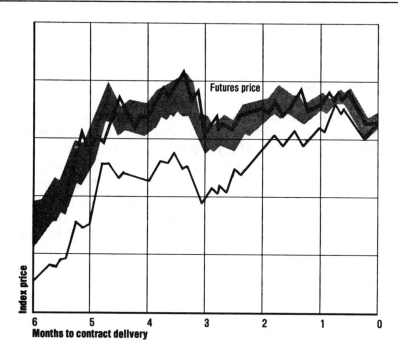

This chart illustrates the convergence of the index futures price and the underlying cash index. The gray band describes the various arbitrageurs' transaction costs, and defines the "fair value" futures price. Any futures price outside the gray band represents arbitrage opportunity.

mission costs, and the time and risk involved in executing so many transactions make pure arbitrage impractical. However, some traders are pursuing quasi-arbitrage, buying or selling smaller portfolios of stocks, designed to have good correlation with the index, against the futures contract.

The yield differential and, less significantly, transaction differences when applied to the current index value form a theoretical fair value for the futures price. More accurately, they form a range because arbitrageurs have different cost factors and return on investment requirements. If heated expectations in the futures market cause the futures price to stray outside this range, or if the interest rate changes causing a change in the yield differential and fair value, arbitrageurs draw the prices back into line.

Trading Opportunities

The most straightforward trading use of futures contracts is to buy them (go long) in anticipation of a rising market and to sell them (go short) in anticipation of a falling market. There are numerous alternatives—choosing different delivery month contracts, spreading between delivery months or using the futures in conjunction with S&P 500 options. To develop a trading strategy, two things are needed: an opinion, formed from fundamental analysis of market factors and/or technical analysis of price trends; and a decision on acceptable levels of risks and rewards.

Professional dealers and traders typically trade the "basis" (the difference between the current cash index price and the futures price). As short-term interest rates change, the yield differential between stocks and other earning assets changes, and so does the basis. Basis traders monitor futures prices and trade small price movements in large volume.

Less active traders typically look for larger-order movements. The primary effects of interest rate changes on the stock market are, after all, more obvious and important than the yield differential basis effects. In addition to various domestic economic indicators, such as consumer sales, capital spending, inflation or money supply, some traders watch the U.S. dollar exchange rate, which has grown in importance with inflationary turbulence. Because the U.S. stock market can become an investment haven at times of dollar strength, large foreign investment flows can have a major effect.

A change in the taxation of dividends, capital gains or corporate profits also can have a large impact on stock prices. Another important market factor is the trading activity of the institutional money managers who invest pension and investment fund resources.

In addition to researching supply and demand factors, many traders analyze the market technically. Technical analysis can take several forms, including charting price movement, and trading volume to focus on buying or selling trends. These "technicians" try to predict trigger points in investor confidence, prices at which money enters or leaves the stock market. Other analysts concentrate on statistical searches of historical prices and economic data, looking for market waves and cycles.

Spreading the Contracts

Spread trading is a reduced-risk trading method that allows small or large traders to focus on the pricing relationship between related contracts. To take a spread position, buy one contract and sell the other; the price difference is referred to as the "spread." Because the contracts are related, both prices tend to move in the same direction, with the spread price changing as they move by different degrees. Because the position includes both a long and a short contract, the spread trader expects to lose on one "leg" of the spread, but to profit more on the other leg.

One type of spread, the "calendar" or "time" spread, can be placed to capture the index/futures yield differential change caused by an interest rate movement. For example, if an investor anticipates rising interest rates, sell the nearby contract and buy a later delivery contract. If short-term interest rates rise levelly, the basis widens more for the later delivery contract because the yield differential is time-related. As a result, he profits more from the distant contract long position than he loses on the nearby contract short position.

The advantage of the spread over an outright long position is that the spread is insulated from index level changes because it includes both long and short contracts. These spreads carry lower margins, and enforce fair pricing in all contract deliveries.

Figure 4   S&P 500 Calendar Spread

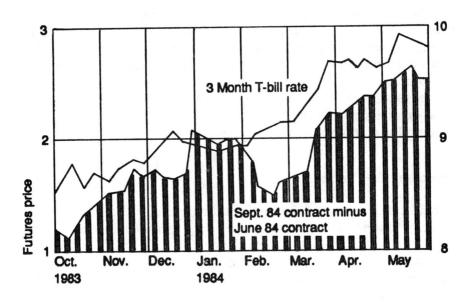

OPTIONS ON S&P 500 FUTURES

If a trader has experience with exchange-traded stock options, he should have little difficulty applying the vocabulary and mechanics to options on S&P 500 futures. These contracts (S&P options, in future references) share the characteristic that makes stock options appealing to many investors: limited risk.

What Is Traded?

When an investor buys an S&P option, he acquires the right to take a position at a specified price in the underlying S&P 500 futures contract at any time before the option expires. There are two types of options: calls and puts. Buying an S&P call option gives the right to take a long position in the underlying S&P futures contract at a specific price; an S&P put option gives the buyer the right to take a short position in the underlying S&P futures contract at a specific price.

An option buyer has the right—but not the obligation—to take positions in the underlying futures contract. The decision whether to enter the futures market is entirely up to the investor. Rather than exercising the option, he may re-sell it in the market, or simply let the option expire if it has no practical value.[2]

The sellers (also called writers) of S&P options assume the obligation of taking a futures position opposite to the option buyer, if the seller is assigned for exercise of the option. In the case of an S&P call, the call writer stands ready to take a short position in the S&P 500 futures contract. In the case of an S&P put option, the put writer stands ready to take a long position in the underlying S&P 500 futures contract. The option writer can liquidate his obligation at any time before he is assigned for exercise by buying an identical contract to close the position. As with futures, the CME clearing house separates the option buyer and seller so that they can act independently.[3]

Strike Prices and Expiration Months

The exercise price (or strike price) of an S&P option is the price at which to take an S&P futures position to exercise the option. Exercise prices are set at 5.00 point intervals, such as 290.00, 295.00 and 300.00. Option contracts are listed for all 12 calendar months. At any point, there are options available for trading that expire in each of the next three calendar months, plus two further quarterly expirations.

---

2 Buying an option does not require the payment of any margin deposit, unless the option buyer exercises and takes a position in the futures market.

3 The writer of an S&P option is required to post a margin deposit when the position is opened because it is the writer who must stand ready to take a futures position at a possibly unfavorable price at any time before the position is closed. The amount of margin required is recalculated daily until the option position is closed.

On the first day of trading for options in a new contract month, exercise prices for puts and calls are listed above and below the settlement price of the underlying futures contract. After the first day of trading, new exercise prices for puts and calls are created based on the upward and downward movement of the underlying futures contract. (No new option is added if it would have less than 10 calendar days remaining to expiration.)

Each option expires in the latter half of the expiration month. The quarter-end expirations (like the underlying futures contracts) terminate trading on the Thursday prior to the third Friday of the contract delivery month at 3:15 p.m. Central Time. The interim month contracts expire on the third Friday at 3:15 p.m.

Exercising Options

An investor may exercise an S&P option on any business day the option is open for trading, including the day on which it is purchased. Exercise of an S&P option contract results in an S&P 500 futures position effective on the next business day. Exercise of an S&P call results in a long S&P futures contract at the call's exercise price. Exercise of an S&P put option results in a short S&P futures contract at the put's exercise price.

Most investors exercise the call only if the current futures price is higher than the call's exercise price, and exercise the put only if the current futures price is lower than the put's exercise price. In either case, he receives a futures position effective on the day following the exercise, and the account is credited the difference between the exercise price and the current futures price. He can hold the futures position, or liquidate it with an offsetting transaction.

If he exercises any of the options that expire within a calendar quarter, he takes a position in the futures contract that delivers at the end of the quarter. So if he exercises a January 300 call, he takes a long position at 300 in the March futures contract.

Exercising a quarter-end S&P option on the last trading day results in a cash settlement because the underlying futures contract terminates trading at the same time, and also results in cash settlement for all open positions. This cash settlement is based on the Special Opening Quotation of the S&P 500 Index on the next day, the third Friday of the contract month. At expiration, the value of a quarter-end S&P call is the amount the S&P 500 Index is above the call's exercise price; the value of a quarter-end S&P put is the amount the S&P 500 Index is below the put's exercise price.

If the Special Opening Quotation of the index is at the same price or at any price below the exercise price of an expiring S&P call, or at the same price or any price above the exercise price of an expiring S&P put, the option expires worthless. The CME clearing house automatically exercises expiring quarter-end "in-the-money" options unless specific instructions are given not to exercise the contract. An in-the-money option has cash value, and to let it expire unexercised is to waste that value.

On the other hand, there is *no* automatic exercise of expiring interim month options because exercise results in a futures position. The inherent risks require that the option holder deliver notice of exercise through his broker in order to exercise an expiring interim month option.

Option Premiums

The premium is the price the buyer of an S&P option pays to the option seller for the right to take a futures position at the exercise price. In order to simplify trading, premiums for S&P options are quoted in terms of index points rather than a dollar value.

The dollar value of an option premium is equal to option index price multiplied by $500. As with the futures contract, the minimum fluctuation in price, or the minimum tick, is .05, or $25 ($500 × .05). To calculate the dollar value of the premium, multiply the quoted premium by $500. Therefore, an S&P option premium quoted as 7.55 equals $3,775.

The premium of an S&P option is related directly to the underlying futures price, rather than to the current cash price of the index. It is the likelihood that the futures will move profitably past the option's strike price that determines the value of the option. This possibility can be defined by the following three factors.

1. **Relationship of the strike price of the option to the underlying futures price.** If the current market price for S&P futures is above the strike price for a call (or below the strike price for a put), the option is said to have intrinsic value.

   The intrinsic value of a call option can be determined by subtracting its exercise price from the underlying futures price or, in the case of a put, by subtracting the futures price from its exercise price. If the difference is positive, the option has intrinsic value.

   An S&P March 290 call has an intrinsic value of 2.30 if the March S&P 500 futures contract is at 292.30; but at this futures price, the March 290 put has no intrinsic value (290.00 − 292.30 = −2.30, or 0). An S&P March 290 put has an intrinsic value of 2.30 if the March S&P 500 futures contract is at 287.70.

   An option with intrinsic value is said to be in-the-money. The option premium equals or exceeds its intrinsic value. An option with no intrinsic value is said to be "out-of-the-money." The distance between the exercise price and the futures price affects the likelihood that the option will move in-the-money and, therefore, affects the market price of the option.

2. **Time.** The more time that remains until an option's expiration, the higher the premium tends to be. The longer time period provides more opportunity for the underlying futures price to move to a point where the purchase or sale of the futures at the strike price becomes profitable. Therefore, an option with six months remaining until expiration has a higher premium than an option with the same strike price/futures price relationship with only three months until expiration. The time component of an option's value tends to be largest when the underlying S&P futures contract is trading near the exercise price of the S&P option—that is, when an option is "at-the-money."

   An option is a wasting asset. As the option approaches

Figure 5   30-Day Historic Volatilities for the S&P 500 Index

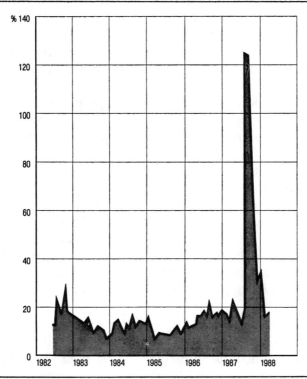

maturity, the time value declines to zero. At expiration, the option's value is only its in-the-money amount.

3. **Volatility.** There is a simple, but significant, relationship between volatility and premium: the greater the volatility or fluctuation in price of the futures, the higher the premium. Higher volatility means a greater chance for the option to move (further) in-the-money by the expiration date.

The "Delta Factor"

How does the changing price of an S&P option relate to changes in the price of the underlying S&P futures contract? The relationship is most often not one-for-one. A price change in the S&P futures usually results in a smaller change in the option's premium. The option's premium is related to the time remaining and to the futures' volatility, as well as to the futures price.

The option's premium is made up of intrinsic value, if any, and time value. The greater the intrinsic value portion of the premium, the more responsive the premium is to a changing futures price. On the other hand, the more time value makes up the premium, the less responsive it is to a changing futures price. The price-change relationship between the option and the underlying futures contract is summarized in what options theorists call the "delta factor."

The delta factor is a measurement drawn from the mathematical option pricing formula, and serves several purposes. Basically, it describes the rate of change of the theoretical value of an option with respect to a change in the underlying futures price. That is, it can be used to gauge the change in the futures price. For instance if a call's delta is 30 percent and the futures price rises quickly by 3.00 points, the call's price should rise by about 0.90 point. If the futures fall, the delta predicts the loss in option value in the same proportion.

Table 1 lists hypothetical deltas for some calls with the S&P futures price at 300.00, and with various lengths of time remaining until expiration. Notice the symmetry represented. Put deltas have a very similar distribution if the strike prices across the top are reversed in order.

For an out-of-the-money call like the 310-strike, it makes sense that as the time to expiration diminishes, so does the delta. With only a week to expiration, a small futures price move does not attract many buyers to the call, so that call's price does not react. On the other hand, with only a week to expiration, the 290-strike call is very likely to finish in-the-money. Even a small futures price change reflects a change in the potential in-the-money amount at expiration; so the call's price varies nearly one-to-one with the futures.

An option's delta also can be considered a rating of the probability that the option will expire in-the-money. The preceding table reflects the influences of time passing and of the futures

Table 1   Hypothetical Call Deltas (with the futures price at 300.00)

call strikes:	290	295	300	305	310
time remaining:					
1 day	100%	99%	50%	1%	–
1 week	97%	83%	50%	18%	4%
1 month	71%	68%	51%	33%	19%
3 months	70%	61%	51%	41%	31%
6 months	64%	57%	51%	43%	37%
Volatility = 13%, interest rate = 6%					

price/strike price relationship; but the probability also is affected by changes in the volatility of the futures price. If the futures price volatility increases, it widens the range of probable outcomes for the futures price at expiration. This increases the time value of the options, and drive all the option deltas toward 50 percent. The table below shows the deltas of the same options as in the prior example, but reflects a much higher level of volatility in the futures price.

A decrease in the volatility of the futures price decreases the time value of the options. The probable range of the futures price at expiration shrinks, and the deltas are driven toward 100 percent and 0 percent. Options that currently are in-the-money have a higher probability of staying in-the-money, and out-of-the-money options effectively are further out-of-the-money.

An option's delta also can be used to indicate the number of futures contracts the holder of a call is long or the holder of a put is short. For example if a call has a delta of .50, then the owner of two such calls is long one underlying futures contract. (The writer of two such calls is short one futures contract.) In this context, the

Table 2   Hypothetical Call Deltas (with the futures price at 300.00)

call strikes:	290	295	300	305	310
time remaining:					
1 day	100%	93%	50%	8%	–
1 week	87%	71%	51%	30%	14%
1 month	71%	61%	51%	41%	31%
3 months	63%	57%	51%	46%	40%
6 months	60%	56%	52%	47%	43%

Volatility = 22%, interest rate = 6%

delta is often referred to as the theoretical or equivalent share position.

OPTIONS STRATEGIES: FLEXIBILITY IN ACTION

Options are attractive because many of their uses involve known and limited risk. But another attraction is flexibility: They can be employed in expectations of rising or falling markets, of stable or volatile markets. The examples below show some ways to use S&P options. However, all of the examples ignore transaction costs and taxes. Obviously, the impact of these factors may be significant. Consult a broker to determine transaction costs, and tax counsel for tax treatment of options on futures transactions.

Buying Call Options

Profiting from a Rising Market   If an increase in the price level of the stock market and a corresponding increase in S&P futures contracts is anticipated, the purchase of a call option is an appropriate strategy.

Consider this example: In October, the stock market begins a major advance and an at-the-money call option with three months left until maturity is bought. With the December S&P futures at 300.00, purchase an S&P December 300 call at a premium of 6.80, or $3,400.

The profit potential on the purchase of the call option is limited only by the increase in the underlying S&P futures contract. The higher the S&P futures contract moves, the more profit realized when the call is sold.

Assume that the price of the futures contract declines and the option moves out-of-the-money. An investor still can recapture a part of the premium by re-selling the option sometime before its expiration for any value it may retain. In no circumstances does the loss exceed the $3,400 premium paid for the option.

The following analysis is a sketch of the profit situation for an array of possible futures prices at expiration. Option profit or loss is calculated by subtracting the premium of the option from the value of the option at expiration. The value of the call at expiration, if any, is the amount by which the futures price exceeds the exercise price of the option (300).

The example assumes the purchase of an at-the-money option with three months to expiration. But there are several call options available for purchase at any time: some with a very short time to expiration, and some with longer periods of time; some with exercise prices approximately equal to or below the underlying futures price, and some with exercise prices above the underlying futures price. How is the right call option selected?

As noted, an option with a longer time until expiration generally costs more than one with a shorter time until expiration. More time until expiration means more time to be correct in forecasting market direction and, hence, more time for the option to become profitable. The pricing of options is such that the time gained through the purchase of a longer-term option is proportionately less costly than that of a shorter-term option.

Figure 6   Long-Call—Profit Profile at Expiration

Profit or Loss at Expiration	
If the December Futures Price is:	The Profit or Loss is:
300.00 or below	6.80-point ($3,400) loss
305.00	1.80-point ($900) loss
306.80	Break Even
310.00	3.20-point ($1,600) profit
320.00	13.20-point ($6,600) profit
330.00	23.20-point ($11,600) profit

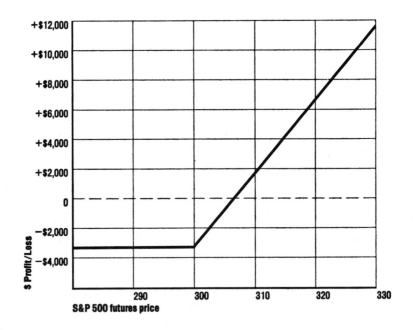

All long calls take this shape, with loss limited to the premium paid. The angle is directly above the strike price, and the break even line is crossed above the futures price that equals the strike plus the premium paid. Such a display of prospective option positions can help to visualize potentials and probabilities.

So decide whether to purchase an in- or at-the-money option, as opposed to an out-of-the-money option. For the same move in the futures price—the dollar amount of profit earned on, for example, an at-the-money option—is greater than that from an out-of-the-money option. But an out-of-the-money option costs less, so any loss is less and should the market move substantially, the rate of return on the out-of-the-money option will be greater than that on an in- or at-the-money option.

Consider further: with the December futures price at 300.00, buy an at-the-money S&P December 300 call at 6.80 ($3,400) or an out-of-the-money S&P December 310 call at 3.20 ($1,600). If on the option's expiration date the closing price for the S&P 500 Index is below 300.00, the entire premium is lost in either case. The loss is less for the out-of-the-money call than for the at-the-money call. However, in a rising stock market climate reflected in rising futures prices, the at-the-money call reaches the break-even point sooner and enjoys a greater dollar profit (but not rate of return) as the futures price increases.

The table that follows locates the break-even points of the two options if held to expiration. (The third column shows the profit/loss for the purchase of two 310 calls, which costs about the same as one 300 call. The out-of-the-money calls provide greater leverage, but the futures have to move further before they become profitable.)

It is evident that the decision of which strike price to use has much to do with the investor's opinion about the magnitude of the expected stock market advance. The following chart displays the profit profiles of the alternatives, as well as that of holding two out-of-the-money calls.

The preceding chart and table represent only expiration values, which are static, and can be predicted with certainty. At expiration, only the relationships of futures price to strike price is important. But over the life of the option, time and volatility play a part in determining the option price.

To further develop a sense of the relative risks and rewards each option represents, observe market prices daily, and keep

Table 3   Profit or Loss Resulting from Purchase of:

Closing Price of the S&P 500 Index at Expiration	December 300 Call	December 310 Call	2 December 310 Calls
300.00 or below	$ 3,400 loss	$ 1,600 loss	$ 3,200 loss
305.00	$ 900 loss	$ 1,600 loss	$ 3,200 loss
306.80	Break Even	$ 1,600 loss	$ 3,200 loss
310.00	$ 1,600 profit	$ 1,600 loss	$ 3,200 loss
313.20	$ 3,200 profit	Break Even	Break Even
315.00	$ 4,100 profit	$ 900 profit	$ 1,800 profit
320.00	$ 6,600 profit	$3,400 profit	$ 6,800 profit
325.00	$ 9,100 profit	$5,900 profit	$11,800 profit
330.00	$11,600 profit	$8,400 profit	$16,800 profit

track of the way futures price movement and the passage of time affect option premiums.

Using Call Options with a Short S&P Futures Position: Call options can be purchased either to lock in the profit or limit the loss on a short futures position. Suppose a December S&P 500 futures contract is sold in anticipation of a drop in the market. By mid-November, the futures indeed has fallen from 311.00 to 295.00, and shows a 16.00 profit ($8,000). Further decline after an upward price correction is expected. To realize profit, rather than buying in the short futures, consider buying a December 295 call for 4.20 ($2,100).

Original position: short S&P 500 Dec futures at 311.00

Current Dec futures price: 295.00

Transaction: buy a Dec 295 call for 4.20 ($2,100)

Figure 7   Alternative Long Calls—Profit Profiles at Expiration

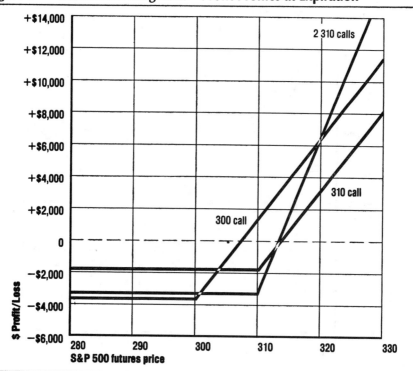

The investor is assured of at least $5,900 profit at expiration, and still can benefit from further downward price movement. The call serves as insurance against an upside move. In a very similar fashion, a long call can be used to limit the loss on a newly-placed short futures position. For either a new or already profitable short futures position with the call having the same expiration as the futures, the minimum profit (or the maximum loss) is defined as: short futures entry price—call strike price—call premium.

The profit profile of the combined position has the same shape as that of a long put, as is demonstrated in the next section. There is, in fact, a third alternative in the case described above: take the futures profits and purchase a put option.

Figure 8   Short Futures/Long Call—Profit Profiles at Expiration

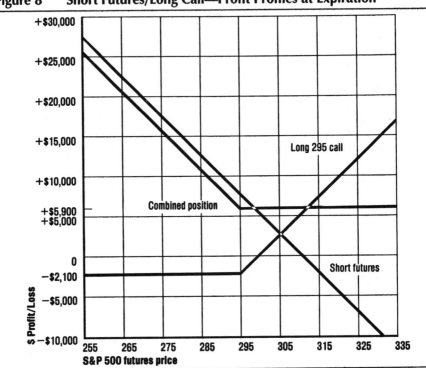

Buying Put Options

Profiting from a Falling Market: The purchase of an S&P put option carries with it the right to take a short S&P futures position; the value of an S&P put option can be expected to increase with falling prices for S&P 500 futures contracts.

In February, the investor believes the stock market will fall. With the March S&P 500 futures price at 302.00, he purchases an S&P March 300 put at a premium of 3.80 or $1,900. The March S&P 500 futures contract declines to 294.00. Reflecting a decrease in the underlying futures price, the put option increases to 8.00, or $4,000. He may sell the put option for $4,000, realizing a profit of $2,100 or the difference between the premium paid originally and the current premium. Or he may hold the put option, hoping for an even greater increase in premium—while recognizing that the time value of the option diminishes as the time to expiration approaches.

Using Put Options with a Long S&P 500 Futures Position: Buying put options in conjunction with a long futures position can set limits to the potential loss or lock in profits from an already profitable futures position. The purchase of the put guarantees, in effect, a selling price for the long S&P 500 futures position. The long put position provides insurance against a drop in the stock market and lower S&P futures prices, thereby placing limits on the loss that might occur from the long futures position alone. The decision concerning which put option to buy depends on investor risk tolerance.

Writing Call and Put Options

Profiting from a Stable or Declining Market: The writer (or seller) of an S&P call option receives payment (the premium) from the buyer of the option in return for the obligation of taking a short position in the futures contract at the exercise price if the option is exercised. (Actually, when an option is exercised, an option writer is randomly chosen and "assigned" to take the short futures position.) The call writer's risk is unlimited, while the call buyer's risk is limited; and the call writer's profits are limited, while the call buyer's profits are unlimited. Note that an option writer can buy in the contract at any time before expiration or assignment to liquidate the obligation. Be sure to understand and have the ability to bear the risk involved in writing uncovered call options.[4]

The principal reason to write call options is to earn the premium. In periods of stable or declining markets, call writing can mean an attractive cash flow from a relatively small capital investment. It is hoped that, at expiration, the settlement price of the

---

4 Call writers must post margin to maintain their positions and may be required to meet margin calls.

Figure 9   Long Futures/Long Put—Profit Profiles at Expiration

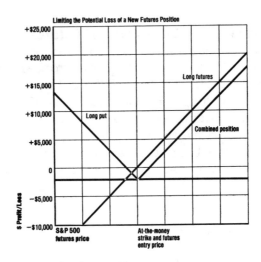

Notice that the shape of the combined position is the same as that of a long call. In fact, call options could be considered as alternatives.

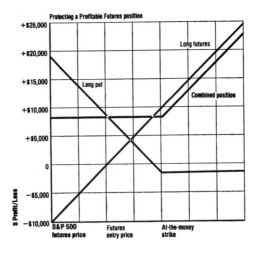

Figure 10   Short Calls—Profit Profiles at Expiration

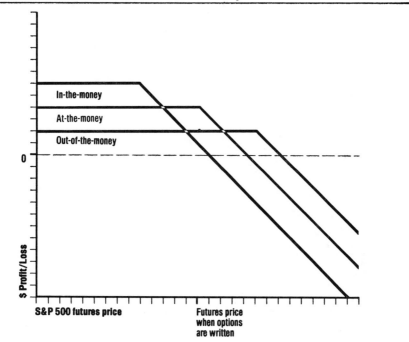

futures contract is at or below the exercise price of the option. The option then expires worthless—and the entire premium can be kept.

Suppose a decline in the stock market is expected and he sells an S&P June 305 call for 5.15, or $2,575. At expiration in June, the S&P 500 index is quoted at 291.20. The S&P June 305 call expires worthless; he retains the entire premium amount of $2,575.

On the other hand, if he holds the short call option position and the futures price at expiration is above the exercise price, he forfeits the in-the-money amount. This results in the loss of at least a portion of the premium, and possibly more than the premium.

If the Special Opening Quotation is at 306.01, he forfeits 1.01, or $505 (futures price settlement of 306.01 minus the exercise price

Figure 11   Short Puts—Profit Profiles at Expiration

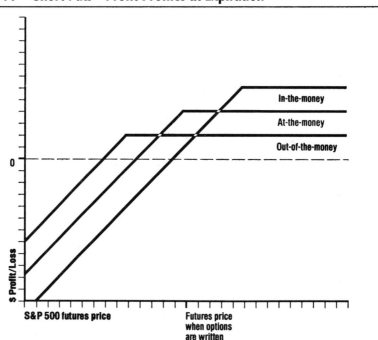

of 305.00). His profit then is reduced to $2,070 (original premium received of $2,575 minus the in-the-money amount of $505). If the index opens at 310.15, he loses the entire premium. If the index opens at any price above 310.15, the result is an absolute loss; he forfeits more than the premium received, to the extent of the actual amount over the premium.

The writer of a call option should keep in mind that he may be assigned at any time during the life of the option. Exercise becomes more likely if an option has a large intrinsic value and little time value. If a call has gone deeply in-the-money and if the writer does not wish to take a futures position, he should consider buying back the call.

Profiting from a Stable or Rising Market: The primary motivation for writing put options is again, to earn the premium. Like the call writer, the put writer is subject to substantial risk in return for earning the premium.[5]

The writer of an S&P put option is obligated to take a long S&P 500 futures position if he is assigned for exercise. The put writer hopes that the futures price is at or above the put's exercise price at expiration. The put option then expires worthless, and the writer keeps the entire premium received for the sale of the put. The risk is that the S&P 500 futures price falls below the exercise price of the put option by an amount exceeding the premium received for the sale of the put option.

Again, a put writer should understand that the option may be exercised by the put holder at any time during the life of the option. Monitor in-the-money puts carefully so as not to take a long futures position.

Income and Limited Protection: Writing a call option against a long futures position is a strategy that can produce an attractive return over the margin required if the stock market stabilizes or rises only slowly. The long futures protects the short call in a rising market to assure that the writer keeps the premium received (less intrinsic value if the call is sold in-the-money). If an out-of-the-money call is sold and the futures price rises, but not through the strike, the premium plus the futures gain both are profit at expiration.

The premium also gives limited protection against a drop in the futures price. The risk is that the futures price might decline by more than the premium received, and the investor may experience a net loss.

A strategy of writing a put against a short S&P 500 futures position similarly can suit the expectation of a stable or slowly declining market. The risk in the combination of short S&P put, short S&P futures is that the futures price may rise by an amount

---

5   Put writers post margin to maintain their positions and may be required to meet margin calls. As in the case of writing calls, writing puts should be undertaken only by thse investors able to bear the risk.

greater than the premium received—causing a loss equal to that of having a short futures position less the premium.

Spreads and Combinations

An investor also can combine options to tailor a position to market expectations. For example, if he expects a limited rise in the stock market, he buys the at-the-money call and sells the call at the next higher strike. The higher-strike call sale reduces the premium cost, and there is no margin required for this position, called a "bull call spread." If the futures prices rises, the lower strike call gains value faster because it has a higher delta factor than the out-of-the-money call. The maximum loss is the net premium cost; at expiration, the maximum gain is the difference between the strike prices less the net premium cost. It is a limited position for limited expectations.

Suppose the market has drifted during the summer, but he expects some economic news that the market can respond to positively. Look for a rally, but not a surge. With the September S&P 500 futures at 299.75, buy the 300-305 bull call spread. Figure 12 is a sketch of the position, with potential risks and rewards defined.

The investor can sell these call spreads (called "bear call spreads") with limited risk, and with profit limited to the net premium received. Put spreads can be formed in the same ways, and there are various permutations to take advantage of either price movement or price stability. The strike prices and premiums of these positions define the costs, risks and rewards.

An interesting option combination is the "long straddle," formed by buying a put and a call at the same strike price. An investor may expect the market to move dramatically, but as is sometimes the case, he can't predict which direction. The straddle is profitable with marked movement in either direction. The passage of time, with little price volatility, is the enemy of such a position.

Figure 12   300-305 Bull Call Spreads—Profit Profile at Expiration

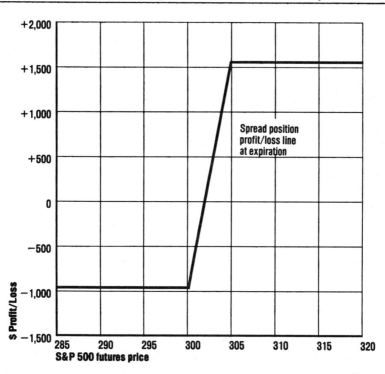

STOCK PORTFOLIO RISK MANAGEMENT

There are benefits and risks in all types of equity ownership: prices of common stocks change and, whether individually or institutionally managed, shares of stock or portfolios are subject to the risks of adverse price moves. The risks of changes in portfolio values are classified in two general categories: diversifiable risk and market risk.

Table 4

	Trade Price	Dollar Equivalent	Option Delta
Buy 1 Sep 300 call	6.00	$3,000	.49
Sell 1 Sep 305 call	4.20	2,100	−.33
Net premium paid	1.80	900	
Net position delta			+.16
Maximum risk (net premium):	1.80	$ 900	
Maximum profit (strike difference less premium):	3.20	$1,600	
Break-even futures price (at expiration, lower strike plus net premium):	301.80		

Diversifiable vs. Market Risk

The stock price of an individual firm is influenced by events and factors unique to that firm: an unexpectedly poor earnings report or a union walkout, for instance. The desire of investors to minimize firm-specific risk was a prime factor in the development of mutual funds.

In a diversified portfolio, unexpected increases in the prices of some stocks are likely to offset unexpected decreases in the prices of others; the portfolio value as a whole may remain fairly constant. Diversifiable risk declines rapidly as the portfolio increases in the number of issues from one to 18 or so, but it is never eliminated completely.

There is a limit to the risk-reduction potential of portfolio diversification. Some events have impact on the economic well-being of the entire market—for example, a change in U.S. monetary policy. This type of price variability is called market risk or systematic risk, and it is the major risk facing holders of diversified portfolios of stock.

Stock index futures and options contracts can adjust the impact of market risk on the portfolio. By holding an appropriate number of futures or option contracts, an investor can insulate his portfolio value from market risk. Gains in the futures or options positions offset losses suffered by the stock portfolio. This approach to risk management is called "hedging." The practice of hedging simply integrates the use of futures or options with the pre-existing or planned stock market investment to offset the change in value of the equity position by the performance of the futures or options positions.

Protecting Stock Investments

Stock portfolio owners may worry about a market decline, but may not be ready to sell stocks—for any of a variety of reasons.

Figure 13   Reduction of Firm—Specific Risk Through Diversification

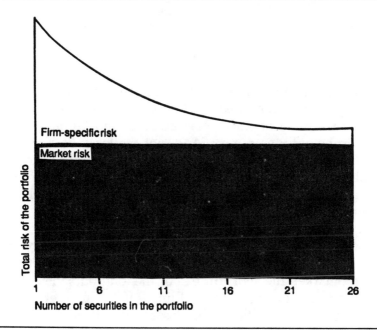

Figure 14   Futures Hedge

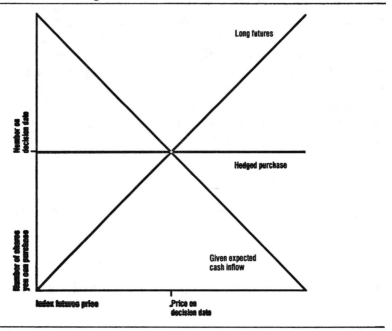

The tax consequences of a sale might be significant, or there may be an opportunity for substantial dividends. The commission cost of selling a variety of stocks may be high, and he may expect the decline to be only temporary. And, not the least, he may have selected the stocks in your portfolio carefully, in order to meet long-term objectives, and believe the reasons for continuing to own the stocks are sound even in the face of a general market decline.

Suppose he is holding a well-diversified portfolio of stocks valued at approximately $2,000,000. He foresees a market decline, but does not want to sell his stocks. He can provide coverage by selling index futures contracts or by buying index put options. In a declining market, the short futures or the long puts yield profits to offset the losses on his stock holdings. If the market rallies, the futures or options position show losses that offset appreciation in

Figure 15   Option Hedge

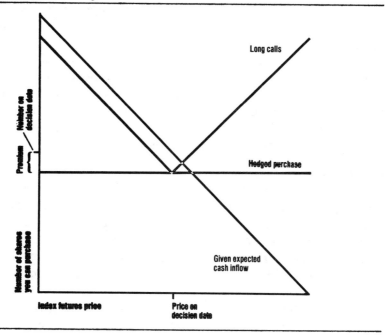

his stock portfolio. The hedged position generally is stabilized in value until he liquidates the hedge.

To provide rough coverage, he divides the portfolio value—$2,000,000—by the current index value times $500. This is the number of contracts that equates in value to the stock portfolio. However, a position of such size can be a fairly inaccurate hedge because his stock portfolio can change in value to a different degree than the stock index.

Limited Hedges: Hedging need not neutralize an entire portfolio. If he is bullish about the market's long-term prospects but foresees stable or declining stock prices just ahead, he can phase in a futures or options hedge. He can immediately initiate, say, 30 percent of the number of contracts for a complete hedge. If his near-

term outlook proves correct and the stock market begins to decline, he may choose to increase his coverage, perhaps to 50 percent of the portfolio value. The hedge is maintained or increased
as the stock market continues its downward movement. When his
bullish outlook returns, he removes the hedge by phasing it out in
a similar manner, or by offsetting the entire position.

Limited hedge techniques offer incomplete protection against
a stock market decline. Their main advantage: if market judgment
proves wrong, the gains from the equity portfolio exceed the
losses generated by the hedge position.

Full Hedge Coverage: To establish exact hedge coverage, first
determine the portfolio beta—a statistic that describes the
portfolio's tendency to rise or fall in value along with the market.
It is a product of the statistical comparison of the portfolio's
changing value over time to the changes in the relevant index
value. An investor (or his trading advisor) uses the past prices of
the stocks he currently holds; and the stock index values for the
same time period.

A portfolio beta of 1.0 indicates that the portfolio value has
moved over time in the same proportion as the index, a beta of .7
indicates that the portfolio value has moved with the index, but
traveled only 70 percent as far on average for each index price
change.

Continuing the example, he regresses his $2,000,000 portfolio
against the S&P 500, and finds the portfolio beta to be 1.14, because the portfolio has tended to move 1.14 times as far as the
index.

Anticipating a falling market, he sells the futures so that they
compensate for stock portfolio losses. To find the number of contracts for full coverage, divide the portfolio value by the current
S&P 500 index,[6] stated in contract value terms, and multiply by
the (beta) hedge ratio. With the S&P 500 index at 285.00, the calculation is:

---

6 The current index price is used, rather than the futures price, so that the hedged position will be
equivalent to the alternative of selling the portfolio and investing in other earnings assets. (See the
Theoretical "Fair Value" section.)

$$\frac{\$2,000,000}{\$500 \times 285.00} \times 1.14 = 16 \text{ contracts}$$

Full coverage with futures requires the sale of 16 contracts. He neutralizes the portfolio, expecting to neither gain nor lose materially on the overall stock/futures position. If he later decides to sell stock from the portfolio, he reduces the hedge position at the same time, recalculating the coverage with current values of the portfolio, the index and beta. As the hedging contracts approach the delivery date, if he wishes to maintain the hedge, he "rolls" the hedge position into a later delivery contract. He buys in the expiring futures (or lets them expire), and sells S&P 500 futures contracts that have three months or more until delivery.

The recalculation of hedge coverage is periodically necessary because the portfolio beta reflects past price behavior and is, therefore, not a perfect predictor. In general, the more diversified the portfolio is, the more constant beta will be. For a portfolio with only a few stock issues, the beta-derived inaccuracy of the hedge can be considerable, and hedge performance should be monitored closely.[7]

Alternatively, he can hedge with options. By buying 16 put options, he can ensure against a large decrease in the portfolio value, and yet maintain profit potential if the market rises. Hedging by buying put options works just like insurance. Simply buy the number of puts dictated by the short futures hedge ratio calculation. The degree of coverage is determined by the choice of the strike price. Higher strike price puts are more expensive than lower strike price puts, but the higher strike puts starts at a higher level to compensate for losses. For example, buying a put with a strike price of 285.00 protects him from a market decline below 285.00. In similar fashion, buying a put with a strike price of 260.00 protects him from a decline below 260.00. The hedger, thus,

---

[7] There is another statistic produced in the regression of the portfolio against the index, R^2, the coefficient of determination, which indicates the reliability of the beta statistic.

has the judgmental business decision about the alternative costs and benefits of the various strike prices available.

Anticipating Future Stock Purchases

Long futures positions or the purchase of call options can protect against a rising market, ensuring that the market does not far outstrip investor ability to make planned stock purchases. Portfolio managers periodically receive funds to invest from various sources, including corporate contributions to pension funds, insurance premium payments from policy holders and dividends on stock holdings. With long futures or calls, investors can pre-position themselves in the market before receiving expected funds and effectively fix the cost of future stock acquisitions.

Figure 16   Futures Hedge

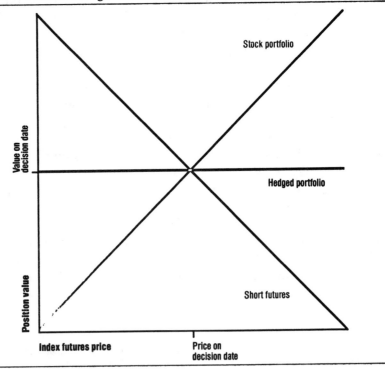

Figure 17   Option Hedge

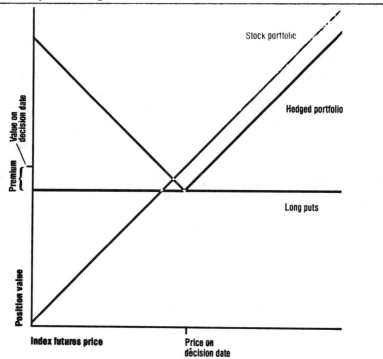

Suppose an investor anticipates receiving a cash payment three months in the future. He plans to purchase a variety of stocks with the cash, but fears that the stock market will advance sharply by that time and that the cash will purchase significantly fewer shares than at current market levels. To establish a price level for the anticipated purchases, he buys futures or calls roughly of the same value as the funds he expects to receive.

Divide the amount of the projected funds by the index value (i.e., current S&P index × $500) to arrive at the number of futures to use. When he knows which stocks to buy, he calculates the beta of the portfolio of purchases, and uses that as the hedge ratio, as in the prior portfolio protection example. If the next futures contract expiration date does not coincide with the date(s) of the planned purchase, he probably buys the following delivery contracts and, as the stock purchases are made, offsets the futures position.

Using options, he can insure against missing a major bull market by buying the same number of calls as futures. He can lock in today's futures price for the planned stock purchase by delta-weighting the number of calls he buys. He then either adjusts the number of calls he holds as the deltas change, or not, depending on whether he wants to avoid all market risk. By deciding not to adjust based on a strong bull market expectation, he profits and can increase the stock purchase in the event the stock market does, indeed, rally. However, a decline or slow rise results in a loss of value (up to the amount of premium paid) through the decay of option time value. So monitor the market and alter the hedge position if the rise does not materialize, certainly before the options have only a few weeks to expiration.

Hedging Risks

Despite the precision involved in the design of some of the hedges described, an investor cannot expect an exact offset to every market move. Three risks must be considered.

By far, the largest risk is that the calculated beta proves to be inappropriate during the hedge period. A portfolio that performed with a given beta in the past may not perform with the same beta in the future. If the beta changes, the hedge performance may not exactly duplicate the change in the value of the portfolio.

Second, the percentage move of the futures price may be somewhat different than that of the underlying indices. This risk—typically referred to as basis risk—may result in some profit or loss, but the dollar amount generally is small relative to the value of the portfolio.

Finally, strict hedging stabilizes and insulates the portfolio value from any change—either up or down—that the market posts. Even so, when losses are generated by the futures position, these losses must be paid in cash, with daily variation margin. Large cash outlays can force short-term borrowing or a premature liquidation of either equity holdings or the futures position. This, of course, does not apply to long option hedges because no margin is required.

While these risks must be recognized, they should not be overstated. An investor must weigh these hedging risks against the risk of adverse price movement that exists by holding any equity portfolio. A decision to hedge can be viewed as the exchange of market risk for a much smaller, more controllable risk.

Writing Calls Against the Portfolio

An investor also can sell S&P 500 call options against his portfolio to earn income when he expects a flat market. This is much like the covered writing of individual stock options, except that beta considerations may be important. For a stock portfolio not very well diversified across industry groups, there is risk that the portfolio will not rise enough in a market rally to completely offset losses on the short calls. There is also basis risk, which can have some effect if interest rates rise markedly. Finally, margins are required on short options; while the option losses should be offset by gains in the stock portfolio, margin calls require cash payment.

Altering Beta and Asset Mix

The application of index futures and options to portfolio management can take many forms. These contracts can be used to extend or neutralize stock market exposure. As a facilitating measure, a short futures position secures a market level while a large sale of stocks is executed in an orderly fashion. Similarly, a long futures position can serve as a temporary hedge while a large purchase is completed.

Index contracts can help to achieve returns from superior selection of undervalued stocks. By eliminating general market risk, the portfolio return appproximates the "risk-free" rate plus the return from superior stock selection.

For market timing, the portfolio beta can be adjusted up or down with index contracts more readily than with cumbersome stock transactions. Long futures and calls add to the portfolio beta; short futures and long puts reduce the total position beta.

The number of contracts needed to adjust the total position beta is defined by the following equation:

$$\text{Number of Contracts} = \frac{\text{current portfolio value} \times (\beta \text{ desired} - \beta \text{ portfolio})}{\text{current index} \times \$500}$$

A positive result indicates the number of long futures to use; a negative result, the number of short futures.

CONCLUSION

Although some examples of hedging and arbitrage techniques may appear complex, do not lose sight of the fact that index futures and options can simplify trading and investments. One trading instrument provides the diversification of an entire market; and one trade establishes a large liquid position, with economy of execution time and commission cost. Speculative traders have in stock index contracts an opportunity to trade markets that react to the most basic economic and political factors.

Investors can increase equity investment and hold it through market down-cycles by using S&P stock index futures and options as a control for market risk. These contracts provide staying power to help achieve the capital gains of productive investment.

APPENDIX I: SUMMARY OF CONTRACT TERMS[*]

	S&P 500 Futures	Futures Options on S&P 500
Description of Index	The S&P 500 Stock Price Index is a capitalization-weighted index comprising 500 of the largest and most-actively traded domestic industrial stocks.	The S&P 500 Stock Price Index is a capitalization-weighted index comprising 500 of the largest and most-actively traded domestic industrial stocks.
Ticker Symbol	Futures: SP Cash: INX	Calls: CS Puts: PS
Contract Size	$500 × the S&P 500 Stock Price Index	One S&P 500 futures contract
Strike Price Intervals	N/A	5.00 point intervals
Minimum Price Change	05 index points = $25.00 per contract	05 index points = $25.00 per contract[**]
Trading Hours	8:30 AM to 3:15 PM Chicago time	8:30 AM to 3:15 PM Chicago time
Contract Months	March, June, September, December	All twelve calendar months[***]
Last Day of Trading	The Thursday prior to the third Friday of the contract month	March, June, September, December: the Thursday prior to the third Friday. Other eight months: the third Friday
Settlement Procedure	Cash settlement. All open positions at the close of the final trading day are settled in cash to the Special Opening Quotation on Friday morning of the S&P 500 Stock Price Index. There is no delivery of securities and the full value of the contract is not transferred. Final gains and losses are charged to the margin accounts, based on the opening values of the 500 stocks. If a stock does not open on Friday, its last sale price is used.	Except on the final trading day of March, June, September and December options, exercise of a call results in a long futures position at the strike price in the underlying contract month; exercise of a put results in a short position at the strike price in the underlying contract month. Any short position open at the end of a trading day is liable to the assignment of a futures position. Exercise of a March, June, September or December option on the settlement day results, in effect, in cash settlement for the in-the-money amount. Expiring in-the-money options for these expirations only will be automatically exercised.
Index Calculation	The Index is calculated using the last sale. The base for the Index is 10.0 (1941-43). Major quote vendors will disseminate this calculation at 15-second intervals throughout the day.	The Index is calculated using the last sale. The base for the Index is 10.0 (1941-43). Major quote vendors will disseminate this calculation at 15-second intervals throughout the day.

[*]All contract terms and conditions herein are subject to change. All matters pertaining to rules and specifications herein are made subject to and are superseded by official Chicago Mercantile Exchange rules. Current CME rules should be consulted in all cases concerning contract specifications. Consult your broker or the CME for verification. These specifications as of 5/15/88.
[**]A trade may occur at a nominal price (.002 = $1) if it results in liquidation for both parties of deep-out-of-the-money option positions.
[***]The underlying instrument for three monthly option expirations within a quarter is the quarter-end futures contract. For example, if you exercise a January, a February, or a March option, you will take a position at the strike in the March futures.

APPENDIX II: MONITORING TRADING ACTIVITY

Trading prices are disseminated instantaneously throughout the world by the various quotation transmission services, and are carried daily in the business pages of most major newspapers. The displays reproduced here are examples of the way *The Wall Street Journal* shows these prices. To convert the quotations to dollar value, simply multiply the quote by $500. For example, a long position in the June S&P 500 futures contract held from the prior day through the close of trading with a change of +4.35 is credited with a 4.35 × $500 or $2,175 profit.

Guide: Table Future Prices

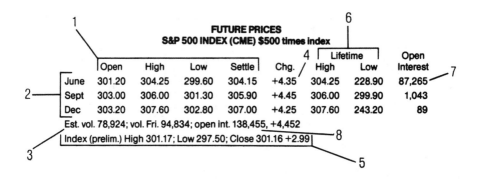

1 Prices represent the open, high, low and settlement (or closing) price for the previous day

2 Contract delivery months that are currently traded

3 The number of contracts traded in the previous two trading sessions

4 One day's change in the settlement price

5 The actual index high, low, close and change

6 High and low prices over the life of the contract

7 The number of contracts still in effect at the end of the previous day's trading session—each unit represents a buyer and a seller who still have a contract position

8 The total of the right column, and the change from the prior trading day

| | | | FUTURES OPTIONS S&P 500 STOCK INDEX (CME) $500 times premium | | | |
| Strike Price | Calls—Settle | | | Puts—Settle | | |
	Jun-c	Jul-c	Aug-c	Jun-p	Jul-p	Aug-p
295	12.90	16.80	18.95	3.80	6.05	8.20
300	9.80	13.85	16.10	5.65	8.00	10.30
305	7.20	11.20	13.55	8.05	10.30	12.65
310	5.10	8.95	11.30	10.95	13.00	–
315	3.50	7.00	9.30	–	–	–
320	2.35	5.40	–	–	–	–

Est. vol. 8,209; Fri vol. 7,565 calls; 4,727 puts
Open interest Fri; 31,335 calls; 14,300 puts

1 Expiration months (most newspapers only show the first three)

2 Most active strike prices

3 Volume of options traded in the previous two trading sessions

4 Closing prices in each option

5 The number of options (each unit represents both the holder and the writer) that were still open at the end of the previous day's trading session

APPENDIX III: GLOSSARY

Arbitrage The simultaneous purchase and sale of equivalent securities and futures in order to benefit from an anticipated change in their price relationship.

Ask   The price at which a party is willing to sell; also called the "offer."

At-the-money   An option with an exercise price equal or near to the current underlying futures price.

Basis   The difference between the futures price and the current index value.

Basis Point   One-hundredth (.01) of a full index point, worth $5.

Beta   The relationship between the movement of an individual stock or a portfolio and that of the overall stock market.

Bear Spread   A spread which is put on with the expectation that the futures price will decline.

Bid   The price at which a party is willing to buy.

Bull Spread   A spread position taken with the expectation that the futures price will rise.

Call Option   An option that gives the holder the right to enter a long futures position at a specific price, and obligates the seller to enter a short futures position at a specific price if he is assigned for exercise.

Cash Settlement   Applies to the expiration of quarterly index options and futures contracts. There is no delivery of securities, and the full value of the contract is not transferred. Final settlement occurs on the morning following the last day of trading when all open positions will be marked to a Special Opening Quotation based on the component stocks in the S&P 500 Index. Expiring options which are in-the-money based on the Special Opening Quotation are automatically exercised. This results, in effect, in cash settlement for the in-the-money amount.

CFTC The Commodity Futures Trading Commission is the independent federal agency created by Congress in 1974 to regulate futures and options trading.

Clearing House An adjunct of the Chicago Mercantile Exchange through which all CME futures and options on futures transactions are made, and through which all financial settlements against those contracts are made.

Covered Writing The sale of an option against an underlying position.

Credit Spread A spread in which the value of the option sold exceeds the value of the option purchased.

Debit Spread A spread in which the value of the option purchased exceeds the value of the option sold.

Delivery The process by which funds and the physical commodity change hands on expiration of a futures contract. (See Cash Settlement.)

Delta A measure of the price-change relationship between an option and the underlying futures.

Exercise Notice A notice tendered by a brokerage firm to the CME clearinghouse that exchanges an option for a futures position.

Exercise Price The price at which futures positions are established upon exercise of an option. Also called "strike price."

Expiration Date The last day that an option may be exercised. (See "Last Trading Day.")

Futures Contract A standardized, transferable legal agreement to make or take delivery of a certain commodity at a specific time in the future. The price is determined by open outcry auction, and is adjusted daily to the current market. (See "Mark-to-Market.")

Hedge To take a position in a futures market opposite to a position held in the cash market to minimize the risk of financial loss from an adverse price change.

In-the-money A situation in which the market price of a futures contract is higher than the exercise price of a call, or lower than the exercise price of a put.

Intrinsic Value That portion of an option's premium that represents the amount an option is in-the-money.

Last Trading Day For the S&P 500 futures and for the quarter-end options, this is the Thursday prior to the third Friday of the contract month. For the eight interim-month expiration options, this is the third Friday of the contract month. If that day is a holiday, it is the preceding business day.

Limit Order An order in which a customer specifies a price; the order can be executed only if the market reaches or betters that price.

Long Position Indicates ownership. In futures, the long has purchased the commodity or security for future delivery. In options, the long has purchased the call or the put option.

Margin Funds that must be deposited with the broker for each futures or written option contract as a guarantee of fulfillment of the contract. Also called Security Deposit.

Maintenance Margin A sum, usually smaller than—but part of—the original margin. If a customer's account with his broker drops below the maintenance margin level, the broker must issue a "margin call" for the amount of money required to restore the customer's balance in the account to the initial margin requirement.

Mark-to-Market Daily, the CME clearinghouse adjusts all open futures and options positions to reflect changes in the settlement price of the contract. Each position is credited with profit or charged with loss.

Market Order   An order to buy or sell at the best price available at that time.

Offset   Any transaction which liquidates or closes out an open contract position.

Open Interest   The number of contracts that have been opened and have not been offset, delivered or exercised. Equal to half of the summed long and short positions.

Out-of-the-money   A situation in which the market price of a futures contract is below the exercise price of a call, or above the exercise price of a put.

Premium   The price of an option agreed on by the buyer and seller in open, competitive trading on the exchange trading floor.

Put Option   An option that gives the holder the right to enter a short futures position, and obligates the seller to enter a long futures position at a specific price if he is assigned for exercise.

Settlement Price   The end-of-day price used to calculate gains and losses in futures market accounts.

Short Position   In futures, the short has sold the commodity or security for future delivery. In options, the short has sold the call or the put and is obligated to take a futures position if he is assigned for exercise.

Spot Price   The current market price of the actual stock index. Also called "cash price."

Spread   Holding a long and a short position in two related contracts to capture profit from a changing price relationship. The term also refers to the price difference between the contracts.

Stop Order   A contingent order to buy futures (buy stop) only if some higher price (the stop price) is reached; or a contingent order to sell futures (sell stop) only if some lower price (the stop price) is reached.

Straddle   The purchase or sale of both a put and a call having the same exercise price and expiration date.

Time Value   That portion of an option's premium that represents the amount in excess of the intrinsic value.

Uncovered Sale   The sale of an option without an underlying futures position.

Volume   The number of transactions in a contract during a specified time period.

Writer   The seller of an option.

SOURCES OF ADDITIONAL INFORMATION

For more information about S&P 500 futures and options, contact a broker. Together, determine what role they should play in an investment strategy. The CME has several other publications available for those interested in financial futures and options. Copies of the following may be obtained by contacting your broker or the CME:

CME Trader's Scorecard

Opportunities in Currency Trading

Opportunities in Interest Rates

Trading in Tomorrows: Your Guide to Futures

Using Currency Futures and Options

Using Interest Rate Futures and Options

Chicago
Chicago Mercantile Exchange
30 South Wacker Drive
Chicago, Illinois 60606
312/930-1000

New York
Chicago Mercantile Exchange
67 Wall Street
New York, New York 10005
212/363-7000

London
Chicago Mercantile Exchange
27 Throgmorton Street
London, EC2N 2AN England
01/920-0722

Tokyo
Chicago Mercantile Exchange
3-3-1 Kasumigaseki
Chiyoda-ku, Tokyo 100 Japan
03/595-2251

The Chicago Mercantile Exchange provides a centralized marketplace for investment and risk management. The CME was established in 1919 as the successor to the Butter and Egg Board which had been created in 1898. The exchange is compromised of three divisions: the Chicago Mercantile Exchange, on which are traded agricultural futures contracts; the International Monetary market (IMM) division established in 1972 for trading of currency and, subsequently, interest rate futures; and the Index and Option Market (IOM) division, activated in 1982 for the trading of equity-related futures, in addition to options on futures.

"S&P," "Standard & Poor's," and "S&P 500" are trademarks of the Standard & Poor's Corporation, which assumes no liability in connection with the trading of any contract based on its indexes.

Chapter 10

Introduction to Stock Index Futures

Bruce Collins
First Boston Corporation

INTRODUCTION

A stock index futures (SIF) contract is an agreement to pay or receive a fixed dollar amount times the difference between the purchase price and (1) the price when sold, (2) the daily futures settlement price (3) or the final settlement price of the underlying index at expiration. SIFs differ from traditional futures contracts in that delivery is in cash. All futures contracts are marked-to-the-market on a daily basis and a payment is made based on the day's price movement. The futures price at the time the contract is initiated represents the price at which the cash transaction will take place at some time in the future.

Because futures are marked-to-the-market, the futures price equals the spot price at expiration.[1] Any difference between the spot price at expiration and the futures price when the contract is

---

1   For traditional commodities, the convergence of the futures price and the spot price at expiration is a consequence of arbitrage. The price of an SIFs contract is equal to the spot price at expiration by contractual agreement.

initiated is exchanged across the expiration cycle. This differs from a forward contract in which no money is exchanged until expiration, or when the forward price is paid for the delivery of the underlying asset. The current futures price equals the forward price with the same terms if interest rates are known and constant over the expiration cycle. In a later section, the pricing of stock index futures is described.

On February 24, 1982, a futures contract on the Value Line Index began trading on the Kansas City Board of Trade (KCBT). The following April, an S&P 500 futures contract began trading at the Chicago Mercantile Exchange (CME). Since that time, other SIF contracts have been listed, including the New York Futures Exchange (NYFE) contract on the New York Stock Exchange's composite index, a futures contract on the Major Market Index (MMI) trading on the Chicago Board of Trade (CBT) and a host of others that have failed.[2]

The success or failure of a futures contract, or of any innovative financial instrument, is directly related to the economic motivation underlying its creation. Furthermore, the instrument must not be redundant. This means that it supplies the market with a valuable investment alternative. The success of a new futures contract also is subject to the market environment for new products. Consequently, market timing is an important issue.

Futures markets serve three fundamental economic functions. They are a means for 1) the economic transfer of risk, 2) the facilitation of capital formation and 3) the facilitation of the price discovery process. SIFs serve a vital economic function by allowing portfolio managers to hedge the market risk of a portfolio by transferring the risk through futures. Moreover, stock index futures facilitate capital formation because market agents can use futures to better manage risk and are, therefore, more willing to hold a portfolio of new issues. In addition, SIFs facilitate the price discovery process because futures prices, formed through competitive bidding, reflect information about future supply and demand conditions, and quickly incorporate new information. Investors can

---

2 The most notable are futures contracts on the Russell Indices, including the Russell 2000 Index.

quickly respond to changing market conditions by adjusting their risk exposure through the futures market. This can be accomplished without altering the composition of their equity portfolio and at a lower cost.

In the sections that follow is a description of the set of existing listed contracts, the characteristics of stock index futures contracts, why they are valuable, the pricing of stock index futures contracts and investment applications.

CHARACTERISTICS OF STOCK INDEX FUTURES CONTRACTS

Contract Specifications

There are four domestic (United States) stock index futures contract that currently trade with sufficient liquidity to warrant coverage in this chapter. These are the S&P 500 futures contract (S&P), The New York Futures futures contract (NYFE), the XMI futures contract (XMI) and the Value Line futures contract (VL). The S&P 500 is by far the most successful. Contract specifications are found in Table 1.

All stock index futures contracts are valued at a multiple of the underlying index value. For example, the multiple for the S&P 500 contract is $500. Furthermore, most contracts profiled in the table have a minimum tick size of .05, trade over the same hours (the XMI opens 15 minutes earlier) and are created across the March expiration cycle (the XMI also trades in the nearest three months).

There are two ways by which a commodities exchange can control price movements: minimum tick size and price controls, which is more severe. Historically, commodities exchanges did not impose price limits on stock index futures contracts, but this changed, however, in the aftermath of the 1987 market crash. An opening price limit was put into effect on the S&P 500 futures contract for the first 30 minutes of trading, and a second adjusted price limit went into effect after the first 30 minutes. The S&P 500

Table 1   Stock Index Futures Contract Specifications

Contract	S&P 500	NYSE Comp.	XMI	Value Line
Ticker	SPX	NYA	XMI	XYL
Exchange	CME	NYFE	CBT	KCBT
Trading hours	9:30am- 4:15pm	9:30am- 4:15pm	9:15am- 4:15pm	9:30am- 4:15pm
Contract size	500	500	250	500
Trading cycle	March	same	same plus 3 nearest months	same
Minimum price change	.05	.05	.05	.05
Daily price limit[1]	30	n/a	n/a	30
Settlement	3rd Friday of contract month-opening	same (close)	same	same

1 The daily price limit is part of a more elaborate regulatory procedure outlined in the text.

---

price limit at the opening was 10 percent versus the previous night close. Following the first 30 minutes, the price limit was 15 percent versus the previous night close.

More recently, the Chicago Mercantile Exchange (CME) imposed a set of price limits on the S&P 500 futures price. These include 1) a five-point opening limit if exceeded trading is suspended for 10 minutes; 2) a 12-point lower price limit when trading can not take place below that level for 30 minutes; 3) a 20-point price limit when trading is suspended for one hour and 4) a 30-point daily price limit.

Other exchanges have taken similar measures in order to restore investor confidence in the marketplace and to prevent the creation of large jumps in the market over short time intervals. Moreover because of arbitrage links between the stock index futures market and the stock market, price limits in the futures market are a response to conditions in the stock market and an attempt to coordinate both markets.

Stock Indices

To understand the value of stock index futures contracts, the underlying cash must be understood as well. Stock indices essentially are summary measures of stock market behavior. A measure of market behavior generates the ability to compare market performance with a variety of economic variables that, according to financial theory, have systematic effects on stock prices. This is particularly important for the investment decision making process and for efficient markets.

Most popular stock indices are a sample of the equity universe. Consequently, several factors go into the construction of an index. First, the choice of what stocks and how many to include in the index must be made. Is the index intended to represent to the entire universe or a specific subset? Second, having decided on what stocks to include, it must decided how to best represent or weight each stock in the index. Is the stock of equal importance (equal weighting) or of relative importance? Third, indices are summary measures of weighted averages, which measure the average price level of a group of stocks. Essentially there are two ways to compute averages, arithmetically or geometrically. Arithmetic indices are most common and easy to replicate. Currently, all major domestic indices are arithmetic averages. However, some are market value weighted (S&P 500, NYSE Composite), others are price weighted (DJIA, MMI) and one is equal weighted (Value Line).

Table 2 presents some of the characteristics of several popular indices, all of which are arithmetic. But the two most popular, the S&P 500 and the DJIA, are weighted differently. The S&P 500 is market value weighted while the Dow Jones Industrial Average (DJIA) is price-weighted. The Major Market Index (MMI) and the DJIA both contain a small segment of the equity universe narrowly focused on large capitalization stocks.

Table 2   Characteristics of Selected Stock Indices

Index	S&P 500	MMI	Value Line	DJIA
Size	500	20	1600	30
Average Price	44	65	30	52
Average Method	arith.	arith.	arith.	arith.
Weight Method	cap.	price	equal	price
SIFs	yes	yes	yes	no

The S&P 500 Index contains 500 names and is more representative. The Value Line Index contains the largest number of stocks but is equally weighted, which gives the same importance to each stock in the index. This index outperforms other indices when small capitalization stocks are outperforming the rest of the market. The S&P 500 futures contracts is based on the S&P 500 Index. It is the most successful contract to date because the underlying index is the most widely used benchmark, which means there are numerous natural hedgers, and because the index is easy to replicate in the cash market. The MMI is the underlying index for the XMI futures contract and has been less successful because of its narrow definition. The Value Line futures contract is the least successful of the surviving stock index futures contracts because the index is difficult to replicate and there are few natural hedgers.

Margin and Leverage

Futures contracts are contractual agreements and, therefore, do not imply ownership of an asset. They give the purchaser of the contract the obligation to purchase the underlying asset at a future date. Consequently, the purchaser of a futures contract need only put up a fraction of the value of the contract. The margin requirement for futures contracts serves a function similar to margin requirements for stocks.

Margin requirements exist as a form of protection for the broker against trading risks and they foster investor confidence in financial markets. However, futures margin differs from stock margin; a futures margin is a performance bond or good-faith deposit, which is only a recognition that the contractual obligations will be honored. In contrast, stock margin is a down payment toward the purchase of a stock. For this reason, margin on futures contracts is significantly lower than margin on stock. Moreover, low margin requirements are important for liquid futures markets. It is the leverage implicit in futures contracts that fosters liquidity, and makes them a viable and efficient form of hedging. It is recognized, however, that margin requirements also must be sufficient to maintain investor confidence in the marketplace. Table 3 presents the current margin requirements for four stock index futures contracts and their accompanying leverage factors.

There are two separate concepts of margin relating to futures contracts: variation margin and initial margin. Variation margin is cash flows debited or credited to a futures account on a daily basis. Initial margin is the good-faith deposit posted when the contract is purchased. Maintenance margin is the minimal margin requirement after the contract has been purchased. If the margin falls below that amount, additional margin must be posted to satisfy the original initial margin requirement. Margin requirements differ for hedgers and speculators. As expected, the margin requirement for speculators is higher to reflect the risk associated with speculation versus hedging. Because of higher margin requirements, speculators receive less leverage through the purchase of a futures contract than hedgers. The existing leverage factor for the S&P 500 futures contract gives a speculator with $100,000 access to $1.34 million in equity exposure. This access is generated because the value of a single stock index futures contract is the product of the index value and a multiplier. The S&P 500 contract, for example, is worth $168,000 (336 × 500) with the index at 336. Because a speculator is required to post only $12,000 per contract,

Table 3   Stock Index Futures Margin Requirements and Leverage Factors[1]

Contract	S&P 500	NYSE Comp.	XMI	Value Line
Hedger				
Initial	$5,000	$3,000	$5,000	$5,000
Maintenance	5,000	3,000	5,000	5,000
Leverage	33	31	26	26
Speculator				
Initial	12,000	6,500	8,000	7,500
Maintenance	5,000	3,000	5,000	5,000
Leverage	14	14	16	17

[1] November 1989 prices and margin

$100,000 then allows the speculator to purchase eight contracts worth $1.34 million.

STOCK INDEX FUTURES PRICING

Cost of Carry Valuation Model

Futures are priced as a function of the cost of financing, the yield on the underlying asset, the price of the underlying asset, the time to expiration and investor expectations. Futures pricing is based on the concept of riskless arbitrage because their valuation is derived from cost of carry considerations underlying the arbitrage argument.

What is the fair value of a futures contract? Fundamentally, economic forces combine to find the equilibrium price. The opportunity cost of not holding the underlying index and the yield received on alternative investments act as the dynamic force behind pricing futures contracts. So the futures price becomes a variation of the spot price, adjusted for the parameters above. Futures prices do not move far out of alignment with spot prices because of the possibility of delivery and arbitrage.

The two most important factors influencing the value of a futures contract are the cost of carry and investor expectations of how that may change over the investment horizon. The fair futures price varies from the spot price by the cost of carry, which is the rate at which an investor can borrow funds to finance the purchase of an asset, adjusted for the yield realized by holding the asset.

For example, the cost of carry associated with a stock investment is the financing rate less the dividend rate. The futures valuation model is referred to the cost of carry valuation model and is based on a set of assumptions:

1. Futures and forward contracts are the same.

2. The underlying asset is perfectly divisible.

3. Dividends are known.

4. Interest rates are known.

5. There are no restrictions on short sales.

6. There are no taxes or transaction costs.

7. The spot price is known.

The reasoning underlying the model is: The purchase of a futures contract is a temporary substitute for a transaction in the cash market; therefore, because the futures contract is not an asset to be purchased but an agreement to enter into a transaction at a later time, no money has to be borrowed today; consequently, the seller must be compensated for incurring the borrowing costs for holding the underlying asset. The futures prices then is adjusted upward by the amount of the borrowing costs:

$$\text{Futures price} = \text{asset price} + \text{cost of borrowing}$$

However, because the buyer of the futures contract does not hold the asset over the life of the contract, the yield from holding the asset is forfeited and the futures contract must be adjusted downward to reflect this. Thus, the formula for the fair futures price, based on cost of carry considerations, is:

$$\text{Futures price} = \text{asset price} + \text{cost of borrowing-yield}$$

In the case of stock index futures, the cost of financing is a short-term credit instrument (STCI) and the yield is the dividend yield on the index. The factors that go into computing fair value are:

- Cash price of index
- Short-term interest rate
- Dividend yield
- Days to expiration

The fair value then is:

$$\text{Fair value} = (\text{index} \times (1 + \text{term rate})) - \text{dividends}$$

For example, assume the index is at 340, there are 60 days to expiration, the financing rate is 8.5 percent and dividends received equals two index points. The fair value calculation is:

$$\text{Fair value} = (340 \times (1 + (0.085 \times 60/365))) - 2.0 = 342.75$$

The futures contract is valued at 2.75 index points above the spot price. Should the spread between the futures and spot price narrow, arbitragers will buy cheap futures and sell the index. The opposite scenario would unfold if the spread widened.

Sources of Mispricing

In practice, the fair value of a futures contract is a range of prices and not a single price, due to several factors that violate the assumptions:

- Uncertain dividend payments
- Varied borrowing and lending rates
- Costs of arbitrage
- Federal funds versus clearinghouse funds
- 360-day versus 365 day years
- Wire transfers and other administrative fees.

The futures price gravitates around fair value because of a viable and active arbitrage mechanism. Arbitrage activity occurs only outside a range surrounding fair value for the reasons listed above. Volatility in the spread (known as "basis") between the futures and spot price may be a consequence of mispricing due to changes in the variables that influence fair value.

Another assumption about futures pricing models is that they are consistent with forward prices—and this is true if the assumption of known interest rates holds. However because futures prices are marked-to-the-market daily, any losses or gains—referred to as variation margin—are immediately realized and a payment is transferred. Moreover at expiration, the price paid by the buyer to the seller is the spot price. Any difference between the spot price at expiration and the futures price when the contract was initiated is exchanged across the expiration period. This differs from forward contracts in which no money is exchanged until expiration when the forward price is paid for the delivery of the underlying asset.

One potential adverse impact on returns may result from financing costs associated with variation margin. An SIFs position outperforms the index in an up market and underperforms in a down market due to variation margin. This increases the volatility of returns and, under some scenarios, adversely affects returns.

Daily losses must be satisfied by cash; they cannot be settled with short-term credit instruments. Consequently, the cash outflow requires financing. A technique referred to as "underhedging" or "tailing" is used to minimize the impact of variation margin on returns. Slightly fewer contracts are bought or sold. The exact number of contracts is a function of interest costs and time to expiration. An adjustment must be made to the strategy as interest rates change and as the time to expiration is reduced. The formula for precise adjustment is:

$$\text{Adjustment factor} = 1/(1 + \text{term interest rate})$$

Use of the adjustment factor is illustrated in the following example. Suppose an investor wants $25,000,000 in equity exposure and decided to accomplish this using stock index futures. The formula for the number of contracts necessary to create a dollar equivalent position is:

$$\text{Number of futures} = 25,000,000 / \text{index price} \times \text{multiplier}$$

For the S&P 500 futures contract, the multiplier is 500; assuming the index is at 333, the number of contracts is $25,000,000/333 \times \times 500$, or 150. The number of contracts is adjusted downward to minimize variation margin risk.

Suppose the financing rate is 8.5 percent and there are 60 days to expiration, the term interest rate is 1.397 percent. The adjustment factor then is 1/1.01397 or .98622. The adjustment factor and the number of contracts yields the adjusted number of contracts. In this example, it is .98622 × 150, or approximately 148 contracts.

Therefore, the number of contracts to satisfy the position is reduced by two.

To see the impact of the adjustment, assume the market declines to 330. A three-point decline requires 3 × 500 × 150, or $225,000 in cash to be delivered to the futures account. The cost of financing the $225,000 for the remaining 59 days is 225,000 × 1.374 percent or $3,091. The effect of tailing is to hold two fewer contracts. The savings from holding two fewer contracts is 3 × 500 × 2, or $3,000, which offsets most of the cost of financing variation margin.

INVESTMENT APPLICATIONS USING STOCK INDEX FUTURES

Hedging Programs

Prior to the introduction of stock index derivatives, a portfolio manager holding a long equity position had to sell off his long position to reduce equity exposure. Stock index futures serve as a valuable hedging instrument for equity portfolio managers. They now are able to hedge systematic risk from their equity position without the need to liquidate any portion of the portfolio itself. The economic importance of hedging is the driving force behind the existence of futures markets.

In the hedging process, the price risk associated with a cash position is transferred from the hedger to speculator. Although hedging is the primary economic motivation for futures transactions, it is the willingness of speculators to assume the price risk that makes the process work. Moreover, the effectiveness of hedging largely is dependent on an effective and efficient arbitrage mechanism. The arbitrage mechanism is crucial to price futures contracts efficiently and, therefore, to the cost of hedging. Mispriced futures can increase the volatility or risk of the hedged position. The absence of an arbitrage mechanism introduces an element of risk to the hedger referred to as "basis risk."[3] Consequently, the act of hedging involves the substitution of basis risk for price risk. The returns to a hedged position should consist of gains (losses) to the cash position and offsetting losses (gains) to the futures position. If the hedge is held until expiration, when the futures price should equal the cash price, and the futures position was secured at a fair price, then basis risk is eliminated, the position is a perfect hedge and the returns over the time period equals the riskless rate.

The effectiveness of the hedging also is influenced by the relationship of the portfolio to the index underlying the futures contract. Hedging an S&P 500 portfolio with futures should be the equivalent of selling the portfolio and investing the proceeds in a riskless security such as treasury bills. However, this assumes that there is no tracking error versus the S&P 500 and that the futures are fair-valued when the hedge is lifted.[4]

The use of stock index futures to hedge an equity portfolio that has positive expected tracking error is regarded as cross-hedging. Cross-hedging involves the use of a like, but not exact, instrument for hedging purposes. The use of SIFs to hedge an equity portfolio with positive tracking error introduces another source of basis risk. The short futures position eliminates market risk but not non-market or unsystematic risk.

In order to hedge, it is necessary to derive the appropriate hedge ratio for a particular portfolio. An effective hedge minimizes the risk to the hedged position. Consequently, the optimal hedge ratio minimizes risk. Any hedge ratio has to address the sources of risk associated with the portfolio and the hedging instrument. Capital market theory has identified two sources of risk associated with an equity portfolio: systematic or market risk, and unsystematic or residual risk. In addition to these sources of risk,

---

3   The basis is the difference between the futures price and the spot price, and should equal the cost of carry.

4   Tracking error is the expected returns differential between the replicating portfolio and the index underlying the futures contract. Mathematically, it is often expressed as the standard deviation of the difference in expected returns.

there is basis risk. These three components of risk can be examined by looking at the returns to a hedged position in this formula:[5]

(1) $$R(h) = R(p) - h \times R(f)$$

The returns to the hedged position should equal the returns to the underlying portfolio, $R(p)$, adjusted by the product of the hedge ratio (h) and the returns to the hedging instrument, $R(h)$. In order to derive the hedge ratio, a functional form of the returns to the equity portfolio and to the hedging instrument must be specified. The returns to the portfolio can be expressed in terms of the market model:[6]

(2) $$R(p) = a + b(p) \times R(m) + e(p)$$

The source of returns for an equity portfolio can be broken down into market related returns ($R(m)$) and non-market returns, $e(p)$.

The returns to a futures position are related to market factors, to the basis ($R(carry)$) and mispricing, $e(f)$. The formula for returns to a futures position are:

(3) $$R(f) = R(carry) + R(m) + e(f)$$

Thus by combining these three equations, the formula for the returns to hedged portfolio is:

$$R(h) = a + b(p) \times R(m) + e(p) - h (R(carry) + R(index) + e(f))$$

---

5   The expression is derived in Figlewski (1984).

6   The market model was developed by Sharpe (1964) and Litner (1965), and is commonly referred to as the Capital Asset Pricing Model (CAPM).

Peters (1986) derived a solution for the risk minimizing hedge ratio, which is the value of h that minimizes the variance of the hedged portfolio:

$$h = b(p) \times b(f)$$

The correct hedge ratio is the product of the portfolio's sensitivity to changes in market returns (beta) and the sensitivity of the index representing the market to changes in the futures returns. This differs from the traditional beta hedge because it takes into account basis risk. The beta hedge is useful when the hedged position is held until maturity. However, for a hedged position with a time horizon that does not coincide with the expiration cycle of the futures contract, the formula above is the correct hedge ratio.

The following example illustrates the use of futures in hedging an equity portfolio. A portfolio manager wants to hedge a $100 million equity portfolio using S&P 500 futures. The beta of the portfolio is one while the beta of the futures is .90. This means that for every dollar of the equity portfolio, $.90 (1 × .90) of futures should be sold. With the S&P 500 Index at 330, the number of contracts to sell equals $100 million × .90/500 × 330, or approximately 545 contracts. The steps are summarized below:

1. Calculate hedge ratio: beta(cash) × beta(futures)

2. Calculate dollar value of hedge: hedge ratio × dollar value of portfolio to be hedged

3. Calculate number of futures contracts: dollar value of hedge/dollar value of single futures contract

Recall that the success of the hedge is affected by the basis when the hedge is implemented versus its value when the hedge is lifted. The risk of hedging using futures is the futures are underpriced when the hedge is initiated (i.e., the basis is narrower than fair value) and either fairly priced or overpriced when the hedge is lifted. There are two scenarios: In the first, assume the hedge is initiated at fair value and held to expiration; in the second, look at a hedge when it is lifted prior to expiration.

Figure 1 shows the outcome of a hedge that is initiated at fair value, contains no tracking risk and is held until expiration. The appropriate hedge ratio is the portfolio beta because there is no basis risk. The hedge is not perfect due to rounding. As the figure indicates in an up or down market, the loss or gain to the hedged position is insignificant and is due only to rounding.

In practice, hedging programs do not always coincide with expiration cycles, portfolios are not exact replicas of the index underlying the futures contracts and frequently the futures are not sold at fair value. Thus, most equity portfolio hedging strategies are subject to basis risk and tracking risk.

The next example is profiled in Figure 2 and assumes the portfolio is similar but not identical to the underlying index and that the hedge is lifted prior to expiration. Suppose the beta of the portfolio is 1.1 and the futures beta remains the same, .90. The number of futures contracts required for hedging is calculated using the steps outlined above

1. Hedge ratio = $1.1 \times .90 = .99$

2. Dollar value of hedge = $.99 \times \$100mm = \$99mm$

3. Number = $\$99mm \: / \: 500 \times 330 = 600$

4. Value of futures = $600 \times 500 \times 332 = \$99.6mm$

Suppose the hedge is lifted after the market index has fallen by 10 percent, with a corresponding 11 percent decline in the portfolio as suggested by the portfolio beta. The loss to the portfolio is $11 million and the return to the futures is $11.1 million, yielding a net gain of $100 thousand. A similar hedge using only the portfolio beta results in a net gain of $211 thousand. Because the net return to hedged position is zero, the first hedge is superior to the beta hedge. A similar outcome is observed should the market increase by 10 percent, and the portfolio value and futures prices behave in the way described in the figure. It turns out that the larger the mispricing risk, the more effective the minimum hedge

Figure 1   Beta Hedge Strategy

Objective: Hedge $100 million S&P 500 portfolio using futures.

Hedge information: Beta (c) = 1
                      Beta (f) = .90
                      Index = 330
                      SIFs = 332
                      Hedge ratio = 1

Hedge: $100 million/500 × 330 = 606 contracts

Expiration Value:	+10%	−10%
Index	297	363
Portfolio	+$10mm	−$10mm
Futures	−9.99mm	+9.99mm
Net	+1,000	−1,000

ratio is versus the beta hedge. In the absence of mispricing, the futures beta approaches unity.

Synthetic Index Fund

Stock index futures can be used to create a synthetic index fund. An investor can purchase futures as a substitute for cash and invest the proceeds in a short-term credit instrument. The risks and returns are identical if the position is held until expiration of the futures contract when the cash and futures prices converge. However, if the position is liquidated prior to an expiration date, the synthetic index fund is subject to greater risks than a comparable cash index fund. (The previous section demonstrates these points.) The returns to a cash index fund consist of price returns and dividends in the following formula:

Figure 2   Minimum Hedge Strategy

Objective: Hedge $100 million portfolio using futures.

Hedge information: Beta (c) = 1.1
                      Beta (f) = .90
                      Index = 330
                      SIFs = 332
                      Hedge ratio = .99

Hedge: $100 million × .99/500 × 330 = 600 contracts

Expiration Value:	–10%	+10%
Index	297	363
Futures	295	367
Portfolio	+$11mm	–$11mm
Futures	–11.1mm	+10.5mm
Net	+100k	–500k

$$R(m) = R(index) + R(dividends)$$

The returns to the synthetic index fund consist of the returns to the STCI plus the returns to the futures:

$$R(s) = R(f) + R(STCI)$$

The returns to the futures can be separated into the returns due to changes in the underlying index, changes in carry (R-Y), or any mispricing in the futures at the time of initiating the index fund:

$$R(f) = R(carry) + R(index) + e(f)$$

Combining the two expressions indicates that returns to a synthetic index fund is the sum of the price returns to the underlying index, the returns due to changes in carry, any incremental returns due to mispricing and the returns to the STCI:

$$R(s) = R(carry) + R(index) + e(f) + R(STCI)$$

Any discrepancy between the returns to the cash index fund and the synthetic index fund using futures can be attributed to mispricing of the futures. To the extent that the mispricing of futures is uncertain, the synthetic index fund is subject to more risk than the cash index fund:

$$R(m) - R(s) = e(f)$$

There are relative advantages and disadvantages to using a synthetic index fund versus a cash index fund, as listed below:

Index Fund	Advantages	Disadvantages
Cash (Long stocks)	dividends restructurings special dividends stock replacement	high initial costs market impact tracking error custodial costs
Synthetic	low costs no tracking error no custodial costs no cash drag	variation margin price risk rolling risk

The risks of holding a synthetic index fund must be compared with the risks affecting a cash index fund. The two sources of risk associated with a synthetic index fund are variation margin risk and price risk. Variation margin risk was described in a previous section that explained a technique for addressing that problem. Price risk exists when the fund is initiated because the futures may be overvalued, which has an adverse impact on returns. The second source of price risk exists if the fund is held over more than one expiration cycle. The risk again is that the futures position may be rolled into the next contract at premium to fair value. Both of these consequences lead to inferior performance.

To illustrate the relative performance of a cash index fund versus a synthetic index fund, refer to Figure 3. If there is $102 million or 600 index fund contracts in the cash or futures markets and three market scenarios are profiled, the outcome is the same regardless of how the index fund is created. However, futures have a cost advantage not reflected in the outcomes; futures have the additional risk, a basis that moves adversely.

In Figure 3, the market is assumed currently at 340, interest rates are 8.5 percent, and dividends to be paid out over a 60-day period until expiration equals two index points. It is further assumed that the futures are fairly priced and the performance is measured through expiration of the near futures contract. A $102 million cash investment is the equivalent of 600 futures contracts. The results indicate that in all three market scenarios the cash index fund and the synthetic index fund yield the same amount.

Asset Allocation

In the 1980s, many institutional investors developed some form of tactical asset allocation model which makes asset shifts using futures contracts. Tactical asset allocation is a short-to intermediate-market timing strategy that attempts to benefit from relative asset class misvaluations. For example, if a TAA model suggests that equities are undervalued relative to bonds, an investor shifts asset exposure from bonds to equities. Stock index futures are particu-

Figure 3   Relative Value In Millions Cash and Synthetic Index Funds

Scenario		Index Fund	
		Cash	Synthetic
Market Unchanged	Initial Value	$102.000	$102.825
	Value at Expiration	102.000	102.000
	Capital Gain (Loss)	0.000	(0.825)
	Interest or Dividend Income	0.600	1.425
	Net Income	0.600	0.600
Market up 5%	Initial Value	$102.000	$102.825
	Value at Expiration	107.100	107.100
	Capital Gain (Loss)	5.100	4.275
	Interest or Dividend Income	0.600	1.425
	Net Income	5.700	5.700
Market down 5%	Initial Value	$102.000	$102.825
	Value at Expiration	96.9.00	96.900
	Capital Gain (Loss)	(5.100)	(5.925)
	Interest or Dividend Income	0.600	1.425
	Net Income	4.500	4.500

larly useful for this purpose because they have a significant cost advantage versus a comparable transaction in the cash market.

There are advantages and disadvantages to using futures for asset allocation shifts. Among the advantages, stock index futures can be bought or sold easily in size with just a few transactions. A comparable transaction in the cash market requires a portfolio transaction involving many individual stock transactions. Second, stock index futures contracts have a broad market exposure, which is desirable for TAA strategies. The most liquid contract, the S&P 500 futures contract, is the most widely used for asset allocation purposes. Third, futures markets are very liquid, which keeps costs down.

Another advantage is that the futures may be purchased or sold at a favorable price relative to the underlying cash instrument. This possibility is particularly relevant for TAA strategies which tend to be contrarian, buying in down markets and selling in up markets when futures frequently are mispriced. Finally, the use of futures eliminates the need to interrupt the underlying cash portfolio, which allows plan sponsors to make asset allocation decisions independent of individual portfolio management decisions. Just as there are advantages to using futures due to mispricing, a disadvantage is that the price may be unfavorable when the time to execute the strategy arises. Furthermore, there is variation margin risk and basis risk. The advantages far outweigh the disadvantages when using futures.

As an example of the use of stock index futures in asset allocation programs, suppose an investor's TAA model is signalling that equities are undervalued relative to other asset classes. The investor decides to increase equity exposure by increasing the dollar exposure and the level of risk in the equity exposure. The amount of desired exposure requires an increase in dollar exposure of $100 million to a total of $700 million and an increase in the level of risk from a beta of 1 to 1.1. There is a formula which can be used to determine the number of futures contracts that must be purchased to accomplish these objectives:

$$N = \frac{(TMV(a) - TMV(o))}{index} \times \frac{beta(p)}{beta(f)} + TMV(a) \times \frac{beta(a) - beta(p)}{beta(f)}$$

TMV(a) = Total market value of adjusted portfolio.
TMV(o) = Total market value of original portfolio.
beta(a) = Beta of adjusted portfolio.
beta(p) = Beta of original portfolio.
beta(f) = Beta of futures versus the index.

This formula has two components. The first component, to the left of the addition operator, captures the number of futures contracts required to change the dollar exposure of the asset class. The second component changes the risk characteristic of the position. If it is further assumed that the index is at 330, the futures beta is one and the multiplier is 500, then the number of futures contracts is calculated as follows:

$$N = \frac{\$100\ \text{million}}{330 \times 500} + \frac{\$700\ \text{million}}{330 \times 500} \times .1$$

$$= 606 + 424 = 1030\ \text{contracts}$$

The number of contracts required to increase the dollar value of equity by approximately $100 million is 606, while the number of contracts required to increase the risk of the equity exposure from a beta of 1 to a beta of 1.1 is 424.

SUMMARY

Stock index futures contracts serve a vital function in equity investment management decision. Moreover, SIFs serve as a powerful risk management tool by allowing equity managers to hedge their portfolios efficiently. Also, the price discovery process is facilitated through the futures markets because of the immediacy of execution and the depth of the market. There are essentially three domestic contracts that have sufficient liquidity to have very useful investment applications. SIFs are priced in a manner similar to other futures contracts based on the cost of carry valuation model. Three investment strategy applications are hedging, synthetic index funds and asset allocation. The importance of the stock index futures market cannot be underestimated for the liquidity it brings to the cash market and the risk management capabilities it brings to the investor.

REFERENCES

Collins, B., "A Comparative Guide to Stock Index Futures Contracts," Chapter 3, in *Stock Index Futures*, eds. Frank J. Fabozzi and Gregory M. Kipnis (Homewood, ILL.: Dow Jones-Irwin, 1989), 39–47.

Collins, B., "Mechanics of Trading Stock Index Futures," Chapter 4, in *Stock Index Futures*, eds. Frank J. Fabozzi and Gregory M. Kipnis (Homewood, IL.: Dow Jones-Irwin, 1989), 58–70.

Figlewsiki, S., "Hedging Performance and Basis Risk in Stock Index Futures," *Journal of Finance* (July 1984), 657–669.

Litner, J., "Security Prices, Risk, and Maximal Gains From Diversification," *Journal of Finance* (December 1965), 587–616.

Peters, E., "Hedged Equity Portfolios: Components of Risk and Return," *Advances in Futures and Options Research*, Vol. 1B, 75–92.

Sharpe, W., "Capital Asset Prices: A Theory of Market Equilibrium under Conditions of Risk," *Journal of Finance* (September 1964), 425–442.

Chapter 11

Managing Cash Flow Risk in Stock Index Futures: The Tail Hedge

Ira G. Kawaller
Chicago Mercantile Exchange

Timothy W. Koch
University of South Carolina

This chapter examines the use of the tail hedge as a means of managing cash flow risk associated with variation margin calls. A tail hedge takes a secondary position in the futures market to offset some of the original futures position. Traders take the opposite futures position with tails, expecting to generate gains that offset the financing costs of variation margin calls. Conversely, potential gains from cash inflows of variation margin offset losses on the tail.[1]

---

[1] When futures prices change favorably, traders can withdraw and invest the excess variation margin. The use of a tail hedge eliminates this potential benefit. Firms that establish separate liquidity reserves gain directly from cash inflows associated with their variation margin position.

BACKGROUND

Stock index futures have existed only since 1981, yet the growth in their trading volume has been dramatic, with the value of index futures trading often exceeding the corresponding dollar value of traditional equity trading.

Speculators, hedgers and arbitrageurs may follow different trading strategies, but all futures market participants face the same practical problem of uncertain cash flow obligations. Specifically, all bear the risk of intermittent cash outflows resulting from variation margin payments required because of adverse price movements of the futures position. At the very least, the cost of financing these dollar flows detracts from the profitability of the futures position. At worst, the cash flow obligation can force premature liquidation and seriously disrupt a well-considered hedging or trading strategy.

Fielitz and Gay (1986) developed a model that portfolio managers can use to establish liquidity reserves against such potential cash outflows. The model determines the amount of funds to be held in reserve given the portfolio's size, its systematic risk (beta), the investment term and management's assessment of an acceptable probability of exhausting the liquidity reserve.

One problem with this approach, however, is that the liquidity reserve is potentially large. In one example, the target reserve equaled 13.8 percent of the total portfolio to provide a 99 percent probability that the fund could handle margin calls over a twenty-day period. If the investment term doubled to forty days, say, the required liquidity reserve increases to 19.6 percent, which amounts to $9.8 million for a $50 million equity portfolio.

Such a liquidity reserve effectively increases the capital requirements for transacting in futures by a nontrival amount. Moreover because the reserve likely consists of highly marketable securities such as federal funds and Treasury bills, investment in qualifying instruments may alter a firm's desired portfolio risk and return profile. The tail hedge is an alternative means of dealing with this reserve problem.

THE INSTITUTIONAL MECHANICS OF TAIL HEDGES

Futures transactions entail cash flow risk associated with variation margin requirements. Whenever futures prices move against the initial futures position, a trader or hedger must pay cash equal to the change in value of the position to cover the loss.[2] However the payment is financed, the margin requirement imposes both explicit costs that reduce the effective return and implicit costs that the increased monitoring entails. Establishing a liquidity reserve is one approach to handling margin calls, as Fielitz and Gay recommend.

An alternative method of managing this risk is to establish a tail, or underhedge position. The tail is a smaller futures position that offsets a small fraction of the initial futures trade. For example, a trader long 200 contracts without tailing might take a coincident short position in five of the same futures contracts. Ideally, the interest cost of variation margin financing on the long position, should the futures price decline, is offset by gains on the tail. If a trader is short futures initially, a tail calls for a smaller, long offset.

Operationally, the cash flow requirements can be satisfied by establishing a trilateral arrangement among the customer (trader), the futures broker and the bank that handles the cash flows. The arrangement consists of an open line of credit, allowing the customer to take down funds as required, and a companion interest-bearing deposit account. The bank lends the customer funds when margin calls require cash infusions and invests excess margin balances when they occur.[3]

Loans of this type generally require a demand note that stipulates the maximum amount of available funds, a security agreement that establishes a lender's lien on assets used as collateral and the assignment of a hedge account that attaches funds in the brokerage account as collateral. Within this framework, the broker contacts the bank directly when additional margin financing is

---

2 Collins and Fabozzi (1989) describe the mechanics of and institutional requirements underlying variation margin rules.

3 Such lending arrangements are common in the case of agriculture hedge loans to finance initial margin, maintenance margin and brokerage commissions arising from trading futures contracts. See "Risk Management Guide for Ag Lenders."

needed and the bank increases the customer's loan. When prices move favorably and excess margin exists, the bank withdraws the excess to pay down the loan or deposits it in an interest-bearing account. Such an arrangement satisfies liquidity concerns but does not alleviate the risk associated with unknown financing costs.

DETERMINING THE SIZE OF THE TAIL HEDGE

The purpose of a tail hedge is to offset the interest cost associated with financing the line of credit in support of margin calls. The tail should be constructed so that the change in value of financing the original futures variation margin is exactly offset by the change in value of the tail position:

(1) $(i) (d/360) (FP) N = -(FP)n,$

where:

i = the assumed annual interest rate applied to the variation margin payment or receipt

d = the number of days remaining until settlement of the variation margin financing or investment

FP = change in value of a single futures contract

N = the number of contracts in the initial futures position

n = the number of contracts in the tail position

The negative sign indicates that the tail position is opposite in form (short versus long) to the initial futures position. The size of the tail implied by Equation (1) reduces to:

(2) $$n = -(i)\,(d/360)\,N$$

Equation (2) derives from the fact that, when multiplied by the change in the value of a single futures contract, the term on the left equals the expected profit (loss) on the tail, and the term on the right equals the expected interest payment (return) on the variation margin financing (investment). In other words, the tail hedge tries to equate the present value of interest flows on variation margin activity with the present value of gains or losses on the tail. A liquidity reserve, in contrast, imposes an up-front cost that far exceeds the present value cost of variation margin payments.

One difficulty in applying Equation (2) arises because of uncertainty regarding the relevant interest rate and the natural drift in d as the expiration of the futures contract approaches. Two factors complicate the choice of interest rate. First, financing rates applicable when the margin is deficient typically exceed investment yields when surplus margin exists. Because the tail hedger does not know the direction of futures prices over the hedge period, neither rate is better ex ante. Second, variation margin requirements normally are handled daily; so a different interest rate applies each successive day, unless the yield curve remains flat throughout the holding period, and the futures price moves consistently for or against the hedger.[4]

Finally, even if managers knew which interest rate applied, expected interest payments decrease toward expiration date as d approaches zero. Appropriate risk management thus requires that portfolio managers periodically recalculate the size of the tail to ensure that it offsets the interest obligation from variation margin. Because these problems cannot be eliminated, the final tail results only approximately offset the costs or benefits of variation margin flows.

---

4   It is possible that changes in the level of rates can be offset exactly by changes in rates associated with movements along the yield curve.

Chapter 11

AN ILLUSTRATION

Consider the problems faced by an equity portfolio manager who decides to hedge $25 million in equities. The equities exhibit a beta equal to 1.0. The manager is concerned that stock prices will decline over the next six months and so decides to use the S&P 500 futures contract to hedge.[5] At the time of the decision, the S&P 500 futures contract is priced at 205 with 150 days remaining to expiration, and the S&P 500 index is trading at 200. In this instance, the correct base hedge requires selling 250 futures contracts ($25 million/(200)(500) = 250).

If the hedge is maintained until the futures expiration date, the manager can expect to earn an amount equal to the reinvested value of the dividends paid on the equities over the next 150 days plus the basis adjustment.[6] The dollar value of the basis adjustment equals the product of the basis (the futures price minus the spot index value), the number of contracts in the hedge and the multiplier of 500. In this case the dollar amount is $625,000 [($205 − $200)(250)(500)].

Before establishing a tail hedge, the manager must determine the term to settlement day for all variation financing or investing, and the relevant interest rate. Typically, the term of the hedge is set equal to the number of days until the original futures position is expected to be closed; but, in fact, any subsequent day can be used. Similarly, the interest rate is set at the term rate available over the same interval, assuming that the yield curve remains flat during the holding period.

A 10 percent interest rate in this example, with a term of 150 days, requires a tail hedge of ten contracts:

---

5 A beta of 1.0 indicates that changes in the value of the firm's equity portfolio exactly match percentage movements on the S&P 500 index. A portfolio beta different from 1.0 affects the number of contracts that should be used to hedge the initial equity exposure. See Fabozzi and Peters (1989).

6 The target earnings need to be adjusted whenever the projected hedge period ends prior to expiration of the futures contract. The incomplete basis adjustment reduces target earnings by a factor equal to the theoretical basis anticipated at the end of the hedge period.

$$n = 250 \, (0.10) \, (150/360) = -10.4$$

If the base hedge is 250 short contracts, the tail requires ten long contracts because contracts are traded only in unit increments. The net position, therefore, is 240 short contracts.

Table 1 demonstrates the recalculation of the tail every 15 days. It assumes that even though the period for financing or investing decreases every day, the appropriate financing rate remains at 10 percent. Table 2 shows the resulting variation margin changes on the base positions and corresponding offsets generated by the tail under a scenario assuming a rising futures price. The table also assumes that futures prices increase by 250 basis points (2.50 index points) immediately following the adjustment to the tail.[7] Note that the actual tail reflects a rounding of the calculated value for n, as contracts must be bought or sold in whole units. In this example, the rounding consistently caused a somewhat smaller tail than that stipulated by the equation.

At the outset, the objective was to earn the dividends from owning the stocks plus the basis adjustment, where this latter component equals five index points per contract ($625,000) for the base hedge. In this example, the expected outcome is not achieved precisely. In the scenario presented, the original equities appreciate by $4,062,500, reflecting an 18.75 percent increase in the S&P 500 index. The hedge, however, produces a consolidated loss of $3,440,365 made up of 1) the base variation margin ($3,437,500), 2) its associated finance charges ($71,615) and 3) the tail profits ($68,750), which serve to reduce overall hedge losses.

The net result is that the hedger earns $622,135 plus dividends. The tailed hedge position actually earns $2,865 less than the target established when the hedge was initiated. This is a mismatch of less than 0.5 percent of the expected basis adjustment. What is most important, however, is that the earnings would have been $71,615 less, or a mismatch of over 11 percent of that target without the tail.

---

7 This is the worst possible timing sequence of price changes.

Table 1   Calculating the Tail

Days Remaining in Hedge Period (d)	Tail Calculation [n = −250(0.1)(d/360)]
150	10.4 ≈ 10
135	9.4 ≈ 9
120	8.3 ≈ 8
105	7.3 ≈ 7
90	6.3 ≈ 6
75	5.2 ≈ 5
60	4.2 ≈ 4
45	3.1 ≈ 3
30	2.1 ≈ 2
15	1.0 ≈ 1
0	0 ≈ 0

Suppose instead that the S&P 500 futures price decreases by 250 basis points every fifteen days. Interest on variation margin then represents income exactly equal to the amount in Table 2, and the tail position produces losses. In this case, the spot index and futures prices settle at 177.50, and the loss in equity value equals $2,812,500. The original hedge position produces a gain of $3,440,365 net of the tail, for aggregate earnings of $627,865, or $2,865 above the target.

As is true for most hedges, it is difficult to execute the tail hedge with the precision demonstrated in Table 2. The biggest challenge is to match the correct number of base futures contracts with the underlying equities. Any discrepancy, or any missed esti-mate of n, affects the tail hedge results. Still, the tail hedge clearly reduces the variance of expected returns around the target.

Table 2   Simulation

Days Remaining in Hedge	S&P Futures Price	Variation Margin	Interest on Variation Margin[a]	Number of Contracts in Tail[b]	Tail Profit[c]
150	207.50	$312,500	$13,021	10	$12,500
135	210.00	312,500	11,719	9	11,250
120	212.50	312,500	10,417	8	10,000
105	215.00	312,500	9,115	7	8,750
90	217.50	312,500	7,813	6	7,500
75	220.00	312,500	6,510	5	6,250
60	222.50	312,500	5,208	4	5,000
45	225.00	312,500	3,906	3	3,750
30	227.50	312,500	2,604	2	2,500
15	230.00	312,500	1,302	1	1,250
0	232.50	312,500	0	0	0
Cumulative Results		$3,437,500	$71,615		$68,750

[a] [0.10 (days remaining in hedge)/360] (variation margin).
[b] 250 [0.10 (days remaining in hedge)/360]; rounded to nearest integer.
[c] $500 (2.50) (number of contracts in the tail position.)

CONCLUSION

Variation margin requirements on stock index futures transactions increase the cash flow risk that portfolio managers face. Rather than establish a liquidity reserve from which funds can be withdrawn to meet payment obligations, the manager may want to follow an alternative procedure that uses tail hedges. The tail hedge requires a smaller up-front investment, and does not alter a firm's risk and return profile.

REFERENCES

Collins, B., and F. Fabozzi. "Mechanics of Trading Stock Index Futures." Chapter 5 in *The Handbook of Stock Index Futures and Options*, F. Fabozzi and G. Kipnis, eds. Homewood, IL: Dow Jones-Irwin, 1989.

Fabozzi, F., and E. Peters. "Hedging with Stock Index Futures." Chapter 13 in *The Handbook of Stock Index Futures and Options*, F. Fabozzi and G. Kipnis, eds. Homewood, IL: Dow Jones-Irwin, 1989.

Fielitz, B., and G. Gay. "Managing Cash Flow Risks in Stock Index Futures." *Journal of Portfolio Management*, Winter 1986, pp. 74-78.

Kawaller, I. "Going the Extra Mile." *Journal of Cash Management*. July/August 1986.

"Risk Management Guide for Ag Lenders." Chicago: Chicago Merchantile Exchange, 1985.

Chapter 12

Introduction to Stock Options*

Richard M. Bookstaber
Morgan Stanley & Co.

Every security and financial market has its own definitions. Because of its unique characteristics, the option market probably has more than its share. This chapter covers the basic definitions that characterize call and put option contracts. It presents in a brief, conceptual form the options features that have led to their pivotal role in the financial market. It also describes the role options serve and the nature of option pricing and trading.

DEFINITIONS OF CALL AND PUT OPTIONS

Call Option

A call option is the right to buy a given amount of a security at a given price on or before a specific date. A particular call option is characterized by four features: (1) the security to which the option refers,

* Adapted from Chapter 3, *Option Pricing & Investment Strategies, Third Edition,* by Richard Bookstaber (Chicago, IL: Probus Publishing Company, 1991).

(2) the amount of the security that the option holder has the right to buy, (3) the price at which the security can be bought and (4) the time at which the option expires.

The security involved in the option contract is called the underlying security. The price at which the security may be bought is called the exercise price or the striking price. The last date on which the option may be exercised is called the expiration date or the maturity date. The amount of the security controlled by the option contract is standardized on the various option exchanges.

For example, a Polaroid July 40 option gives the holder of the option the right to purchase 100 shares of Polaroid stock at the price of $40 per share on or before the expiration date in July. If the option is exercised, the option holder pays $4000 in exchange for 100 shares of Polaroid stock.

The word right in the definition of the call option deserves some emphasis. It is the use of right rather than obligation that makes the option market so interesting. Because a buyer has the right but not the obligation to exercise an option, the buyer only exercises the option when it is profitable to do so. If the stock never rises above $40 a share, the buyer obviously does not exercise the option because the stock can be purchased at a lower price in the market. The cost of the option contract is lost. On the other hand if the stock price rises above $40, then the buyer profits from exercising the option. The $40 per share stock can be sold at the higher market price. If the market price goes to $45, the buyer can sell it for $4500, making $500 less the cost of the option. So an option gives the buyer the potential for large gains, while limiting losses to the cost of the option contract itself.

The profit profile for the option buyer is illustrated in Figure 1. The option giving the holder the right to buy 100 shares of stock is assumed to cost $600. The profit is expressed in per-share terms. If the stock price is below the exercise price of $40 on the expiration date, the option expires worthless; the investor loses the initial investment in the option, which comes out to $6 per share of stock. If the stock price is above $40 per share, the investor gains the difference between the cost of buying the stock and the higher market price at which the stock can be sold. The buyer's profit is

Figure 1   Payoff of a Call Option

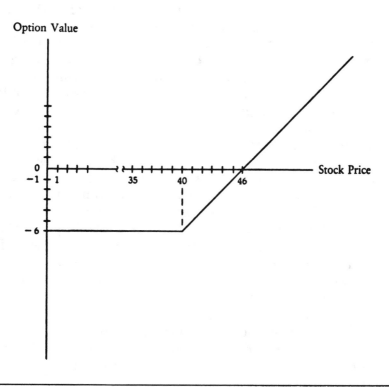

equal to the final stock price minus the $40 exercise price less the initial cost of the option. So, if the stock rises to $50, the investor's net profit is $50 – $40 – $6 = $4 per share of stock, for a total profit of $400.

Call Option Writing   An option agreement is initiated between two parties. When an investor buys an option contract, there is someone on the other side of the contract who is agreeing to sell the buyer the security at the exercise price. This person is called the option writer.

If the security rises above the exercise price, the option is exercised, and the writer does not make any gain above that price. If the writer owns the Polaroid stock and writes the Polaroid July 40, he needs to part with the stock at $40 per share even though the stock is going for more than that in the market. On the other hand if the stock drops in price, the option writer is left holding the bag—the option buyer walks away without exercising, and the writer absorbs all of the loss: the writer has all of the potential loss from the stock, but has given all of the gain above the exercise price to the option buyer.

The writer may want to issue the option contract without holding the underlying stock. In this case, the writer is said to write a naked option, which means the writer does not have the stock that he has agreed to sell to the buyer. Unlike the covered option writer who holds the stock on the option written, the writer of a naked option does not lose if the stock drops in price. However, there is considerable risk if the stock increases in value. For example, if Polaroid goes up to $45, the writer has to buy the stock at $45 a share and then sell it to the option buyer at the exercise price of $40 a share: he realizes a loss of $5 a share, for a total loss on the 100-share contract of $500.

The writer receives the option premium at the time the option is issued. If the going price for the Polaroid July 40 is $600 for an option contract of 100 shares, the writer gets $600 at the time that the contract is issued.

The profit profile for the writer of the Polaroid July 40 is shown in Figure 2. This figure shows the return for both the covered (solid line) and naked (dotted line) option writer.

Put Option

A put option is the right to sell a given amount of a security at a given price on or before a specific date.

The put option differs from the call option only by replacing the word buy with sell. If the investor buys a Polaroid July 40 put option and the stock drops to $35, the investor can buy 100 shares of the stock in the market for $3500, and then turn around and sell

Figure 2   Payoff of a Call Option Writer

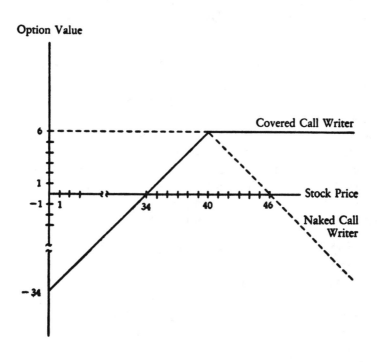

it to the writer at $40 per share, for a net gain of $400. But if the stock is above $40 per share, the investor does not exercise the option because the stock can be sold in the market for a higher price than it can through the option contract. While the call option increases in value as the security increases in price, the put option increases in value as the security decreases in price.

Once again, the use of the word right is important. If the contract involved the obligation rather than the right to sell the stock, it would be the same as selling the stock short at $40. (A short sale involves selling stock the investor does not currently own, with the anticipation of covering the sale by buying the stock later at a lower price.) If the stock drops in value, the short sale yields a profit; but if the stock goes above $40, the short sale involves a loss because the investor has to buy the stock at the higher price and sell at the lower price. But with the option, the investor does not face the same potential for loss from the stock rising in price; the stock does not have to be sold at the exercise price. The investor does so only if it is profitable. The maximum loss is the cost of buying the option.

The profit profile for the put option buyer is shown in Figure 3. If the stock price is above $40, the option is not exercised and the buyer does lose the initial cost of the option. If the stock is below the exercise price, the investor's profit is $40 minus the stock price minus the option price. Assuming the Polaroid July 40 put option is bought for $500, if the stock price drops to $35 a share, the investor breaks even, with the proceeds of the option equaling the $5 per-share cost of the option contract.

Put Option Writing Like the call option, for every put option bought there is an investor on the other side of the transaction who has written the contract. If the put option is exercised, the option writer buys the stock at the $40 exercise price, even though the going market price is lower. In return for this unfavorable possibility, the writer receives a premium from the buyer for issuing the put option.

THE ROLE OF OPTIONS

Individual investors and market traders dominated the option markets in the first decade of its existence. These traders use options to make plays on the underlying securities or form arbitrage strategies on the options themselves. Over the past few years, a second role of options has become increasingly prominent. This is the use of options to mold return distributions, to form a more complete market that can better match the investment objectives of portfolio managers, pension plan sponsors and financial institutions with asset/liability needs. This second role, while slower in

Figure 3   Payoff of a Put Option

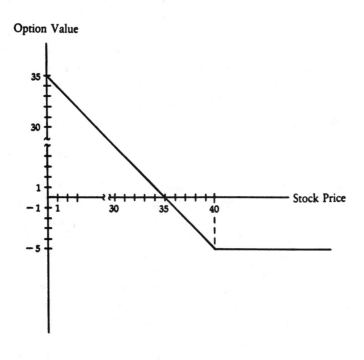

unfolding, is the more important of the two. The principal justification for options and for the application of option theory is to create payoffs and returns that meet the needs of the market.

Two key propositions provide the statement of the role options and option theory play in the financial markets:

Proposition 1 Any feasible payoff can be created with the appropriate set of options.

Proposition 2 Any option can be created through the appropriate trading strategy.

Using Options to Create Payoffs to Meet Investment Objectives

A stock option may appear to be nothing more than a side bet on the price of the underlying security. Certainly a company on which an option is listed receives no income from the option contract. And the two parties that enter into the option agreement appear to be in a zero sum game—the "winner" gains at the expense of the "loser." Are options just an instrument for the speculators and gamblers, or does having this derivative claim on the stock serve a useful function? To answer this question, take a closer look at the motivation for making investments.

The process of investing takes place in two stages. First, the investor makes an appraisal of the most likely course of events and then chooses investments that will pay off if those events occur. An investor may make an analysis of General Motors and come to the conclusion that G.M. will be very profitable over the next year. To take advantage of this assessment, the investor buys a security that will appreciate should G.M. be profitable. In the ideal financial market, there is a range of securities available to give the investor flexibility in making investments that precisely follow this assessment, as well as the flexibility to take advantage of the events that the investor perceives will most likely occur.

If G.M. stock is the only security available for trading on the investor's perceptions of G.M., the investor is limited in the range of events that can be met with a market position. The investor can buy the stock in the belief that the company will do well and can sell the stock in the belief that it will do poorly. But what if the investor's analysis is more precise than this? For example, what if the investor is convinced G.M. will go up between 20 and 50 percent? This is a more precise appraisal than simply saying the stock will go up; but the only way the investor can take advantage of this analysis is to buy the stock. The individual is forced to follow a diluted appraisal, taking a position that the stock might go up 5 percent or 80 percent along with his actual belief that the stock appreciation will be in the 20 percent to 50 percent range. The nature of the stock itself limits the precision with which perceptions can be acted on in the market. Faced with the inability to match personal beliefs exactly through a market transaction, the investor is forced into a suboptimal investment strategy, and so may fail to invest as much as if a tailor-made security existed.

The ideal market has a range of financial instruments available to enable investors to meet their investment objectives exactly. There is a security that gives a payoff if the stock appreciates between 20 and 50 percent and that gives no payoff if any other return is realized. The ideal market permits the investor to cover any contingency in the market, to fine-tune a portfolio to meet personal investment objectives and perceptions exactly. Options create such a market.

To see how such a payoff can be created, suppose an investor buys a call option with an exercise price of 55, writes an option with an exercise price of 60, writes another option with an exercise price of 75 and then buys yet another call option with an exercise price of 80. The result of this strategy is shown in Figure 4. The payoff (exclusive of the options' cost) is $5 for prices between 60 and 75, and tapers off quickly to no payoff for prices outside of that range. Therefore, it represents a close-to-ideal strategy for this investor.

(To see how this combination of options leads to the payoff depicted in the figure, note that as the stock price moves from 55 to 60, the option with the 55 exercise price gains $5. At 60, the second option written offsets further gains in the first option. So for prices above 60, the combination of these two options leads to a payoff of $5. The option with the 75 exercise price loses dollar for dollar with an increase in the price of G.M. above 75; by the time G.M. gets up to 80, the combination of this third option with the other two leads to a net payoff of zero. The option with the exercise price of 80 then nets out the impact of this third option, leading to no payoff for any stock price above 80. The payoff can be brought down to zero more quickly by using endpoint options with exercise prices closer to 60 and 75.)

This example shows that options expand the set of alternatives that can be met through investment strategies, and options expand the number of contingencies that can be met through investments in the financial market.

**Figure 4   An Option Strategy Payoff
                (Strategy Cost = $.50)**

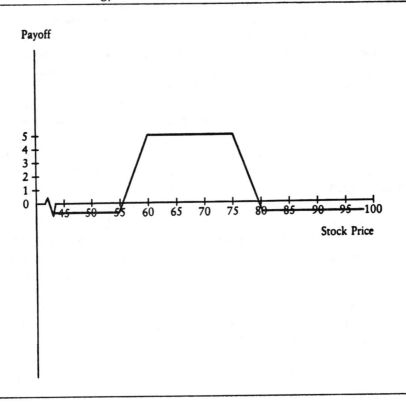

Creating Options through Trading Strategies

In the extreme case where options are available with exercise prices equal to every possible stock price, every possible investment contingency can be covered. Of course, the complete set of options also needs to be available for a range of securities that cover every variable of concern to the investor; not just G.M. stock, but IBM stock and AT&T stock; and not just stocks, but foreign exchange rate, interest rates and the overall market. And the time to expiration of the options needs to be consistent with the investment horizon of the investor. The reality is that options are available with some exercise prices, with some times to expiration and on some financial assets. So while the option market increases the flexibility of the market in meeting the needs of the investor, it does not cover all possible contingencies.

However, investors are not limited by the availability of options in the marketplace. It is possible to construct options through trading strategies in other instruments. If an instrument can be easily and liquidly traded, it is possible to make a tailored option with the desired time to expiration and exercise price. If they cannot buy it in the market, they can build it using the security underlying the option as the raw material. The procedure for doing this is the foundation of option pricing and strategies.

To illustrate how a trading strategy can replicate an option payoff, suppose an investor wants to create an option on 100 shares of G.M. with 1 year to expiration and an exercise price of 60. To create the option, ask the question at every point in time, "If this option were trading efficiently in the market, how much would its price change with a change in the underlying value of G.M.?" As is explained later in the chapter, this is a question that is answered through the use of option pricing models.

Suppose that at the current stock price of $60 a share, the option changes in value by $.50 with every $1.00 change in the price of G.M. To create a payoff that matches that of the option, then, the investor needs to buy 50 shares of stock. Having done this, if G.M. stock changes by a quarter of a point, the position changes by an eighth of a point. An observer looking at the price behavior of this position is unable to differentiate its performance from the price performance the investor would have had if he actually had purchased the option in the marketplace rather than had created it.

The exposure to the stock required to replicate the option changes over time and with changes in the price of the stock. For example if the stock moves up to $80 a share, the call option is far in the money, and moves nearly dollar for dollar with the stock. To replicate the price movement of the option may then require an increase in stock exposure to 95 shares. The replication process, therefore, is dynamic in nature. If day by day the investor continues to mirror the price movements of the option he is seeking to replicate, at the time of expiration that investor also replicates the payoff of the option.

The dynamic trading technique can not only be used to create options to meet investment objectives, it also can be used to arbitrage options that are available in the marketplace when these options are incorrectly priced.

Suppose an investor finds a listed option on G.M. selling for $7 and working through an option pricing model, finds that same option payoff can be created for only $5. By writing the market option for a cash inflow of $7 and then spending the $5 to create the same payoff using the dynamic trading methods, at the time of expiration the payoff of the replicated option matches the payoff of the option the investor wrote leaving no net obligation. However, the investor has pocketed $2 at the outset because of the mispricing of the listed option. The investor has created an option for one price and sold it in the marketplace for another price.

This type of a strategy is called an arbitrage strategy, because it leads to a profit for no net investment and no risk. Obviously, the notion of no risk is not quite correct, because the replication may be imperfect; but generally such strategies can be done with low enough risk to make this a widespread, though sophisticated, investment strategy. In fact, there are a number of sophisticated trading firms that specialize in such arbitrage strategies.

PRICING OPTIONS

The most important breakthrough in option analysis has been the development of option pricing models. These models give the price of an option as a function of observable variables, such as the security price and security price volatility, the exercise price, the time-to-maturity of the option and interest rates. Option models are one of the most powerful tools in finance. The analytical method they use can be applied to virtually any financial security, opening up a new era in understanding and pricing financial instruments.

Because the variables used in the models are observable, the use of the option pricing models has been of practical value to the investment profession at large. However, the number of people who use these models exceeds the number who understand them. The models were derived originally using advanced mathematical methods that obscured the intuition behind the formula. The practical implications of the models for profiting from mispriced options and for deriving hedges in more complex strategies has remained unexplored until recently.

This is an explanation of the methodology behind the option pricing models and shows how to exploit profit opportunities if the market price of the option differs from the option model price. Appendix I presents a derivation of the option pricing formula that uses only elementary algebra, progressing from the simple one-period formula to a many-period formula. Later sections use option pricing techniques to describe trading strategies.

A One-Period Example

Suppose a stock is priced currently at $100 a share, and in one period it will be worth either $95 or $110. There is a call option available on the stock with an exercise price of $100 and one period to expiration. The current price of the option is $800. (See Figure 1.) The riskless interest rate for both borrowing and lending is 5 percent over the one time period.

Consider the following portfolio strategy. The investor writes three call options, receiving an income of $2400, and buys 200 shares of the stock at $100 per share. The net initial position is $17,600. Assume the investor can then borrow at the 5 percent rate to cover the position, so that the net initial investment is zero (the stock is being purchased entirely from the proceeds of the option sale and the borrowed funds). What will the investor's return be at the end of the period?

If the stock drops to $95 by next period, the option expires worthless. The investor then needs to repay $18,480 (the $17,600 plus 5 percent interest to the bank), and holds $19,000 worth of stock. The net position is $19,000 − $18,840 = $520. Because the

Figure 5   A Call Option with One Period to Expiration

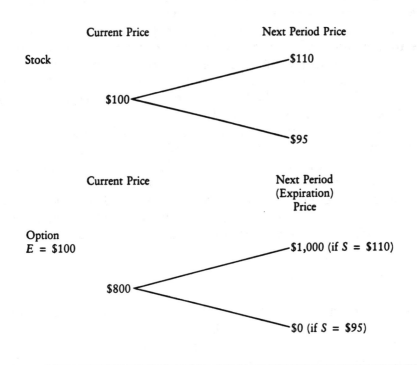

initial investment is zero, the investor makes a profit if the stock drops.

If the stock increases in value to $110, $3000 is needed to cover the option position, and the stock is worth $22,000. With the cost of the borrowed funds, the investor's net position is $22,000 - $3000 – $18,480 = $520. Once again the strategy nets a profit. This strategy is illustrated in Table 1.

This transaction is remarkable because not only is a profit made in either case, but the profit is riskless—it is exactly the same no matter which way the stock moves. Also, the profit is made for no net investment. A profit that is obtained at no risk and for no initial investment is called an arbitrage profit. If any amount of

Table 1   Trading Strategy When the Option Price is $800

Current Position		End-of-Period Position	
		S = 95	S = 110
Write 3 call options	2,400	0	(3,000)
Buy 200 shares	(20,000)	19,000	22,000
Borrow at 5 percent	17,600	(18,480)	(18,480)
Net Profit	0	520	520

arbitrage profit is possible, then an investor can make unlimited profits. Given a chance to make a certain profit of $520 with no investment, the investor's position needs only to increase by x times and make x times as great a profit risklessly and with no initial investment.

There is only one price for the option that eliminates this profit opportunity. As Table 2 shows, if this strategy is followed when the option is priced at $635, there is no arbitrage profit. If the price is below $635, the reverse strategy of buying three options, selling short 200 shares of stock and placing the proceeds of the transaction into the riskless asset yields an arbitrage profit. The results of this strategy are illustrated in Table 3 for an option price of $500.

In this simple example, the option price of $635 is the correct option price. If the option is at this price in the market, there is no arbitrage opportunity. If it is mispriced, there is the possibility of obtaining large profits for no risk. The option pricing formula in the next section gives this correct option price under far more realistic assumptions than those used in this example. There is no law that requires the market price to equal this correct option price. But if it does not, then the knowledgeable investor can make large profits for little or no risk by taking the appropriate position in this mispriced option and the underlying stock.

Table 2   Trading Strategy When the Option Price is $635

Current Position		End-of-Period Position	
		S = 95	S = 110
Write 3 call options	1,905	0	(3,000)
Buy 200 shares	(20,000)	19,000	22,000
Borrow at 5 percent	18,095	(19,000)	(19,000)
Net Profit	0	0	0

Table 3   Trading Strategy When the Option Price is $500

Current Position		End-of-Period Position	
		S = 95	S = 110
Buy 3 call options	(1,500)	0	3,000
Sell short 200 shares	20,000	(19,000)	(22,000)
Lend at 5 percent	(18,500)	19,425	19,425)
Net Profit	0	425	425

The existence of an arbitrage profit puts a mechanism into action that drives the option price to the value that eliminates the profit opportunity. For example if the option is initially priced at $800 and more and more investors follow the arbitrage strategy by selling options, the option price needs to drop in order to entice others to buy the increased supply of options. If the option price is below the correct value, the option price is driven up as investors try to buy more options. The pressure on the option price continues in either case until the option is priced at $635.

Note that any of the three securities—the stock, the option or the interest rate—can adjust to eliminate the profit opportunity. Just as the arbitrage strategy puts pressure on the option price, it also tends to move the other securities in the direction that eliminates the arbitrage profit. As investors follow the arbitrage strategy to take advantage of an overpriced option, they buy stock, raising the price of the stock, and they borrow more funds, putting upward pressure on the riskless rate of interest. So the option price is set by relative, not absolute, prices.

If an arbitrage profit is possible, the option is no more mispriced than the underlying security or the interest rate. Given any values for two of the securities, there is a unique price for the third security that eliminates the profit opportunity. Because the option market usually is thinner and more elastic than the other markets, it adjusts to a relative price discrepancy before the underlying security or the riskless asset does. So, for convenience, the option is said to be mispriced.

Anatomy of an Arbitrage: Making $1.5 Million at the State Fair

To understand how arbitrage works, take a more down-to-earth example. Imagine a refreshment stand at the state fair. There are three other stands there, one selling hot dogs for 50 cents each, one selling nine-ounce cups of cola for 30 cents and another selling hot dogs with a six-ounce cup of cola for 75 cents.

It is apparent that a buyer can package the hot dogs and six-ounce cola for less than the going price 75 cents. He purchases hot dogs from the one stand and cola from the other in the proportions of two colas for every three hot dogs, and repackages the two to match the product of the third stand.

If the market is competitive, he can sell all the servings of hot dogs and six-ounce colas at 75 cents. The cost of the package is only 70 cents; so by buying the parts and packaging them as the whole, he makes a sure profit. If the pricing went the other way so that the hot dog-cola combination cost only 60 cents, he buys the package and resells it separately. The relationships are shown in Table 4.

Table 4   How to Make $1.5 Million at the State Fair

1. *Buy*		*Going price*	
	3 hot dogs	$.50 each =	$1.50
	2 nine-ounce coals	.30 each =	.60
	Total		$2.10
2. *Repackage and sell*		*Going price*	
	3 hot dog-six-ounce cola jumbos	$.75 each =	$2.25
	Profit		$ .15
3. *Repeat 10 million times*			

The fact that two items can replicate the third indicates that the two must be priced in a certain proportion relative to the third. In particular, to eliminate this profit opportunity it must be that three hot dogs and two of the nine-ounce colas must sell for the same price as two of the hot dog-cola combinations.

The pricing of the options relative to the stock and the riskless asset is determined in the same way. The combination of the short position in the call option and the long position in the stock replicates the riskless asset, in that the return from the position is riskless. Because the option and stock can be packaged in a particular proportion that replicates the riskless asset, it must be that the portfolio of the two sells for the same amount as the riskless asset. If it does not, then construct a "homemade" riskless asset by taking the appropriate position in the option and the stock, with the homemade riskless asset costing less to produce than the going market price for the riskless asset.

Or, combine the stock and the riskless asset in a proportion that yields the same payoff as the option at the time of expiration. Still another possibility is to combine the option with the riskless asset to ensure a return that is the same as the return to the stock at the end of the period.

For example, if the investor combines a long position in three options with $18,095 in the riskless asset, the return is the same as if 200 shares of the stock are held. If the stock drops to $95 a share, the investor receives $18,095 (1.05) = $19,000; if the stock goes up to $110 a share, the investor receives $19,000 from the riskless asset and $3000 from the option, for a return of $22,000. Because the portfolio of the options and the riskless asset exactly replicates the payoff of the stock at the end of the period, it must be that the portfolio of the two is priced so that it equals the stock price at the start of the period. Otherwise, profit opportunities are possible by taking a long or a short position in the portfolio.

The fact that any two of the assets can be combined to produce a portfolio with the same payoff as the third is the key to the arbitrage opportunity. If the relative price of the three is such that the replicating portfolio for any of the assets has a different price than the price of the asset itself, then an arbitrage opportunity exists. By simultaneously buying at the lower price and selling the asset at the higher price, it is possible to get a positive return for no net investment.

The example shown here obviously is simplified to deal with one time period to expiration and with stock price movements that are unrealistic. However, this example does provide the basis for option pricing in the more realistic setting. The extension of this example to a more realistic setting is treated in Appendix I to the chapter. The formation of the riskless hedge and the possibility for arbitrage profits are the motivating principles for option pricing in the more complex setting.

THE OPTION PRICING MODEL

The option example used in the previous section is unrealistic. A security can take on any number of values, not just one of two values as assumed. Nor is trading done on a period-by-period basis. Markets operate continuously during trading hours.

However, a more realistic approach can be developed by extending the example. If the example is extended to many periods rather than to one period and the length of each time period becomes small (for example, 180 periods of one-day duration rather than two periods of three-month duration each), then trading conditions are more realistic. If it is further assumed that the security price can take on any number of values in a given period of time, then the objection of the two-state security price movement is removed as well.

These assumptions are far less restrictive, and it is possible to fashion an example such as the one used in the previous section with these assumptions. There is still a correct option price, and it still is the case that an arbitrage profit is possible if the option price differs from the correct price. The extension of the illustration to the many-period case and the derivation of the option pricing formula is left to the chapter's Appendix I.

The correct option price in this more realistic case is due to Black, Scholes and Merton, and is called the Black-Scholes formula. The formula determines the option price that is necessary to eliminate the possibility of profit opportunities. As in the one-period example, if the option price does not conform to this price, there is the opportunity to make large profits by using the correct hedging strategy with the option and the stock. Unlike the example, the Black-Scholes formula finds the correct price under assumptions that more closely resemble the actual trading price.

The Black-Scholes formula is:

$$C = SN(d_1) - Ee^{-rT}N(d_2)$$

where

$$d_1 = (\ln S/E) + (r + \tfrac{1}{2}\sigma^2)T)/\sigma\sqrt{T}$$

and

$$d_2 = d_1 - \sigma\sqrt{T}.$$

In this formula, in is the natural logarithm, e is the exponential, (e = 2.718) and σ^2 is the instantaneous variance of the security price, which is the measure of security return volatility in the formula (so σ is the standard deviation of the returns). $N(\cdot)$ is the normal distribution function, which is tabulated in most probability and statistics texts. The other variables are defined as before.

Computing the Correct Option Price

The use of the formula requires the input of five variables: the price of the underlying security, the exercise price, the time of maturity, the interest rate and the volatility of the security price. To illustrate the use of the formula, particular values for these variables are specified to calculate the value of an S&P 100 (OEX) option that has 90 days to expiration:

$$
\begin{aligned}
S &= 236 \\
E &= 235 \\
T &= 90/365 = .247 \text{ years} \\
r &= 6 \text{ percent per annum} \\
\sigma &= 18 \text{ percent}
\end{aligned}
$$

The first three variables are easily observable from the option quotation. The time-to-maturity is obtained by counting the number of calendar days until the time of maturity, and then dividing it by 365 to get the time-to-maturity in annual terms. The method for estimating the volatility is described in Appendix II of this chapter. T, r, and σ all are expressed in annual terms. Recalling the formula and substituting the appropriate variables, the option price is:

$$
d_1 = \frac{\ln(236/235) + (.06 + .18^2/2)\,.247}{.18\sqrt{.247}}
$$

$$
= .023/.089 = .258
$$

$$
d_2 = .258 - .18\sqrt{.247} = .168
$$

Using the normal distribution tables, it is found that:

$$N(d_1) = N(.258) = .60169$$

$$N(d_2) = N(.168) = .56684$$

The values for $N(.258)$ and $N(.168)$ are tabulated in most elementary probability and statistics texts, and are found also in mathematical handbooks. Using these values, we obtain the call option price

$$C = 236 \times .60169 - 235 \times e^{-.01479} \times .56684 = 10.75.$$

The option formula gives the correct option price in the sense that if the option price differs substantially from this price, there are arbitrage profit opportunities.

The correct option price as given by the formula depends on the security price, the exercise price, the time to expiration, the riskless interest rate and the volatility of the security. In terms of practical usefulness, what the formula does not depend on is almost as important as what it does depend on. In particular, the formula is not contingent on any assessment of the future or expected security price. Also, it does not depend on investor attitudes toward risk. Because these are not observable, any formula that requires them as inputs is of little practical value. The fact that the option formula is independent of expectations and other subjective measures bodes well for its applicability.

Options on Dividend-Paying Stock

A stock dividend can be used to finance partially the borrowing cost for the option strategy, leading to a lower cost for the option. To see this, modify the option strategy presented at the start of the chapter to have the stock pay out a three percent dividend. While the premium from writing the option still can be invested at the market interest rate of five percent, the effective borrowing rate for the stock drops to two percent, because the dividend payout compensates for three percent of the borrowing cost. As shown in Table 5, the option is less expensive than the $635 of the example presented in Table 1 because the implied borrowing cost for the option is lower.

THE HEDGE RATIO

Going back to the initial example, the detection of the mispriced option is just the start of the arbitrage strategy. A position not only was taken in the option, a position was taken in the security as well. This position gave the investor a hedge against unfavorable security price movements; no matter which way the security price moved, the value of the investor's position and the profit were unchanged.

As this suggests, a successful option strategy not only involves taking the appropriate position in a mispriced option, it also involves the second step of taking the appropriate hedge position in the underlying security. The option position allows the investor to profit from the mispriced option, and the hedge position

Table 5   Trading Strategy for an Option on a Stock with a 3 percent Dividend

Current Position		End-of-Period Position	
		S = 95	S = 110
Write 3 call options	1,333	0	(3,000)
Buy 200 shares	(20,000)	19,000	22,000
Borrow at 2% effective rate	20,000	(20,400)	(20,400)
Lend at 5%	(1,333)	1,400	1,400
Net Profit	0	0	0

in the security allows the profit to be obtained risklessly, unaffected by shifts in the security price.

This hedge is of critical importance later on in the chapter. Because the calculation of the proper hedge is related to the option formula, it is introduced now.

Suppose an investor feels that a particular option currently selling at 7 is overpriced in the market. If it is overpriced, the investor gets a premium for writing it that is above the fair premium. But once the option is written, the investor is subject to the risks of later changes in the security price. The option may be overpriced now; but if the underlying security increases a few points, the option rises in price. If the investor's position in the option is not covered, a substantial amount is lost because of the security price changing, even if the investor initially was correct about the mispricing.

Suppose the option price changes by half as much as any change in the security price. If the security rises by one point, the option rises by half a point. A one-point rise in the security means the value of the investor's short option position drops. To cover the position after the security rise, the option that the investor originally sold for only $700 needs to be bought back for $750. The .5 point rise in the option, therefore, means a loss of $50.

The investor can guard against this possible loss by taking a hedge position in the security. By buying 50 shares of security, the investor is hedged against a shift in the security price; if the security rises (or drops), the total position is unaffected. If the security rises by one point, the option position drops by $50; but the security position increases in value by $50—the $1 increase in the security price multiplied by the 50 shares of security held long.

If the security drops a point, then the option position increases in value by $50 because the option sold for $700 can now be bought back for $650. However, the security position drops by $50 from the one-point decline in the security price. In either case, the net position is unchanged—the investor has been insulated from movements in the security price.

If the investor is buying the option rather than writing it, the position in the option is hedged by selling the security short rather than by buying the security. So the hedge position in the security is always the opposite direction of the position in the call option. If long in the call option, the investor is short in the security. If short in the call option (that is, if the investor writes the option), then a long position should be taken in the security to hedge.

The position is always opposite for a call option because the call option moves in the same direction as the security price; in a hedge, the option and security position must move in opposite directions. If the security and the option are held in the right proportions, the movements exactly counterbalance each other so that the investor's total position is unchanged. On the other hand because a put option moves in the opposite direction of the underlying security, the proper hedge for a long put option is a long position in the security. Thus, the hedge position in the security is always the same direction as the position in the put.

The change in the price of an option with a dollar change in the price of the underlying is called the delta of the option, denoted by Δ. (In the example just given, the delta of the call option is .5). If the hedge ratio is set according to the value of delta so that Δ times as much security is held in a position opposite to the position of the call option (that is, with the security held long if the call option is written, and with the security sold short if the call option is bought or Δ times as much of the security is held in a position the same as the put option, then the movement in the option position exactly counteracts any movement induced by shifts in the security price and the value of the investor's position is unchanged on net.

In summary, then, the ideal hedge ratio from the standpoint of eliminating the investor's exposure to the risk of the security is to hold $-\Delta$ shares of security for every option. In the Black-Scholes model, the value of Δ for a call can be computed using the first term of the formula:

$$\Delta = N(d_1)$$

When N(·) is the cumulative normal distribution function, and when d_1 is defined as in the Black-Scholes formula. For the generalized option model, the delta of a call option is:

$$\Delta = e^{-\delta T}N(d_1)$$

Using the S&P 100 option from the example of the Black-Scholes model in the previous section, compute the delta for that option as:

$$\Delta = N(.258) = .602$$

This delta means that if the S&P index changes in value by one point, the value of the call option changes by just over .6 points. If the index goes from 236 to 237, the option goes from 10.75 to 11.35. So if .6 units of the index are used to hedge each call, the change in the index value counterbalances any change in the option price and the investor's position is unaffected by the movement in the index (see Table 8).

Using the put-call parity relationship, the delta of a put option in the Black-Scholes model and the generalized option model, is, respectively:

$$\Delta = N(d_1) - 1$$

and

$$\Delta = e^{-\delta T}N(d_1) - e^{-\delta T}$$

Once a mispriced option is discovered, the investor can form a riskless hedge by buying Δ shares of security for each option writ-

Table 8   Effect of Security Price Change on Hedge Position

Current Price	
S&P 100 Index	236
S&P 235 Call Option	10.75
New Price	
S&P 100 Index	237
S&P 235 Call Option	11.35
Initial Delta	.60
Strategy	
Buy one 235 Call	
Sell short .60 units of the S&P 100	
Effect of Price Change on Position	
Profit on option position	11.35 − 10.75 = .60
Profit on index position	−.60 (237 − 236) = −.60
Net change in position	0

ten (if the option is above its correct price) or by selling short Δ shares of security for each option bought (if the option is below the correct price).

The hedge position for the option changes as the underlying security price changes. It also changes as the time to expiration changes. So the hedging strategy involves a dynamic hedge. The ratio must be reevaluated frequently and the riskless hedge adjusted whenever the security price changes significantly, and as the time to expiration declines. Also, the delta is a local measure. That is, it represents a riskless hedge only if the security price moves by small amounts. If the security price suddenly jumps 5 or 10 points, the ratio does not ensure that the riskless hedge is maintained. This means that the possibility of jumps in the security price that cannot be covered by adjusting the hedge affect the riskiness of the hedging strategy.

APPENDIX I: THE DERIVATION OF THE OPTION PRICING FORMULA

While this chapter permits some intuition about the option formula, this appendix presents a more detailed look at the derivation of the formula. First, a one-period option formula is derived and then extended to a many-period formula. The resulting option pricing model, known as the binomial model, is not only easy to derive and intuitively appealing, it is also the most widely-used model among professional option strategists.

The binomial model also provides a basis for understanding the derivation of the continuous-time formula. Indeed, the continuous-time formula is simply an extension of the binomial model to the case when the length of the time periods used is very small.

The Option Pricing Formula: A Simplified Case

As an introduction to the development of the option model, the example presented is expanded in the first section of the chapter.

Consider a security with a current price of S that changes by either a factor u or d by the next period. In the example of the first section of the chapter, $S = 100$, $u = 1.1$ and $d = .95$. By the next period when the option reaches its expiration date, the security either increases to uS or decreases to dS. The option price on expiration is uniquely related to the value of the security at expiration, being worth $C_u = MAX(0, uS - E)$ if the security rises by a factor of u percent or $C_d = Max(0, dS - E)$ if the security drops by a factor d of its initial price.

The values for the security and the related values for the option are presented in Figure A–1. This figure is the same as Figure 1, with the numbers replaced by symbols.

Figure A–1   One-Period Option Pricing

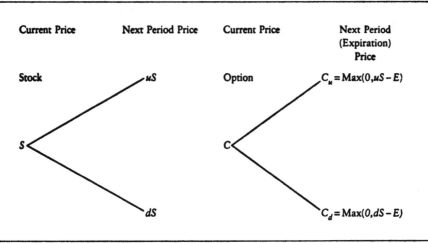

| Current Price | Next Period Price | Current Price | Next Period (Expiration) Price |

Stock → uS ; Option → $C_u = \mathrm{Max}(0, uS - E)$

S ; C

dS ; $C_d = \mathrm{Max}(0, dS - E)$

Using this specification for the behavior of the security price, the option price with one period to expiration is given by:

(1) $$C = (pC_u + (1 - p)C_d)/r$$

where

> r = one plus the riskless interest rate and
> $p = (r - d) / (u - d)$

The associated delta is:

(2) $$\Delta = \frac{C_u - C_d}{(u - d)S}$$

This formula was used in constructing the example in the preceding chapter. The delta for that example can be derived directly from Equation 2; the option price can be determined from Equation 1. Using that example to illustrate the formula:

$$u = 1.1, d = .95, S = 100, r = 1.05$$

$$C_u = \text{Max} (0, (1.1 \times 100) - 100) = 10$$

$$C_d = \text{Max} (0, (.95 \times 100) - 100) = 0$$

The delta is computed as:

$$\Delta = \frac{C_u - C_d}{(u - d)S} = \frac{10 - 0}{(1.1 - .95)\,100} = \frac{2}{3}$$

Thus, the proper hedge ratio is to write calls against the security in a ratio of 3 to 2.

To compute the correct option price, use Equation 1, with:

$$p = \frac{1.05 - .95}{1.1 - .95} = \frac{2}{3}$$

Therefore:

$$C = (\frac{2}{3} \times 10 + \frac{1}{3} \times 0)\,\frac{1}{1.05} = 6.35$$

If the option is not priced according to the pricing formula given in Equation 1, then an arbitrage profit is possible. If the option price is higher than the formula states, then the investor makes arbitrage profits by following the strategy of writing calls and buying the security in the ratio Δ and financing the difference between the option premium and the price of the security through borrowing at the riskless rate. If the market price for the call is below the price given by the equation, then the reverse strategy of buying calls and selling the security short in the proportions dictated by the delta and putting the proceeds into the riskless asset yield an arbitrage profit.

The Delta-Neutral Hedge: The first step in constructing the option model is creating a delta-neutral hedge—a position that guarantees the same return no matter what the security price is at the end of the period. This position is formed by writing one call option against Δ units of the security. With this position, the initial cost is the cost of the shares, ΔS, minus the income from the option, or $\Delta S - C$. At the end of the period, the position is worth either $\Delta uS - C_u$ or $\Delta dS - C_d$, depending on whether the security rises or falls in value.

What determines the size of the hedge? To get a riskless position, choose a hedge that ensures that the position is the same no matter which way the security moves. That is, choose a Δ so that:

$$\Delta uS - C_u = \Delta dS - C_d$$

(3)

Solving for Δ, this implies that the delta should be

(4)
$$\Delta = \frac{C_u - C_d}{(u - d)S}$$

The One-Period Option Formula: With this ratio of the security held to options written, there is a return that is certain no matter which way the security moves. This portfolio, therefore, replicates the riskless asset. Because the return is riskless, it must be that it yields the riskless rate of interest. That is, the value of the security-option position at the end of the period must equal the initial investment in the position brought forward by one period's interest, or:

(5)
$$\Delta = uS - C_u = r(S\Delta - C)$$

In this equation, r equals one plus the riskless rate. Rewriting this equation and substituting for Δ from Equation 4:

(6)
$$C = \left(\frac{(r-d)}{u-d} C_u + \frac{(u-r)}{u-d} C_d \right) / r$$

Defining $p = (r - d) / (u - d)$, rewrite Equation 6 in the simpler form:

(7)
$$C = (pC_u + (1-p)C_d) / r.$$

This is the equation for the price of a call option with one period to maturity.

There is valuable insight into the option pricing formula by thinking of the variable p as a probability. If p is the probability the security will go up and $(1 - p)$ as the probability the security will go down, the current option price in Equation 7 simply equals the expected future option price discounted by the riskless interest rate. Keep in mind that the value of p is not obtained as a probability of the security price going up or down. In fact as already noted, one of the attractive features of the option pricing formula is that the probability of the security price moving up or down is not needed as an input. But it turns out that p is the probability of the security going up if the expected return to the security is set equal to the riskfree rate. That is, if p equals the probability of the security going up to uS and if the expected return of the security is set equal to the risk-free return, then:

$$p(uS) + (1 - p)(dS) = rS$$

Solving for p in this equation, $p = (r - d)/(u - d)$. For the purpose of option pricing, the riskless hedging argument indicates that the expected return of the security equals the riskless rate of return. This is because the hedge eliminates any risk from the security price, and so the option pricing problem can be approached from a risk-neutral perspective. This means that when a riskless hedge exists, the price of an option can be calculated as the present value of its expected return assuming the expected return to the security equals the risk-free rate.

Note that the call option price is a function of the price of the security, the exercise price, the riskless interest rate and the range of the future security price as represented by u and d. These are the same variables that determine the option value in the Black-Scholes formula. In this case, the parameters u and d provide a measure of volatility.

Put options are priced in the same way as calls; the only difference is in the specification of the end-of-period payoff. While for a call option $C_u = \text{Max}(0, uS - E)$ and $C_d = \text{Max}(0, dS - E)$, for a put option we have $P_u = \text{Max}(0, E - uS)$ and $P_d = \text{Max}(0, E - dS)$. Indeed, in addition to calls and puts, a wide set of contingent claims can be priced by this arbitrage relationship by specifying the terminal value of the claim as a function of the underlying asset.

The Two-Period Option Formula: The one-period case is unrealistic because the security price may move many times between a given date and the time the option expires. However as previously described, the same arbitrage principle can be applied in the many-period case, although the computations become more tedious. To obtain the pricing formula for many periods, first extend the technique to the two-period case. Go back one period from the formula derived and see what the pricing formula is when there are two periods before the option expires.

Let the price of the security two periods before the expiration be S. With one period to expiration, the security is worth either uS

or dS dollars (assuming that the security follows the same binomial process for price changes each period). At the time of maturity of the option, the security again goes up by u or down by d.
At the time of maturity, then, its price is uuS (if it goes up by u
both times), udS (if it goes up one time and down one time) or
ddS (if it drops by d percent both times). Note that udS = duS, so
that the price of the security at expiration is the same regardless of
which period it goes up and which period it goes down.

The price of the option when there are two periods to expiration can be denumerated in a similar way. If the price of the option with two periods to expiration is C, then by the next period it
will have a price of C_u or C_d depending on whether the security
goes up or down. On expiration its price is C_{uu} = Max $(0, u^2S - E)$ if
the security rises both periods, C_{ud} = Max $(0, udS - E)$ if the security goes up one period and down the other, and C_{dd} = Max $(0, d^2S
- E)$ if the security drops both perriods. The possible movement of
the security price and the related movement of the option price are
illustated in Figure A–2.

The value of the options with one period left can be derived
by the same methods that are used in the one-period case. If the
value of the option with one period left is C_u, then it is worth
either C_{uu} or C_{ud} at maturity depending on whether the security is
worth U^2S or udS at maturity. Relating back to Equation 7, it is
apparent that if the security price with one period left is uS, the
option price is:

(8) $$C_u = (pC_{uu} + (1 - p)C_{ud})/r$$

and if the security price is dS, the call option is worth:

(9) $$C_d = (pC_{du} + (1 - p)C_{dd})/r$$

Moving two periods back from the time of expiration, the
same reasoning is applied again. With two periods left, the security price is S and the security price the next period is either uS or

Figure A–2 An Example of Two-Period Option Pricing

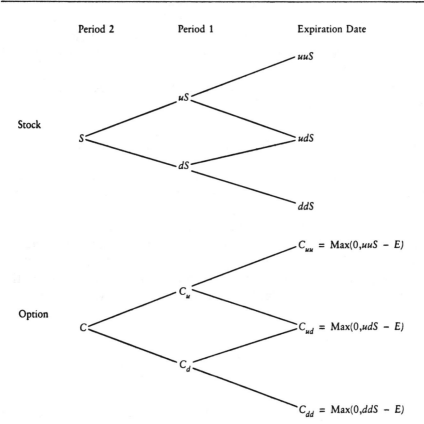

dS. The related options prices are C_u and C_d. The option then is priced with two periods left to expiration according to Equation 7:

(10) $$C = (pC_u + (1 - p)C_d)/r$$

When C_u and C_d already have been determined given by the application of Equations 8 and 9.

This recursive solution method permits pricing a two-period option by repeated application of the one-period formula. As with option pricing in the one-period setting, the price here is expressed in terms of known parameters, S, E, r, u and d. Because the possible values of the option at maturity are known, the two-period value can be determined exactly.

The use of the two-period case can be illustrated by extending the one-period example.

Profiting from Mispriced Options: A Two-Period Example

If the security is at $100 with two periods to go, its values with one period left is 95 or 110, and at expiration the security is worth either uuS = (1.1)(1.1)100 = 121, udS = (1.1)(.95)100 = 104.50 or ddS = (.95)(.95)100 = 90.25. The option at maturity is worth either zero or the final security value at expiration minus the exercise price of $100, C_{uu} = 21 C_{ud} = 4.5 or C_{dd} = 0. Working back to one period before expiration, the option price can be obtained by using the one-period option formula. If the security is at 110 with one period left, then C_u = 21 and C_d = 4.5, so that:

$$C = (\frac{2}{3} \times 21 + \frac{1}{3} \times 4.5)/1.05 = 14.76$$

If the security is at 95 with one period remaining, the option price can be computed as:

$$C = (\frac{2}{3} \times 4.5 + \frac{1}{3} \times 05)/1.05 = 2.86$$

The price of the option with two periods remaining now can be obtained by again applying the one-period formula, with the values for C_u and C_d being 14.76 and 2.86, respectively. The resulting value is:

$$C = (\frac{2}{3} \times 14.76 + \frac{1}{3} \times 2.86)/1.05 = 10.28$$

The security prices and the related option prices are shown in Figure A–3. The delta is placed in parentheses below the option prices in that figure. The delta is calculated using Equation 2.

Depending on the market price of the option, the delta dictates either buying Δ shares of a security for each option written or selling short h shares of security for reach option bought. Denoting the market price of the option C_m, trading strategies are:

Period 1
If $C_m > C$, buy 79.3 shares for each 100 call options written
If $C_m < C$, sell 79.3 shares for each 100 call options bought

Period 2
S = 110
If $C_m > C_u$, buy 100 shares for each 100 call option written
If $C_m < C_u$, sell 100 shares for each 100 call options bought
S = 95
If $C_m > C_d$, buy 31.6 shares for each 100 call options written
If $C_m < C_d$, sell 31.6 shares for each 100 call options bought

To illustrate the strategy, take a particular path for the security price. Suppose the security goes from 100 to 110, and that the option price in the market, C_m is $11.

The period-by-period steps in the strategy are:

Period 1
S = 100, C = 10.28, Δ = .793

Write 100 options at 11	1,100
Buy 79.3 shares of security at 100	(7,930)
Borrow (7,930 – 1,100) at 5 percent	6,830
Net position	0

By the next period, the security is at $110. Say that the option goes to $16. It, therefore, remains overpriced. The investor main-

Figure A–3 An Example of Two-Period Option Pricing

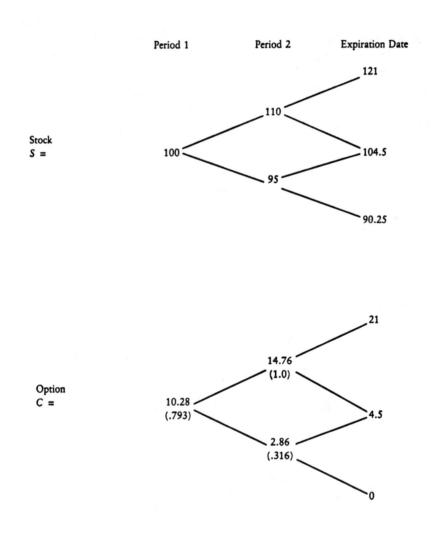

tains a short position in the option, but with a delta of 1. By buying 20.7 more shares of security in Period 2, revise the delta to the
prescribed 100 shares of security per 100 options.

Period 2
S = 100, C = 14.76, Δ = 1.0

Buy 20.7 shares of security 110	(2,277)
Borrow 2,277 at 5 percent	(2,277)
Net position	0

Following this strategy through to expiration date, the final
profit is $79 no matter which direction the security moves on the
expiration date:

Expiration date
S = 121, C = 21

Sell 100 shares of security at 121	12,100
Buy 100 options at 21	(2,100)
Repay loan of 6,830 $(1.05)^2$	(7,530)
Repay loan of 2,277 (1.05)	(2,391)
Net Profit	79

S = 104.5, C = 4.5

Sell 100 shares of security at 104.5	10,450
Buy 100 options at 4.5	(450)
Repay loan of 6,830 $(1.05)^2$	(7,530)
Repay loan of 2,277 (1.05	(2,391)
Net profit	79

The delta changes from period to period, requiring constant
updating of the portfolio position. Over the two periods, the delta
moved from .793 to 1.0. Because of the constant updating of the
hedge position, this strategy is called a dynamic hedging strategy.
In order to maintain the riskless position, the ratio of options to
security must change as the time to expiration gets closer and as
the security price changes. If the delta is not adjusted, the once-

riskless position becomes risky, and the opportunity for an arbitrage profit is lost.

Option Pricing When There May Be Early Exercise

Most listed options are American options, options that can be exercised any time on or before the expiration date. For call options that do not have discrete cashflows it turns out that the value of an American call option is the same as that of a European call option. However for call options with dividends or other cashflows and for put options in general, it may be optimal to exercise early. The American option then has a greater value than its European counterpart.

The possibility of early exercise adds substantial complexity to option pricing. Rather than evaluating the exercise value of the option only at expiration, a check now must be made at every time period to see if the option is worth more exercised than not, and the option price must take on the greater of these two values. Fortunately, the numerical procedure of the binomial pricing method provides a natural way for making this check because the solution already involves a pricing calculation at every time period. When the one-period option pricing formula is applied at every time period, just include a second check to compare the resulting option price with the value the option will have if it is exercised, and then use the greater of these values as the option price.

For American options, evaluate each period whether the option is worth more dead than it is alive. The value of the option dead is simply its intrinsic value: the maximum of 0 or S - E for a call option, the maximum of 0 or E - S for a put option. The value of the option alive is the value brought back by the recursive pricing methodology described earlier:

$$C = [p\, C_u + (1-p)\, C_d]/r$$

At each node in the option model, rather than solving recursively for the option value as shown in Figure A–2, take the greater of the value of the option dead or alive. For an American call option, then, the value at each node is:

$$C = Max\ (C_{dead},\ C_{alive})$$

$$= Max\ (S - E,\ [p\ C_u + (1 - p)\ C_d]/r)$$

The Black-Scholes Model as a Limiting Case of the Binomial Model

The binomial formula approximates reality better as more time periods are used. That is rather than splitting six months into six periods of one month each, split six months into 26 periods of one week each. The objections to having the security follow a simplistic binomial price change are reduced with further time periods because over those time periods the security can take on a wide range of values. The most important question for application then is how many time periods are necessary to get a good approximation of reality. Table A–1 answers this by comparing the binomial model for various volatilities, times to expiration and exercise prices. It also compares the price from the binomial formula with the price of its continuous time counterpart, the Black-Scholes formula. The table looks at the binomial approximation with only five periods and with 25 periods.

   In the limit as each time period becomes smaller and smaller and the number of time periods used in the binomial formula approaches infinity, the binomial formula approaches the Black-Scholes formula. (The Black-Scholes formula has the drawback, however, of not being able to consider the possibility of early exercise.) But from Table A–1, it is clear that the number of time periods does not need to get too large for the formula values to coincide closely. For 25 periods, the two formulas are often within a few pennies of each other. So for practical purposes, as few as 25 periods may be sufficient.

Table A–1   Comparison of the Binomial and Black-Scholes Models

(Stock price = 50; Riskfree interest rate = 10%)

Model	Days to Expiration	σ = .2 Exercise Price			σ = .4 Exercise Price		
		45	50	55	45	50	55
Binomial	30	5.38	1.40	.07	5.87	2.60	.83
with	120	6.74	3.21	1.12	8.03	5.53	3.06
N = 5	210	7.95	4.59	2.14	10.00	7.58	5.15
Binomial	30	5.37	1.36	.08	5.82	2.50	.78
with	120	6.70	3.13	1.08	8.23	5.35	3.29
N = 25	210	7.93	4.49	2.14	10.07	7.35	5.21
Black-Scholes	30	5.39	1.36	.08	5.83	2.49	.77
(Binomial with	120	6.75	3.15	1.09	8.25	5.35	3.27
N = ∞)	210	8.02	4.54	2.21	10.11	7.36	5.22

APPENDIX II: VOLATILITY ESTIMATION

The five principle inputs into the option pricing formula are the price of the underlying security, the exercise price of the option, the time to expiration of the option, the riskfree interest rate and the security's price volatility. The first three are determined immediately by the terms of the option contract; the riskfree interest rate can be proxied by the Treasury bill rate or the certificate-of-deposit rate prevailing for the time until the expiration of the option. The critical input that remains for the successful use of the option pricing formula is volatility.

In theory, there is little problem in getting an adequate volatility estimate. Unlike attempts to estimate the direction of the security price, the estimation of price volatility does not require any divination into the future course of the price or into the mind set of other investors in the market. Volatility estimators are simply a reflection of how variable price movement is expected to be. The direction of the security movement does not matter. A security can be just as volatile going up 20 percent in value as it can when it is trading up and down in a 10 percent trading range.

In practice, volatility estimation is complicated by a number of factors. The most significant problem is the instability of volatility over time. Figure B–1 traces the volatility for the S&P 500 over a nine-year period. Each of the estimates in this figure was made using data over 60 trading days. The volatility has a mean of approximately 15 percent; but there are times when the market heats up and volatility takes sudden jumps—at two points, the volatility went to nearly 24 percent, over one and one half times the average volatility. This instability exacerbates volatility estimation methods that rely on past data. If volatility shifts about erratically, there is no reason to expect volatility estimated over the past to reflect current volatility.

Volatility Estimation Using Past Prices

Because volatility is a measure of the standard deviation of security returns, the estimators for volatility are essentially variance estimators. Indeed, the most straightforward volatility estimator, which uses closing stock prices, is simply the maximum likelihood variance estimator from elementary statistics. But estimating volatility with only closing prices ignores other valuable information in the price summary data. The high and low prices also contain information about the variability of prices, and after the close-to-close estimator is described, a more powerful volatility estimator that uses high and low prices is outlined.

Estimating Using Close-to-Close Price Changes

Letting C_t be the closing price of the security for period t, the security return R_t is defined as the price relative between period $t - 1$ and period t, $R_t = C_t/C_{t-1}$. To approximate the continuously compounded returns, use the natural log of R_t in the computations. Denoting the mean return over n time periods by m:

Figure B–1   S&P 500
            60-Day Volatility

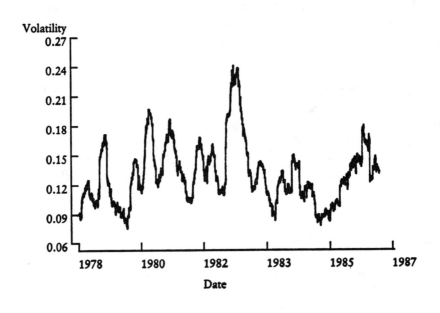

$$m = \frac{1}{n} \sum_{t=1}^{n} \ln R_t$$

the variance can be computed using the standard maximum likelihood variance estimator:

$$\sigma^2 = \frac{1}{n-1} \sum_{t=1}^{n} (\ln R_t - m)^2$$

Volatility is obtained as the square root of σ^2. Note that the sum is divided by $(n - 1)$ rather than n. This is necessary to obtain an unbiased estimate of the variance.

From this, volatility is seen simply as the square root of the variance of returns. Volatility should be adjusted to give an annualized value. If weekly closing prices are used in the variance calculation, then resulting volatility is multiplied by the square root of 52. If daily closing prices are used, daily volatility must be multiplied by the square root of the number of trading days in the year. While this varies from year to year, it is approximately 250 days.

A precise estimate of the volatility over any time period is possible with only a moderate number of observations. The accuracy of the estimate of past volatility is not the critical problem. Since market volatility may vary substantially over short time periods, critical problem is whether that volatility estimate, based as it is on past prices, reflects the current volatility.

Volatility Estimation Using the Volatilities Implied in Option Prices

For investors who have a high regard for the wisdom of the market, the ideal estimate of volatility comes from polling those who are trading in the market. The volatility estimates of the traders might be averaged together, perhaps with more weight given to the larger and assumably better-informed traders. Unfortunately, no such poll is taken; and in any event, the more successful traders probably would not be forthcoming with their estimates. But the result of the poll—the weighted average of the volatility estimates held by those in the market—is readily available; it is embedded in the market price of every option.

It is already known that fair option value is a function of the security price, the time to expiration and exercise price of the option, the riskless interest rate, and the security's price volatility. Given the values of the other parameters and the market price of the option, a unique volatility can be solved that leads to that market option price. If the market price of the option is taken to be the correct price, the volatility backed out of the formula is the best estimate of the correct volatility. Put another way, since in the aggregate the market takes the market price to be correct, the volatility implied by the market price is the market's opinion of what the volatility should be.

This volatility estimate is called implied volatility, which can be derived using an option formula. If the option formula C (S,T, E, r, σ) is known as well as the current market price, denoted by C_m, then the implied volatility is that volatility σ that sets the formula value equal to the market value; the implied volatility is the value σ* that solves the equation:

$$C_m = C\ (S, T, E, r, \sigma^*)$$

The resulting implied volatility obviously depends on the option model used.

The implied volatility is an attractive shortcut to volatility estimation. It lets the market do the work, leaving the final calculation to depend only on the current stock and option quotes, and the choice of the model. But there are obvious problems in using the implied volatility as presented here for finding mispriced options. Putting implied volatility into the option pricing formula always shows the option to be correctly priced, because the implied volatility came from setting the formula price equal to the market price in the first place. This identity between the market option price and the formula price can be avoided by using the average of the implied volatilities of a number of options on the same stock. Also, implied volatility can be used directly in pinpointing mispriced options without reentering implied volatility into the option pricing formula.

Implied Volatility Also Provides a Method for Finding Mispriced Options

There is only one volatility for each security. If implied volatility for one option on a particular security is 24.8 percent and the implied volatility for another option is 21.5 percent, both volatilities cannot be correct. There is no way to know which of the two volatilities is closest to the truth without further investigation; but for some option trading strategies, it is enough to know that the two volatilities differ significantly. Because a higher option price leads to a higher implied volatility, it is clear the option with 24.8 percent volatility is over-priced relative to the option with 21.5 percent volatility; a profitable spread may be executed by buying the underpriced option and writing the overpriced option against it.

The implied volatility already has all the information necessary to find relatively mispriced options. If two options have a wide spread in implied volatilities, a profit opportunity may exist. If the implied volatility on one option is far out of line with the implied volatilities on the other options, that alone may be enough to indicate a mispricing. It must be kept in mind that implied volatility is only as correct as the option formula that was used to find it. If the option formula does not allow for early exercise or does not include dividends, implied volatility reflects that misspecification. But in some cases, misspecifications affect all of the option prices in the same way and the variations in implied volatilities of the options still may reflect relative mispricing. If the magnitude of the specification errors does not vary greatly from option to option, the spreads in the implied volatilities can still lead to the discovery of profit opportunities.

Chapter 13

Equity Warrants[*]

Sidney Fried
Editor, *RHM Survey of Warrants,*
Options and Low Price Stocks
Editor, *RHM Convertible Survey*

Stock options and index options are highly-leveraged speculative short-term instruments in the equity market. Warrants, on the other hand, are highly-leveraged long-term instruments. Just as with options, warrants are also amenable to mathematical logic. A good understanding of the warrant market and how they work can result in the ability to determine potential profit opportunities. Whereas index options react to the market as a whole, stock options and warrants are inextricably tied to the movement of the associated common stock.

A warrant is issued by the corporation itself and represents the right to buy a share of common stock of the company at a specific price, for a specific period of time. This "time" period is always measured in years, 3 years, 5 years, at times even 10 years, in contrast with Index Options which have a life measured in

[*] Reprinted with permission from *Investment and Speculation with Warrants, Options and Convertibles,* by Sidney Fried (Glen Cove, NY: R.H.M. Press).

months. When a company gets into trouble, the common stock can decline sharply, but the warrant can fall to a very low figure—even pennies. Then, when the company gets out of trouble, the common stock will recover, but the warrant can soar in percentage terms. The most important characteristic of a warrant is its leverage, its ability to appreciate at a far greater rate than its respective common stock.

At this point, however, let us consider the crucial difference in behavior between a warrant that is selling "in the money"—that is, having intrinsic value because the common stock price is above the exercise price of the warrant—and a warrant that is selling "out of the money,"—the common stock price being below the exercise price of the warrant.

Let us consider an XYZ warrant that is the right to buy XYZ common stock at $10 per share, and also consider that XYZ common is selling at $15. The XYZ warrant must sell at least at $5 in this instance, because if the warrant were to sell significantly below $5, "arbitrageurs" would step in to make a riskless profit.

To explain this, suppose the XYZ warrants were selling at $3 when the common is at $15, even though each warrant can be turned in to the corporation with $10, to receive one share of common stock. An arbitrageur could buy one warrant for $3, turn the warrant in to the company with $10 payment, for a total outlay of $13, and then turn around and sell the share of stock he duly received, for $15. His profit would be $2, and there would have been no risk in the transaction.

Indeed, the arbitrageur would not wait to receive his share of stock from the company before selling it in the open market, because during the time he was waiting to get that share, the market price of the stock could go through some changes. Instead, as soon as he had purchased his warrant at $3, he would have sold one share of XYZ common short at $15, thereby locking in his profit.

Having established that with XYZ common selling at $15, the XYZ warrant, exerciseable at $10, must sell at least at $5, it is further true that the warrant can sell above its straight exercise value, to reflect the additional exercise life still remaining. So a warrant can sell above its straight exercise value—at a premium—, but cannot sell below its straight exercise value—at a discount.

What is the case, however, when the common stock is selling below the exercise price of the warrant? Here, the XYZ warrant is still the right to buy XYZ common stock at $10, but the current market price of that XYZ common is, say, $7. No one would exercise a warrant at an expenditure price of $10, if he can buy that same share of common stock in the open market for $7, without a warrant. Here, there is no objective criterion for fixing a minimum price for an out of the money warrant. It can sell down as far as it wants to as far as the arbitrageur is concerned—it has no minimum.

Because this is so, emotion can have full sway with an out of the money warrant, erring on the side of pessimism, or on the side of optimism. If the general market is on a steady course, or is heading higher, the warrant may be generously priced, but if the company that issued the warrant is doing poorly—or is even in serious trouble—and the general market is on the downside, the warrant can sell down to a very low price, getting down to a few dollars, or one dollar, or even the "pennies" level, because investors have little faith that the applicable common stock can ever get up to a sufficiently high price so that the warrant will have any value. The deeper the market slide, the deeper the pessimism, and the lower the warrant will move.

THE EVALUATION OF A WARRANT

Over many years of following hundreds of warrants, we have found the following "formula" to be quite helpful in determining whether a warrant, given the existing market price for warrant and common, is overvalued, undervalued, of "fairly" valued. The following steps are involved:

1. Assume a 50% advance in the common stock.
2. Assume another 50% advance in the common stock.

3. Assume, after the second 50% advance for the common, that the warrant is selling for its straight exercise value.

4. Take one-half of that exercise value.

5. Now take one-half of what resulted from Step (4).

At this point you have the existing "fair value" for the warrant, and you compare it to the price at which the warrant is actually selling. If the warrant is selling well below the "fair value," it is undervalued. If it is selling quite close to the "fair value," it is fully priced. If it is selling well above the "fair value," it is overvalued.

In March 1986, Eli Lilly issued a warrant which started trading around the $8 level, with Eli Lilly common selling at $59.25. Each warrant could be exchanged for one share of common stock upon payment of $75.98 until March 31, 1991, when the warrant would expire. Following the above formula, and taking the beginning prices for Eli Lilly common and warrants, we now:

1. Assume a 50% advance for Eli Lilly common from $59.25 to $88.875.

2. Assume a second 50% advance from $88.875 to $133.31.

3. The Eli Lilly warrant being the right to buy at $75.98, we deduct $75.98 from $133.31 to arrive at an exercise value of $57.33.

4. One-half of that $57.33 exercise value is $28.66.

5. One-half of $28.66 is $14.33, which is the "fair value" of the Eli Lilly warrant, with the common at $59.25 and an exercise right at $75.98.

But the Eli Lilly warrant was selling at $8. It was considerably undervalued and, therefore, proceeded to far outstrip Eli Lilly common on the upside, while, at the same time, protecting capital on the downside.

ASARCO '91 WARRANTS

In May 1989, Asarco[1] common stock was selling at $28-7/8 and the Asarco warrant was selling at $12-7/8. Asarco is a leading producer of copper, silver, lead and zinc, among other operations, and the warrant represents the right to buy one share of Asarco common stock for $16.09, this privilege to last to August 15, 1991, when the warrant will expire.

Given these figures, is the warrant undervalued, overvalued or somewhat in-between?

Following the formula:

1. We multiply $28.875 by 1.5 (a 50% advance) and get $43.31.

2. We multiply $43.31 by 1.5 and get 64.97.

3. We deduct the exercise price ($16.09) from $64.97 and get $48.88, which is the straight exercise value of the warrant.

4. We take one-half of that exercise value and get $24.44.

5. We take one-half of the result in step 4 and get $12.22, and that is the fair value for the Asarco warrant when the common is at $28-7/8, and the fair value was $12.22, the warrant could be termed "fairly valued."

We can make the point that even at its "fairly-valued" price, the Asarco warrant still promised to advance twice as fast as Asarco common. That is, Asarco common goes from $28.1875 to $43.31, up 50%, while the Asarco warrant goes from $12.875 to $24.44, not much less than 100%.

It is not enough, however, to calculate what the warrant will do on the upside. What if Asarco declines by 50% from $28.875 to $14.43? Will the Asarco warrant also decline only by 50% from $12.875 to $6.44? We do not think so. We feel we would more likely find the Asarco warrant selling closer to, say, the $4 level, possibly lower.

---

1 See the May 29, 1989 issue of the R.H.M. Survey of Warrants, Options and Low Priced Stocks.

What conclusion should we draw from this? The conclusion would be that a fairly-valued warrant is still likely to advance about twice as fast as the common stock on the upside, but is also likely to decline considerably faster than the common stock, on a percentage basis. Given that prospect, one could not say in May 1989 that the Asarco warrant was an attractive purchase.

A very important first step in considering the potential of a warrant is also a very simple one: divide the common price by the warrant price. If you get a low number, the warrant is not likely to represent a purchase opportunity. If you get a high number, the warrant has passed its first test of being attractive for purchase.

Thus far in our "Evaluation" of warrants, we have ignored the length of life still remaining for exercise. Obviously, this is a very important factor, but we excluded it for the moment, to get our major point across.

Our experience has been, where our Evaluation Equation is concerned, that if warrants have more than two years of exercise life remaining, the "time" question has only marginal influence, and we can take the conclusion of the "Equation" without hesitation.

Once we get under the two-year mark, we should "shade" our results to some small extent, and once we get under the 18-month mark, we should use the Evaluation Equation only as a very rough guide, giving greater weight to other factors.

The time factor with warrants is of the utmost importance, but with very low-price warrants, it is considerably less important than with high-price warrants.

CAPITAL CITIES/ABC WARRANTS

It is quite appropriate (and educational!) that we should go from discussing a warrant selling at $1.4 (the earlier price of the Southwest Airlines warrant) to a warrant selling initially in the $30 range!

Also, there is the great contrast between a Southwest Airlines warrant being the right to buy stock at $35 per share, and a Capital Cities/ABC warrant being the right to buy stock at $250 per share. Since we, at different times, recommended that both should be purchased, it is evident that warrant "arithmetic" works in any price range.

In March 1985, American Broadcasting Companies ("ABC") was merged into Capital Cities Communications, the new entity being known as Capital Cities/ABC.

Warrants should almost always be bought as soon as they begin trading, because the warrants are completely unfamiliar to most investors, and they proceed to sell them at prices which typically later prove to be bargain prices. This is true whenever stockholders receive warrants because of a merger, acquisition, or some other financial event.

It was no different with ABC stockholders when they received warrants as part of the acquisition package from Capital Cities Communications. Each warrant (and there were 2.85 million of those warrants) represented the right to buy one share of the newly combined companies—Capital Cities/ABC—for $250—the warrants to expire on July 29, 1988. Thus, it was only a two year warrant.

In April 1986, the new Capital Cities/ABC warrant was trading at $30.50 and the common at $228.50.[2] We can apply the evaluation equation as follows:

Divide the common price by the warrant price (228.50 divided by 30.50), and we get 7.49, which is a number sufficiently high to mark the warrant as worth looking into as a purchase, from that initial criterion.

We then apply our Evaluation Equation, as follows:

1. We multiply 228.5 by 1.5 and get 342.75.

2. We multiply 342.75 by 1.5 and get 514.13.

3. We deduct the exercise price of the warrant (250) from 514.13 and get 264.13, which is the straight exercise value of the warrant when the common is at 514.13.

---

2 See RHM survey, April 18, 1986.

4. We take one-half of the exercise value, and get 132.06.

5. Finally, we take one-half of the result in step 4 and get 66.03, which is the fair value of the warrant when the common is at 228.50, as it was in April 1986.

So the Capital Cities/ABC warrant was selling at $30.50 when its fair value was $66.03. That is quite an undervaluation, and demonstrates again how new warrants resulting from mergers and acquisitions, very often start trading at bargain levels because the stockholders who received the warrants have little comprehension of their true long-term value.

Capital Cities Communications, after acquiring American Broadcasting Companies, had become a media giant, revenues jumping from $1 billion to $4 billion as the newspapers, shopping guides and myriad other publications were added to the television and radio networks of ABC.

In subsequent years, the fine outlook for the combined companies was demonstrated by strong earnings gains, jumping from $11.20 per share in 1986 to $16.46 per share in 1987, and to $22.31 per share in 1988. The common stock of the new Capital Cities/ABC proceeded to move sharply higher, as shown on the chart (see the following page—figure courtesy of Securities Research).

Prior to the October 1987 market break, the common stock reached $450, and the warrant, being the right to buy at $250, sold at its exercise value of $200. The reason for the lack of a premium over exercise value was that the warrant had only a 2-year life to begin with, and by its 1987 high, the exercise life was already less than one year. Furthermore, high-priced warrants—and $200 is a high price (!)—always sell at lower premiums over exercise value than do lower-priced warrants.

From the April 1986 prices, the common stock had advanced from $228.50 to $450.00, an advance of 97%, while the warrants had advanced from $30.50 to $200.00, and advance of 556%. Illustrating the fact that high-priced warrants can act very much like low- priced warrants do, when both are favorably situated, recall that the Southwest Airlines warrant had advanced 600% while the

Figure 1   Capital Cities/ABC, Inc. ICCBI

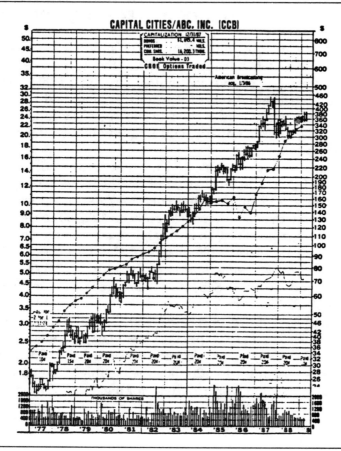

Capital Cities/ABC warrant had advanced 555%, as we have just recounted.

And what has also been demonstrated once again is the likelihood of a new warrant, emanating from a merger or an acquisition, selling at a very attractive price in the early stages of its trading activity when it comes upon the market. This has led us to almost always recommend immediate purchase of such warrants, as soon as trading begins.

THE CLEAR ADVANTAGE OF THE CAPITAL CITIES/ABC
WARRANT OVER CAPITAL CITIES/ABC COMMON STOCK

It is necessary to fully understand how superior a well-situated warrant can be, when compared with the respective common stock. In recent years, and continuing through to this day, there have always been hundreds of warrants trading, and if you buy a common stock without first checking to see if there is a warrant trading for the same company, you might willingly embrace some severe disadvantages.

Let us go through the relevant warrant "arithmetic" with Capital Cities/ABC to add further emphasis to these very important concepts. We are dealing with a common/warrant price relationship which saw the common stock go from $228.50 to $450.00, and the warrant go from $30.50 to its straight exercise value of $200.00.

If we had purchased 100 shares of Capital Cities/ABC common stock at $228.50, we would have expended $22,850, and when the common advanced to $450, the 100 shares were worth $45,000, for a gain of $22,150.

Alternatively, if we purchased 350 Capital Cities/ABC warrants at $30.50 (the market price of the warrants when the common was at $228,50), we would have expended $10,675, and when the warrants advanced to $200.00 (their straight exercise value), the 350 warrants were worth $70,000, for a gain of $59,325.

$22,850 invested in the common stock had produced a profit of $22,150;

while less than half that amount, or $10,675 invested in the warrants had produced a profit of $59,325.

The Capital Cities/ABC warrants were far ahead of the common stock on the upside. But what about the downside? Suppose the advantage of the warrant on the upside was offset by poor performance on the downside. We know, of course, that this will not be so, from our former example of Eli Lilly warrants, and when we go through the relevant "arithmetic," that is exactly what we find.

If the common stock of Capital Cities/ABC lost half its value, from $228.50 to $114.25, there would be a loss of $11,425.

Since the entire investment in the Capital Cities/ABC warrants was $10,675, there could not be a greater loss for the warrants than the common, even if the warrants had gone to zero! But our estimate is that with the common at $114.25, the warrants would be selling at about the $15 level, or a $15.5 loss on 350 warrants, which comes to $5,425.

So on the downside, we find a loss of $10,675 for the common stock, but only $5,425 for the warrants.

Upside or downside, an investment in the Capital Cities/ABC warrants, when they were selling at $30.5, was a far better investment than Capital Cities/ABC common stock. And this again emphasizes that with hundreds of warrants trading, and new warrants steadily coming on the scene, always check the warrant list whenever you are considering the purchase of a common stock.

A COMMON/WARRANT HEDGE POSITION WITH CAPITAL CITIES/ABC

A short position in a stock can be hedged with a warrant. Conversely, a warrant can be hedged with a short position in the underlying stock. However, short selling is not a popular strategy.

What makes even investors with some knowledge of short-selling justifiably nervous about that market maneuver is the following: if you buy a security, the maximum loss is what you paid for the security. But if you sell a security short, there is no maximum, for there is no limit, theoretically, to the increase in price which a security can attain. And to the extent that the shorted security goes up, your loss goes up.

For example, you buy 100 shares of ABC Inc. common stock at $50, laying out $5,000. The maximum loss you can sustain is—$5,000—which assumes ABC common has gone to Zero. The loss cannot be any greater.

Now, instead, you sell 100 shares of ABC common short, at $50. If ABC common goes to $100, and you cover your short, you have a loss of $5,000. That is, you took in $5,000 when you sold the stock short, and must pay $10,000 to buy 100 shares of ABC common at $100 to replace the stock you sold short at $50, to terminate the position.

If ABC common goes to $200, you have a loss of $15,000, if to $300, a loss of $25,000. It is all open-ended. Theoretically, your potential loss is unlimited. And it is that open-ended possibility of loss with a short-sale that correctly frightens investors.

Now observe how short-selling Capital Cities/ABC common stock not only does not threaten you with open-ended loss, but actually eliminates possible loss! Recall that Capital Cities/ABC is selling at $228.50 and the warrant is selling at $30.50. Each Capital Cities/ABC warrant is the right to buy the common stock at $250 per share.

We now set up the following Hedge position:

A. We buy 350 Capital Cities/ABC warrants at 30.50, laying out $10,675.

B. We sell short 100 shares of Capital Cities/ABC common stock at 228.50, taking in $22,850.

We know that in actuality, Capital Cities/ABC common stock ran up to $450 in 1987, so the 100 shares we sold short at $228.50 would show a loss of $45,000 minus $22,850, or a loss of $22,150.

But, at $450 for the common stock, the Capital Cities/ABC warrant, being the right to buy common at $250, must sell at a minimum of $200, and that is where it actually sold. Our 350 warrants, purchased at $30.50 for $10,675, are now worth 350 × $200 × or $70,000.

Deduct $10,675 from $70,000, and our gain is $59,325.

Gain of $59,325 on the long position in the warrants, and loss of $22,150 on the short position in the common stock, and our net gain is $37,175.

And no matter how high Capital Cities/ABC common might go, because we were short 100 shares, and long 350 shares via the warrants, our net profit would have to climb higher and higher, because the net position was actually long 250 shares of common stock.

THE DOWNSIDE

If Capital Cities common went to zero, our short-sale of 100 shares at $228.50, for $22,850 would, of course, result in a profit of $22,850. Since the entire cost of our long position in 350 warrants was $10,675, our net gain would have to be $12,175.

Now, to make a more reasonable assumption, say that Capital Cities/ABC common went down 50%, from $228.50 to $114.25. We would have a gain of $11,425 on our short position in 100 shares common at $228.50. Since this amount is still larger than the total investment in 350 Warrants—$10,675—there could be no net loss on the position. But since it is reasonable, from experience, that with the common at $114.25, the warrants should sell at about $15, the actual loss in the warrants would be 15.5 points on 350 warrants, or $5,425.

In this instance, gain of $11,425 on the short-sale of 100 shares common, and loss of $5.425 on the long position in 350 warrants, and our net gain would be $6,000.

CONCLUSION

The Hedge position we have just outlined of short Capital Cities/ABC common stock, and long Capital Cities/ABC warrants, had to show a substantial profit whether Capital Cities/ABC common stock went up or down!

There are several very important additional factors to consider here. When you sell a security short, you do not have to put up any funds to accomplish the transaction. All short-sales are automatically accomplished in a "margin account," and if you are carrying fully-paid securities in that margin account (if needed, fully-paid securities can simply be switched from your "cash" account to a "margin account"), in excess of the size of the short-sale, that would satisfy the requirements for selling short and would not require you to put up any additional funds at the inception of the position.

Therefore, you might own General Motors common stock, or Treasury securities, or any other security, and if these are reposing in your margin account, they are not affected in any manner, but they serve the purpose of allowing you to take short positions without putting up additional funds.

Thus, the net profit that eventuates is a very high return on the actual cash invested, because the only portion that required putting up cash is the long position in the 350 warrants.

That being so, if that warrant long position involved $10,675 (350 warrants at $30.50), a gain of $37,175 on the upside, or $6,000 on the downside, would be a very large percentage profit on the actual cash involved, and earned without risk! Even on more modest moves in a warrant/common Hedge position than we have just described for Capital Cities/ABC, the net return would still be riskless and large.

Therefore, when a warrant is selling at a favorable price in relation to the common, along the lines we have been discussing with Eli Lilly and Capital Cities/ABC, think seriously about setting up the type of Hedge position we have just described. We are fully aware that the vast majority of investors do not like to sell short, and find "Hedge" positions "too complicated," but we trust that we have demonstrated that the potential rewards are so large, and the diminution or elimination of risk so welcome, that the reader should overcome those fears and prejudices!

ANOTHER FACTOR ENTERS OUR WARRANT EVALUATION EQUATION

Thus far we have seen that the time factor (exercise life still remaining), must often be considered with our Warrant Evaluation Equation, which tells us what the "fair value" of a warrant is, so that this price may be compared with the current price of a warrant in which we may have an interest.

Now we enter another area which is at least equally important—the anticipated volatility of the common stock price, and the time frame for the profit horizons for the company itself. These additional factors do not take anything away from what the Equation can provide for us in the way of guidance; they add to the value of the guidance. Analyses of the fundamentals of a stock[3] are an indispensable part of arriving at the value of a warrant.

SALLIE MAE WARRANTS

In July 1986, the Student Loan Marketing Association (Sallie Mae) sold 300,000 Units, bringing in net proceeds of $296,940,000 to the company, and "blazing a trail" in that two different warrants were part of the offering, including Put warrants.

That is, each Unit consisted of $1,000 principal amount of a 5.60% Note, 12 Call warrants and 6 Put warrants. Each Call warrant represented the right to buy one share of Sallie Mae, which traded on the New York Stock Exchange, for $100, until August 1, 1991, when the warrant would expire.

Each Put warrant, to quote the Prospectus: ". . . entitles the holder to tender to Sallie Mae one share of Nonvoting Common Stock for mandatory purchase by Sallie Mae at a price of $51 . . . until August 1, 1991."

So, if Sallie Mae common would subsequently decline in the marketplace to, say, $30, the Put would be worth a minimum of $51 minus $30, or $21. For just as we previously explained about the role of the professional arbitrageur, ever alert for such opportunities, if the Put would sell for less than $21, with Sallie Mae common at $30, the arbitrageur could buy the Put, and one share of Sallie Mae common in the open market, and sell the combination to the company for $51.

---

3   For a detailed illustration, please see Sidney Fried, *Warrants, Options and Convertibles*, RHM Press, New York 1989.

COMPANIES SELLING "NAKED" WARRANTS

Thus far we have seen companies raising capital by selling warrants attached to new Bond issues and to issues of common stock, but Intel Corp. went in quite another direction by selling warrants attached to nothing! This is why we call them "naked."

On March 25, 1987, 3,500,000 warrants were sold at a price of $10 each, and after allowances for "Underwriting Discount and Commissions," Intel received a net $33,250,000 on the sale.

This felt so good, and made so much sense, that less than four months later, Intel was doing the same thing again, except that this time they sold 6,000,000 warrants at $10 each, bringing in a net $57,480,000.

Something else happened with the last-named warrant issue, which was the right to buy at $45 per share to August 15, 1988. It was only a one-year warrant, and the ability of the company to sell a warrant issue of such short duration illustrates the appetite of investors for warrants—a point we shall have more to say about.

ADJUSTING WARRANT EXERCISE TERMS FOR STOCK SPLITS

In September 1987, Intel split its common stock 3-for-2. This meant that every 200 shares became 300 shares, and the warrant terms were adjusted for that event. The warrant that had been sold in March 25, 1987 became the right to buy 1.5 shares at $30 per share, whereas it had previously been the right to buy 1 share for $45.00.

And a 10-year warrant which had originally been sold in May 1985 became the right to buy 1.5 shares at $26.67 per share to May 15, 1995. The right to have warrant terms adjusted for stock splits or, in many cases, even for smaller stock dividends, is very important to maintaining the value of a warrant.

SOME ADDITIONAL SIGNIFICANT POINTS

The one-year warrant that Intel had sold in August 1987, reached the end of its life in August 1988 as the right to buy 1.5 shares for each warrant, at $30 per share. Or, to put it another way, each warrant could buy 1.5 shares for $45.

Now, in early-August 1988, Intel was selling at $35, so 1.5 shares were worth $52.50. The right to buy a package worth $52.50 for $45 is worth $7.50, which meant that anyone holding the warrants rushed to exercise them prior to the expiration date of 8-15-88, because if they did not do so, they lost the difference between $52.50 and $45.00.

GEICO WARRANTS

One could begin describing the high-leverage opportunity that developed for GEICO warrants by asking the question: How could a $500 investment in one common stock warrant become worth $608,000 in a few years?

And there is an answer to that question that will be meaningful for hundreds of warrant opportunities when the next large downturn for the stock market comes on the scene.

High-leverage warrant opportunities occur when the company that issued the warrants gets into trouble, and then gets out of trouble. This, of course, is exactly what will happen in many instances when, first, recession hits, along with a falling stock market, which will cause many companies to get into trouble.

This will be followed by all-out Federal Reserve Board and Washington action, which will get many of those companies out of trouble and very probably also get the stock market "out of trouble." What is coming, then, is a "down- then-up" stock market, which is always the best setting for high- leverage warrant events.

A close look at how the GEICO warrant situation developed will be highly instructive for these later warrant opportunities to come.

If you want to see GEICO's common stock collapsing, look at the chart on the next page (courtesy of Securities Research), and note the toboggan slide from $60 in 1972 to about $3-1/8 in 1976, with the company having suffered heavy losses in 1975 and 1976 - a loss of ($7.00) per share in 1975 alone.

Figure 2   GEICO Corp. (GEC)

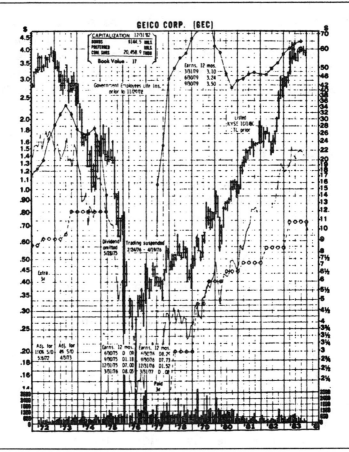

A reorganization, during which existing warrants got an extension of life to 1983, put the company on the road to recovery under the leadership of Chairman John J. Byrne, and earnings got back on the upswing trail.

Dividend payments were reinstated during that period, and climbed year-by-year, and the result for the common stock is shown on the chart by a V-like recovery, so that during 1983, GEICO common stock actually returned to its old high at $60.

The major reason that the greatest profit opportunities in warrants come when the company that issued the warrants gets into trouble, is that the pessimism engendered by the sinking of the common stock, and often the real threat of bankruptcy, causes the warrant to fall to very low prices, very often to the "pennies" level.

If the company is then able to get out of trouble and get back to profitability, a rising stock market will very often take the common stock to a high level of recovery, and the warrant then suddenly has a large market value because of its right to be exchanged for that common stock, at a specific price for a specific period of time. (The definition of a warrant!)

This is exactly what happened to the GEICO warrant. In 1978, when GEICO was in a very weakened position, the records of the National Quotation Bureau show a low for the GEICO warrant of 1/16 (6-1/4 cents), which rebounded to $1-5/8 in 1979 as the reorganization took hold and the threat of bankruptcy faded.

As earnings and the common stock climbed, the warrant advanced. Finally, in 1983, with each warrant representing the right to buy 2.08 shares of GEICO common at $24 per share, when the common stock hit its high of $60 that year, the right to buy one share at $24 had a minimum worth of $60 minus $24 or $36, and the right to buy 2.08 shares for each warrant meant the warrant had a minimum value of 2.08 times $36, or $74.88, with the actual recorded high for the warrant being $76.00.

The leverage here proved to be literally enormous.

Thus, if anyone was so fortunate as to have put $500 into 8,000 GEICO warrants at the 6-1/4 cents low, by the time the warrant it $76, as it had to once the common stock reached $60, that $500 speculation had become worth $608,000.

Even a mere $62.50 in 1,000 warrants became worth $76,000 in that same period of time.

This, then, is the kind of remarkable profit potential which develops with a long-term warrant when there is the process of the company that issued the warrants first getting into trouble, and then getting out of trouble.

It emphasizes the fact that the reader should be carefully watching a host of developing warrant opportunities over the next year or two, while the country as a whole gets into trouble, and then gets out of trouble. Opportunities, among the hundreds of warrants trading today, with new warrants coming on the scene in a regular flow, will range from the moderate, but still very rewarding and the extremely high leverage we have just described with GEICO warrants.

We expect warrant opportunities over the next year or two to be of an historic nature.

Chapter 14

Americus Trust Scores[*]

Sidney Fried
Editor, RHM Survey of Warrants,
Options and Low Price Stocks
Editor, RHM Convertible Survey

In 1987, a new type of "warrants" were created called the Americus Trust Scores. The quotation marks denote that these warrants had very special characteristics, all of which we shall soon explain, but, to begin with, let us understand that, as with all Warrants, they were highly-leveraged. This factor was very important because these Warrants represented the right to buy 26 of the very top blue chips on the New York Stock Exchange. All Scores trade on the American Stock Exchange, and we shall begin by pointing out that each Score is found in the table as A- followed by the symbol of the blue chip, followed by "sc." Thus, the **IBM** Score is carried as A-ibm sc, the **General Electric** Score is carried as A-ge sc etc. We shall shortly list all the blue chips with their symbols, so that they may be easily found.

---

[*] Reprinted with permission from *Investment and Speculation with Warrants, Options and Convertibles,* by Sidney Fried (Glen Cove, NY: R.H.M. Press).

Since we expect large market swings to come in subsequent markets, including a deep market decline to be followed by a new bull market, it is obvious that the reader will want to know all about Scores, and how they provide such a leveraged response to movement of their blue chip common stocks. What follows aims at supplying that knowledge.

SCORES (WARRANTS) ON 26 TOP BLUE CHIPS

In exactly the same time period:

Du Pont common moved from 79 to 105   . . . up **33%**

while the **Du Pont Score** moved
from 7-1/8 to 23-7/8   . . . up **235%**

Why did the Du Pont Score **advance 7 times faster** than Du Pont common?

This, of course, is nothing unusual for a Warrant, as we have certainly demonstrated. But they were all "American-style" Warrants, which could be exchanged for common stock at any time up to expiration date, whereas the Du Pont "Score" was a "European-style" Warrant, where the Warrant could be exchanged for common stock only on the last day of its life, which was years hence.

The Du Pont Score was nevertheless able to advance sharply, because of the way it was created—and that creation included something called an "Americus Trust" and a "Prime" along with the Score. A remarkable speculative medium, with high promise of capital appreciation was created when "Americus Trust," "Prime" and "Score" came into being, so let us explain the whole process from the beginning before we get into what we deem to be the high profit potential for investors who understand how to use these new market instruments.

The creation of a new investment entity is never initiated from an altruistic viewpoint—it comes about because there is profit in it. And, first and foremost, the Americus Trust concept came into being because the institutional investors and funds that held the blue chip stocks, the individuals who conceived the approach, and the investment banking houses that brought the concept to life, all expected to make money, each in their own way.

A. Joseph Debe and his company were among the prime movers of the concept, and Alex Brown & Sons was the investment banker for almost all of the Trusts, and the back cover of each Prospectus set forth what had been created, in condensed form.

As each Prospectus spelled out, the intent was to take a blue chip share of stock and break it down into two components; one component representing the right to receive dividends, and the other component representing the right to the capital appreciation that might be expected to flow from the investment.

Towards this end, large holders of blue chips—basically institutional holders—were approached to exchange shares of blue chip common stocks for Units in an Americus Trust.

A separate Americus Trust was set up for each successful offer, which would hold the blue chip shares tendered and exchange each share for one Americus Trust Unit which consisted of one rime and one Score. The Unit certificates could be immediately separated; the holder able to sell off either the Prime or the Score, and retain the part that was desired.

All three parts, the Unit itself, the Prime and the Score would trade separately on the American Stock Exchange, providing a market for any later approach desired.

The Prime was the income component of the Unit, entitled to receive all dividends paid. Such dividend payments were made by the blue chip company to the Americus Trust for that stock, since the original shares tendered were now owned by the Trust. When the trust received the dividends, they would pay them out to the holders of the Primes, retaining only 5 cents per share per annum, to meet the modest expenses of the Trust.

The Score was not entitled to receive any dividends, but would receive all appreciation in the common stock beyond a stated price, in a manner we shall now describe.

Each Americus Trust had a stated life of five years, which the Prospectus calls the "Termination Date." We happen to be looking at the Prospectus for the "Americus Trust for IBM Shares," and on the third page of the Prospectus, the "Termination Date Of The Trust" is given as June 30, 1992.

There is also something called the "Termination Claim," and it is the price therein stated which gives meaning to Prime and Score as the underlying common stock fluctuates in the marketplace.

Thus, the Termination Claim for the IBM Americus Trust is $210, which has relevance as follows: On June 30, 1992, the Americus Trust for IBM shares will go out of business, and its assets (almost all assets consisting of the original shares of IBM that had been tendered) would be distributed to the holders of Primes and Scores.

Each Prime would be entitled to receive assets up to the Termination Claim which, remember, was $210. Thus, if IBM common was selling at $210 on the Termination Date (June 30, 1992), each Prime would get value in IBM stock of $210, which would account for all the shares available for distribution, while the Score would receive nothing.

If IBM common was selling below $210 on the Termination Date, the Primes would still be getting all the shares, but they would be worth whatever the market price of IBM happened to be on that Termination Date, while the Scores would still get nothing.

If, however, IBM common was selling above $210 on the Termination Date, the Prime would get its maximum value in IBM shares of $210—and the Score would get all the rest.

Thus, if IBM common would be selling at $300 on the Termination Date, the Prime would get only its maximum of $210 in value, while the Score would get the difference, or $90 in value.

This, of course, is what makes the Score a Warrant, since it has a specific life (to the Termination Date), and a specific exercise price (the Termination Claim). Where the Score differs from an American Warrant is that the American Warrant, in almost all instances, can be exchanged for common stock (exercised) at any time, while the Score can be exercised only on the Termination Date of the applicable Americus Trust.

At this point, we go back to the beginning and consider the question as to why an institutional holder would be willing to exchange blue chip shares fore Prime/Score Units in the first place.

Take such an institutional holder that was primarily interested in the dividend yield, and only secondarily in the possible appreciation of the stock, and consider that they could tender the shares, sell off the Scores, retain the Primes, and thereby put themselves in an excellent position, as follows:

The Prime was entitled to the same dividend as the common stock, less the miniscule five cents per share per annum, but in selling off the Score, the cost of the Prime was now less than the common stock.

We can see what this means by looking at the price of IBM common stock, as we are writing, and the price of the IBM Prime, on the American Stock Exchange. IBM common closed at 120-7/8, and pays dividends of $4.40 for the year, while the IBM Prime closed at 110-1/4 and pays $4.35 for the year.

The yield on the common stock is 3.64%, while the yield on the Prime is 3.95%. This might not seem like much incentive for a speculatively minded investor interested in building capital, but to an institutional investor to whom return on invested capital is supremely important, that difference in yield is quite significant. Further, the funds received upon originally selling the Score could be invested in additional Primes, which would increase the return still further.

And would giving up appreciation potential beyond the $210 Termination Claim dissuade the institutional investor? Not in most cases, since IBM moving from 120-7/8 to 210 would be quite satisfactory from a conservatively approached investment standpoint.

So the institutional investor who originally tendered shares was, from that point of view, very comfortably situated with the remaining Primes, receiving the considerably higher yield for the 5-year life of the Americus Trust, and still guaranteed the substantial capital gain, if the stock went up from the price where the shares were tendered to the Termination Claim five years hence.

And the exchange of blue chip stock for the Americus Trust Unit was ruled by the Internal Revenue Service to be a tax-free exchange. Responding to all of the above logic, Americus Trusts

Table 1

Name	Term Date	Term Price
American Express (axp)	8-92	50.00
Amer Home Prod (ahp)	12-91	90.00
AT&T (att)	2-92	30.00
Amoco (an)	3-92	105.00
Atl Ritchfield (arc)	7-92	116.00
Bristol-Myers (bmy)	2-92	110.00
Chevron (chv)	7-92	75.00
Coca-Cola (ko)	7-92	56.00
Dow Chemical (dow)	5-92	110.00
Du Pont (dd)	3-92	110.00
Eastman Kodak (ek)	3-92	92.00
Exxon (xon)	9.90	60.00
Ford (f)	6-92	104.00
GTE (gte)	7-92	44.00
General Electric (ge)	5-92	140.00
General Motors (gm)	6-92	107.00
Hewlett-Packard (hwp)	7-92	90.00
IBM (ibm)	6-92	210.00
John & John (jnj)	6-92	118.00
Merck (mrk)	4-92	200.00
Mobil (mob)	6-92	60.00
Philip Morris (mo)	7-92	110.00
Procter & Gamble (pg)	6-92	105.00
Sears (s)	7-92	64.00
Union Pacific (unp)	4-92	87.00
Xerox (xrx)	7-92	97.00

for 26 blue chip stocks were successfully launched, and below we give the salient information on those 26 Americus Trusts.

THE PROFIT POTENTIAL OF THE AMERICUS TRUST SCORES

If the Score was not exerciseable for the underlying common stock until the Termination Date, it would not be such a remarkable investment instrument. But, in what we consider to be a stroke of genius, the originators of the whole concept, with Mr. Debe in the forefront, instituted a provision which applies to each and every Americus Trust; the provision stating that at any time, one Prime plus one Score could be turned in to the appropriate Americus Trust, and be exchanged for one share of common stock.

This made each Score a truly exciting vehicle for capital appreciation, on a par with any American-style Warrant, and, indeed, even more so, because the Scores represented Warrants on 26 top blue chips, which we enumerated in the table previously presented.

It is important that the reader follow the reasoning carefully, as to why the Scores have become so promising, because of this provision. We will use the example of the *Du Pont Score* for our explanation.

To begin with, for at least the time period since the October 1987 crash, when Scores were driven down to quite low price levels, the equation has persisted in unanimous fashion for all the Prime/Score situations, that one Prime plus one Score just about equals the current price of the underlying common stock.

To demonstrate this, we look at closing prices for a representative selection of Common/Prime/Score for July 26, 1989, do the necessary arithmetic, and once again make the findings (we have checked this many times on previous occasions) that the current prices of one Prime plus one Score does indeed approximately equal the common stock price.

If we go back to the November 1988 prices for Du Pont common, Prime and Score, we can see this "equation" in operation. Du Pont common was then selling at 79, the Du Pont Prime was selling at 72-1/8 and the Du Pont Score was selling at 7-1/8.

Table 2

Name	Prime	Score	Prime plus Score	Common
Amer Exp	29.87	6.37	36.25	35.50
AT&T	25.87	14.37	40.28	39.37
Coca-Cola	45.00	18.87	63.87	63.62
Dow Chem	75.12	18.25	93.37	90.75
Du Pont	88.75	26.62	115.37	115.00
GTE	39.87	17.87	57.75	57.87
Hlt Pack	44.75	8.12	52.87	52.12

Add 72-1/8 and 7-1/8 and you get 79-1/4, only 1/4 point more than Du Pont common.

And in our observation throughout, for all the 26 blue chips with Primes/Scores trading, the combination of Prime plus Score prices has always just about equaled the common stock price.

Now it is necessary to understand why the Du Pont Score went from 7-1/8 to 23-7/8, up 235%, when Du Pont common went from 79 to 105, up 33%; the Score advancing 7 times faster than Du Pont common. To do that we must understand what makes a Prime attractive, or less attractive, for purchase.

To begin with, as we have noted in previous paragraphs, the Prime gets the same dividend as the common stock (less that 5 cents fee), but sells at a lower price than the common stock; hence the yield is larger. The advantage may be only 1% or so, but to those who invest for yield—particularly institutional investors—that 1% can be quite important.

At this point, it will be useful for the reader to look at the next two pages which show Du Pont common and the Du Pont Score facing one another. Both charts are courtesy of *Daily Graphs*.

The reader should take note of the fact that although Du Pont common and the Du pont Score seemed to parallel one another in moving to the upside, we are talking of a common stock which reached the 110 area, and a Score which reached the 25 area. The leverage of the well-selected Score is very clear.

Figure 1 Warrants, Options and Convertibles

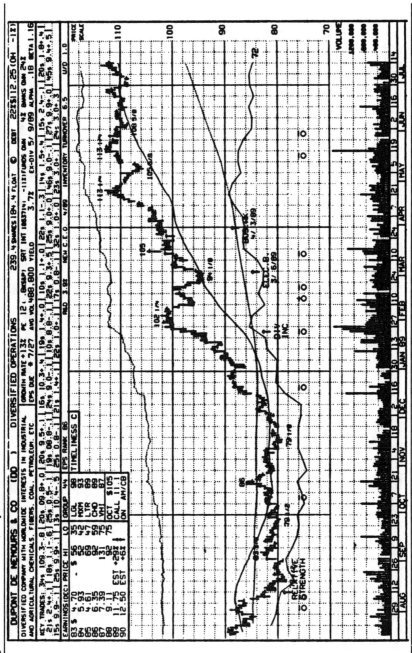

Figure 2 Scores

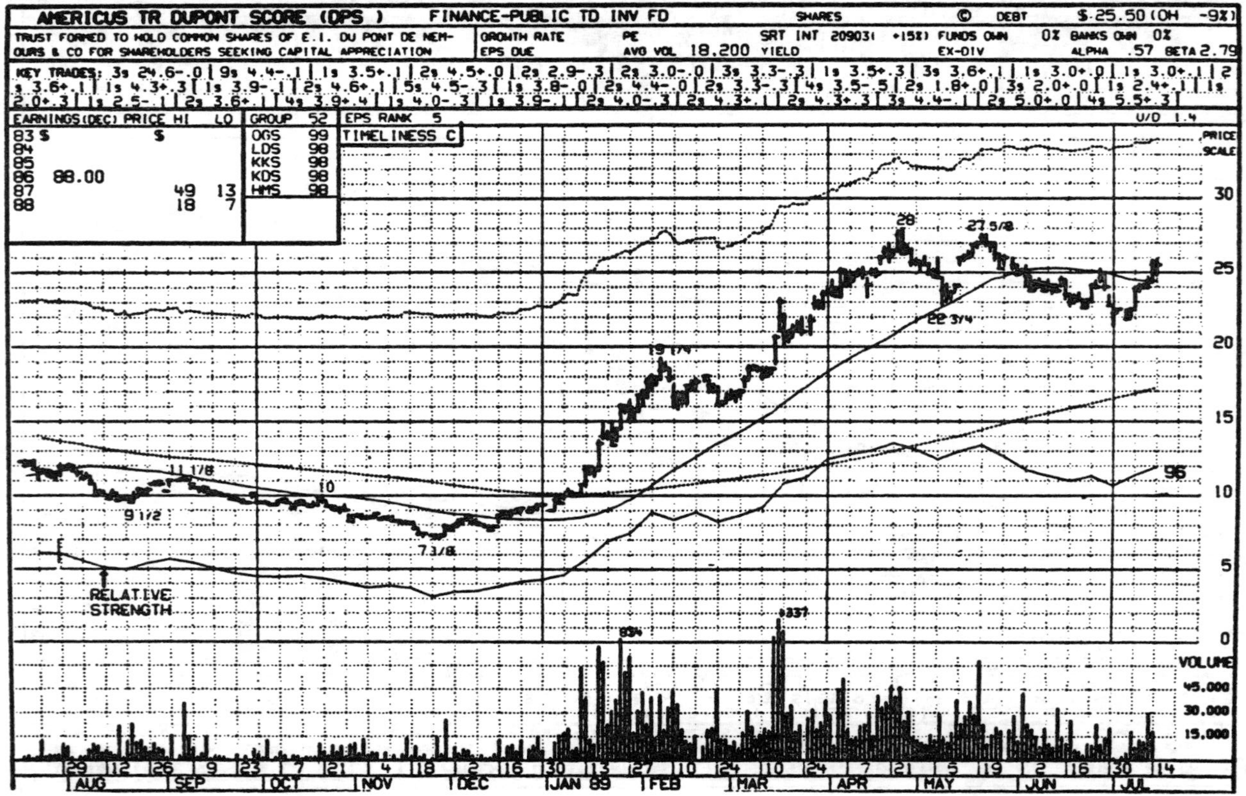

Continuing now with our discussion of the Du Pont Prime and Score, we look at the most important factor: the hoped-for capital gain when Termination Date arrives and the assets of the Americus Trust are distributed among Prime and Score.

Recall that the Prime is entitled to receive up to the Termination Claim price. If, then, the common stock and therefore, the Prime, are selling considerable below the Termination Claim price, the potential for capital gain is large, making it attractive for purchase. While if the Prime is selling much closer to the Termination Claim price, the capital gain potential is smaller, making the Prime that much less attractive for purchase.

In the case of Du Pont in November 1988, the Prime was selling at 72-1/8 while the Termination Claim price was $110. As Du Pont common rose in December 1988 and January 1989, and in the months following, the Prime rose as well. But as Du Pont came closer and closer to the $110 Termination Claim price, the capital gain potential of the Prime (the Difference between the Termination Claim price and the Prime price), became less and less, so the Prime rose less and less rapidly in relation to the common.

Since the "equation" reads: one Prime plus one Score just about equals one share of common stock, if the Prime lagged the common stock in its advance, the Score must make up the difference, which means advancing more rapidly.

That is why, between November 1988 - March 1989:

Du Pont common rose from 79 to 105   . . . up 33%

Du Pont Prime rose
from 72-1/8 to 82-1/4   . . . up 14%

while the Du Pont Score
rose from 7-1/8 to 23-7/8   . . . up 235%

A VALUABLE MEASURING TOOL FOR SCORES

What we have just described for Du Pont common, Prime and Score is one of the most important factors affecting this relatively new market instrument.

If the common stock is a considerable distance from the Termination Price, we would expect the Prime to keep pace with the common stock on any upside move, thereby giving the Score only limited scope for an appreciable advance.

If, on the other hand, as we saw in the late-1988-early-1989 months with Du Pont, the common stock approaches the Termination Price by dint of a substantial rise, then we should become very interested in the Score. Because any further rise in the common stock would find the Prime lagging in its advance, while the Score must advance, close to point-for-point with the common stock, giving it the kind of excellent leverage that we saw demonstrated with the Du Pont Score.

Because this factor is so important, from time to time, we present the Table 3 in which we calculate the common stock price as a percentage of the Termination Price.

The closer the individual Americus Trust is to the top of the table, the more likely it is that the Prime will lag, and the Score will begin to move rapidly to the upside on a percentage basis, if the common stock continues to move higher.

This does not mean that the Americus Trust Scores near the middle or the bottom of the list are to be ignored. The kind of moderate, even gentle, fluctuation they provide, with the similar fluctuation of the common stock, could be quite valuable in profitable trading techniques.

There is a whole range of profit-promising positions[1] that can be taken with the 26 scores on top blue chip companies, whether for leveraged profit on the up side or for short-term trading. We feel certain that close attention paid by investors to scores will be well rewarded.

---

1 For a detailed illustration, please see Sidney Fried, *Warrants, Options and Convertibles*, RHM Press, New York 1989.

Table 3

Name	Common Price	Termination Price	Common Price as % of Termination Price
Exxon	89.50	60.00	149.16%
Ford	105.25	104.00	101.20%
GTE	44.37	44.00	100.85%
AT&T	29.00	30.00	96.67%
Philip Morris	102.75	110.00	93.41%
American Home Products	81.87	90.00	91.00%
Merck	181.87	200.00	90.94%
Proctor & Gamble	87.37	105.00	83.21%
Du Pont	91.50	110.00	83.18%
General Motors	87.87	107.00	82.13%
Dow Chemical	89.62	110.00	81.48%
Bristol-Myers	88.50	110.00	80.45%
Coca-Cola	44.50	56.00	79.46%
Mobil	47.62	60.00	79.38%
Union Pacific	67.12	87.00	77.16%
Amoco	78.12	105.00	74.40%
Eastman Kodak	67.31	92.00	73.16%
Atlantic Richfield	84.50	116.00	72.84%
Johnson & Johnson	85.37	118.00	72.35%
Sears	41.75	64.00	65.23%
Chevron	48.50	75.00	64.67%
General Electric	89.75	140.00	64.11%
Xerox	59.12	97.00	60.95%
IBM	124.25	210.00	59.17%
Hewlett-Packard	52.50	90.00	58.33%
American Express	27.87	50.00	55.75%

Source: RHM Survey.

Chapter 15

Pricing Convertible Bonds

Thomas Ho
G.A.T.

INTRODUCTION

The convertible bond market is an important part of the fixed-income sector. The convertible bond offers the holder the option to convert a corporate bond into a specified number of shares of the firm, usually any time up to the maturity of the bond. Other features include:

- The call provision that allows the firm to buy back the bonds at prespecified prices
- The sinking fund requirement that obligates the firm to redeem the bonds over a period of time
- The put option that gives the investor the right to sell the bond back to the firm at a predetermined price

These features often dramatically affect the bond's behavior and value. Although similar to nonconvertible corporate bonds, convertible bonds represent a spectrum of vastly different securities. Because convertibles are hybrids of bonds and stocks, they must inherit all the complexities of the underlying instruments and behave in an often complicated fashion as a mix of two securities. While convertible securities offer many opportunities for investing and for formulating portfolio strategies, they are also relatively complicated to analyze. So, this chapter provides a basic framework for analyzing these securities given their diverse characteristics. It offers an analytical framework that enables bond issuers and investors to deal with these difficulties in a systematic fashion.

The description shows how the complex structure of a convertible may be broken down into five basic components: the underlying bond, the latent warrant, the latent call option, the sinking fund option and the put option. Then each component is analyzed separately, including the value and behavior of each part and how it affects the convertible bond. The analytical approach provides valuable insights into the convertible bond's behavior and demonstrates how the analysis yields fair value of a convertible bond.

THE BASIC FRAMEWORK

A description of the basic assumptions of the model uses the standard framework for studying securities pricing to derive the fair value of a convertible bond so the determining factors of the bond price must be considered in a specific way using perfect capital market assumptions.

It ignores all types of transaction costs: the commissions, the bid/ask spreads, the issuance costs and all the explicit costs that are involved in a transaction. The reason is that the price at which an investor can buy or sell a bond is not relevant; what is relevant is the price that the bond should be sold at equilibrium in order to determine the bond price if the market is functioning perfectly (i.e., at fair value).

These assumptions focus on the options aspect of the pricing problem, ignoring topics such as tax implications of the convertible, marketability of the issues, and corporate strategies. Although these issues are important to the bond pricing, they are beyond the scope of this chapter.

So the question here is, given the stock price and the investment value, how should a convertible bond be priced in a perfectly functioning market?

An Illustrative Example

There are many terminologies and notations used to describe a convertible bond. An example is Corroon and Black (CBL), 7.5, June 1, 2005. The bondholder can convert each $100 face value bond into 3.5714 Corroon and Black shares any time up to the maturity. (For the purposes of this chapter, $100 face amount denominations and the associated conversion values are used instead of the commonly used $1000 denomination). The issuer can call back the bond at 107.5 percent of par in year 1985. The call schedule then decreases linearly to 100 percent in 1994 and remains on that level until maturity. However, the firm cannot call the bonds before June 1, 1987 unless the common stock trades above 140 percent (the call trigger) of the conversion price at the time of call. The bond also has a sinking fund. The firm is obligated to retire 7.5 percent of the amount issued in each of the years 1995 through 2004.

On November 15, 1986, the stock was traded at $35/share and the bond was $131. The stock at that time was paying $0.65 dividend/share. The credit risk of the bond is given by the Moody's rating of A2. The information below is summarized with the notations of each item given in the first column:

Corroon and Black (CBL)

T	=	the bond maturity	6/1/2005
c	=	the bond coupon rate	7.5%
k	=	the conversion ratio	3.5714
t	=	the call trigger	140%
B	=	the market bond price	$131
S	=	the market stock price	$35
d	=	the dividend	$0.65
R	=	the rating	Moody's A2

Given this information, some other parameters can be calculated.

$$P = \text{parity (conversion value)}$$

The parity, or conversion value, is the value of the bond if the holder decides to convert. It is, therefore, the equity worth of the convertible bond; the share price is not important. More important is the parity, the product of the conversion ratio and the share price:

$$P = kS \text{ or } (3.5714 \times 35) = \$124.99$$

The conversion price, Cp, is the price of a share that creates parity value of \$100. That is,

$$100 = kCp$$

In this case, Cp equals \$28/share.

The investment value (I) is the value of the bond, ignoring the possibility of converting the bond to equity. The investment value is, therefore, the underlying bond value given by the present value of the bond cash flow (coupons and principal) adjusted for the credit risk, the sinking fund provision and other bond related features.

Basics of the Convertible Bond

The convertible offers the investor the upside return when the common stock value increases. This is possible because, when the stock value becomes high, the investor can convert the bond to equity. But that does not mean that the investor must convert to capture the price appreciation of the equity. When the parity value is high, the convertible trades like equity, and the convertible bond value appreciates in step with the stock price. If the stock value drops, the investor, at worst, still receives the coupons and principal. That is, the investor still holds the bond or has the investment value. As a result, the downside risk of the investment is protected.

In short, the convertible offers the upside return and protects the investor from the downside risk. The investor, in essence, is holding a straight bond and a warrant. A warrant is an instrument that provides the holder with the right to purchase a prespecified number of shares of stock at a specific price. Although this is a useful way of thinking about a convertible, it does not describe accurately most of the convertible bonds traded in the U.S. market.

With most bonds, investors are expected to be forced to convert to stocks in a relatively short time period. For this reason, it is more appropriate to think of the convertible bond as the parity value (the equity value) plus the present value of the coupons net of the present value of the dividends that the investor can receive before being forced to convert. This alternative way of viewing a convertible bond can affect the analysis of the bonds significantly.

However, this description of a convertible bond is incomplete because the estimate of the inflow of coupons net of dividends is inadequate to describe the option-like feature of the bond. The firm, at its option, can force the bondholders to convert the bond to equity, (It is the option of the firm,) and such an option must be priced. Below is a formal analysis of this and other option aspects of the problem.

THE CONVERTIBLE BOND MODELS

The simplest possible convertible bond model captures the essential features of the convertible; gradually, other features of the bond are incorporated to create a model that can describe adequately total bond behavior.

The Latent Warrant

First is the simplified version of the Corroon and Black (CBL) bond. To determine the fair value of the bond, assume that the bond has no call or sinking fund provisions, and has no credit risk. For the time being, even assume that the bond pays no coupon and the stock gives no dividends.

The important observation here is that, although the bondholder can convert the bond to stocks any time up to maturity, there are no economic incentives to do so. The argument is quite simple. If the investor converts the bond, then at maturity the investor has the prevailing value of the parity value. On the other hand if the investor holds the bond to maturity, the bond can be converted whenever it is beneficial to do so. Indeed when the parity value is above the bond value, the bondholder would convert. That is, the bondholder has the stock return, but also is guaranteed the minimum value of the bond par value (investment value). For this reason, it is always advantageous to hold the bond to maturity because there is value in retaining the option to convert. Even if the parity value is high and the convertible bond is traded like equity, the convertible bond still offers the protection of the downside risk. Once the conversion is effected the downside protection is eliminated.

Recognizing that there is no value to the early exercise, now focus on what the investor optimally should do at maturity. As described, when the parity is above par, the investor gives up the principal and receive the shares. But that is precisely the same as receiving the principal and using the amount to exercise a warrant. In sum, the convertible bond is the same as the basic bond plus a warrant when the exercise price of the bond is par value and the expiration date is the bond's maturity. This warrant is called the *latent warrant*.

To illustrate the latent warrant, refer to the CBL bond. It has a warrant that gives the holder the right, but not the obligation, to buy 3.5714 shares on 6/1/2005 for $100. Therefore, the latent warrant is a long-term American option.

Coupon and Dividends

So far, the analysis assumes that there are no coupon and dividends. But that assumption is made for the clarity of exposition,
and relaxing the assumption affects little of the analysis. The crux
of the argument is to recognize whether or not the warrant would
be exercised early. When the bond pays coupons, there is even less
incentive to exercise early because, in holding onto the bond, the
investor receives all the coupons in addition to retaining the option to the last minute. This ignores the dividends on the stock; in
fact, if the investor converts the bond to equity, he receives the
stock dividend. But it is clear that as long as the coupon payments
are higher than the dividends, the warrant would not be exercised
early. Luckily, most convertible bonds pay coupons that yield significantly more than the dividends on the stock. For this reason
the arguments apply for nearly all convertible bonds. For example
in the case of CBL, the annual dividend on the parity is given by
the product of the conversion ratio and the dividends ($0.65 \times
3.5714 = \$2.3214$). It is significantly less than the \$7.50 earned on
each \$100 par bond. Note that this ignores the growth rate of the
dividend/share for illustrative reasons.

As the investor holds the bond until maturity, the convertible
bond value should be equal to the consolidated investment value
of the underlying bond plus the latent warrant. The latent warrant
is denoted by W in a simple formula:

(1) $$B = I + W$$

It is instructive to represent the convertible bond value dia-
grammatically; the diagram is called the value diagram.

The Value Diagram

The value diagram is a graphic representation of the security's
value as a function of the parity value at any time before the

bond's maturity. This shows how the underlying bond value, latent warrant, the convertible bond and other related instruments change values as parity value varies.

On the value diagram, the y-axis is the value of any instrument, and the unit of measure is in dollars. The x-axis is the parity value, also in dollars. First, the underlying bond curve, which is the investment value of the bond. When the parity is high (stock value is high), presumably the bond has little credit risk; for this reason, the curve should be flat, taking the value of the present value of the coupons and principal.

However when the parity is low, the share value has dropped, reflecting a drop in the firm value. In this case, the bond credit risk increases and the bond value drops. The bond curve in Figure 1 depicts the behavior of this bond. The 45 degree line through the origin is called the parity line. It represents the convertible bond value at the instant that the bond is converted to equity (conversion value).

Note that the investor always converts when it is advantageous to do so. Because it is never advantageous for bondholders to convert the bond early, the convertible bond fair value must lie above both the underlying investment value and the parity value. For this reason, the curve that is the higher of the bond curve and the parity line represents the formula prices. The formula prices are the lower bound of the values of the convertible bond. Turning to the latent warrant, the formula value of the warrant is the higher of the following two lines: the 45 degree line starting from the exercise price (par value) and the horizontal line on the x-axis from the origin to the par value. The formula price curve represents the minimum value of the warrant.

Standard option theory shows that the minimum warrant value is in fact the 45 degree line that intersects the x-axis at the present value of the exercise price, or the present value of the par value, in this case. Given this argument, the warrant curve in Figure 2 can be sketched.

So the convertible bond is the sum of the bond curve and the warrant curve. It is represented in Figure 3, where the curve XY represents the convertible bond value. Figure 3 also depicts the

Figure 1 Bond Curve and Parity Line

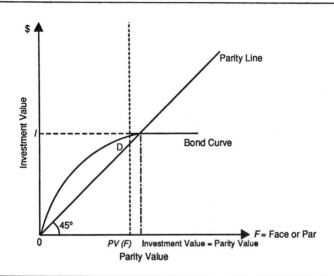

Figure 2 Warrant Curve

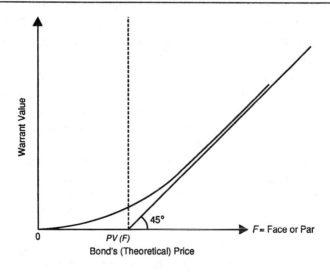

Figure 3   Composition of the Convertible Bond Value

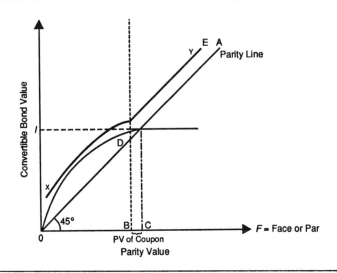

composition of the convertible bond value. The line OA is the parity line. However when the parity value is high, the convertible bond value does not converge to the parity line, instead it converges to the parallel line of DE. The distance of point D from the y-axis (the distance is the same as OB) is the present value of the face value of the bond. Because the bond value, or investment value, is the sum of the present value of the face value and the coupon value, it follows that the distance between the parity value and the line DE is the present value of the coupon. Therefore, the convertible bond value must exceed the higher of the investment value, or the sum of the parity value and the present value of the coupons. The level of excess is the term premium of the intent warrant. This excess is the cost to the convertible bondholder for having a position that participates on any upside return of the stock and is limited on the downside to the investment value of the bond.

Because the latent warrant is a long-term stock option, this excess value is very sensitive to the estimate of the stock return volatility. Unfortunately, the stock return volatility is not observable (as a price is observable). As a result, the market has to determine the precise value of the term premium, and convertible bond models can prove only relatively rough estimates of fair value.

If there is any dividend on the stock, the description can be altered by considering the present value of the coupon net of the dividends, instead of just the coupon. Many analyses of convertible bonds tend to focus on the latent warrant value. Unfortunately, this analysis is far from complete. As in the case of straight corporate bonds, the call provision must be taken into account in analyzing the convertible bond value.

First, the minimal value of the warrant is estimated by assuming that there is no early exercise of the dividend-paying stock. Then the option value is greater than the stock value (parity) net of both the present value of the stock dividends that the option holder will not receive and the present value of the strike price. In the case of the convertible bond in the earlier example with a 7 percent discount rate, the present value of the strike price over 19 years is $27.65. Assuming constant dividends (a conservative estimate) of $2.3214 per year, the present value of all the dividends in the next 19 years is the product of $2.3214 and the presaent value annuity factor at 7 percent for 19 years. The value is $26.3144. Therefore, the warrant value should exceed $71.025 ($124.99 − $27.65 − $26.3144).

Now the investment value of the bond can be estimated. It is shown that the investment value of the bond cannot be greater than the convertible bond traded price net of the lower bound value of the warrant. So the investment value cannot exceed $59.975 ($131 − $71.025).

The Call Feature

The call provisions on convertible bonds are quite homogeneous and in many ways are similar to the call provisions of industrial corporate bonds. The call provision allows the issuer to call back the bonds in part or in whole at the prespecified price, or the call price. The call schedule tends to decline linearly, reaching the lowest call price, or the par value, some time before maturity. But the similarities between the call provisions in the convertibles and the corporates end here.

Although the convertible bond call provision also has a call protection period, it is implemented differently. Most convertible bonds issued after 1985 have a call trigger price stated typically in percentages (140 percent, as in the case of CBL). In these cases, the firm cannot call the bond unless the common stock is traded above the product of the call trigger price and the conversion price. This restriction of calling the bonds applies only for a period of time, typically two to three years. After this call protection period, the firm can call the bonds whenever it is advantageous to the issuer. But that does not mean that the firm would call the bonds when they are traded slightly above the call price.

In fact for bonds with a coupon rate similar to those of the current new issues, a firm usually calls the bonds only when they are traded 20 to 25 percent above the call price. There are many arguments to explain this observation. For example when the bond is called, the investor has one month to decide whether to convert the bond into stock or surrender it for cash based on the call price.

If it cannot be sure whether the investors will decide on cash or shares, the firm must prepare to issue the shares as well as to pay cash. This scenario may create administrative complications. However if the firm waits until the market price of the stock reaches a level that makes it obviously more advantageous to convert rather than to accept cash, then the firm calls its bonds. In line with this reasoning, the firm would have to decide that, over the one month period, there would be a small probability that the stock price would drop to a level causing investors to change their minds and select cash.

Notice here that calling the bond is motivated by the rise in the parity value. There is also another reason: it may be an optimal call period. Market interest rates have fallen significantly, then the firm may call the bond to refinance the issue at a lower interest cost. In this case, there is no need to consider the complexities involved in forced conversion. The firm may call the bond because it is economically optimal.

Without dwelling on this issue, note that the convertible bonds usually are called when the bonds are traded significantly above the call price for whatever reason.

When the bond is called, the parity value must be high or the bond would not be traded at such a high premium. For this reason, the investors always prefer to convert into equity than to receive that call price. This calling of bonds is called *forced conversion* and is the most important aspect of the call provision of the convertibles. The provision is used by the firm to force the bondholders to convert the bond into equity.

This forced conversion feature significantly affects the pricing of the convertible. Suppose there is a market consensus that when the convertible bond trades above a price, called the *implicit call price*, i.e., the bond is to be called. Also note that the more volatile the stock, the higher this implicit call price is. So from the previous description, the spread between the implicit call price and the stated call price depends on the stock return volatility.

No investor would pay a price higher than the implicit call price, no matter how high the parity value rises. Refering to the value diagram, note that when the convertible bond rises in step with the higher parity value, it must rise at a slower rate as the value approaches the implicit call price. When the bond value reaches the implicit call price, the bond price must be the parity value because the investor should be indifferent about whether to hold the bond or to convert to equity. Referring to Figures 3 and 4, note how the call provision affects the bond values.

In Figure 4, the convertible bond value must be capped by the implicit call price. As the parity value rises, the convertible bond value rises in step. But as the convertible bond value approaches the implicit call price, the market anticipates the firm's calling the bond and the bondholders convert the bonds to the parity value.

For this reason, the market still trades the bond at the parity value. Figure 4 depicts this relationship between the parity value and the convertible bond value.

Figure 4   Effect of the Implicit Call Price

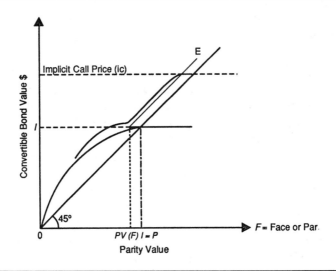

The Latent Call Option

The forced conversion of the bond introduces another option built into the convertible bond, the *latent call option*, denoted by C. This time, the issuer decides the optimal exercise of the option. In exercising the option, the issuer forces bondholders to convert the bond to equity. In so doing, the firm saves the present value of the coupons in subsequent years. If the convertible bond value does not rise above the implicit call price, the firm does not call the bond and the call option has little value. Therefore, the latent call option is valuable to the firm for saving the interest costs.

The most striking feature of the latent call option is that the option pricing behavior has to be significantly different than the stock option. The major difference is that no matter how high the underlying asset value (in this case, the convertible bond value), the value of the option is capped. It does not rise unbounded like the stock option because the latent call option allows the firm to save the interest cost which has a maximum value.

In the presence of the call provision, the convertible bond has three components. The pricing formula is:

$$(2) \qquad\qquad B = I + W - C$$

The impact of the call option on the convertible bond price is best illustrated by the example of the CBL bond again.

From Equation 2:

$$(3) \qquad\qquad C = I + W - B$$

But it was argued earlier that the warrant value must exceed the parity value net of the present value of the dividends and the preset value of par. So $C > I + P - PV(d) - PV(\text{par}) - B$. But by definition,

$$(4) \qquad\qquad C > P + PV(c) - PV(d) - B$$

Here, P is the parity value, $PV(c)$ the present value of the coupons out to the bond maturity, $PV(d)$ the present value of the dividends out to the bond maturity and PV (par) the present value of par.

Now estimate the numbers for B, P, c, d, and $PV(\text{par})$. B is $131. P is $124.99. Assume a 7 percent discount rate (the prevailing ten-year rate) and a conservative estimate of a constant dividend of $2.3214 per year. The present value of the annuity of the coupon net of the dividends over 19 years is $58.696 (the present value annuity factor is 11.3343). Therefore using Equation 4, the latent call option has a value of more than $52,686.

In the presence of the call provision, investors no longer believe they can hold the bond to maturity, as described above. They expect to be forced to convert. Therefore, the convertible bond price is not the sum of the parity and the present value of all the coupons. In the presence of the call provision, it is the sum of the parity and the present value of the coupons up to forced conversion. This line of argument can be used to calculate when the bond would be forced to convert. Let the time be b years. The present value of the coupons and dividends in b years is PV(coupons) and PV(d). The bond value is B and the parity value is P. Therefore, the following equation must hold.

(5) $B = P + PV(\text{coupons}) - PV(d)$

Using Equation 3 and the time b, it is relatively straightforward to calculate that the market expects the bond to be called. Notice that this is precisely the breakeven analysis often used by convertible investors. Although this approach seems tractable and useful, there are several assumptions. Indeed, Equation 3 can be derived from Equation 2 if several assumptions are made. First, the latent warrant is traded sufficiently in-the-money that its value is approximated by the formula price of $P - PV(\text{strike price})$. Noting that the strike price is the par value:

(6) $W = P - PV(\text{par value})$

Also if the premium of the latent call option is negligible (the market is quite certain about when the firm will call the bonds), the C (option value) is the present value of the coupons not paid to the investors.

(7) $C = PV(\text{coupon after } b)$

Combining Equations 3, 6, and 7, Equation 5 is calculated.

The above analysis shows that if the break-even analysis is-sued to determine the expected time of forced conversion, it must be assumed that the warrant is very much in-the-money and the volatility of the latent call option is negligible.

THE PREMIUM DIAGRAM

Now consider two polar cases. When the stock prices are high so that the parity value is significantly higher than the investment value, the market should anticipate a forced conversion. For this reason, the convertible bond should be traded very near the parity value. On the other hand when the stock value drops significantly so that the bondholder does not expect to convert the bond to eq-uity, then the convertible bond would trade near its investment value. These two polar cases of the convertible bond's perfor-mance are relatively straightforward.

Of course, the important part of pricing the convertible bonds occurs when the parity value is close to the investment value. In this region, the convertible bond value is influenced greatly by the latent warrant value and the latent call value; therefore, the con-vertible bond value is no longer a simple relationship to the parity and investment value. Pricing the convertible bond value, in this case, requires the modeling of the warrant value and the call op-tion value.

There is much insight into the bond behavior if the fair value of the bond in the premium diagram, which is derived from the value diagram, is analyzed. While the value diagram is concerned with the absolute value of the bond, the premium diagram is con-cerned with the parity value and the convertible bond value as percentages to the investment's value (ratio). This way, the pre-mium diagram focuses on the region where the parity value is close to the investment value. Also by normalizing the convertible bond values around the investment value it is possible to cross-compare different convertible bond pricing behaviors. Figure 5 provides a summary depiction.

Specifically, the x axis of the premium diagram is defined as the ratio of the parity value and the investment value. For example, when the x value is unity, the parity value is the same as the investment value. The y axis of the premium diagram is the ratio of the convertible bond value to the investment value. In essence, the premium diagram depicts the relationship between the convertible bond value and the parity value normalized by the investment value of the bond.

The Intrinsic Value

The premium diagram can be derived from Figure 4. The striking result is that the premium seems to represent a call option, as the normalized convertible bond value rises monotonically from 1 to a 45 degree line. Perhaps this is the source of confusion in defining the latent warrant because the value curve looks somewhat similar to a warrant value curve. But as the analysis has shown, this curve represents two options. And this curve is not specified by the standard parameters: expiration date, exercise price and volatility.

To illustrate this point, it is instructive to consider a special and somewhat unrealistic case. Assume that there is no stock return uncertainty. And for simplicity, assume that the stock does not pay any dividend. To be consistent with the no arbitrage argument, the stock must appreciate at a risk-free rate, which also is assumed with certainty. Now the premium diagram of a convertible bond can be constructed.

The bond behavior is analyzed in four regions. First when the parity value is low, the bond-to-the-investment-value ratio is unity; therefore, the value curve is depicted by AB in Figure 5. Point C is the present value of the exercise price of the latent warrant (divided by the investment value). When the parity ratio goes beyond point C, the bondholder is expected to convert the bond to equity at the bond maturity. That is, the convertible bond must now incorporate the intrinsic value of the latent warrant value. For this reason, the value curve must increase along the 45 degree line, depicted by line CD.

As the parity ratio increases, the value curve also increases in step. But the value curve cannot go beyond the implicit call price. Indeed when the bond value reaches the call price, the bond price

Figure 5   Premium Diagram

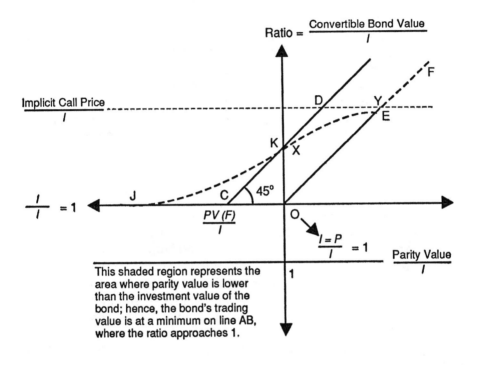

This shaded region represents the area where parity value is lower than the investment value of the bond; hence, the bond's trading value is at a minimum on line AB, where the ratio approaches 1.

remains at the value even if the parity value continued to increase. This behavior is depicted by the line DE, which indicates when the call option has value to the issuer. In this case, the issuer can call back the bonds, and eliminate the ability of the bondholder to collect the coupons on the bond and to convert the bond to equity at maturity.

Finally, remember that the convertible bond cannot be traded below the parity value. Therefore when the line DE meets the parity line, the convertible bond trades at parity. The explanation is quite simple. When the parity value is sufficiently high, the bond simply is traded at the parity anticipation of a forced conversion.

When the firm calls the bond, the bondholder converts the bonds to equity without losing any value. In this region, the bond curve is represented by the line EF.

The piecewise linear graph ABCDEF represents the intrinsic value of the convertible bond. To construct the intrinsic-value graph requires the (estimated) value of the parity, present value of the warrant exercise price, the investment value and the call price (or implicit call price). The important point is that all these parameters, in principle, can be measured, so the intrinsic-value graph can be constructed without developing complex mathematical models.

The Fair Value

The intrinsic value of the convertible bond is derived by assuming no uncertainty. In the presence of uncertainty, the convertible bond fair-value curve deviates from this intrinsic-value graph. It is a smooth curve because it is reasonable to assume that the uncertainty is resolved in a continuous and smooth manner. For this reason, the convertible bond value must relate to the parity value in a smooth fashion.

Such a fair-value curve is depicted in Figure 5 by XY. The curve must originate from point F because, under uncertainty, the bond is called when it reaches the implicit call price; at this point, the bond must be worth only the parity value. As the parity value drops, the bond value must drop because, in the world of uncertainty, the bond value can be, at most, the implicit call price. Meanwhile if the parity value drops significantly to the region CD, the bond value also drops. For this reason, the bond value has to come down instead of remaining at the call price as in the certainty case.

On the other hand, consider the region OA. In this instance, the minimum value of the bond is the investment value. But if the parity value increases substantially, the bond also incorporates the warrant intrinsic value. For this reason, the bond trades above the investment value. This resulting fair-value curve is depicted by JK.

The complete fair-value curve must link curves XY and JK smoothly, as depicted by YJ.

The precise fair-value curve is determined by the level of the stock-return uncertainty: the higher the uncertainty, the smaller the curvature of the fair-value graph. But in any case, the intrinsic-value graph provides a valuable frame of reference for pricing or analyzing a convertible bond. Also, what is clear from this analysis is that the convertible bond fair-value curve is not a simple option-value curve because it is a combination of the latent warrant and the latent call option. Analysis that focuses on either the warrant value or the call option value (by using the breakeven analysis) is misleading. The two aspects of the problem have to be studied together, and the convertible bond intrinsic-value graph provides such a framework.

SUMMARY

This chapter provided a framework for ascertaining a convertible bond's fair-value. It was shown that, for most convertible bonds traded in the market, the bond value incorporates both the warrant and call option values. It also was shown that, by constructing a graph depicting the intrinsic value of the convertible bond under different stock values, the capability of identifying and analyzing the effects of the warrant and call options is enhanced.

PART III

INVESTMENT, HEDGING AND TRADING STRATEGIES

Chapter 16

Using Currency Futures and Options

Chicago Mercantile Exchange

INTRODUCTION

Trading in currency futures at the International Monetary Market® (IMM) division of the Chicago Mercantile Exchange (CME) began on May 16, 1972. The opening bell at the IMM signaled the beginning of a new era in futures trading—currency futures represented the first step in the development of financial futures.

The rapid growth in the use of currency futures is indicative of the utility that these markets have for a variety of users—foreign and domestic banks, foreign exchange brokers, institutional traders, corporate treasurers and public investors. These contracts provide a mechanism for price "discovery" and hedging, which are the most important economic benefits of an organized futures exchange.

Over the next decade, speculative, arbitrage and hedge trading increased liquidity in currency futures; in early 1984, the CME introduced options on those futures.

Also in 1984, the Singapore International Monetary Exchange (SIMEX) opened trading in Deutsche mark, British pound and Japanese yen futures. The contracts are identical to those traded on the CME, and are cleared through a mutual offset system, whereby a position can be opened at one exchange, and held or offset at the other. Options on Deutsche mark and Japanese yen futures also are traded at SIMEX. The effect of this arrangement is that the trading hours are expanded greatly, allowing hedgers and traders to adjust positions to late-breaking news during hours when the more local exchange is closed.

Foreign exchange traders are finding that by using futures and options on futures, they are able to reduce the exposure of a spot or forward position, or temporarily substitute futures and options positions for cash transactions they plan to make at a later date.

The exchange provides three elements essential to futures and options trading:

- An efficient central market, which brings together differing viewpoints of future values
- An open market available to all participants
- A market that eliminates certain credit risks. The clearing house acts as the seller to every buyer and as the buyer to every seller in each futures and options transaction

MONITORING CME CONTRACT PRICES

The exchange quotes all currency futures and options prices in "American terms," which is the dollar price of each foreign currency unit (e.g., $.6000 per Swiss franc). Those familiar with European terms (e.g., SF 1.6667 per dollar) need to convert to American terms by taking the reciprocal of the European quote. For example, SF 1.6000 per dollar is equivalent to $.6250 per Swiss franc.

$$\left(\frac{1}{1.6000} = .6250 \right)$$

Figure 1   IMM Currency Futures Trading Volume

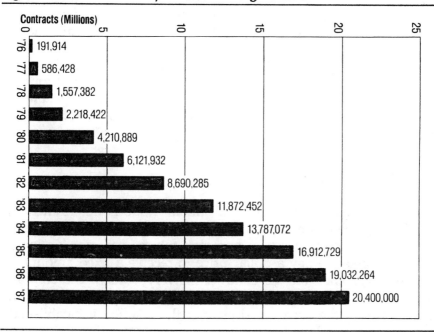

Figure 2   Options on IMM Currency Futures Volume

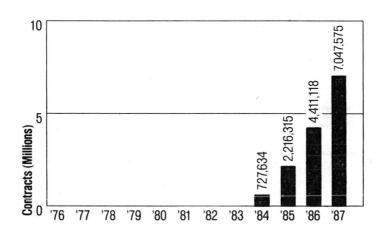

CME currency contract price activity can be monitored daily in the business pages of most major newspapers. The displays reproduced below are examples of the way these prices are shown in *The Wall Street Journal*.

An easy way to calculate the dollar value of a price change or an option premium is to ignore the decimal point, and multiply by the value of one point, listed in Appendices I and II. For example, a Deutsche mark price change of .0011 represents 11 × $12.50, or $137.50.

CURRENCY FUTURES CONTRACTS

A currency futures contract's total dollar value is determined by multiplying the contract amount (i.e., DM 125,000) by the price of the contract. The buyer of a currency futures contract (a "long" position) agrees to pay a dollar price to receive a fixed amount of the other currency on the contract delivery date (if the contract position has not been "offset" by resale). The buyer profits, if the dollar price of the currency rises after the position is established. For example, if a long September Swiss franc position is taken at

Table 1   Futures

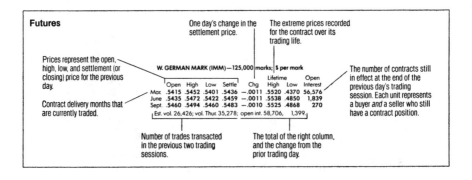

Table 2   Options on Futures

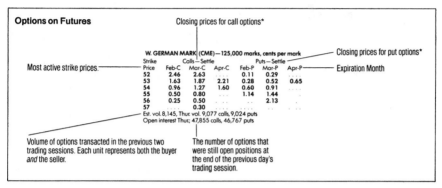

| Options on Futures | | | Closing prices for call options* | | | | |

W. GERMAN MARK (CME)—125,000 marks, cents per mark — Closing prices for put options*

Most active strike prices.

Strike	Calls—Settle			Puts—Settle			Expiration Month
Price	Feb-C	Mar-C	Apr-C	Feb-P	Mar-P	Apr-P	
52	2.46	2.63	....	0.11	0.29	....	
53	1.63	1.87	2.21	0.28	0.52	0.65	
54	0.96	1.27	1.60	0.60	0.91	....	
55	0.50	0.80	....	1.14	1.44		
56	0.25	0.50	....	....	2.13	....	
57	....	0.30	....	....			

Est. vol. 8,145, Thur. vol. 9,077 calls, 9,024 puts
Open interest Thur; 47,855 calls, 46,767 puts

Volume of options transacted in the previous two trading sessions. Each unit represents both the buyer *and* the seller.

The number of options that were still open positions at the end of the previous day's trading session.

*The dollar price represented by a premium quotation equals the quote multiplied by the number of currency units covered in the underlying futures. For example, a quote of 0.50 for a 55 call represents a dollar premium of 0.50¢ x DM 125,000 = $625.

.4200 and the price then rises to .4220, the long is credited a profit of $250. The contract value has risen from $52,500 ($.4200 × SF125,000) to $52,750 ($.4220 × SF125,000). The seller of the contract, the "short," agreed to deliver 125,000 Swiss francs, and is debited a loss of $250.

Futures prices are related closely to "spot" (or cash) exchange rates, but there is a difference which is due to different delivery times. This difference—the futures price minus the spot price—is called the "basis." The basis tends toward zero as the delivery day for the futures contract approaches; as a result, the futures delivery ultimately becomes a spot delivery. They become perfect substitutes for each other, hence they should have equal value. This principle is very important in a futures market because it is the essence of the use of the futures for "forward pricing" or fixing of costs in advance.

In foreign exchange, the basis reflects the interest-rate differential between countries. If there are no restrictions for trade and capital flow, forward rates vary inversely with the interest-rate differential between two countries. For example, if interest rates are two percent higher in Canada than in the United States, the for-

Figure 3   The Convergence of Spot and Futures Prices

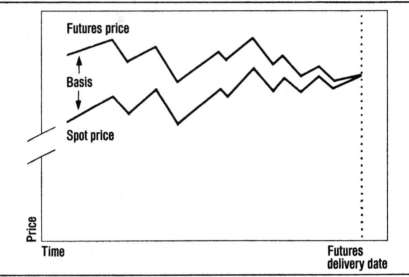

ward price for Canadian dollars should be at a two percent discount on an annual basis in terms of U.S. dollars.

Basis Trading

A trader can test current market prices to see if they properly reflect the interest-rate differential. A general formula for calculating the basis derived from those rates is:

Equation for Equilibrium Basis

$$\left(\begin{array}{c} \text{Spot} \\ \text{Exchange} \\ \text{Rate} \end{array}\right) \times \left(\begin{array}{c} \text{Euro--} \\ \text{dollar} \\ \text{Rate} \end{array}\right) - \left(\begin{array}{c} \text{Euro--} \\ \text{currency} \\ \text{Rate} \end{array}\right) \times \left(\begin{array}{c} \text{Days to} \\ \underline{\text{Delivery}} \\ 360^* \end{array}\right)$$

* A 360-day denominator is used. This would be correct for Deutsche marks, French francs, Japanese yen and Swiss francs; but the basis for British pounds, Australian dollars and Canadian dollars is calculated using a 365-day denominator, a commonly accepted conversion.

The spot exchange rate here is quoted American-style, as dollars per unit of the other currency. The Eurodollar and Eurocurrency interest rates used are those for the maturity that coincides with the delivery date of the futures contract.

Given a calculation of the equilibrium basis, the "theoretically correct" futures price is the spot price plus this basis. Any discrepancy between the theoretical futures price and the actual price available in the futures market means that a profitable arbitrage opportunity exists.

Consider the following assumptions, for example:

> Spot market value date: March 19
> Delivery date for June British pound futures: June 18
> Spot three-month Eurocurrency rates**
>   E$9 7/8%
>   E£9 5/16%
> Spot value of the British pound: $1.4570

The equilibrium basis for the June British pound contract is computed as follows:

$$\text{Equilibrium Basis} = 1.4570 \, (.098750 - .093125) \times \frac{91}{365}$$

$$= \frac{1.4570 \times .005625 \times 91}{365}$$

$$= +.0020$$

The equilibrium basis is added to the spot rate for British pounds to determine a theoretical futures price of 1.4590. If the actual futures price is less than 1.4590, the trader sells spot British pounds and buys futures; if the actual futures price is greater than

---

** The decision to use the bid or offered side of the market would depend on whether or not trader were a bank dealer. Thus the theoretical futures price may be slightly different for different market participants.

1.4590, he buys spot and sells futures. Of course, a sufficient differential is needed to compensate for transactions costs; but these account for only a few price ticks.

Spread Trading

Basis analysis can be used to profit directly from the futures market, excluding any cash market transaction. Once the trader knows the equilibrium basis from spot to each contract month, the interdelivery spread that brings parity is simply additive. For example:

June-to-Sept. basis = Spot-to-Sept. basis – Spot-to-June basis

If the actual difference between June and September futures prices is positive, but less than the expected June-to-September spread, the trader can buy September and sell June futures. When June and September prices return to a normal relationship (monitoring the interest differentials which are relevant to June and September deliveries), the trader buys back the June and sells back the September futures, gaining the difference between the actual and the expected spread.

Figure 4   Dollar Price of the Deutsche Mark

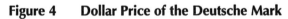

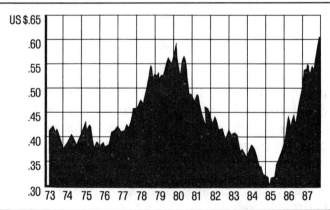

Figure 5   Dollar Price of the British Pound

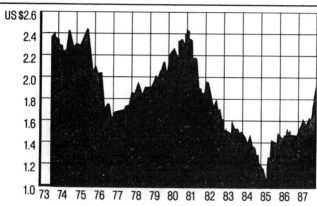

Figure 6   Dollar Price of the Swiss Franc

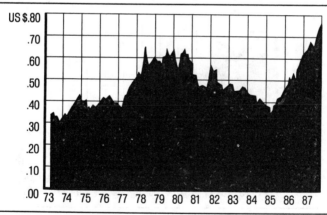

Lower margin requirements for futures spread positions make this style of trading attractive. Another advantage is that brokerage commissions usually are lower on a per-contract basis for spreads.

Figure 7   Dollar Price of the Japanese Yen

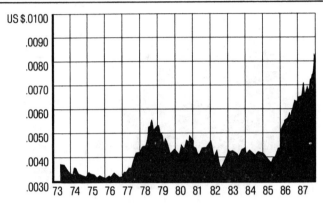

Figure 8   Dollar Price of the Canadian Dollar

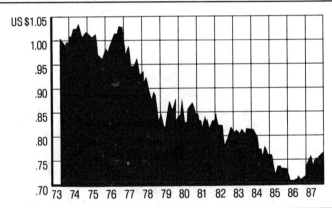

Comparison of the Currency Futures Market With the Interbank Market

Dealers in the Interbank market offer forward contracts, which provide benefits that are similar to those of futures contracts. But

Figure 9   Dollar Price of the Australian Dollar*

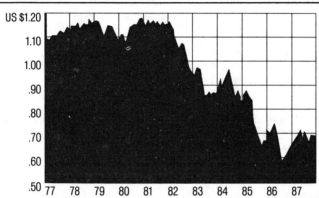

the two types of contracts have distinct differences. The following summarizes the major differences between the two markets.

Futures Market	Spot & Forward Interbank Market
1. Trading is conducted in a competitive arena by "open cry" of bids, offers and amounts.	1. Trading is done by telephone or telex, with banks generally dealing directly with other banks, foreign exchange brokers or corporations.
2. Participants are either buyers or sellers of a contract at a single, specified price at any given time.	2. Participants usually make two-sided markets (quoting two prices that indicate a willingness to buy at the lower price and sell at the higher price) for both spot and forward prices.

* These graphs plot the currencies' dollar exchange rate in the cash market. They all reflect "American terms" (dollars per unit of currency) as do IMM currency futures prices.

Futures Market	**Spot & Forward Interbank Market**
3. Non-member participants deal through brokers (Exchange members) who represent them on the trading floor.	3. Participants deal on a principal-to-principal basis, either directly or through brokers.
4. Market participants usually are unknown to one another, except when a firm is trading its own account through its own brokers on the trading floor.	4. Participants in each transaction always know the other trading party.
5. Participants include banks, corporations, financial institutions, investment companies, individual investors and speculators.	5. Participants are banks dealing with each other, and other major commercial entities. Access for individuals and smaller firms is limited.
6. Trading prices of currency futures are disseminated continuously by the CME.	6. Indicated bids and offers, as opposed to actual prices, are available throughout the Interbank market.
7. The exchange's clearinghouse becomes the opposite side to each cleared transaction; therefore, credit risk is reduced substantially.	7. Each counter-party with whom a dealer does business must be examined individually as a credit risk, and credit limits set for each. As such, there may be a wide range of credit capabilities of participants.
8. Margins are required of all participants.	8. Margins are not required by banks dealing with other banks, although for smaller, non-bank customers, margins may be required on certain occasions.
9. Settlements are made daily via the exchange's clearinghouse. Gains on position values may be withdrawn and losses are collected daily.	9. Settlement takes place two days after the spot transaction (one day in the U.S. for the Canadian Dollar). For forward transactions, gains or losses are realized on the settlement date.

Futures Market	**Spot & Forward Interbank Market**
10. All positions, whether long or short, can be liquidated easily.	10. Forward positions are not as easily offset or transferred to other participants.
11. Standardized dates are used for all contract months, concentrating liquidity to produce maximum price competition.	11. Settlement of forward contracts can be at any date agreed upon between the buyer and seller.
12. Contract size is standardized in terms of currency amount.	12. Participants can trade any amount agreed upon between the buyer and seller.
13. Prices are quoted in U.S. terms (dollar units per one foreign currency unit).	13. Prices are quoted in European terms (units of local currency to the dollar) except for British pounds and some Commonwealth currencies.
14. A single roundturn (in and out of the market) commission is charged. It is negotiated between broker and customer, and is relatively small in relation to the value of the contract. Commissions are business expenses and generally are tax-deductible.*	14. No commission is charged if the transaction is made directly with another bank or customer. A commission is charged to both the buyer and seller, however, if transacted through a foreign exchange broker. Commissions are business expenses and generally tax-deductible.*

OPTIONS ON CURRENCY FUTURES

Taking a position on a currency by buying a call or a put option requires no margin. The price (also called the premium) paid for the option is the absolute limit of the buyer's risk. As an option buyer, there is the right, but not the obligation, to take a position

* Traders should consult their tax counsel before entering the market.

in the underlying futures contract.[1] A futures position can be taken by "exercising" the option, re-selling it in the market, or simply letting the option expire if it has no value.

Buying a call option gives the right to buy the underlying futures at a specific price, even if the current price is higher. Calls gain value when the futures price rises quickly. Buying a put option gives the right to sell the futures at a specific price, even if the current price is lower. Puts gain value when the futures price falls quickly.

Calls and puts are distinct contracts, and there is a seller for every buyer of either. The option "writer," who sells the option to open a position, assumes the obligation of taking a futures position opposite to the option holder, if the option is exercised. The call writer stands ready to take a short futures position. The put writer stands ready to take a long futures position.[2]

The option writer sells the right to exercise in order to earn the premium income. Such a position carries unlimited risk, but can be liquidated at any time before expiration by buying the same option. Many option writers limit their risks by writing the option against an opposite futures, cash or option position. This enables any loss on the written option to be offset by profit from the other position.

Strike Prices And Expirations

Calls and puts are always available at various "strike" prices. The strike (or exercise) price of an option is the price at which a futures position is taken upon exercise. Strike prices are listed for trading both above and below the current futures level; when the futures price changes significantly, new strike prices are listed accordingly.

---

1   Upon taking a futures position, a margin deposit will be required.

2   The writer of an option is required to post a margin deposit when the position is opened. The amount of margin required is recalculated daily as the option's market price changes. The writer of an option must post margin because it is the writer who must stand ready to take a futures position at a possibly unfavorable price at any time before the position is closed.

Option expirations are listed for every calendar month. The three monthly expirations within a quarter are all exercisable into the quarter-end futures contract. For example, for January, February and March options, exercise will result in a March-delivery futures position.

While currency futures are very straightforward, currency options allow a choice of long or short, call or put, strike price and expiration. The option trader has the flexibility of choosing the length, the probabilities and the leverage of the position.

Option Prices

Each option covers one futures contract, and the "tick," or minimum price change, is worth exactly the same dollar amount for either. If the decimal in either quotation is ignored and multiplied by the value of one point (see Appendices I and II), the dollar value of the prices and price changes can be determined easily.

The price of a currency option is directly related to the underlying futures price, rather than to the current exchange rate. The option price is shaped by the following three factors.

1. **Relationship of the strike price of the option to the current underlying futures price.** If the current futures price is higher than a call's strike price, the call is said to be "in-the-money." If the call holder exercises it today, he takes a long futures position at the strike price. The difference between the futures price and the strike price is the amount he will be credited, and is termed the option's "intrinsic value."

   Similarly, if the futures price is lower than the strike price of a put, that put is "in-the-money." The exercise of an in-the-money put results in a sale of the futures at an above-market price.

   In general, the greater an option's intrinsic value, the higher that option's premium. If the option is "out-of-the-money" (currently has no intrinsic value because the futures price is lower than the call's strike or higher than the put's strike) the more out-of-the-money it is, the lower the option premium.

2. **Time.** The more time that remains until an option's expiration, the higher the premium tends to be. The longer time period provides more opportunity for the underlying futures price to move to a point where the purchase or sale of the futures at the strike price becomes profitable. Therefore, an option with three months remaining until expiration has a higher price than an option with the same strike price/futures price relationship and with only two months until expiration. The time component of an option's value tends to be largest when the underlying futures contract is trading near the exercise price of the option—that is, when an option is "at-the-money."

   An option is a wasting asset. As the option approaches maturity, the time value declines to zero. At expiration, the option's value is only its in-the-money amount.

3. **Volatility.** The more the underlying futures price tends to fluctuate, the higher the potential profit on the option. Volatility is a measure of the degree of fluctuation in the futures price. If volatility increases with all else remaining the same, the option price rises; and if it declines, the option price falls.

The "Delta Factor"

Delta is the rate of change in the option premium in relation to the change in the underlying futures price, expressed in percentage terms. Because option premiums do not always move by the same amount as the underlying futures price, this delta factor is used.

Generally, a price change in the underlying futures results in a smaller change in the option premium. Suppose that a Deutsche mark's futures price rises by 25 points, and the call option on that futures contract rises by 12 or 13 points. It is obvious that the option premium gained only about half of what the futures price did. This indicates that particular call option's delta is 50 percent. If the futures price were to fall, the delta factor helps predict a similar loss in the value of the option premium.

Deltas range from zero percent (for deep out-of-the-money options) to 100 percent (for deep in-the-money options). At-the-money options have delta factors of approximately 50 percent.

So deltas change with the futures price: as futures move from in-the-money to at-the-money to out-of-the-money, the delta gets smaller. Conversely, the delta becomes larger as the futures move from out of- to at- to in-the-money. Changes in delta are influenced by such factors as time left until expiration and the implied volatility.

The table below lists hypothetical deltas for some calls with the Japanese yen futures price at .6100, and with various lengths of time remaining until expiration. Notice the symmetry represented. Put deltas have a very similar distribution if the strike prices across the top are reversed in order.

For an out-of-the-money call like the 63¢-strike, it makes sense that as time to expiration diminishes, so does the delta. With only a week to expiration, a small futures price move does not attract many buyers to the call, so that call's price does not react. On the other hand with only a week to expiration, the 59¢-strike call is very likely to finish in-the-money. Even a small futures price change reflects a change in the potential in-the-money amount at

Table 3   Hypothetical Call Deltas (with the futures price at .6100)

Call strikes:	59¢	60¢	61¢	62¢	63¢
Time remaining:					
1 day	100%	100%	50%	–	–
1 week	99%	86%	50%	14%	2%
1 month	86%	71%	51%	31%	16%
3 months	74%	63%	51%	39%	29%
6 months	68%	60%	52%	43%	35%

volatility = 11%, interest rate = 9%

expiration, so, the call's price varies nearly one-to-one with the future's price.

An option's delta also can be considered a rating of the probability that the option will expire in-the-money. The preceding table reflects the influences of time passing and of the future's price/strike price relationship, but the probability also is affected by changes in the volatility of the futures price. If the futures price volatility increases, it widens the range of probable outcomes for the futures price at expiration. This increases the time value of the options, and drives all the option deltas toward 50 percent. The table below shows the deltas of the same options as in the prior example, but reflects a much higher level of volatility in the futures price.

A decrease in the volatility of the futures price decreases the time value of the options. The probable range of the futures price at expiration shrinks, and the deltas is driven toward 100 percent and 0 percent. Options that are currently in-the-money have a higher probability of staying in-the-money, and out-of-the-money options effectively are further out-of-the-money.

Table 4   Hypothetical Call Deltas (with the futures price at .6100)

Call strikes:	59¢	60¢	61¢	62¢	63¢
Time remaining:					
1 day	100%	94%	50%	6%	–
1 week	89%	73%	50%	28%	12%
1 month	73%	62%	51%	40%	30%
3 months	65%	59%	52%	45%	39%
6 months	62%	57%	53%	48%	44%

volatility = 20%, interest rate = 9%

BASIC OPTION STRATEGIES

Options are attractive because many of their uses involve known and limited risk. But another reason for the attractiveness of options is their flexibility: options can be employed in expectation of rising or falling markets, or of stable or volatile markets.

Buying Call Options

An investor who anticipates an increase in a given currency's exchange rate (in American terms) and a corresponding increase in the price of the futures contract, may find the purchase of a call option an appropriate strategy.

The profit potential on the purchase of a call option is limited only by the increase in the underlying futures contract. The higher the futures contract moves, the more profit the investor realizes when the call is sold.

How should an investor choose which call option to purchase? An option with a longer time until expiration generally costs more than one with a shorter time until expiration. However, the option with a longer maturity obviously gives the investor more time to be correct in his forecast of market direction and, hence, more time for the option to become profitable. In pricing options, the time gained through the purchase of a longer-term option is actually less costly, proportionately, than that of a shorter-term option. Ultimately, the decision about whether to buy a call with a nearby expiration date or pay a higher premium for one with a more distant expiration date depends on the investor's opinion of when the exchange rate may rise.

Investors also must decide whether to purchase an in- or at-the-money option, as opposed to an out-of-the-money option. For example, given the same move in the futures price, the dollar amount of profit earned on an at-the-money option is greater than that from an out-of-the-money option. But an out-of-the-money option costs less, so any loss is less; and, assuming the option expires in-the-money, the rate of return on the out-of-the-money option is greater than that on an in- or at-the-money option.

Buying Put Options

The investor who anticipates a falling exchange rate and correspondingly lower futures prices may purchase puts to realize a profit. Recalling that the purchase of a currency put option carries with it the right to take a short futures position, the value of a put option can be expected to increase with falling prices for the futures contract.

If the investor is incorrect in his estimate of exchange rate movement, all, or a portion, of the premium paid for the put option is lost. But again, the loss is limited to the purchase price for the put option. On the other hand, should the investor be correct in predicting an overall decline in the currency's value, the profit potential of the put option is limited only by the decrease in the underlying futures contract price. The lower the futures contract moves, the more profit the investor realizes when the put is sold.

Writing Call Options

The writer (seller) of a call option receives payment (the premium) in return for the obligation of taking a short position in the futures contract at the exercise price if the option is exercised. If the writer of the option does not have a long position in the futures market, he is called an uncovered (or naked) writer. The profit profile of the uncovered call writer is the opposite of that of the call buyer: The call writer's risk is unlimited, while the call buyer's risk is limited; and the call writer's profits are limited, while the call buyer's profits are unlimited.

The principal reason for writing call options, then, is to earn the premium. And in periods of stable or declining markets, call writing can provide an attractive cash flow from a relatively small investment of capital. The writer of a call option hopes that, at expiration, the settlement price of the futures contract is at or below the exercise price of the option. The option then expires worthless, and the call writer keeps the entire premium.

If, on the other hand, the futures price at expiration is above the exercise price of the call option, the call writer is forced to assume a short position in the futures contract at the strike price. The writer loses the in-the-money amount when the short futures position is subsequently marked-to-market. This results in the loss of at least a portion of the premium, and possibly more than the premium.

The writer of a call option should keep in mind that the holder may exercise at any time during the life of the option, and exercise becomes more likely if an option has a large intrinsic value and little time value. Therefore in these cases, the call writer who does not wish to take a futures position should consider closing his options position.

Writing Put Options

As in writing call options, the primary motivation for writing put options is to earn the premium. However, the put writer is subject to substantial risk in order to earn the premium.

Because the put writer is obligated to take a long futures position, he hopes that the futures price at expiration is at or above the exercise price of the put. The put option then expires worthless, and the writer keeps the entire premium received for the sale of the put. The risk is that the futures price will fall below the striking price of the put option by an amount exceeding the premium received.

Again, the put writer should understand that the option may be exercised by the put holder at any time during the life of the option, and should monitor the position carefully if he does not wish to take a futures position.

Dynamic Strategies

Profitable options strategies can be designed to meet nearly any forecast of market conditions. Options on currency futures, like the futures themselves, can be used to take a position in the market, or to protect an already established position. However, with the choice of strike price and of buying or writing puts or calls, the degree of exposure to the market can be varied to reflect the relative certainty of a given forecast of market conditions. The trading decision can be refined from an absolute timing decision to one in which the commitment can be limited and quantified.

Following is a description of "straddles" and "strangles," positions that convey the flexibilities that options bring to currency trading.

Strategies for Volatile Markets

The simultaneous purchase of both call and put options with the same strike price—a straddle position—can profit from or protect against anticipated sharp movement in either direction. The straddle earns a profit if the futures price moves significantly in either direction, and the maximum cost of the straddle is realized if the futures price remains constant.

The profit profile of a straddle follows in the chart on the next page. This straddle is placed by buying a June call and a June put option, both with a 56¢ ($0.56) strike price. Assume that June Deutsche mark futures are at $.5600, and the premium paid for each option is .5¢ ($.0050) per Deutsche mark covered, or $625.

If the straddle is held until expiration, the dotted line describes the profit or loss on the straddle combination at every settlement price for the underlying futures. If the futures price at expiration is .5600, the dealer pays 1¢ per unit of currency for the price protection. If the futures price is at .5500 or .5700, the straddle breaks even; and if it is at .5400 or .5800, there is a profit of 1¢ per DM.

The solid line in the chart represents the profit profile for the same straddle held for only one day. Since the trader maintains the straddle only under volatile and uncertain market conditions, the insurance cost (the erosion of the options premiums) is minimized by the trader's resale of the options the following day.

A "strangle" is similar to a straddle because the trader buys both puts and calls, but they are bought at differing out-of-the-money strike prices. If the current June DM futures price is .5550, between the option strike prices, a strangle with puts at the next

Figure 10   Long Straddle Position

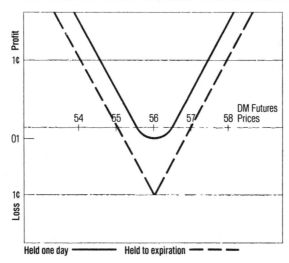

lower strike price, .55, and calls at the next higher strike price, .56, act much like the straddle just described. The premiums are cheaper and the futures have to move further to produce a profit.

The strangle, placed at well out-of-the-money strike prices, can be a lower-cost form of insurance against large moves in the currency because out-of-the-money option prices are less. For short holding periods, such a strangle serves much the same purposes as the straddle, but generally is less responsive to small currency fluctuations. It offers higher leverage, but expires worthless more often if held to expiration.

Profiting from a Stable Market

Selling a straddle or a strangle brings a profit if the futures price is fairly stable over the period that it is held. The time value portion of the premiums diminishes as time passes and as volatility decreases. The profit profile of a short straddle is shown here.

Figure 11   Short Straddle Position

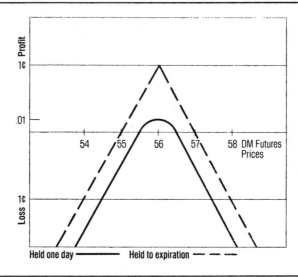

Often a trader has a view of the expected range for a currency's price. Options positions can improve the basic strategy of buying at the low end of the range and selling at the high end. Selling the strangle (i.e., selling out-of-the-money calls and puts) brings a profit if the market trades within the range of the striking prices, as the time value of the options erodes. If the futures price moves to either end of the range, the trader is in the same position that he would have been in without the option. By selling the option combination, the trader has agreed to buy at the low end and sell at the top of the range.

HEDGING CURRENCY RISK WITH FUTURES AND OPTIONS

The difference between hedging and speculating involves risk. The speculator starts with no risk, and buys or sells options or futures contracts, assuming risk in order to make profits. The hedger starts with a pre-existing currency risk generated from the normal course of business; options or futures are used to reduce or eliminate that pre-existing risk.

For example, the U.S. exporter who contracts to accept payment in Deutsche marks bears the risk that the value of the Deutsche mark may fall before payment. In this case, any strategy that provides profits from a declining Deutsche mark (up to the total amount of the pre-existing exchange rate risk) is a hedge.

Futures contracts may be used to hedge some or all pre-existing risk by essentially locking in a rate in a forthcoming foreign exchange transaction. Once hedged with futures, the position is insulated from the effects of subsequent changes in the spot exchange rate—either beneficial or adverse. Options contracts provide alternative hedging approaches with different characteristics.

For a given risk (i.e., either the risk of a declining exchange rate or a rising exchange rate) options can be used to offset risk or generate income in one of two ways. For example, to hedge against declining exchange rates (rising value of the dollar), buy an appropriate number of put contracts or sell an appropriate number of calls. Similarly, during a period of rising exchange rates (a declining dollar) hedge by buying calls or by selling puts.

In general, the option-buying hedge can be viewed as purchasing insurance with a deductible clause. The options protect against losses after they reach a certain point. The precise threshold point is determined by the option chosen (i.e., by the selected strike price). An option-selling hedge, on the other hand, offers protection with a maximum coverage equal to the value of the options sold. If losses from the pre-existing risk exceed the receipts of the option sale, those "excess" losses are not protected by the hedge.

Example: Hedging the Risk of Declining Deutsche Mark Exchange Rates (Rising Dollar)

On July 1, a company makes a sale for which it will receive DM 125,000 on September 1. The firm wants to convert these Deutsche marks to dollars, so the transaction is exposed to the risk that the exchange rate will decline in the meantime. If they do not hedge, such a decline means that they will own fewer dollars on September 1. The firm might hedge in any one of three ways:

1. Selling futures
2. Buying puts
3. Selling calls

Table 5 shows possible results for each choice using options with strike prices just above and just below the spot exchange rate of July 1. The example assumes a 6.4 percent drop in the spot exchange rate for Deutsche marks and the consequent price adjustments of associated futures and options contracts.

In this example, a decision to remain unhedged would yield a loss of 125,000 × (.5922 − .5542) or $4,750. The various hedge result possibilities are shown in Table 6.

Table 6 also demonstrates several differences among the various hedge strategies.

1. The futures hedge offers the closest offset to the loss due to the decline of the spot exchange rate.

2. The purchase of the in-the-money put (the 60 strike price) offers greater protection than the out-of-the-money put (the 58 strike price).

Table 5   Declining Exchange Rate Scenario

	July 1	September 1
Spot	$.5922	$.5542
Sept. futures	.5956	.5558
Sept. .58 put	.0059	.0250
Sept. .60 put	.0144	.0447
Sept. 58 call	.0225	.0004
Sept. 60 call	.0120	.0001

Table 6   Hedging Alternatives: Offsetting a $4,750 Loss Due to a Declining Spot Exchange Rate (Rising Dollar)

Short Futures Hedge Result

(5956 − 5558) × 12.50 = $4,975.00 profit

Long Put Hedge Results

58 put: (250 − 59) × 12.50 = $2,837.50 profit
60 put: (447 − 144) × 12.50 = $3,787.50 profit

Short Call Hedge Results

58 call: (225 − 4) × 12.50 = $2,762.50 profit
60 call: (120 − 1) × 12.50 = $1,487.50 profit

3. The sale of the in-the-money call (the 58 strike price) offers a greater offset than the out-of-the-money call (the 60 strike price).

Note that if the decline of the exchange rate had continued even further, the put buying hedges would have continued to appreciate, while both call selling hedges already provided an offset near their maximums.

A complete assessment of the option hedge strategies comes only by examining the results that follow from a rise in the exchange rate or a stabilization. While the company decided to hedge because of an expected decline in exchange rates, what would have happened had the expectation proved wrong? To answer this question, assume the hypothetical conditions in Table 7.

In this case, the spot exchange rate rise is a benefit to the cash position of (.6338 − .5922) × 125,000, or $5,200; and all of the hedge alternatives generate hedge losses in varying degrees.

In Table 8 the futures hedge again provides the closest offset; however, with these hedges generating losses, the bottom line in this instance is better served by the smallest offset. Under rapidly

Table 7   Rising Exchange Rate Scenario

	July 1	September 1
Spot	$.5922	$.6338
Sept. futures	.5956	.6374
Sept. .58 put	.0059	.0001
Sept. .60 put	.0144	.0001
Sept. 58 call	.0225	.0580
Sept. 60 call	.0120	.0375

rising exchange rates, the company benefitted most from hedging with a long put position.

The final scenario described is that of a relatively minor movement in the exchange rate. Table 9 shows a smaller decline in the rate from July 1 to September 1.

The cash position has suffered a loss of (.5922 − .5850) × 125,000, or $900, with the various hedge positions showing mixed results.

As Table 10 shows, the futures position best mirrors the cash risk. However, either short call more than compensates for the cash market loss. In general, the long options perform better as hedges with large price moves (in either direction) and short option positions perform better during a smaller price move; but the futures tend to offer the closest to dollar-for-dollar offset.

A comparable case can be constructed for a firm or individual facing risk from rising exchange rates—a U.S. importer who pays for goods in foreign currency or a non-U.S. exporter who receives dollars—but the conclusions are the same. Hedging with futures insulates the hedger from the effects of subsequent exchange rate moves (either adverse or beneficial). Buying options (puts to protect against an exchange rate decline or calls to protect against a rise) is like insurance purchased for one-way protection. And as a third alternative, selling options (calls or puts) offers protection for

Table 8   Hedging Alternatives: Offsetting a $5,200 Gain Due to Rising Spot Exchange Rates (Declining Dollar)

Short Futures Hedge Result

(6374 − 5976) × 12.50 = $4,975.00 loss

Long Put Hedge Results

58 put: (59 − 1) × 12.50 = $725.00 loss
60 put: (144 − 1) × 12.50 = $1,787.50 loss

Short Call Hedge Results

58 call: (580 − 225) × 12.50 = $4,437.50 loss
60 call: (375 − 120) × 12.50 = $3,187.50 loss

Table 9   Moderate Exchange Rate Scenario

	July 1	September 1
Spot	$.5922	$.5850
Sept. futures	.5956	.5875
Sept. .58 put	.0059	.0010
Sept. .60 put	.0144	.0156
Sept. 58 call	.0225	.0064
Sept. 60 call	.0120	.0004

a small market move, but leaves the hedger exposed to larger exchange rate fluctuations.

Options As Contingency Hedges

Long option positions confer the right, but not the obligation, to buy or sell a currency contract. If a forthcoming exchange of cur-

Table 10   Hedging Alternatives: Offsetting a $900 Loss Due to a Moderately Declining Spot Exchange Rate (Rising Dollar)

Short Futures Hedge Result

$(5956 - 5875) \times 12.50 = \$1,012.50$ profit

Long Put Hedge Results

58 put: $(59 - 10) \times 12.50 = \$612.50$ loss
60 put: $(156 - 144) \times 12.50 = \$150.00$ profit

Short Call Hedge Results

58 call: $(225 - 64) \times 12.50 = \$2,012.50$ profit
60 call: $(120 - 4) \times 12.50 = \$1,450.00$ profit

rencies is possible, but not definite, long put or call positions can be safer hedges than either futures or forward positions.

For example, assume that a U.S. company makes a firm Deutsche mark bid on a German investment, with the bid acceptance announcement in three months' time. If the firm wishes to hedge the dollar cost of the bid, it buys futures contracts, so that if the Deutsche mark strengthens, the futures position contributes profits to offset the increased dollar costs of the prospective investment. But if the bid eventually is rejected and if the Deutsche mark has fallen in the meantime, losses from the long futures position have no offset.

Options on currency futures provide a better hedge in such a case. Purchasing DM calls provides protection against a rising Deutsche mark; and yet, if the bid is rejected and the Deutsche mark falls, the uncovered hedge loss is limited to the premium paid for the calls.

At the point that the contingency becomes a certainty, the hedge position should be reevaluated. The hedger should consider the various alternatives described in the previous section. In this example, if the bid is accepted, the investor might decide to maintain the long calls or to change to other strike prices, to a long futures position, or to a short put position, depending on the market view and hedging objective. Note that an investor in the opposite position, such as a German hedging the Deutsche mark cost of a dollar bid, should use long DM puts rather than short call positions to provide the safest hedge.

NOTES ON THE EXCHANGE TRADING PROCESS

The CME is a classic example of the auction market process at work. All bids and offers on currency and other financial futures and options contracts are made by open outcry in a competitive arena—one of the largest and most modern trading facilities in the world.

Unlike some securities exchanges that utilize the specialist system, the CME confers no special responsibility on individual trading members and makes certain that all participants have equal access to the market. This philosophy has allowed competition among traders to flourish and has fostered an efficient market environment that consistently seeks the best price for a given currency futures contract and a constant flow of bids and offers.

The cornerstone of this trading system is the Chicago Mercantile Exchange's membership—more than 2,500 independent traders, members of partnerships and representatives of brokerage firms. These members perform two important market functions: floor broker and floor trader.

A *floor broker* serves as a "broker's broker," responsible for executing orders for the accounts of one or more of the exchange's member firms. These orders may be for member firms or for customers of those firms.

A *floor trader* is analogous to a market-maker in the securities markets. As individuals trading for their own accounts or for those of organizations they represent, floor traders are an important factor in creating market interest and in assuring that bids and offers always are available.

Together, floor traders and floor brokers are the marketplace for trading currency and other futures. The trading tactics and strategies they employ, combined with their knowledge and expertise, contribute significantly to successful, liquid markets.

Exercise of a Currency Option

Options expire at 7:00 p.m. on the last trading day. However, a broker may set a considerably earlier cut-off time for exercising expiring options. Note that there is no automatic exercise of expiring in-the-money options.

An option buyer may exercise on any trading day, if the buyer's clearing member presents an exercise notice to the clearing house by 7:00 p.m. on the day of exercise. The option buyer receives a futures position (long for a call, short for a put) marked-to-the-market from the strike price the following trading day. Initial margin is required before trading begins on the second day following exercise.

By a process of random selection, the clearing house assigns exercise notices to clearing members, which then assign them by an approved selection process to their clients. Notice of assignment is given to the clearing member before trading begins on the day following an exercise notice. Call writers who are assigned receive short futures positions; put writers who are assigned receive long futures positions. The futures is assigned at the strike price and is marked-to-market at the end of trading on the day following the long option holder's notice of exercise. Initial margin is required before trading begins on the second day following the tender of an exercise notice.

IMM Currency Delivery System

Though relatively few holders of currency futures contracts ever take actual delivery of a currency, the integrity of the contracts rests heavily on the exchange's ability to provide accurate, timely delivery when called upon to do so.

The IMM delivery system is structured so that neither currency involved in the delivery-exchange has to leave its home country. The long futures position holder delivers U.S. dollars in the United States, and receives the contract currency in its home country. The short futures position holder delivers the contract currency in its home country, and receives dollars in the United States.

Prior to the last day of trading, there is an exchange of bank-related information among the various participants: the contract-holder, the holders' clearing member, the clearing house and the clearing house's agent bank. Through a pre-arranged banking transfer system, each buyer pays the settlement price for the currency in U.S. dollars and receives the contract amount of currency, both on the Wednesday following the last day of trading. On that same day, the seller pays the contract amount of the currency, and receives the settlement price in U.S. dollars.

APPENDIX I: CURRENCY FUTURES CONTRACT SPECIFICATIONS[1]

	Australian Dollar (AD)	British Pound (BP)	Canadian Dollar (CD)	Deutsche Mark (DM)	French Franc (FR)	Japanese Yen (JY)	Swiss Franc (SF)	European Currency Unit (EC)
Trading Unit	AD100,000	BP62,500	CD100,000	DM125,000	FR250,000	JY12,500,000	SF125,000	ECU125,000
Quotations	US$ per A$	US$ per pound	US$ per C$	US$ per mark	US$ per franc	US$ per yen	US$ per franc	US$ per ECU
Minimum Price Change	.0001	.0002	.0001	.0001	.00005	.000001	.0001	.0001
Value of 1 point	$10.00	$6.25	$10.00	$12.50	$2.50	$12.50	$12.50	$12.50
Price Limits[2]	150 Points	400 Points	100 Points	150 Points	500 Points	150 Points	150 Points	150 Points
Months Traded	March, June, September, December							
Trading Hours[3] (Chicago Time)	7:20am-2:00pm	7:20am-2:00pm	7:20am-2:00pm	7:20am-2:00pm	7:20am-2:00pm	7:20am-2:00pm	7:20am-2:00pm	7:10am-2:00pm
Last Day Hours	7:20am-9:16am	7:20am-9:16am	7:20am-9:16am	7:20am-9:16am	7:20am-9:16am	7:20am-9:16am	7:20am-9:16am	7:10am-9:00am
Last Day of Trading	Two business days before the third Wednesday of the delivery month							
Delivery Date	Third Wednesday of the delivery month							

[1]Contract specifications are subject to change. All matters pertaining to rules and specifications herein are made subject to and are superseded by official Chicago Mercantile Exchange rules. Current Chicago Mercantile Exchange rules should be consulted in all cases concerning contract specifications. Check with your broker to confirm this information.
[2]Price limits are in effect from 7:20 am to 7:35 am each day based on change of price from previous day's settlement.
[3]Trading will end at 12:00 noon on the business day before a CME holiday and on any U.S. bank holiday that the CME is open. 10/12/88

APPENDIX II: OPTIONS CONTRACT SPECIFICATIONS

	Australian Dollar	British Pound	Canadian Dollar	Deutsche Mark	Japanese Yen	Swiss Franc
Ticker Symbols	Calls: KA Puts: JA	Calls: CP Puts: PP	Calls: CV Puts: PV	Calls: CM Puts: PM	Calls: CJ Puts: PJ	Calls: CF Puts: PF
Option Coverage	One AD futures contract (AD 100,000)	One BP futures contract (BP 62,500)	One CD futures contract (CD 100,000)	One DM futures contract (DM 125,000)	One JY futures contract (JY 12,500,000)	One SF futures contract (SF 125,000)
Strike Price Intervals	US 1¢	US 2.5¢	US .5¢	US 1¢	US .01¢	US 1¢
Quotations	US $ per A dollar	US $ per pound	US $ per C dollar	US $ per mark	US $ per yen	US $ per franc
Minimum Price Change[2]	.0001	.0002	.0001	.0001	.000001	.0001
Value of 1 point	$10.00	$6.25	$10.00	$12.50	$12.50	$12.50
Months Traded[3]	Jan, Feb, Mar	Apr, May, Jun		Jul, Aug, Sep		Oct, Nov, Dec
Underlying Futures	Mar		Jun	Sep		Dec
Price Limit	None					
Trading Hours[4] (Chicago Time)	7:20am-2:00pm	7:20am-2:00pm	7:20am-2:00pm	7:20am-2:00pm	7:20am-2:00pm	7:20am-2:00pm
Last Day of Trading	Two Fridays before the third Wednesday of the contract month					

[1]Contract specifications are subject to change. All matters pertaining to rules and specifications herein are made subject to and are superseded by official Chicago Mercantile Exchange rules. Current Chicago Mercantile Exchange rules should be consulted in all cases concerning contract specifications. Check with your broker to confirm this information.

[2]A trade may occur at a nominal price (=$1) if it results in position liquidation for both parties.

[3]Options on currency futures are listed for all 12 calendar months, with each exercisable into the following quarterly-delivery futures contract. For example, January, February and March options are exercisable into the March futures contract, and it is the March futures price that is relevant for the pricing of the three sets of options. At any point in time, you can choose from options that expire in the next three calendar months, plus the following two quarter-end expirations.

[4]Trading will end at 12:00 noon on the business day before a CME holiday and on any U.S. bank holiday that the CME is open   10/12/88

SPECIFICATIONS COMMON TO ALL CME OPTIONS ON CURRENCY FUTURES

Strike Prices   Strike prices for puts and calls are available at 1/2-cent intervals above and below the current futures prices. In response to futures prices moving to the new levels as well as expirations and new listings for futures contracts, new option strikes will be added.

Last Day of Trading   Two Fridays before the third Wednesday of the contract month. If that Friday is an exchange holiday, the last trading day is the immediately preceding business day.

Minimum Margin   No margin required for put or call option buyers, but the full premium must be paid in cash. Check with a broker for margin on short option positions and combination option/futures positions.

Exercise Procedure   Option buyers may exercise on any trading day. Check with a brokerage firm for its exercise procedure.

Exercise results in a long futures position for a call buyer or a put seller, and a short futures position for a put buyer or a call seller. The futures position is effective on the trading day immediately following exercise, and is marked-to-market to the settlement that day. Initial margin is required before trading begins on the second day following the long option holder's notice of exercise. If the futures position is not offset prior to the expiration of trading in the futures contract, delivery of physical currency results or is required.

Expiration   Options expire at 7:00 p.m. (Chicago time) on the last trading day. However, a broker may set a considerably earlier cut-off time for exercising expiring options. Always check with a broker for exercise deadlines.

There is no automatic exercise of the expiring in-the-money currency options by the CME clearing house.

APPENDIX III: GLOSSARY

Arbitrage The purchase and sale of a currency in different markets to benefit from price disparities.

Assign To designate an option writer for fulfillment of his obligation to sell a futures (call option writer) or buy a futures (put option writer).

At-the-Money An option with an exercise price equal to or near the current underlying futures price.

Call Option An option that gives the holder the right to enter a long futures position at a specific price, and obligates the seller to enter a short futures position at a specific price if the option is exercised.

Cash or Spot Market The market for the cash commodity (as contrasted to a futures contract), taking the form of: (1) an organized, self-regulated central market; (2) a decentralized over-the-counter market; or (3) a local organization, which provides a market for a small region.

CFTC The Commodity Futures Trading Commission is the independent federal agency created by Congress to regulate futures trading. The CFTC Act of 1974 became effective April 21, 1975. Previously, futures trading had been regulated by the Commodity Exchange Authority of the USDA.

Clearinghouse An adjunct to a futures exchange through which transactions executed on the floor of the exchange are settled using a process of matching purchases and sales. A clearing organization also is charged with the proper conduct of delivery procedures and the adequate financing of the entire operation.

Clearing Member A member firm of the clearing house or organization. Not all members of the exchange are members of the clearing organization, however, all trades of a non-clearing member must be registered with, and eventually settled through, a clearing member.

Closing Price (Range)   The high and low prices, or bids and offers, recorded during the period designated as the official close of the market.

Contract Month   The month in which futures contracts may be satisfied by making or accepting delivery (same as ""delivery month"); or the month in which the option contract expires.

Convergence   The movement of a futures price toward the price of the underlying currency as the delivery date approaches. Until the settlement date draws near there is a natural difference between the cash and futures price due to the cost or yield from holding the other currency.

Delivery   The process by which dollars and the contracted currency change hands upon expiration of a futures contract.

Forward Contract   A contractual agreement between two parties to exchange a currency at a set price on a future date. Differs from a futures contract in that most forward commitments are not actively traded or standardized and carry the risk from the creditworthiness of the other side of the transaction.

Futures Contract   A standardized contract, traded on an organized exchange, to buy or sell a fixed quantity of a defined commodity at a set price in the future. Positions easily can be offset (closed out) by taking the other side in the open outcry auction; and positions are marked-to-market and settled in cash, daily.

In-the-Money   A term describing any option that has intrinsic value. A call option is in-the-money if the underlying future is higher than the striking price of the call. A put option is in-the-money if the future is below the striking price.

Intrinsic Value The value of an option if it were to expire immediately with the underlying futures at its current price; the amount by which an option is in-the-money. For call options, this is the difference between the futures price and the striking price if that difference is a positive number, or zero otherwise. For put options, it is the difference between the striking price and the futures price if that difference is positive, and zero otherwise.

Limit Order An order, given to a broker by a customer, that has execution restrictions. The order specifies a price and can be executed only if the market reaches or betters that price.

Long One who has bought a futures or options contract to establish a market position and who has not yet closed out this position through an offsetting sale.

Margin Funds that must be deposited with the broker for each futures transaction as a guarantee of fulfillment of the obligation.

Mark-to-Market The daily adjustment of an account to reflect profits and losses.

Market Order An order for immediate execution given to a broker to buy or sell at the best obtainable price.

Minimum Price Fluctuation Smallest increment of price movement possible in trading in a given contract (also called "tick").

Open Interest Number of open futures or options contracts. Refers to unliquidated purchases or sales.

Opening Price (or Range) The range of prices at which the first bids and offers were made or first transactions were completed.

Out-of-the-Money A term describing an option with no intrinsic value. A call option is out-of-the-money if the underlying futures price is lower than the strike price; a put is out-of-the-money if the underlying futures price is higher than the strike price.

Put Option   An option that gives the holder the right to enter a short futures position, and obligates the seller to enter a long futures position at a specific price should the option be exercised.

Settlement Price   The price determined at the close of each trading session; the closing price, if there is only one closing price. If there is a closing range, the midpoint of that range. Settlement prices are used to determine gains, losses, margin calls and invoice prices for deliveries.

Short   One who has sold a futures or options contract to establish a market position and who has not yet closed out this position through an offsetting purchase.

Strike Price   The price at which the option holder may buy or sell the underlying futures, as defined in the terms of his option contract. It is the price at which the call holder may exercise to buy the futures or the put holder may exercise to sell the futures (same as "exercise price").

Time Premium   The amount by which an option's total premium exceeds its intrinsic value.

Volatility   A measure of the amount by which an underlying futures price has fluctuated or is expected to fluctuate in a given period of time.

Chapter 17

Hedging Long Term Commodity Swaps with Futures*

David Apsel
Chase Manhattan Bank

Jack Cogen
Chase Manhattan Bank

Michael Rabin
Chase Manhattan Bank

INTRODUCTION

In the past decade the financial community has developed an assortment of risk management techniques. The most successful tool has been the swap. Interest rate and currency swaps have grown into a three trillion dollar market (notional principal outstanding). Corporations have been able to manage their exposures to fluctu-

* The Global Finance Journal, Volume 1, Number 1, pages 77–93.
Copyright © 1989 by JAI Press, Inc.
ISSN: 1044-0283

ating financial markets. This has facilitated the planning process and allowed corporations to focus on their primary business. Now these same techniques can be applied to commodity price risk.

The commodity swap market differs from the interest rate swap market in two ways. First, the commodity swap user is more likely to be the purchasing manager than the corporate treasurer. Second, the instruments available to the commodity swap dealer to use for hedging are typically limited to futures contracts that cover a period of up to one year at best, whereas the rate swap dealer has a large variety of instruments including 30 year bonds.[1]

In this chapter we describe the commodity swaps market. We start with a description of the product and the marketplace. Then we discuss the difficulties of hedging a commodity swap from the dealer's perspective and develop a hedging model for the strategy of replicating long-dated forwards with only short futures contracts. The techniques described here are applicable to any commodity that has a liquid futures market, but most of the discussion used the oil market as an example. Currently, expanding the swap market into petroleum products has been the focus of major commercial and investment banks.

DESCRIPTION OF A COMMODITY SWAP

A commodity swap is a financial contract between two counterparties that effectively fixes the price of a commodity for a period of time. The parties agree to the length of the swap, the settlement periods within the swap, the quantity of the commodity swapped per settlement period, and the fixed price of the commodity. At each settlement period, one side pays the fixed price multiplied by the quantity of the commodity, the other side pays the then current spot price of the commodity. The structure is nearly identical to an interest rate or currency swap except that the index is copper or oil instead of LIBOR.

For example, consider an airline that wants to hedge its jet fuel price risk. The airline could enter into a two year swap where

---

1 Since this paper was written, crude oil futures contracts beyond one year have been introduced.

it pays a fixed cost of $170 per metric ton of jet fuel, for 5,000,000 tons of fuel per settlement, with semi-annual settlements. A total of 20,000,000 tons are therefore swapped. The airline then proceeds to buy its fuel through its normal channels (see diagram on page 00). If the price of fuel goes up, then the airline will pay more for the fuel but receive a cash payment at the swap settlement. If the price of fuel goes down, then the airline will pay less than expected for the fuel, but it will have to pay more on the swap. The effect is to fix the all in cost of fuel.

MARKET PARTICIPANTS

Commercial users of commodity swaps are consumers of the commodity who cannot immediately offset an increase in their commodity cost with a like increase in their revenue. Likewise, producers of the commodity use swaps if they cannot decrease their production costs when the price of the commodity that they produce, and hence their revenue, falls.

With oil swaps, the major consumer industry groups using them have been airlines, utilities, shipping companies, and petrochemical companies. On the producer side, oil exploration companies have used swaps.

Oil refineries buy crude oil and produce petroleum products whose pricing is highly correlated with the crude. Their exposure is not to changes in price level, but rather to changes in the spread between crude and product. Recently, the market for swaps on spreads has begun to develop.

Interest rate and currency swaps have been used for years by the corporate treasure, but commodity swaps are often used by the purchasing manager. As in the beginning of the rate swap market, the sale cycle is very long due to the education process. There is also an institutional problem in many companies. The swap is technically a financial instrument, normally under the purview of the treasurer. The purchasing manager may not have authority to enter into the transaction. Often the first commodity swap must be specifically approved by the board of directors.

There is also a professional dealer market. The dealers have been of two types. There are commodity trading firms, including subsidiaries of the Wall Street houses, who trade the swaps against their cash positions. There are also commercial banks, who match counterparties or hedge in the futures markets. The commercial banks bring credit intermedication skills and credit appetite to the market. Due to the longer nature of the swap, with many transactions having a term of five years, credit worthiness becomes an important consideration. Many end users only want to deal with commercial banks for long transactions. Similarly, many trading houses prefer commercial bank credit as well.

HISTORY OF THE OIL SWAP MARKET

Oil swaps were first discussed in the financial community in the early 1980s as a means of restructuring LDC debt. Nations that produced oil could lock in a high price for their oil and use the guarantee price to support their loans. Although accepted in principle, no one could agree on the value of the oil. Few, if any, deals were done.

The business grew after 1985 when a few commercial and investment banks tried to arrange swaps between commercial users and producers of oil. The first deals were done by getting a user and a producer to agree on a price, with a bank standing in the middle to arrange the deal and guarantee credit and anonymity. The growth of the business was restricted by the need for the bank to find two counterparties at the same time who agreed on the size, tenor, and price of the swap.

The first rule of arranging a swap transaction is that buyers only want to buy on a downtick in the market and sellers only want to sell on an uptick. The swap dealer must be able to do one side of the transaction, hedge the position, and then look for the offsetting transaction at a later time. Since 1987 the dealers have been actively hedging one-sided transactions using futures contracts.

FUTURE OF THE MARKET

As the market matures, commodity swaps are being combined with other techniques to create new financial instruments. For example, a firm with no oil exposure can issue an oil indexed note and swap the coupon from oil into LIBOR. The purchasers of the note are fund managers who want oil exposure and will pay a premium for a non-oil company name because of credit considerations. A similar credit arbitrage drives the interest rate swap market.

Long-term options on commodities are also becoming more liquid. Again, this is following the pattern set in the interest rate market. First there were interest rate swaps, then interest rate caps and floors followed. Now swaps on copper, aluminum, zinc, gold, silver, and petroleum caps and floors are available with increasing frequency.

WHAT MAKES A GOOD COMMODITY SWAP INDEX?

There are five conditions that are needed for a commodity index to be successful as a swap index. First, there must be a large pool of users of the commodity that would have interest in receiving a fixed price. Oil attracts diverse interest, titanium has a narrower market.

Second, the index used must be published by an independent source. for interest rate swaps, six months LIBOR has become the standard index because the average of a number of banks' offer rates are compiled by Telerate and Reuters. In petroleum products there are daily publications like Platt's Oilgram Price Report, and the daily closing price of futures contracts can be used as well.

Third, relating to the first two points, the index must not have the potential to be manipulated by a market player.

Fourth, there must be some way for the swap dealer to hedge his exposure. For a swap on crude oil, there is the New York Mercantile Exchange (NYMEX) West Texas Intermediate (WTI) crude oil contract. To hedge a specific petroleum product where a futures contract does not exist requires trading the commodity itself or accepting the basis risk between the product and a futures index. This limits the number of dealers willing to swap on that product.

Fifth, there must be market volatility. If the market is calm and predictable, there is really no advantage in doing a swap. Luckily for the swap dealer, we live in uncertain times.

DETERMINING THE PRICE OF A COMMODITY SWAP

The price of a swap, whether the underlying index is a floating interest rate such as LIBOR or the price of oil, depends on the cost of hedging the index at each of the settlement dates. The fixed amount in the swap calculation is the average amount (adjusted for the time value of money) at which the swap dealer expects to break even plus a premium for credit exposure, agency value, and the possible variance of the realized cost from expectation. Such a variance will arise due to the imperfection of available hedging strategies.

In the case of interest rate swaps, the cost of hedging a LIBOR payment at any time forward can be inferred from the term structure of interest rates observed in the U.S. Treasury bond market. These implied rates are derived from a mathematical model of the cash-and-carry arbitrage that could be done to lock in the desired forward rate. In practice, the hedge is imperfect since not all points on the yield curve are actually traded and the forward spread between Treasuries and LIBOR can vary, and this spread is not observable.

When the interest rate swap market first began, the bid/offer spread was very wide, and it has narrowed over the years. One reason for the narrower spread was a reduction in the risk premium needed to compensate for the imperfections in the hedge. This risk has declined because more and more instruments have become available to hedge the forward rates (FRAs, liquidity in swaps, caps, floors, collars, swap options, cap options, OTC Treasury options, etc.).

The term structures of forward prices for most commodity prices, unlike interest rates, are not observable beyond a few months. For crude oil the term structure is observable through the West Texas Intermediate (WTI) futures contract traded on the New York Mercantile Exchange (NYMEX). This contract is the world's second most liquid futures contract. It has contracts covering one year into the future. Beyond one year a model must be used.

The term structure of forward prices for any commodity is bounded by the cash-and-carry arbitrage relationship. If the forward price is too high in relation to the spot price, then the arbitraguer could sell at the forward price, borrow money and buy the physical commodity, store the commodity, and deliver in into the market when his forward contract comes due, using the proceeds to repay his loan. The difference between the forward price and the spot price must cover his storage, insurance, net interest costs, plus return on capital for the transaction to be worthwhile.

If the forward price is too low in relation to the spot price the reverse arbitrage should be possible. But it requires borrowing the commodity and selling it at spot. In some commodities markets this is possible (e.g. gold) but in others the market goes into steep backwardation that goes beyond the arbitrage threshold. The lack of arbitrage in commodity futures markets has been extensively discussed elsewhere [see for example, Williams, Jeffery, "The Economic Function of Futures Markets," Cambridge University Press, 1986].

Given a commodity with only a few months of liquid futures contracts, and where the cash-and-carry arbitrage can not necessarily be carried out, a hedging strategy for long-dated swaps needs to be developed. The rest of the paper addresses this problem. First an example of a strategy that rolls futures contracts to hedge the swap is presented. A discussion of a model of the strategy follows.

EXAMPLE OF ROLL STRATEGY

Let us suppose that there are three dates, time 0, time 1, and time 2. Let S(i) and F(i) be the spot and one period future price of oil at time i. There is a future market for oil one period in the future. Here, a future contract will be an agreement to receive one barrel of oil, one period in the future, for a specified price. Thus at time i we can buy spot oil at price S(i) or future oil at price F(i) (note: in this case there is no distinction between a future and a forward).

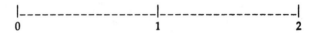

Let us consider the following problem: at time 0 we know that we require one barrel of oil for time 1, and one barrel of oil for time 2. The price of oil at time 0 is $15, and the forward price is $16. At time 1, the price of oil is $20, and the forward price is $21. At time 2, the price of oil is $25.
    Thus we have

$$S(0) = \$15 \qquad F(0) = \$16$$

$$S(1) = \$20 \qquad F(1) = \$21$$

$$S(2) = \$25.$$

For simplicity we assume an interest rate of zero. The obvious strategy is, at time 1, buy one barrel of oil at $20, then at time 2, buy one barrel of oil at $25. The total cost is

$$\$20 + \$25 = \$45.$$

Now consider an alternate strategy. At time 0, buy two future contracts at $16. At time 1, sell one barrel of spot oil at $20 and buy one future contract at $21. For this strategy, at time 0 there is no cash flow. At time 1, we pay 2 × ($16) = $32, and collect $20. At time 2, we pay $21. The total cost is

$$\$32 - \$20 + \$21 = \$33.$$

Our cost has been reduced in a predictable way. In particular, we were able to lock in the cost of oil for time 1 and time 2.[2] The lock in at time 1 is obvious, we simply buy the future and lock in the cost. The lock in at time 2 is achieved by constructing a two period synthetic forward by rolling one period futures. The cost of this synthetic forward is

$$Q(2) = [F(0) - S(1)] + F(1)$$

$$= S(0) + [F(0) - S(0)] + [F(1) - S(1)]$$

$$= S(0) + d(0) + d(1)$$

Where $d(i)$ is the slope of the forward price curve at time i. In our case the slope is constant and equal to $1 per time period. Thus $Q(2) = \$17$. Of course, $Q(1) = F(0) = \$16$, and thus our total cost is

$$Q(1) + Q(2) = \$33.$$

Assuming that the slope is constant, the forward price of oil can be locked in. In general, this strategy eliminates price risk, but leaves one exposed to slope risk.

THE FUTURES ROLL STRATEGY

We consider first the problem of hedging a long maturity short forward position, that is, an agreement to, at a specified date in

---

2   The lock-in for time 2 is valid only because we are assuming a constant slope.

the future, receive a fixed payment in return for a unit of the commodity (or with cash settlement, the spot value of a unit of the commodity). In the next section we make the extension to swaps.

To simplify we assume there are only two liquid markets, a spot market and a one month futures contract. The hedge involves holding a long position in the futures, offsetting the position the following month at the spot price, and rolling into a new long position in the next month's futures contract.

Let m index months and suppose the forward agreement is initiated at month zero for settlement at month T. The net cash flows on the hedged position at month m, CF(m), are:

(1)
$$
CF(m) = \begin{cases} 0, & m = 0 \\ N(m-1)\big[S(m) - F(m-1)\big], & 0 < m < T \\ N(T-1)\big[S(T) - F(T-1)\big] + \big[P(T) - S(T)\big], & m = T. \end{cases}
$$

where

S(m) = spot price at month m
F(m) = one month out futures price at month m
N(m) = long futures position at month m
P(T) = forward price for settlement at month T.

A futures position initiated at month m in an amount N(m) produces a cash flow on N(m) [S(m + 1) – F(m)] at month m +1, as the one month futures price converges to spot. For simplicity, we have assumed that the futures price change occurs at the end of the month. The present value of the net cash flows discounted at a constant continuously compounded interest rate, r, is

(2)
$$
V(T) = \sum_{m=0}^{T} R^{-m} CF(m)
$$
$$
= \sum_{m=1}^{T} R^{-m} N(m-1)\big[S(m) - F(m-1)\big]
$$
$$
+ R^{-T}\big[P(T) - S(T)\big].
$$

where $R = e^{r/12}$.

The relationship between the spot and futures prices is assumed to be give by a simple linear model:

(3)
$$F(m) = CS(m) + D(m), \quad m = 0, \ldots , T$$

where the $D(m)$'s represent adjusted cash futures price spreads, which for now are only assumed to be independent of the $S(m)$'s. The constant, C, represents the systematic impact of a change in spot on the futures price, i.e.,

$$C = \text{Cov}\left[F(m), S(m)\right]/\text{Var}\left[S(m)\right].$$

In market in which the cash-and-carry arbitrage is available in both the long and short direction we would expect to see $C = e^{(r + h)/12}$, where h is the continuously compounded rate of proportional holding costs net of dividend payments, if any, on the spot commodity. Then $D(m)$ can be interpreted as a deviation from the arbitrage cash futures price relationship, i.e., a carry adjusted cash futures basis. As an alternative interpretation of the model, the special case $C = 1$ represents the situation where the forward price curve tends to shift in parallel without regard to arbitrage considerations, and $D(m)$ measures the simple spot futures price spread that, in this case, has no systematic relation to the level of spot. For commodities futures markets where arbitrage is often not fully effective, it is frequently possible to estimate C econometrically from a time series for spot and futures prices.

Our hedging strategy is to choose the futures hedge amounts $N(m)$ to immunize the value of $V(T)$ to variations in the future spot prices $S(m)$, $m - 1,...,T$.[2] Substituting (3) into (2) we can write

---

3 This is not the same as choosing the hedge amounts to minimize the variance of $V(T)$, but it presents comparatively reduced information requirements since there is no need to specify the covariance structure of the $S(m)$'s. The two approaches, spot immunization and variance minimization converge when the uncertainty over spot dominates the uncertainty over the spot-futures spread. This is typically the case empirically.

(4)
$$V(T) = \sum_{m=1}^{T} R^{-m} N(m-1)\left[S(m) - CS(m-1) - D(m-1)\right]$$
$$+ R^{-T}\left[P(T) - S(T)\right].$$

Differentiating V(T) with respect to each of the unknown S(m)'s for m − 1, . . ., T and setting each derivative to zero implies that the futures hedge amounts must satisfy

$$N(m-1) - CN(m)/R = 0, \quad m = 1, \ldots, T-2$$

and,
$$N(T-1) - 1 = 0,$$

which implies,

(5)
$$N(m) = (C/R)^{(T-m-1)}, \quad m = 0, \ldots, T-1.$$

Substituting the immunizing hedge amounts from (5) into (4) we get

(6)
$$V(T) = R^{-T}\left\{\left[P(T) - C^T S(0)\right] - \sum_{m-1}^{T} C^{(T-m)} D(m-1)\right\}.$$

Due to hedging, the only terms appearing in (6) that are unknown at month zero are the adjusted spreads, D(m) for m - 1,...,T. There is no remaining exposure to spot.

Equation (6) can also be rewritten in terms of Q(T), the break-even value of P(T) which makes V(T) in (6) equal zero.

(7)
$$Q(T) = C^T\left[S(0) + \sum_{m-1}^{T} C^{-m} D(m-1)\right].$$

If the D(m)'s were known with certainty, Q(T) is the forward price that could be 'locked in' through the futures roll strategy.

If we interpret C as a 'net carry' factor, then the term $C^T S(0)$ in (7) represents the traditional forward price enforced by a cash-

and-carry arbitrage. The formula for Q(T) can then be viewed as reflecting the deviations induced by the D(m)'s in a situation in which the cash-and-carry arbitrage is not available and the long forward must be synthetically created by rolling the futures.[3]

EXPECTED HEDGE COST AND RISK

In general the D(m)'s can only be estimated with err and it is necessary to characterize the remaining exposure to spread risk in the roll strategy. This requires further assumptions about the stochastic process generating the adjusted spreads. For a parsimonious but flexible specification we assume the D(m)'s follow a simple mean reverting process

(8) $$D(m) - D(m - 1) = k \left[U - D(m - 1) \right] + e(m),$$

where,

(9) the e(m)'s are uncorrelated and identically distributed with,
$$E\left[e(m) \right] = 0 \text{ and } Var\left[e(m) \right] = W^2,$$
for m = 0, . . . ,T.

The parameter U represents the long run average spread to which the D(m)'s ten to revert, while k determines the speed of reversion. For k = 0, the D(m)'s follow a random walk with no tendency to revert to a mean, while k = 1 implies that the D(m)'s are them-

---

4 Cash-and-carry arbitrage does not eliminate the backwardation in many commodity markets. For example, on May 4, 1989 the WTI June future contract on the NYMEX closed at $20.58 per barrel. The June 1990 contract closed at $17.01 per barrel. This would allow an arbitrageur to profitably borrow oil, sell it into the June 1989 contract, and buy it back in the June 1990 contract at any oil rate of interest below 17 percent per annum.

selves random draws around a mean of U. Intermediate behavior is obtained for $0 < k < 1$.[4]

Using the model in (8) and (9) we obtain (see Appendix A for details)

(10)

$$E\left[Q\left(T\right)\right] = C^T\left[S\left(0\right) + G\left(T\right)\right],$$

and,

$$\mathrm{Var}\left[Q\left(T\right)\right] = W^2 C^{2T} H\left(T\right),$$

(11)

where,

$$G\left(T\right) = \sum_{m=1}^{T} C^{-m}\left[D(0)\left(1 - k\right)^{m-1} + kU\sum_{j=1}^{m-1}\left(1 - k\right)^{j-1}\right],$$

$$H(T) = \sum_{m=1}^{T-1}\left[\sum_{j=m+1}^{T} C^{-j}\left(1 - k\right)^{j-(m+1)}\right]^2.$$

Given specific values for the parameters C, k and U, and initial values S(0) and D(0), it is simple to compute the expected cost and variance of the synthetic long forwards using formulas (10) and (11). This information could be used by a dealer to quote on long-dated forwards on the basis of expected cost plus an allowance for risk. Some sample computations are given in Table 1.

SWAPS

A standard swap involves periodic receipt of a predetermined fixed amount and corresponding periodic payment of the spot value of a unit of the commodity. The swap can be regarded as a portfolio of forward contracts, one for each payment date, and each written at the same forward price. For example, the value,

---

4   For the NYMEX crude oil futures, preliminary analysis suggests k values between 0.2 and 0.4 in a monthly model.

Table 1   One Year Forward

S(0) = 20	D(0) = 0	r = 0.1	C = 1	W = 0.2	U = –0.10
k =	.1	.3	.5	.7	.9
E[Q] =	19.59	19.22	19.10	19.04	19.01
STD[Q] =	2.87	1.70	1.16	0.88	0.70

S(0) = 20	D(0) = 0	r = 0.1	C = 1	W = 0.2	k = 0.5
U =	–0.2	–0.1	0	0.1	0.2
E[Q] =	18.20	19.10	20.00	20.90	21.80
STD[Q] =	1.16	1.16	1.16	1.16	1.16

denoted X(N), of a swap with N monthly payments[5] and a fixed side of P is just

$$(12)$$

where V(t,P) is as defined in (2) with the dependence on P shown explicitly. The hedge of the swap will be the sum of the hedges of the individual forwards. Substituting (6) into (12) we obtain

---

5 We consider the case of a monthly pay swap purely for notational convenience. In the general case it is necessary to distinguish the periodicity of the swap from that of the rolls in the hedge strategy, but otherwise the analysis in the paper goes through unaltered.

(13)

$$X(N) = \sum_{t=1}^{N} R^{-t} \left\{ \left[P - C^t S(0) \right] - \sum_{m=1}^{t} C^{t-m} D(m-1) \right\}$$

$$= AP - \sum_{t=1}^{N} (C/R)^t \left[S(0) + \sum_{m=1}^{t} C^{-m} D(m-1) \right]$$

where,

$$A = \sum_{t=1}^{N} R^{-t} = (1 - R^{-N})/(R - 1).$$

The first term, AP, in (13) represents the present value of the stream of fixed payments, while the second is the present value of the outlays involved in synthetically creating the floating side using the futures roll strategy. The break-even value for the fixed side, is denoted Z(N) and defined by the condition that X(N) be zero when P equal Z(N). From (13) we have

(14)
$$Z(N) = A^{-1} \sum_{t=1}^{N} (C/R)^{-t} \left[S(0) + \sum_{m=1}^{t} C^{-m} D(m-1) \right].$$

Given our assumption (8) of a mean reverting process for the D(m)'s the mean and variance for Z(N) can be derived. (See Appendix B for details).

(15)
$$E\left[Z(N) \right] = A^{-1} \sum_{t=1}^{N} (C/R)^{-t} \left\{ S(0) + \sum_{m=1}^{t} C^{-m} \left[(1-k)^{m-1} D(0) \right] \right.$$

$$\left. + kU \sum_{j=1}^{m-1} (1-k)^{j-1} \right] \right\}$$

(16)
$$Var\left[Z(n) \right] = (W/A)^2 \sum_{t=2}^{N} \left[\sum_{m=t}^{N} C^{-m} (1-k)^{m-t} \sum_{i=m}^{N} (C/R)^i \right]^2$$

Some sample values are given in Table 2.

Table 2   One Year Swap

S(0) = 20	D(0) = 0	r = 0.1	C = 1	W = 0.2	U = –0.10
k =	.1	.3	.5	.7	.9
E[Z] =	19.86	19.70	19.62	19.58	19.56
STD[Z] =	1.15	0.77	0.56	0.43	0.35
S(0) = 20	D(0) = 0	r = 0.1	C = 1	W = 0.2	k = 0.5
U =	–0.2	–0.1	0	0.1	0.2
E[Z] =	19.25	19.62	20.00	20.38	20.75
STD[Z] =	0.56	0.56	0.56	0.56	0.56

OTHER MODELLING ISSUES

In practice, it is frequently possible to improve the pricing model by considering features of particular commodity futures. For example, a dealer may have knowledge of certain peculiarities or liquidity features which are expected to affect futures price spreads in the near term. Or there may be a regular seasonal component to spread variations. The model can be readily generalized to handle these issues. Since the cost of the roll strategy depends on the spreads at which the rolls are done, any additional information about future spreads can only improve the accuracy of the estimate of hedging costs.

CONCLUSION

We have examined the commodity swap market's dynamics. The swap product offers another risk management tool to corporations.

The decision makers in the corporations have been expanded from the treasury department to the purchasing management department. Dealers have entered the market, first on a fully matched basis, but recently they have added a book running capability based on their ability to hedge with futures contracts.

We have examined a hedging strategy that protects the dealer from price level changes by offsetting long-dated forwards with futures contracts. The model assumes that the forward price can be described with a systematic factor that is related to the spot price and a mean reverting random variable that is independent of the spot price.

In many commodity futures markets cash-and-carry arbitrage is not available, and so the dealer is exposed to unexpected and dramatic changes in the shape of the price forward curve. The model can be used to help the dealer price his risk on a swap. This model assumes that the dealer holds the swap to its maturity and he does not take an offsetting swap position to reduce his risk. As the market develops liquidity, the dealer will be able to unwind his transactions earlier, and therefore his risk will be reduced. This will be reflected in narrower bid/offer spreads to the customer.

APPENDIX A

Substituting (9) into (7) we get

$$Q\,(T) = C^T \left\{ S\,(0) + \sum_{m=1}^{T} C^{-m} \left[kU \sum_{j=1}^{m-1} (1-k)^{j-1} + (1-k)^{m-1}\,D\,(0) \right] \right\}$$

$$+ C^T \left[\sum_{m=1}^{T} C^{-m} \sum_{j=1}^{m-1} (1-k)^{m-1-j}\,e\,(j) \right].$$

A little algebra gives,

$$Q(T) = C^T \left\{ S(0) + \sum_{m=1}^{T} C^{-m} \left[kU \sum_{j=1}^{m-1} (1-k)^{j-1} + (1-k)^{m-1} D(0) \right] \right\}$$
$$+ C^T \left[\sum_{h=1}^{T-1} e(h) \sum_{j=h+1}^{T} C^{-j} (1-k)^{j-(h+1)} \right].$$

It now follows that

$$E\left[Q(T)\right] = C^T \left\{ S(0) + \sum_{m=1}^{T} C^{-m} \left[kU \sum_{j=1}^{m-1} (1-k)^{j-1} + (1-k)^{m-1} D(0) \right] \right\}$$

and

$$\text{Var}\left[Q(T)\right] = W^2 \, C^{2T} \sum_{h=1}^{T-1} \left[\sum_{j=h+1}^{T} C^{-j} (1-k)^{j-(h+1)} \right]^2.$$

APPENDIX B

Substituting (8) into (14) we get

$$Z(N) = A^{-1} \left\{ \sum_{i=1}^{N} R^{-i} C^i \left[S(0) + \sum_{m=1}^{i} C^{-m} \left[kU \sum_{j=1}^{m-1} (1-k)^{j-1} + (1-k)^{m-1} \right. \right. \right.$$
$$\left. \left. \left. D(0) \right] \right] + \sum_{i=1}^{N} R^{-i} C^i \sum_{m=1}^{i} C^{-m} \sum_{j=1}^{m-1} (1-k)^{m-1-j} e(j) \right\}.$$

This can be written as

$$
Z(N) = A^{-1} \left\{ \sum_{i=1}^{N} R^{-i} C^{i} \left[S(0) + \sum_{m=1}^{i} C^{-m} \left[kU \sum_{j=1}^{m-1} (1-k)^{j-1} + (1-k)^{m-1} \right. \right. \right.
$$

$$
\left. \left. \left. D(0) \right] \right] + \sum_{h=1}^{N-1} e(h) \sum_{j=h+1}^{N} C^{-j} (1-k)^{j-(h+1)} \sum_{i=j}^{N} R^{-i} C^{i} \right\}.
$$

It now follows that

$$
E \left[Z(N) \right] = A^{-1} \left\{ \sum_{i=1}^{N} R^{-i} C^{i} \left[S(0) + \sum_{m=1}^{i} C^{-m} \left[kU \sum_{j=1}^{m-1} (1-k)^{j-1} \right. \right. \right.
$$

$$
\left. \left. \left. + (1-k)^{m-1} D(0) \right] \right] \right\}
$$

and

$$
\mathrm{Var} \left[Z(N) \right] = A^{-2} \, \mathrm{Var} \left[e(\cdot) \right] \sum_{h=1}^{N-1} \left[\sum_{j=h+1}^{N} C^{-1} (1-k)^{j-(h+1)} \sum_{i=j}^{N} R^{-i} C^{i} \right]^{2}.
$$

Figure 1   Commodity Swap

Chapter 18

Yield Opportunities and Hedge Ratio Considerations with Fixed Income Cash-and-Carry Trades

Ira G. Kawaller[*]
Chicago Mercantile Exchange

Timothy W. Koch[*]
University of South Carolina

Prices of nearby futures contracts on fixed income securities are determined by an arbitrage activity commonly called cash-and-carry trade. With this trade, an arbitrageur buys or sells the deliverable spot instrument, takes the opposite position with a nearby futures contract and compares the resulting rate on this synthetic instrument with the prevailing Treasury bill repo rate (or reverse repo rate). If the difference is sufficiently large, the arbitrageur borrows at the lower rate and invests at the higher rate.

Under certain yield conditions, the cash-and-carry trade offers an opportunity that enhances potential returns. Whether the opportunity exists, however, depends on the arbitrageur's hedging

[*] We appreciate the helpful comments of Alex Arapoglou of Chemical Bank as well as those of an anonymous reviewer.

435

objective which, in turn, determines the appropriate hedge ratio. Managers who want to equate daily changes of values due to changing interest rates use a hedge ratio that exceeds the hedge ratio used by an arbitrageur who attempts to equate changes in values over longer periods. The first foregoes any yield enhancement opportunity; the second retains it.

This chapter demonstrates the nature of yield opportunities in cash-and-carry trades involving Treasury bills and explores implications regarding the choice of the appropriate hedge ratio. The fundamental conclusion is that the appropriate hedge ratio depends on the choice of the hedge value date and on the maturity of the instrument being hedged. Yield enhancement opportunities exist only when arbitrageurs (a) finance their position overnight or for any maturity less than term and (b) use hedge ratios based on the futures delivery date. The first section describes the cash-and-carry trade with Treasury bills and explains characteristics of the opportunity more fully. The second section examines the choice of hedge ratio and its implications. Results are summarized in the final section.

YIELD OPPORTUNITIES IN TREASURY BILL CASH-AND-CARRY TRADES

It is generally recognized that prices on nearby Treasury bill futures contracts reflect cash-and-carry trading activity (Kawaller and Koch, (1984); Gendreau, (1985); and Allen and Thurston, (1988)). Here an arbitrageur identifies the appropriate deliverable security or the optimal spot market instrument that meets the futures contract specifications upon expiration. The purchase of this security coupled with the simultaneous sale of the futures contract synthetically shortens the maturity of the deliverable instrument and establishes a holding period yield over the time horizon from the value date of the purchase to the futures delivery date.

This yield, designated the implied repo rate, is then compared to the prevailing repo rate in the spot market. When the implied repo rate exceeds the actual repo rate, arbitrageurs borrow at the prevailing repo rate, buy the deliverable bill and sell the futures contract to yield the implied repo rate. The net return equals the implied repo rate less transactions and financing costs. Alternatively when the actual repo rate exceeds the implied repo rate, arbitrageurs borrow by selling the deliverable bill, buy the futures contract then invest via a reverse repo transaction. The net return here equals the effective term repo rate minus the implied repo rate net of transactions cost.

Kawaller and Koch (1984) demonstrated that for Treasury bills the implied repo rate equaled the actual repo rate, on average, from 1977 to 1982 due to arbitrage activity. For Treasury bonds, in contrast, the implied repo rate has been shown to be consistently below the prevailing repo rate (Klemkosky and Lasser, (1985); Kolb, Gay and Jordan, (1982); and Resnick and Hennigar, (1983)). Most of the studies attribute the difference to the fact that sellers of Treasury bond futures have a choice of which long-term security to deliver at expiration, along with several timing choices as to when to deliver. Because these delivery choices have value and favor the short futures position, the futures price is depressed relative to what it would be if no delivery choices existed.[1]

The nature of the yield opportunity in the cash-and-carry trade can be demonstrated by analyzing the specific features of a traditional transaction involving three-month Treasury bill futures. An arbitrageur identifies the currently traded cash Treasury bill that has three months' remaining maturity at the first delivery day of the futures contract. This security currently has a maturity greater than three months. The traditional arbitrage consists of buying the cash bill and simultaneously selling futures to establish an implied repo rate for a holding period from the present to the first delivery day of the Treasury bill futures contract.

Assume a spot value date of April 1 and a nearby futures delivery date of June 23. On April 1, the deliverable cash Treasury bill has a 174-day maturity, segmented as 83 days remaining to delivery plus 91 days from delivery until maturity on September

---

1 The difference between the implied repo rate and actual repo rate reflects the value of this delivery option.

24. The purchase price of the deliverable bill (Pb) is determined by the traditional formula;

(1) $$P_b = \text{Par}[1 - R(d/360)]$$

where Par equals the par value of the Treasury bill at maturity. R is the discount rate, and d is the number of days to maturity. With a $1 million par value and discount rate on the deliverable bill of 6.50 percent, the invoice price determined by substituting the appropriate values in equation (1) is $968,583.33.

The sale of a June futures contract establishes a projected price at delivery, also determined by equation (1), but with the futures discount rate substituted for the cash rate and only 91 days to maturity. Assuming a futures rate of 6.40 percent, the projected futures invoice price is $983,822.22. The implied repo rate, therefore, equals the projected futures price minus the purchase invoice price expressed as an annualized money market rate. In this example, the 83-day holding period yield, or implied repo rate, is determined as:

$$\text{Implied repo rate} = \left(\frac{\$983,822.22 - \$968,583.33}{\$968,583.33}\right) \times \left(\frac{360}{83}\right) = 6.824\%$$

An arbitrageur earns this precise implied repo rate only if the futures and cash rates equal 6.40 percent at expiration of the futures contract. Slight discrepancies usually occur because rates vary between the initial transactions and expiration. Table 1 demonstrates the potential magnitude of these discrepancies when rates alternatively fall and rise.

Consider a decline in the June futures and cash rate to 4.40 percent at delivery (column 1). With lower rates the futures position produces a cumulative loss of $5,000 equal to $25 for each basis point times the two percent change in rates. The cash Treasury bill, in contrast, increases by $5,055.56 over its initial projected value to $988,877.78 as each basis point is valued at $25.28.[2] The difference reflects the fact that the cash Treasury bill has 91 days remaining to maturity rather than the 90 days assumed in futures pricing. So the unanticipated gain on the cash position exceeds the loss on the futures position by $55.56, thereby improving the realized return to 6.849 percent.

The data in column 3 similarly demonstrate the effect of an increase in rates on the realized return from this series of transactions. With rising rates, the futures position increases in value but the $5,000 gain is less than the $5,055.56 decline in the value of the cash bill below its projected value. The realized return thus drops to 6.799 percent.[3]

The implication of Table 1 is simply that the implied repo rate is largely insensitive to changes in the general level of interest rates so traders can anticipate the outcome of their position with a high degree of reliability. This assumes, however, that arbitrageurs finance their position to term or use term reverse RPs. If they use overnight RPs instead or any maturity instrument less than term, the net return from the trade may vary from expectations. Specifically, the realized profit declines when rates rise above expectations and rises when rates fall below expectations with the traditional cash-and-carry trade. The opposite relationship holds for the reverse cash-and-carry trade combination.

Yield Enhancement Through Early Unwinding

Kawaller and Koch's (1984) results support the use of overnight financing or overnight reverse RP investing. Allen and Thurston's (1988) results are more consistent with transactions to term. Only in the case of overnight or less-than-term transactions can arbitrageurs enhance yields from the cash-and-carry trade through early unwinding.

---

2 $1,000,000(.0001)(91/360) = $25.28.

3 Arbitrageurs do not normally view these changes in returns as a significant problem or benefit with the cash-and-carry trade.

Table 1   The Effect of Interest Rate Changes on the Realized Return to the Cash-and-Carry Trade

| | *Interest rate Changes After the Initial Transaction* | | |
	1. Lower Rates	*2. No Change in Rates*	*3. Higher Rates*
Settlement Rate	4.400%	6.400%	8.400%
Settlement Price	$988,877.78	$983,822.22	$978,766.67
Purchase Price	968,583.33	968,583.33	968,583.33
Gain on Cash	20,294.44	15,238.89	10,183.34
Final Futures Price	95.60	93.60	91.60
Futures Profit/Loss	−5,000.00	0.00	5,000.00
Net Gain on Combined Position	15,294.44	15,238.89	15,183.34
Return on Investment	6.849%	6.824%	6.799%

The yield enhancement opportunity in a cash-and-carry trade derives from the difference between the change in values of the deliverable Treasury bill versus the futures position. This difference becomes exaggerated during the period prior to the futures expiration. Whenever interest rates decline, after the implementation of the traditional cash-and-carry trade, an arbitrageur may have the opportunity to liquidate the combined positions prior to futures expiration and earn a substantially higher rate of return, albeit for a shorter holding period.[4]

When interest rates increase, the arbitrageur can hold the position to futures expiration and earn the implied repo rate, plus or minus the several basis point discrepancy per Table 1. In this case, however, the arbitrageur faces higher financing costs. Implicitly, the initial rate discrepancy between implied repo and actual repo rates should cover the *effective* term repo rate expected, even if overnight financing is utilized. If rates increase more than originally expected, profit declines. The opposite holds with the reverse cash-and-carry trade.

---

4 The owner of any cash Treasury bill has the same option.

Ignoring the financing uncertainties, consider, for example, how the previous cash-and-carry trade changes in value if cash and futures rates change sharply within the course of a day. The first column in Table II demonstrates that an arbitrageur realizes an annualized overnight return of almost 50 percent if both cash and futures rates fall by 50 basis points the day after the cash-and-carry trade is implemented.

$$\text{Realized return} = \left(\frac{\$1,333.33}{\$968,583.33}\right) \times \left(\frac{360}{1}\right) = 49.557\%$$

Because the deliverable Treasury bill has 173 days to maturity and not the 90 days assumed in futures pricing, the bill's value increases by $2,583.33 while the loss on the futures position (increase in futures variation margin) totals just $1,250. If such a liquidation is effected, additional financing charges are not realized and the arbitrageur liquidates the combined position, earning $1,333.33 overnight.

The second column in Table II shows that an increase in rates produces the opposite result. Specifically, a 50 basis point jump in rates generates a consolidated loss of $972.22 if the position is liquidated.[5] Instead, the cash-and-carry trader holds this position until either rates drop back down or futures expire. Still, the trader might need additional collateral if the deliverable Treasury bill is used as a self-financing vehicle because the decline in value exceeds the gain from the futures position.[6]

This yield opportunity exists for both the direct cash-and-carry trade described above and the reverse when an arbitrageur sells the deliverable Treasury bill and buys futures. A reverse is justified whenever the actual repo rate exceeds the implied repo

---

5 The table is not meant to suggest that a parallel rate shift is expected. Clearly, the relationship of the two rate moves would depend on whether the basis were normal or inverted and whether rates were rising or falling. For example, with futures rates above spot rates in a declining rate environment, one would expect slightly higher rate moves on the part of the futures. Given the same basis conditions in a rising rate environment, one would expect the opposite ordering.

6 The terms of repurchase agreements may not provide for additional credit extension in response to rising collateral requirements.

Table 2   The Effect of Overnight Interest Rate Changes on the Realized Return to the Cash-and-Carry Trade

	1. Lower Rates	2. Higher Rates
Initial days to maturity	174 days	174 days
Initial discount rate	6.500%	6.500%
Initial invoice price	$968,583.33	$968,583.33
Next-day's days to maturity	173 days	173 days
Next-day's discount rate	6.000%	7.000%
Next-day's invoice price	971,166.67	966,361.11
Change in invoice value	2,583.33	−2,222.22
Initial futures price	93.60	93.60
Next-day's futures price	94.10	93.10
Profit/loss on futures	−1,250.00	1,250.00
Consolidated profit/loss	1,333.33	−972.22
Overnight R.O.I. (annual rate)	49.557%	−36.135%

rate. Constructing a reverse cash-and-carry trade effectively creates a liability or borrowing facility. Whenever the positions are held to maturity, the realized term financing rate equals the initial implied repo rate plus or minus the small adjustment for rate changes, similar to that in Table 1. In contrast with the traditional cash-and-carry trade, however, the reverse carries a yield enhancement opportunity that increases in value when interest rates rise. Higher rates potentially lower the effective borrowing rate when the gain on the deliverable bill exceeds the loss on futures, though the financing period is shortened. The fact that the yield opportunity applies equally for direct and reverse cash-and-carry trade suggests that it exerts a price-neutral effect on futures prices.

Although these examples use Treasury bills, the same opportunities exist with virtually any commodity for which a cash-and-carry trade can be constructed. Occasionally, however, there are complications. In the case of Treasury bonds and notes, for example, implementing a cash-and-carry trade is complicated by the conversion factor system in pricing futures and determining the deliverable bond. Brennan and Schwartz (1987) explain a similar position for stock index futures arbitrage. In this case, however, perturbations that foster price shifts in stock index hedging and arbitrage tend to produce changes of roughly equivalent values for the underlying stocks and futures contracts. This suggests that the value of the timing opportunity should be substantially smaller for stock index/futures arbitrage versus that for fixed income/futures arbitrage. Moreover within the realm of fixed income arbitrage, the most pronounced opportunities exist for short-term instruments. This is because the passage of time creates a greater change in the value of a basis point when the time in question represents a "significant" share of the maturity of the security. For example, 15 days hardly affect the value of a basis point on a 10-year bond; but it dramatically changes the value of a basis point on a three-month bill.

THE CHOICE OF HEDGE RATIO

Profit opportunities with the cash-and-carry trade vary with the objectives and strategies of each arbitrageur. The previous description implicitly assumes that the arbitrageur prices the cash and futures transactions with the futures expiration day (designated the anticipated trade date). If a position is financed on an overnight basis, the trade offers a yield opportunity to the arbitrageur. If financed to term, no such opportunity exists. Similarly, the correct hedge ratio is determined by the remaining maturity of the deliverable bill at delivery. So even if the current maturity of the bill is 174 days when the arbitrage is initiated, the appropriate hedge ratio is one futures contract for each $1 million par amount.

This hedge ratio is determined by comparing the value of a basis point associated with the deliverable Treasury bill upon the delivery date to the value of a basis point ($25) on a Treasury bill futures contract.[7] In general for nondelivery date circumstances, the value of a basis point (V) can be determined from:

---

7 This assumes that the discount rate on a cash bill moves one-for-one with the associated futures rate.

$$(2) \qquad V = \text{Par}(.0001)\left(\frac{d}{360}\right)$$

when d equals the number of days until maturity. The one-to-one hedge ratio assumed earlier was obtained by dividing a basis point value of \$25.28 for the cash Treasury bill by \$25; but this ratio clearly exceeds unity for Treasury bills with maturity beyond three months.[8] Suppose, for example, that the objective is to hedge the overnight exposure of the same deliverable Treasury bill rather than the exposure until the futures expiration. Implicitly, the goal is to equate changes in cash and futures values on a daily basis. To achieve this end, the hedge ratio should reflect the next day's maturity. Hedging interest rate risk in the previous example now requires calculating the revised value of a basis point as the original Treasury bill changes from a 174-day to a 173-day instrument. In this case, the value of a basis point for the cash bill equals \$48.06 and the appropriate hedge ratio becomes 1.92 futures contracts per \$1 million of par value bills.[9]

As structured, the hedge ratio necessarily decreases as time passes until it reaches unity at delivery. So a trader who wants to hedge changes in values on a daily basis must rebalance the hedge continuously. Toevs and Jacob (1986) essentially make this point by distinguishing between "strong form" and "weak form" hedges. In general, a trader who chooses to hedge to a value date other than delivery day uses a different hedge ratio determined by the targeted value date.

Features of Value-Equating Hedges

Such value-equating hedges have several unattractive features. Hedge traders using this type of hedge forego the yield enhancement opportunity inherent in the traditional cash-and-carry trade

---

8 See footnote 2.

9 With Treasury bonds/notes the value of basis point must be calculated for the cheapest to delivery security using the present value formula, multiplied by the conversion factor.

because changes in cash values due to interest rate changes are exactly offset by changes in futures values. Also, the hedge does not take into account price changes in the cash Treasury bill due solely to the passage of time and the natural accretion of price to par. Therefore, a hedger still might realize substantial losses on the combined position.

Consider a government securities dealer who decides to hedge a deliverable bill with a current maturity of 180-days. The appropriate value-equating hedge requires two futures contracts per $1 million dollars par. The value of the basis point on the cash bill is $50 vs. $25 for the futures. Over the next three months assuming away rounding problems, the hedge ratio is reduced systematically to unity by the delivery day due to the declining maturity and declining value of a basis point. Assume that immediately after initiating the hedge, interest rates rise by X basis points and remain at the higher level until the final hedge ratio adjustment. Then when the actual hedge ratio is one-to-one, rates fall by the same X basis points. In this case, the interest rate induced price effect on the cash market instrument is zero, given that the initial rate change ultimately is reversed. In contrast, the consolidated hedge profits are nonzero. When rates rise, twice as many contracts are maintained compared to when rates fall. So even though the hedge ratio is designed to equate these changes in cash values with futures profits (losses) on a day-to-day basis, the objective is not always realized over time.

The above situation may not be relevant for a government bill dealer who maintains an inventory of bills to service customer orders and wants to eliminate interest rate exposure. Here the hope is to profit solely from high turnover so the dealer can earn the bid-ask spread. Clearly, hedging with a value date that corresponds to the futures delivery date is inappropriate because the cash market basis point value is not likely to be $25. Hedging with the next-day's value of a basis point as the determining feature similarly may have the undesirable cumulative effects described previously. While no perfect solution exists, a dealer can estimate the average holding period length that defines the relevant hedge value date, and hedge the position to that date. Earlier sales necessarily mean insufficient hedge coverage and later sales mean excessive coverage; but, if the average is reasonably reliable and if the size of the inventory remains fairly stable, the imbalance should even out over time.

SUMMARY

Cash-and-carry trading links futures prices with cash prices on deliverable securities. Arbitrageurs who finance their positions on an overnight basis or for any period less than term retain a yield enhancement opportunity. For arbitrageurs who buy the deliverable instrument and sell futures, the opportunity arises when interest rates fall. Those that initiate the reverse cash-and-carry trade see this opportunity arise when interest rates rise. This opportunity is available whenever arbitrageurs employ a hedge ratio determined by targeting the futures delivery date as the specific trade date. It is not available for traders who want to hedge changes in cash and futures values on a daily basis.

BIBLIOGRAPHY

Allen, L., and Thurston, T. (1988, October): "Cash-Futures Arbitrage and Forward-Futures Spreads in the Treasury Bill Market," *Journal of Futures Markets*.

Brennan, M., and Schwartz, E. (1987, July): "Arbitrage in Stock Index Futures," Working paper.

Gendreau, B. (1985, Fall): "Carrying Costs and Treasury Bill Futures," *Journal of Portfolio Management*.

Kawaller, I., and Koch, T. (1984, Summer): "Cash-and-Carry Trading and the Pricing of Treasury Bill Futures," *Journal of Futures Markets*.

Klemkosky, R., and Lasser, D. (1985, Winter): "An Efficiency Analysis of the T-Bond Futures Market." *Journal of Futures Markets.*

Kolb, R., Gay, G., and Jordan, J. (1982, Fall): "Are There Arbitrage Opportunities in the Treasury Bond Futures Markets," *Journal of Futures Markets.*

Resnick, B., and Hennigar, E. (1983): Volume 2, Number 1: "The Relationship Between Futures and Cash Prices for U.S. Treasury Bonds," *Review of Research in Futures Markets.*

Toevs, A., and Jacob, D. (1986, Spring): "Futures and Alternative Hedge Ratio Methodologies," *Journal of Portfolio Management.*

Chapter 19

Universal Hedging: Optimizing Currency Risk and Reward in International Equity Portfolios*

Fischer Black
Goldman, Sachs & Co.

Investors can increase their returns by holding foreign stocks in addition to domestic ones. They can also gain by taking the appropriate amount of exchange risk. But what amount is appropriate?

Assume that investors see the world in light of their own consumption goods and count both risk and expected return when figuring their optimum hedges. Assume that they share common views on stocks and currencies, and that markets are liquid and there are no barriers to international investing. In this perfect world, it is possible to derive a formula for the optimal hedge ratio.

This formula requires three basic inputs—the average across countries of the expected returns on the world market portfolio; the average across countries of the volatility of the world market portfolio; and the average across all pairs of countries of exchange rate volatility. These values can be estimated from historical data.

---

* This article appeared in *Financial Analysts Journal* 45 (July/August, 1989).

The formula in turn gives three rules. (1) Hedge foreign equity. (2) Hedge less than 100 per cent of foreign equity. (3) Hedge equities equally for all countries. The formula's solution applies no matter where an investor lives or what investments he holds. That's why it's called "the universal hedging formula."

In a world where everyone can hedge against changes in the value of real exchange rates (the relative values of domestic and foreign goods), and where no barriers limit international investment, there is a universal constant that gives the optimal hedge ratio—the fraction of your foreign investments you should hedge. The formula for this optimal hedge ratio depends on just three inputs:

- the expected return on the world market portfolio
- the volatility of the world market portfolio
- average exchange rate volatility

The formula, in turn, yields three rules.

- Hedge your foreign equities.
- Hedge equities equally for all countries.
- Don't hedge 100 per cent of your foreign equities.

This formula applies to every investor who holds foreign securities. It applies equally to a U.S. investor holding Japanese assets, a Japanese investor holding British assets, and a British investor holding U.S. assets. That's why we call this method "universal hedging."

WHY HEDGE AT ALL?

You may consider hedging a "zero-sum game." After all, if U.S. investors hedge their Japanese investments, and Japanese investors hedge their U.S. investments, then when U.S. investors gain on their hedges, Japanese investors lose, and vice versa. But even though one side always wins and the other side always loses, hedging *reduces risk* for both sides.

More often than not, when performance is measured in local currency, U.S. investors gain on their hedging when their portfolios do badly, and Japanese investors gain on their hedging when their portfolios do badly. The gains from hedging are similar to the gains from international diversification. Because it reduces risk for both sides, currency hedging provides a "free lunch."

WHY NOT HEDGE *ALL*?

If investors in all countries can reduce risk through currency hedging, why shouldn't they hedge 100 per cent of their foreign investments? Why hedge less?

The answer contains our most interesting finding. When they have different consumption baskets, investors in different countries can all add to their expected returns by taking some currency risk in their portfolios.

To see how this can be, imagine an extremely simple case, where the exchange rate between two countries is now 1:1 but will change over the next year to either 2:1 or 1:2 with equal probability. Call the consumption goods in one country "apples" and those in the other "oranges."

Imagine that the world market portfolio contains equal amounts of apples and oranges. To the apple consumer, holding oranges is risky. To the orange consumer, holding apples is risky.

The apple consumer could choose to hold only apples, and thus bear no risk at all. Likewise, the orange consumer could decide to hold only oranges. But, surprisingly, each will gain in expected return by trading an apple and an orange. At year-end, an orange will be worth either two apples or 0.5 apples. Its expected value is 1.25 apples. Similarly, an apple will have an expected value of 1.25 oranges. So each consumer will gain from the swap.

This is not a mathematical trick. In fact, it is sometimes called "Siegel's paradox."[1] It is real, and it means that investors generally want to hedge less than 100 percent of their foreign investments.

---

1 J.J. Siegel, "Risk, Interest Rates, and the Forward Exchange," *Quarterly Journal of Economics*, May 1972.

Table 1   Siegel's Paradox

Quarter	Start-of-Quarter Exchange Rates		Percentage Changes in Exchange Rates	
	mark / dollar	dollar / mark	mark / dollar	dollar / mark
1Q84	2.75	.362	−5.58	5.90
2Q84	2.60	.384	7.18	−6.69
3Q84	2.79	.358	9.64	−8.79
4Q84	3.06	.326	3.66	−3.52
1Q85	3.17	.315	−1.83	1.84
2Q85	3.11	.321	−2.25	2.30
3Q85	3.04	.328	−13.04	15.01
4Q85	2.64	.377	−7.59	8.21
1Q86	2.44	.408	−4.46	4.67
2Q86	2.33	.427	−6.80	7.29
3Q86	2.17	.459	−7.16	7.73
4Q86	2.02	.494	−5.19	5.46
1Q87	1.91	.521	−5.11	5.41
2Q87	1.81	.549	0.49	−0.49
3Q87	1.82	.547	1.09	−1.08
4Q87	1.84	.541	−14.00	16.28
1Q88	1.58	.629	4.29	−4.12
2Q88	1.65	.603	9.83	−8.95
3Q88	1.82	.549	2.27	−2.22
4Q88	1.86	.537	−4.88	5.12
Average			−1.97	2.47

To understand Siegel's paradox, consider historical exchange rate data for deutschemarks and U.S. dollars. Table 1 shows the quarterly percentage changes in the exchange rates and their averages. In each period and for the average, note that the gain for one currency exceeds the loss for the other currency.

WHY *UNIVERSAL* HEDGING?

Why is the optimal hedge ratio identical for investors everywhere? The answer lies in how exchange rates reach equilibrium.

Models of international equilibrium generally assume that the typical investor in any country consumes a single good or basket of goods.[2] The investor wants to maximize expected return and minimize risk, measuring expected return and risk in terms of his own consumption good.

Given the risk-reducing and return-enhancing properties of international diversification, an investor will want to hold an internationally diversified portfolio of equities. Given no barriers to international investment, every investor will hold a share of a fully diversified portfolio of world equities. And, in the absence of government participation, some investor must lend when another investor borrows, and some investor must go long a currency when another goes short.

Whatever the given levels of market volatility, exchange rate volatilities, correlations between exchange rates and correlations between exchange rates and stock, in equilibrium prices will adjust until everyone is willing to hold all stocks and until someone is willing to take the other side of every exchange rate contract.

Suppose, for example, that we know the return on a portfolio in one currency, and we know the change in the exchange rate between that currency and another currency. We can thus derive the portfolio return in the other currency. We can write down an equation relating expected returns and exchange rate volatilities

2 See, for example, B.H. Solnik, "An Equilibrium Model of the International Capital Market," *Journal of Economic Theory*, August 1974; F.L.A. Grauer, R.H. Litzenberger and R.E. Stehle, "Sharing Rules and Equilibrium in an International Capital Market Under Uncertainty," *Journal of Financial Economics*, June 1976; P. Sercu, "A Generalization of the International Asset Pricing Model," *Revue de l'Association Francaise de Finance*, June 1980; and R. Stulz, "A Model of International Asset Pricing," *Journal of Financial Economics*, December 1981.

from the points of view of two investors in the two different currencies.

Suppose that Investor A finds a high correlation between the returns on his stocks in another country and the corresponding exchange rate change. He will probably want to hedge in order to reduce his portfolio risk. But suppose an Investor B in that other country would increase his own portfolio's risk by taking the other side of A's hedge. Investor A may be so anxious to hedge that he will be willing to pay B to take the other side. As a result, the exchange rate contract will be priced so that the hedge reduces A's expected return but increases B's.

In equilibrium, both investors will hedge. Investor A will hedge to reduce risk, while Investor B will hedge to increase expected return. But they will hedge equally, in proportion to their stock holdings.

THE UNIVERSAL HEDGING FORMULA

By extending the above analysis to investors in all possible pairs of countries, we find that the proportion that each investor wants to hedge depends on three averages—the average across countries of the expected excess return on the world market portfolio; the average across countries of the volatility of the world market portfolio; and the average across all pairs of countries of exchange rate volatility. These averages become inputs for the universal hedging formula:[3]

$$\frac{\mu_m - \sigma_m^{\,2}}{\mu_m - \frac{1}{2}\sigma_e^{\,2}}$$

where

---

3 The derivation of the formula is described in detail in F. Black, "Equilibrium Exchange Rate Hedging" (National Bureau of Economic Research Working Paper No. 2947, April 1989).

μ_m = the average across investors of the expected excess return (return above each investor's riskless rate) on the world market portfolio (which contains stocks from all major countries in proportion to each country's market value);

σ_m = the average across investors of the volatility of the world market portfolio (where variances, rather than standard deviation, are averaged); and

σ_e = the average exchange rate volatility (averaged variances) across all pairs of countries.

Neither expected changes in exchange rates nor correlations between exchange rate changes and stock returns or other exchange rate changes affect optimal hedge ratios. In equilibrium, the expected changes and the correlations cancel one another, so they do not appear in the universal hedging formula.

In the same way, the Black-Scholes option formula includes neither the underlying stock's expected return nor its beta. In equilibrium, they cancel one another.

The Capital Asset Pricing Model is similar. The optimal portfolio for any one investor could depend on the expected returns and volatilities of all available assets. In equilibrium, however, the optimal portfolio for any investor is a mix of the market portfolio with borrowing or lending. The expected returns and volatilities cancel one another (except for the market as a whole), so they do not affect the investor's optimal holdings.

INPUTS FOR THE FORMULA

Historical data and judgment are used to create inputs for the formula. Tables 2 through 8 give some historical data that may be helpful.

Table 2 lists weights that can be applied to different countries in estimating the three averages. Japan, the U.S. and the U.K. carry the most weight.

Table 2 Capitalization and Capitalization Weights

	Domestic Companies Listed on the Major Stock Exchange as of December 31, 1987[1]		Companies in the FT-Actuaries World Indices™ as of December 31, 1987[2]	
	Capitalization (U.S. $ billions)	Weight (%)	Capitalization (U.S. $ billions)	Weight (%)
Japan	2700	40	2100	41
U.S.	2100	31	1800	34
U.K.	680	10	560	11
Canada	220	3.2	110	2.1
Germany	220	3.2	160	3.1
France	160	2.3	100	2.0
Australia	140	2.0	64	1.2
Switzerland	130	1.9	58	1.1
Italy	120	1.8	85	1.6
Netherlands	87	1.3	66	1.3
Sweden	70	1.0	17	0.32
Hong Kong	54	0.79	38	0.72
Belgium	42	0.61	29	0.56
Denmark	20	0.30	11	0.20
Singapore	18	0.26	6.2	0.12
New Zealand	16	0.23	7.4	0.14
Norway	12	0.17	2.2	0.042
Austria	7.9	0.12	3.9	0.074
Total	6800	100	5300	100

[1] From "Activities and Statistics: 1987 Report" by Federation Internationale des Bourses de Valeurs (page 16).

[2] The FT-Actuaries World Indices™ are jointly compiled by The Financial Times Limited, Goldman, Sachs & Co., and County NatWest/Wood Mackenzie in conjunction with the Institute of Actuaries and the Faculty of Actuaries. This table excludes Finland, Ireland, Malaysia, Mexico, South Africa and Spain.

Table 3   Exchange Rate Volatilities, 1986–1988

	Japan	U.S.	U.K.	Canada	Germany	France	Australia	Switzer- land
Japan	0	11	9	12	7	7	14	7
U.S.	11	0	11	5	11	11	11	12
U.K.	9	10	0	11	8	8	14	9
Canada	12	5	11	0	12	11	12	13
Germany	7	11	8	12	0	3	15	4
France	7	11	8	11	2	0	14	5
Australia	14	11	14	12	14	14	0	15
Switzerland	7	12	9	13	4	5	15	0
Italy	8	10	8	11	3	3	14	5
Netherlands	7	11	8	11	2	3	14	5
Sweden	7	8	7	9	5	5	12	7
Hong Kong	11	4	11	6	11	11	11	12
Belgium	9	11	9	12	6	6	14	8
Denmark	8	11	8	11	4	4	14	6
Singapore	10	6	10	8	10	10	12	11
New Zealand	17	15	16	15	17	17	14	18
Norway	9	10	9	10	7	7	13	9
Austria	8	11	9	12	5	5	15	7

Table 3 to 5 contain statistics for 1986–88 and Tables 6 to 8 contain statistics for 1981–85. These subperiods give an indication of how statistics change from one sample period to another.

When averaging exchange rate volatilities over pairs of countries, we include the volatility of a country's exchange rate with itself. Those volatilities are always zero; they run diagonally through Tables 3 and 6. This means that the average exchange rate volatilities shown in Tables 5 and 8 are lower than the averages of the positive numbers in Tables 3 and 6.

The excess returns in Tables 4 and 7 are averages for the world market return in each country's currency, minus that country's riskless interest rate. The average excess returns differ

Table 3   Exchange Rate Volatilities, 1986–1988 (Continued)

Italy	Nether-lands	Sweden	Hong Kong	Belgium	Denmark	Singa-pore	New Zealand	Norway	Austria
8	7	7	11	9	8	10	17	9	8
10	11	8	4	11	11	6	15	10	11
8	8	7	11	9	8	10	16	9	9
11	11	9	6	12	11	8	15	10	12
3	2	5	11	6	4	10	17	8	5
3	3	5	11	6	4	10	17	7	5
14	14	12	11	14	14	12	14	14	14
5	5	7	12	8	6	11	18	9	7
0	3	5	11	6	4	10	17	7	5
3	0	5	11	6	4	10	17	7	5
5	5	0	8	6	4	8	16	6	5
10	11	8	0	11	11	5	14	10	11
6	6	6	11	0	6	10	17	8	6
4	4	4	11	6	0	10	17	7	5
10	10	8	5	10	10	0	15	10	10
17	17	15	14	17	17	15	0	16	17
7	7	5	10	8	7	10	16	0	7
5	5	5	11	6	5	10	17	8	0

between countries because of differences in exchange rate movements.

The excess returns are *not* national market returns. For example, the Japanese market did better than the U.S. market in 1987, but the world market portfolio did better relative to interest rates in the U.S. than in Japan.

Because exchange rate volatility contributes to average stock market volatility, σ_m^2 should be greater than $\frac{1}{2}\sigma_e^2$. Exchange rate volatility also contributes to the average return on the world market, so μ_m should be greater than $\frac{1}{2}\sigma_e^2$ too.

AN EXAMPLE

Tables 5 and 8 suggest one way to create inputs for the formula. The average excess return on the world market was 3 percent in the earlier period and 11 percent in the later period. We may thus estimate a future excess return of 8 percent.

The volatility of the world market was higher in the later period, but that included the crash, so we may want to use the 15 per cent volatility from the earlier period. The average exchange rate volatility of 10 per cent in the earlier period may also be a better estimate of the future than the more recent 8 percent.

This reasoning leads to the following possible values for the inputs:

Table 4   **World Market Excess Returns and Return Volatilities in Different Currencies, 1986–1988**

| | Excess Return | | | Return Volatility | | |
Currency	1986	1987	1988	1986	1987	1988
Japan	8	−12	21	14	26	15
U.S.	29	12	14	13	25	11
U.K.	23	−14	16	14	26	15
Canada	26	4	5	14	24	11
Germany	8	−5	30	15	27	14
France	11	−7	27	14	26	14
Australia	23	−2	−6	19	25	14
Switzerland	8	−8	36	15	27	15
Italy	2	−6	23	15	27	14
Netherlands	8	−7	30	15	27	14
Sweden	16	−6	19	13	25	13
Hong Kong	30	13	17	13	25	11
Belgium	7	−8	28	15	27	14
Denmark	8	−10	26	15	27	14
Singapore	36	6	16	12	25	12
New Zealand	15	−22	13	20	29	14
Norway	19	−11	15	14	26	12
Austria	7	−6	30	15	27	14

Table 5   World Average Values, 1986–1988

	Excess Return	Return Volatility	Exchange Rate Volatility
1986	17	14	9
1987	-3	26	8
1988	18	13	8
1986–88	11	18	8

$$\mu_m = 8\%$$
$$\sigma_m = 15\%$$
$$\sigma_e = 10\%$$

Given these inputs, the formula tells us that 77 per cent of holdings should be hedged:

$$\frac{0.08 - 0.15^2}{0.08 - \frac{1}{2}(0.10)^2} = 0.77$$

To compare the results of using different inputs, we can use the historical averages from both the earlier and later periods:

$$\mu_m = 3\% \text{ or } 11\%$$
$$\sigma_m = 15\% \text{ or } 18\%$$
$$\sigma_e = 10\% \text{ or } 8\%$$

With the historical averages from the earlier period as inputs, the fraction hedged comes to 30 per cent:

$$\frac{0.03 - 0.15^2}{0.03 - \frac{1}{2}(0.10)^2} = 0.30$$

Table 6   Exchange Rate Volatilities, 1981–1985

	Japan	U.S.	U.K.	Canada	Germany	France	Australia	Switzerland	Italy	Netherlands
Japan	0	12	13	11	10	10	12	11	9	10
U.S.	11	0	12	4	12	13	11	13	10	12
U.K.	12	13	0	12	10	11	14	12	11	10
Canada	11	4	11	0	11	12	10	12	10	11
Germany	10	12	10	12	0	5	13	7	5	2
France	10	13	11	12	4	0	12	8	5	5
Australia	12	10	13	10	12	12	0	13	11	12
Switzerland	11	14	12	13	7	8	14	0	8	7
Italy	9	10	11	10	5	5	12	8	0	5
Netherlands	10	12	10	11	2	5	12	7	5	0

Table 7   World Market Excess Returns and Return Volatilities in Different Currencies, 1981–1985

Currency	Excess Return	Return Volatility
Japan	3	17
U.S.	−1	13
U.K.	10	16
Canada	2	13
Germany	8	15
France	7	16
Australia	7	18
Switzerland	9	16
Italy	4	15
Netherlands	8	15

Using averages from the later period gives a fraction hedged of 73 per cent:

$$\frac{0.11 - 0.18^2}{0.11 - \frac{1}{2}(0.08)^2} = 0.73$$

Generally, straight historical averages vary too much to serve as useful inputs for the formula. Estimates of long-run average values are better.

OPTIMIZATION

The universal hedging formula assumes that you put into the formula your opinions about what investors around the world expect for the future. If your own views on stock markets and on exchange rates are the same as those you attribute to investors generally, then you can use the formula can be used as it is.

Table 8   World Average Values, 1981–1985

Excess Return	Return Volatility	Exchange Rate Volatility
3	15	10

If your views differ from those of the consensus, you may want to incorporate them using optimization methods. Starting with expected returns and covariances for the stock markets and exchange rates, you would find the mix that maximizes the expected portfolio return for a given level of volatility.

The optimization approach is fully consistent with the universal hedging approach. When you put the expectations of investors around the world into the optimization approach, you will find that the optimal currency hedge for any foreign investment will be given by the universal hedging formula.

A NOTE ON THE CURRENCY HEDGE

The formula assumes that investors hedge real (inflation-adjusted) exchange rate changes, not changes due to inflation differentials between countries. To the extent that currency changes are the result of changes in inflation, the formula is only an approximation.

In other words, currency hedging only approximates real exchange rate hedging. But most changes in currency values, at least in countries with moderate inflation rates, are due to changes in real exchange rates. Thus currency hedging will normally be a good approximation to real exchange rate hedging.

In constructing a hedging basket, it may be desirable to substitute highly liquid currencies for less liquid ones. This can best be done by building a currency hedge basket that closely tracks the basket based on the universal hedging formula. When there is tracking error, the fraction hedged should be reduced.

In practice, then, hedging may be done using a basket of a few of the most liquid currencies and using a fraction somewhat smaller than the one the formula suggests.

The formula also assumes that the real exchange rate between two countries is defined as the relative value of domestic and foreign goods. Domestic goods are those consumed at home, not those produced at home. Imports thus count as domestic goods. Foreign goods are those goods consumed abroad, not those produced abroad.

Currency changes should be examined to see if they track real exchange rate changes so defined. When the currency rate changes between two countries differ from *real* exchange rate changes, the hedging done in that currency can be modified or omitted.

If everyone in the world eventually consumes the same mix of goods and services, and prices of goods and services are the same everywhere, hedging will no longer help.

APPLYING THE FORMULA TO OTHER TYPES OF PORTFOLIOS

How can you use the formula if you don't have a fully diversified international portfolio, or if foreign equities are only a small part of your portfolio? The answer depends on why you have a small amount in foreign equities. You may be

(a) wary of foreign exchange risk;

(b) wary of foreign equity risk, even if it is optimally hedged;

(c) wary of foreign exchange risk and foreign equity risk, in equal measure.

In case (a), you should hedge more than the formula suggests. In case (b), you should hedge less than the formula suggests. In case (c), it probably makes sense to apply the formula as given to the foreign equities you hold.

If the barriers to foreign investment are small, you should gain by investing more abroad and by continuing to hedge the optimal fraction of your foreign equities.

Foreign Bonds

What if your portfolio contains foreign bonds as well as foreign stocks?

The approach that led to the universal hedging formula for stocks suggests 100 per cent hedging for foreign bonds. A portfolio of foreign bonds that is hedged with short-term forward contracts still has foreign interest rate risk, as well as the expected return that goes with that risk.

Any foreign bonds you hold unhedged can be counted as part of your total exposure to foreign currency risk. The less you hedge your foreign bonds, the more you will want to hedge your foreign stocks.

At times, you may want to hold unhedged foreign bonds because you believe that the exchange rate will move in your favor in the near future. In the long run, though, you will want to hedge your foreign bonds even more than your foreign equities.

CONCLUSION

The formula's results may be thought of as a base case. When you have special views on the prospects for a certain currency, or when a currency's forward market is illiquid, you can adjust the hedging positions that the formula suggests.

When you deviate from the formula because you think a particular currency is overpriced or underpriced, you can plan to bring your position back to normal as the currency returns to normal. You may even want to use options so that your effective hedge changes automatically as the currency price changes.

Chapter 20

Understanding Option Replication Technology

Richard M. Bookstaber
Morgan Stanley & Co.

INTRODUCTION

Options appear in many financial settings. They are embedded in callable bonds and mortgage securities. They appear as caps and floors in swap transactions. They form the basis of investment strategies such as portfolio insurance and dynamic hedges. And, of course, they exist in a wide set of listed and over-the-counter markets.

Options are an essential ingredient in many investment strategies because they can mold investment returns to meet many contingencies. Options are written to increase current yield, and are purchased to protect portfolios against loss. More complex option strategies are used to hedge out the negative convexity of mortgage-backed portfolios and callable bonds. Option strategies are used to hedge the multifaceted exposure of swap portfolios and liabilities incurred through financial offerings, and to manage the exchange risk of foreign investments. And options form the basis for many of the most sophisticated trading and arbitrage strategies.

The flexibility available with options goes far beyond these examples. Indeed, one of the central propositions of finance is that it is possible to create and to hedge any payoff with the proper set of options. The limited availability of the proper options appears to be the key limitation in altering investment payoffs and hedging investment risks. However, even the limitations that might be imposed by the restricted set of options available in the market can be overcome: any option can be created through the proper trading strategy rules in buying and selling an asset, it is possible to replicate any option-like payoff in that asset.

This chapter provides a simple exposition of the technology that allows option replication. This technology fills a role in finance similar to the role filled by genetic engineering in biology. Just as the technology of genetic engineering allows biological components to be combined to create new substances that do not exist in nature, option replication technology allows financial instruments to be combined to create payoffs that cannot be obtained directly with any instruments available in the marketplace. Just as the biological substances can be used to create new immunological agents, resulting payoffs can be constructed for hedges and investment objectives that would not otherwise be attainable.

Here, the mechanics of option replication—the mechanics used widely by option trading and arbitrage houses, over-the-counter option market-makers and hedging operations—are described. Their applications extend to cover a wide variety of strategies in the fixed income markets. These include:

Asset/Liability Management

Many products offered by financial institutions have embedded options that must be managed explicitly to assure an asset/liability match. For example, most Single Premium Deferred Annuities (SPDA) and Guaranteed Investment Contracts (GIC) offered by insurance companies include a prepayment or redemption option that gives the holder an early termination right. Consumer loans offered by banks also usually provide for early payment. Because these products leave the financial institution with a portfolio of short options, the assets backing the liabilities must contain long option exposure to prevent an asset/liability mismatch in the face of interest rate swings.

Portfolio Hedging Strategies

Hedges can employ options and option replication strategies to provide minimum floor returns. This type of strategy is sometimes referred to as portfolio insurance. Portfolio hedges also can be used to address more complex, multidimensional risks. For example, an option-based hedge might be used by a Japanese investor holding U.S. Treasury bonds who wishes to implement a hedge to assure that his dollar investment does not drop below a specified yen value.[1]

Arbitrate Trading Strategies

In option arbitrage, an investor might buy an option priced in the market at an implied volatility of 15 percent, believing the actual volatility over the life of the option will be 20 percent. If he writes the option in the marketplace immediately at that higher volatility while buying it at the lower volatility, he has an arbitrage profit: He has bought an option at one price and simultaneously sold it in the market at a higher price. However even if the option is not available in the market, he can create it through the proper dynamic strategy. If he is correct about the course of volatility, his cost in creating the short position in the option is the same as his cost in writing the option at 20 percent in the market; he realizes the same arbitrage profit.

---

1 An even more complex option-related hedge can be created to achieve a total return in yen based on the dollar-based total return of the bonds; that is, to translate into yen, at a prespecified exchange rate, any gains realized in the dollar investment. A straight foreign exchange hedge cannot provide foreign exchange protection against a risky investment position because the total amount of the hedge that is necessary is not known until the investment period has come to a close. Furthermore, there are no existing option contracts to facilitate this sort of hedge, so an option-based dynamic hedging strategy must be used to create the required option payoffs.

Mortgage-Related Trading Strategies

Each mortgage-backed security contains a portfolio of short prepayment options that are triggered by a sufficient drop in rates (and occasionally by demographically based prepayment decisions). Indeed, most of the incremental yield of a mortgage-backed security over the Treasury can be attributed to the fact that the mortgage-backed holder has written a portfolio of call options and, like any call option writer, enjoys greater current yield because of the related rate exposure.

Options can be used to manage the convexity risk that arises because of this portfolio of short option positions embedded in mortgaged-backed securities. Options also can be used to facilitate trades on mispriced mortgage-backed securities. For example if the premium of the options embedded in the mortgage-backed securities is greater than the cost of replicating them, the institution can buy the securities and employ dynamic hedging technology to hedge the convexity risk of the embedded options. Because the option hedge costs less than the premium received from the overpriced embedded options, the transaction is an arbitrage strategy just like the option arbitrage. Such a strategy is akin to the popular risk-controlled arbitrage transaction.

HOW DYNAMIC HEDGING AND OPTION REPLICATION WORKS

The objective of option replication is to create a payoff that is the same as the payoff of the target option. For example to replicate a call option with an exercise price of $100 and one year to expiration, the objective must be to create a portfolio that pays off a maximum of zero or the asset price minus $100 in one year.

Suppose the price of this call option today will change 60 percent as much as the price of the underlying asset. If the asset goes up by $1.00, the call option increases in price by $.60; if the asset price drops by $1.00, the call option's price drops by $.60. (The dollar change in the option price per dollar change in the underlying asset is called the option's *delta*.) To mirror the price character-istics of the target option, take a 60 percent position in the under-lying asset.

If tomorrow the asset has risen by two dollars, the position will have risen by $1.20. An observer looking at the way the port-folio is moving will not be able to distinguish the position's perfor-mance from the performance that would have occurred had if the target option actually had been purchased in the marketplace.

Option replication proceeds by asking the same question each day: "If I had actually bought the target option, how would its price change with a change in the price of the underlying asset?" The hedge then is adjusted to make the position of the replicating strategy have the same movement as the option itself would have. Because day by day the price movement of the option is mirrored, the option price is matched as the time to expiration arrives. At the end of the program, the same payoff exists as if the option had been purchased.

Delta-Neutral Hedging

Delta-neutral hedging is illustrated in Figure 1. It shows the value of the target call option as a function of the price of the underlying asset. Becuase the target option is a call option, its price increases at an increasing rate with a change in the price of the underlying asset. The slope of its price diagram at the current asset price is its delta. In this example, the slope is .60.

It is this payoff diagram that the hedging strategy must repro-duce. At its current price, it can be done by buying 60 percent of the underlying asset. As the tangent line illustrates, doing so mim-ics the price movements of the option around the current price level. By attempting to match the slope, or delta, of the underlying payoff, this hedge is called a delta-neutral hedge.

It is readily apparent that this hedge will fail to match the target option if there is a significant price movement. The option payoff has positive curvature—its delta increases as the asset price increases—while the underlying asset has constant exposure. This

Figure 1   Creating an Option with the Asset

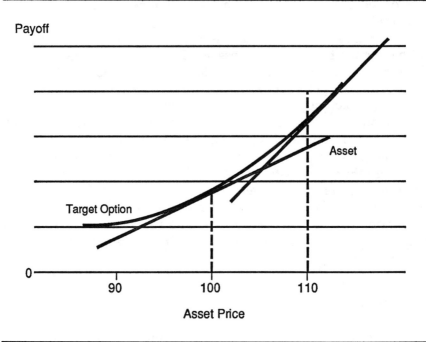

Payoff

Asset

Target Option

0

90   100   110

Asset Price

curvature is called the *gamma* of the option.[2] It means that the hedge must be adjusted as the asset price changes.

For example if the asset increases from 100 to 110, the delta might increase from .60 to .80. The asset position held in the hedge needs to increase from a .60 position to an .80 position, as illustrated by the second tangent line in the exhibit. The hedge must be adjusted frequently with asset price changes so that the tangent lines trace out facets of the curvature. The more frequently the

2   The gamma is the change in the delta of the option induced by a small change in the price of the underlying asset. Thus while the delta is the first derivative of the option price with respect to the underlying asset price, the gamma is the second derivative of the option price with respect to the price of the underlying asset. Because the underlying asset always moves one-to-one with itself, its delta is equal to 1 and its gamma is equal to 0.

hedge is adjusted, the smoother the facets will be and the better the match of the curvature of the target option.

It should be noted that the payoff curve itself shifts from day to day as the option moves closer to expiration. The change in the option price with the passage of time, referred to as the option's *theta*, requires a periodic recalculation of the option price and all the option's exposure measures, even if no other variables change.

Delta-Gamma Neutral Hedging

The fact that the option price has this curvature while the underlying asset has no curvature leads to errors in the hedge. Because in practice the hedge cannot be adjusted every instant the asset price changes, the delta-neutral hedge only approximates the actual option payoff. The hedge can be improved by introducing a hedging instrument that, itself, has curvature.

One method of doing this is illustrated in Figure 2, which presents the payoff of both the target option and a second call option that is available to use in the hedge. The second call option has a shorter time to expiration than the target option and because of this, has greater gamma. By combining the higher-gamma option and the zero-gamma underlying asset in the hedge, a hedging portfolio can be formed that matches both the slope and the curvature of the target option. Just as the delta-neutral hedge can match the slope of the target option only at the current asset price, the delta-gamma neutral hedge can match both the slope and curvature only at the current asset price. A sufficient change in price or simply the passage of time still leads to inaccuracies in the hedge. However as is clear from the exhibit, this hedge leads to smaller hedging errors than does the delta-neutral hedge.

There are variables other than the price of the underlying asset that affect the option price, such as interest rates and volatility. The option replication question can, therefore, be made more complete by generalizing it to ask: "If I had actually bought the target option, how would its price change with a change in the underlying asset price, interest rates, volatility and other variables?"

Figure 2   Using Options in the Hedge

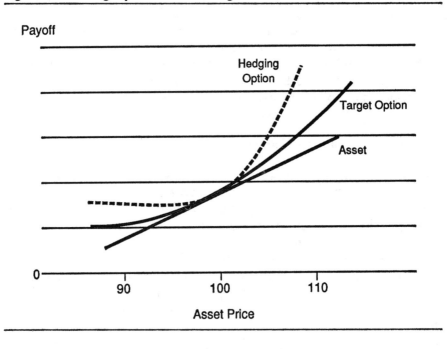

The function of the option pricing model is to answer this question. If the model is wrong, following its prescriptions day by day leads to a payoff different from what is intended. Indeed, the best measure of an option model is how closely it matches the specified payoff when its day-to-day hedging prescription is followed. Because so much has been written about option models elsewhere, in this report the model is given with the assumption that its pricing and exposure measures are correct.[3]

_____

3 Note that the majority of discussion of option models has never addressed the replication issue itself. When an option pricing model states than an option should have a particular price, it is stating that the option's payoff can be created for that cost if the hedging prescription of the model is followed. It would seem, then, that a natural test of an option model would be to follow repeatedly its hedging instructions over actual data, and track the errors between its actual and target payoffs for a given estimate of volatility. (One might want to use the actual volatility realized over the hedging period, so as to move away from a joint test of the option model and volatility prediction capability.)

A DAY IN THE LIFE OF A DYNAMIC HEDGE

To illustrate the use of dynamic hedging, note the mechanics of a single dynamic hedging adjustment in replicating a one-year call option on a hypothetical 30-year Treasury bond. The Treasury bond is assumed to have a 9 3/8 percent coupon and is initially priced at par. The target option to be replicated is a one-year call option with an exercise price of $95. Assume the carrying cost for the option position (the interest rate at which the asset used in the hedge can be borrowed or the proceeds of the hedge can be loaned out) is 8.25 percent and the price volatility of the underlying Treasury bond is 18 percent.

The specifications of the bond, and its critical exposure measures, are presented in Table 1. The option price and the associated "Greeks" are derived from the standard Black-Scholes option pricing model.[4,5] While it is well known that this model is not completely appropriate for pricing fixed income instruments, its wide availability makes it easier for those who are interested in reproducing and extending the results in the following examples.[6]

---

4 In reproducing these calculations, it is important to note the convention of adjusting for the coupon payment of the Treasury bond in the option pricing model by replacing the current bond price in the model with the bond price minus the present value of the coupon paid and its accrued interst from the bond's settlement date to the option's expiration date.

In particular, for the prices and exposure measure in Table 1 and elsewhere in the underlying Treasury bond price in the option pricing formula by its market price minus $8.80, giving an underlying asset value for option pricing purposes of $91.20. In later examples when the Treasury bond is assumed to rise to $101 or $110, likewise subtract $8.80 from those prices when doing the option calculations.

5 Delta and Gamma have been briefly defined in Section I. *Kappa* is the dollar change in the option value per 1 percent change in volatility (e.g., volatility changing from 18% to 19%). Kappa is also sometimes referred to as *vega*. *Rho* is the dollar change in the option price per 1% change in the interest rate that reflects the option carrying cost. Another measure, not explicitly treated in this analysis, is the *theta* of the option position. The theta measures the change in the option price with the change in time to expiration, i.e., the itme decay of the option.

A discussion of these exposure measures is provided in various sources, including *Option Pricing and Investment Strategies*, R. Bookstaber, Probus Publishing, Chicago, IL, 1987, pp. 125-126. This reference also includes the formulas for calculating the measures.

6 The particular problems with the model include its assumption of constant interest rates, which clearly is unrealistic for fixed income instruments, and its failure to take yield curve variations into account. These and other shortcomings are discussed in a number of publications, including "The Arbitrage-Free Pricing of Options on Interest-Sensitive Instruments" in *Advances in Futures and Options Research*, Frank Fabozzi, editor, JAI Press, Greenwich, CT, 1986, pp. 1-23.

This example is quite straightforward; but, nonetheless, it contains the essentials for applying dynamic hedging and option replication in many settings, including those described earlier. For example, it is a simple matter to replace the values for the exposure measures of the one-year Treasury option with the exposure measures of a longer-term option or a portfolio of options, and carry forward in an exactly analogous manner.

Furthermore, because both the prices and the exposure measures of a portfolio of options can be aggregated, a portfolio of options can be treated in the same manner as the single option position in the cases in this chapter. For example, to hedge a portfolio of options in a trading position or a portfolio of options embedded in a mortgage-backed position, apply an option model to solve for the exposure measures of each of the options individually, and then add up the individual measures to obtain an aggregate delta, gamma, kappa and rho. Then treat the resulting aggregates as if they represented the exposure of a single option delta because the delta of a portfolio of options is the weighted average of the individual option deltas.

Thus while the particular numbers differ, all of the analysis of the one-year call option is immediately applicable to other types of options and to other strategies—such as hedging an option book or a portfolio containing securities with embedded options—that may involve a large set of options. Indeed once a computer has done the aggregation and computed the total exposures, it is no harder to hedge a position with many options than it is to hedge a single option.

Case 1: Delta Hedging

Because (as Table 1 shows) the delta of the one-year option is .6264, if the underlying Treasury bond increases in price from 100 to 101, the option should increase in price from \$8.44 to \$9.07. To mimic the behavior of the delta of the option, take a position in .6264 Treasury bonds. The result of this hedge is illustrated in part

Table 1   Target Option Specification

Underlying Bond:	On-the-run 30-year Treasury, with a coupon = 9.375% and initially priced at par
Exercise price:	$95
Interest rate:	8.25%
Time to maturity:	1 year
Price volatility of the underlying bond:	18%
Exposure Measurements:	
Call price:	$8.44
Delta:	.6264
Gamma:	.0231
Kappa:	.0035
Rho:[1]	.0049

[1] For simplicity, assume there is no change in the price of the underlying bond due to a change in the carrying cost of the option. That is, assume the short-term interest rate and the long-term yield on which the bond price is based are independent.

A of Table 2. According to the option model, the price of the target call should move by $.64 from $8.44 to $9.09. The delta position moves from $62.64 to 63.27, for a change in price of $.63. The target option is tracked to within $.01.

The $.01 error occurs because, like all the exposure measures of the option model, the delta is a local measure. That is, it provides the relative price change between the option and the underlying asset only for very small changes in price. Even at $1.00 move in the underlying bond is sufficient to change the delta of the option from .6264 to .6491. So while the hedge position is correct for the first small movement in the option, it is slightly off over the remainder of the one-point move. To get things exactly correct would have required increasing the hedge continuously as the bond moved from 100 to 101. While the error here is insignificant, it points to the potential for far greater errors.

This potential is illustrated in part B of Table 2. Here, the same .6264 hedge is maintained while the bond moves from $100 to $110. Over the course of this 10-point move, the delta changes from .6264 to .8161. Because the hedge is maintained at the initial level, there is an error of $1.03. This is a direct manifestation of the hedging errors illustrated in Figure 1. The same tangent exposure to the option payoff is maintained, while the option price has moved up the curve. The $1.03 error is the difference between the tangent line and the option curve once it is 10 points from the tangent point.

Case 2: Delta-Gamma Hedging

The mistracking of the delta hedge is symptomatic of violations in the continuous hedging assumption that underlies the option pricing model. It results from the failure to adjust the hedge because of gap moves, or from the accumulated impact of repeatedly ad-

Table 2   Delta Hedging

A. Bond Price Moves from 100 to 101

	Initial Value	New Value	Change in Value
Target call	8.44	9.08	.64
Δ of bond	62.64	63.27	.63
Error			−.01

B. Bond Price Moves from 100 to 110

	Initial Value	New Value	Change in Value
Target call	8.44	15.73	7.29
Δ of bond	62.64	68.90	6.26
Error			−1.03

justing the hedge after a number of relatively small moves.[7] Recalling Figure 2, when the underlying asset is hedged, this error occurs because of the failure of the tangent line to match the curvature of the option being replicated. The curvature of the option payoff is measured by the gamma of the option. For example, the gamma of the one-year option is .0231. This means that the delta of the option changes by .0231 per one-point change in the underlying bond.[8]

To hedge against the curvature or gamma risk, an asset that has gamma exposure must be employed—that is, one which itself has a delta that changes as the bond price changes. The underlying bond has zero gamma—it always changes one-for-one with itself—so the investor must look elsewhere to hedge against the gamma risk. The natural place to look is to other options.[9]

Table 3 presents the characteristics of an option to be used as a hedging candidate to address the gamma exposure: a call option with three months to expiration and the same $95 exercise price as the target call option.[10] Because this option has a shorter time to expiration, its payoff curvature, and hence its gamma, is greater than that of the one-year option, or 0389 versus .0231.

There is a two-step process to use this option in the hedge. First, purchase enough of the short-term options to match the gamma of the target option. This can be done by buying

---

7   The failure of many U.S. equity portfolio insurance programs on October 19 and 20, 1987 can be attributed to gamma exposure. The rapid drop in prices did not allow timely adjustments in the delta, thus leading to a failure of the option replication. While volatility also rose over the period, it reverted back to near-historical levels after a few weeks, and thus did not have as substantial an impact on longer-term positions.

8   As with the delta, the gamma changes with changes in the price of the underlying asset and is therefore only a precise measure for very small incremental changes in the asset price. Even a one-point change in the asset will lead to enough of a change in the value of gamma to lead to a small error.

9   One way to see why it makes sense to use other options in the hedge is to go back to the objective stated earlier of matching the price changes of the target option that are induced by changes in other variables. The more similar a hedging instrument is to the target option and the more these other variables affect its price, the better it will mirror the target option's sensitivity.

10 The same conventions are followed in applying the Black-Scholes model to this three-month option as are followed for the one-year option. The bond price is discounted to $97.68 to adjust for the present value of the coupon and accrued interest, and the days to expiration used is $365/4 = 91.25$ days.

Table 3   Target Option Specification

Underlying Bond:	Same as target call
Exercise price:	$95
Interest rate:	7.25%
Time to maturity:	3 months
Price volatility of	
the underlying bond:	18%
Exposure Measurements:	
Call price:	$6.06
Delta:	.7111
Gamma:	.0389
Kappa:	.0017
Rho:	.0016

.0231/.0389 = .594 of the three-month option. Second, use the Treasury bond to hedge the aggregate delta of these two option positions. The aggregate delta is equal to the delta of the target option minus the delta of the three-month option already purchased.[11] This process is illustrated in Table 4. The result is a position that is both delta and gamma neutral—that is, a position that matches both the slope and the curvature of the target option payoff at the current Treasury bond price.

Parts A and B of Table 5 illustrate the performance of this hedge in matching the target payoff for the two cases considered in the delta hedging strategy. For a one-point move in the bond price, the hedge performs to an accuracy of better than $.01. For a 10-point move, the hedge has a $.17 tracking error—less than one-fifth the error of the delta-neutral hedge. However, it is important

Table 4   Steps in Delta-Gamma Hedge

Step 1: Eliminate Gamma Exposure

	Delta	Gamma	Kappa	Rho
Target call option	.6264	.0231	.0035	.0049
.594 3-month call options	.4224	.0231	.0010	.0010
Remaining exposure	.2040	0	.0025	.0039

Step 2: Eliminate Delta Exposure

	Delta	Gamma	Kappa	Rho
.204 of underlying bond	.2040	0	0	0
Remaining exposure	0	0	.0025	.0039

to note that even the delta-gamma neutral hedge does not perform perfectly for large moves in the price of the underlying bond because the curvature is matched precisely only at the current bond price of $100.

The performance can be enhanced by proper selection of the option used in the hedge. The closer the characteristics of the hedging option are to the target option (the closer the gamma of the two options, for example), the wider the range of asset prices and parameter variations where the hedge will be secure. The hedge also can be improved by combining two options, one with a shorter and one with a longer time to expiration than the option to be replicated.

It is easy to imagine tightening the hedge further by not only matching the slope and the change in the slope, or curvature, of the target option, but also by using more options to match the change in the curvature, the change in the change in the curvature and so on. Alternatively, additional instruments can be used to match the delta and gamma along the curve, not just at the current bond price. In theory, the only limit is the number of options in the marketplace. The tradeoff is between the frequency of hedge

---

11 The calculation for the delta hedge is

$$.204 = \Delta_{long} - \frac{\Gamma_{long}}{\Gamma_{short}} \times \Delta_{short}$$

adjustments and the number of options that must be purchased and managed because the better the match, the less frequency hedge adjustments are needed.

As a practical matter, adding too many options to the arsenal results in hedge improvements that look better on paper than when actually executed. First, option models are imperfect, and those imperfections become more manifest the greater the number of disparate options the model combines. If five or 10 different options with widely varying times to expiration and exercise prices are aggregated, the cumulative error in the model may exceed the theoretical improvement in the hedging fit. Second, generally only near-the-money options with a short time to expiration are liquid. Adding options to the arsenal gives a tighter fit, but may end up doing so at an upfront cost that exceeds the potential cost of mistracking. Part B of Table 5 gives some idea of what this mistracking is because a 10 percent price gap leads to less than three-sixteenths of a point of mistracking for even the simplest delta-gamma neutral hedge.

Part C of Table 5 illustrates the impact of interest rate changes on hedging performance.[12] It shows the same delta-gamma neutral hedge of part B, but now under the assumption that the carrying cost of the option drops by 100 basis points, from 8.25 percent to 7.25 percent.[13] The differing times to expiration of the three-month and one-year call cause them to be affected differently by the drop in the carrying cost. While the target call drops an additional $.67 in price, the three-month call drops by only an additional $.13.

---

12 Assume throughout this example that the shift in carrying cost is independent of the interest rate for the underlying Treasury bond. In practice, the carrying cost interest rate and the 30-year bond yield is correlated, and the shift in the short-term rate is likely to be accompanied by a change in the price of the Treasury bond. Option models applied to fixed income instruments generally take this correlation into account. However, as already noted, we maintain the convention of using the Black-Scholes model and of shifting the short-term rate independently of the Treasury bond price to make the examples that form the body of this report easily reproducible.

13 The carrying cost of the option is the cost of funding the security position used in the replication. It is a short-term interest rate which, as was noted earlier, for expositional purposes is independent of the underlying bond price.

Table 5   Delta-Gamma Hedging

A. *Bond Price Moves from 100 to 101*

	Initial Value	New Value	Change in Value
Target call	8.44	9.08	.64
.594 of 3-month call	62.64	63.27	.63
.204 of bond			.20
Error			.00

B. *Bond Price Moves from 100 to 110*

	Initial Value	New Value	Change in Value
Target call	8.44	15.73	7.29
.594 of 3-month call	3.60	8.68	5.08
.204 of bond	20.40	22.44	2.04
Error			−0.17

C. *Bond Price Moves from 100 to 101 and the Carrying*
   Cost of the Options Drops 100bp

	Initial Value	New Value	Change in Value
Target call	8.44	15.06	6.62
	3.60	8.55	4.95
Δ of bond	20.40	22.44	2.04
Error			.37

This differential is apparent by comparing the rhos of the respective options: .0016 for the three-month and .0049 for the one-year option. The net result of the interest rate drop is to cause the hedging error to more than double, from $.17 to $.37.

Case 3: Delta-Gamma Rho Hedging

As seen in part C, the delta-gamma neutral hedge has a shortcoming in not controlling for changes in the carrying cost of the option position. The option pricing model requires an interest rate assumption that measures the costs of financing the hedge position. For a call option, an increase in interest rates increases the carrying cost and causes the option price to increase. For many hedging applications, an instrument to address this interest rate risk explicitly is required.[14]

Just as the gamma error was hedged by introducing a hedging vehicle that contained gamma exposure, the interest rate error can be hedged by introducing a hedging vehicle that has interest rate exposure. The hedging instrument for this example is a Eurodollar futures contract.[15] The specifications for the Eurodollar futures are presented in Table 6.

The most interesting characteristic from a hedging perspective is that, because it is assumed the short-term interest rate and the bond price are independent, the futures contract focuses on interest rate risk without affecting the delta, gamma or kappa. This means that to hedge the interest rate risk, proceed in two steps as above for the delta-gamma hedge. Then add a third step of matching the aggregate rho with an appropriate Eurobond futures position. The sequence of steps is presented in Table 7.

The result of including the Eurodollar futures in the hedge is shown in Table 8. The hedging error is cut by more than one-third, to only $.11. This is remarkable given the specter of a 10 percent gap in price and a 100-basis-point drop in rates.

---

14 This risk is increasingly important the longer the time to expiration of the option, because the interest rate effect increases exponentially with time. Indeed for longer-term options, interest rate considerations can outweight those of volatility. Because the mean-reverting nature of volatility tends to make it increasingly predictable over longer hedging periods, the impact of its misspecifications grows less slowly than interest rate misspecification does.

15 The rho also can be addressed by simply adding a second option into the hedge. Because all options have some degree of exposure to carrying cost, the weights in a portfolio of two options and an underlying asset can be set to maintain delta-gamma-rho neutrality.

Table 6   Hedge Futures Specification

Eurodollar Futures Specifications::
    Interest rate: 7.25%

Exposure Measurements:
    Price: 92.75
    Delta: 0
    Gamma: 0
    Kappa: 0
    Rho: -.001[1]

[1] Assumes that the interest rate is expressed in the same form as the rate from which the Eurodollar futures are priced (e.g., semiannual, bond equivalent).

Case 4: Delta-Gamma-Kappa-Rho Hedging

So far, exposure from sudden gaps and interest rate shifts has been covered. Next is exposure to volatility changes. The impact of volatility shifts is measured by the position's kappa, which measures the dollar cost of a 1 percent change in volatility. For example, a target option has an assumed volatility of 18 percent and a kappa of .0035. A 1 percent increase in the volatility, from 18 percent to 19 percent increases the option price by $.35.[16]

By widening the set of options in the hedge, it is possible at any point in the hedging process to construct a hedge for volatility

16 As with the other exposure measures, kappa measures the impact of very small changes. If even a 1 percent change in volatility changes the value of kappa, the computation of the option cost from the model is slightly different from the computation obtained by multiplying the kappa for an 18% volatility by the 1% change.

Table 7   Steps in Delta-Gamma-Rho Hedge

Step 1: Eliminate Gamma Exposure

	Delta	Gamma	Kappa	Rho
Target call option	.6264	.0231	.0035	.0049
.594 3-month call options	.4224	.0231	.0010	.0010
Remaining exposure	.2040	0	.0025	.0039

Step 2: Eliminate Delta Exposure

	Delta	Gamma	Kappa	Rho
.204 of underlying bond	.2040	0	0	0
Remaining exposure	0	0	.0025	.0039

Step 3: Eliminate Rho Exposure

	Delta	Gamma	Kappa	Rho
.256 of Eurodollar futures	0	0	0	.0039
Remaining exposure	0	0	.0025	0

in a manner similar to the way delta or gamma is hedged.[17] The key difference between delta or gamma hedges and volatility hedges is that there is an incremental cost to hedging volatility. The cost of hedging delta and gamma, by contrast, is already part of the theoretical option price. Furthermore, there is no instrument available to address directly the volatility risk for a predetermined cost over the life of the option. Because the cost of the volatility

---

17 In particular by holding the underlying asset and three options, it is possible to solve a system that gives the proper weights to hedge delta, gamma, kappa and rho. The system to solve can be expressed in matrix form as:

$$
\begin{bmatrix}
1 & \Delta_2 & \Delta_3 & \Delta_4 \\
0 & \Gamma_2 & \Gamma_3 & \Gamma_4 \\
0 & \Gamma_2\,(t_2-t) & \Gamma_3\,(t_3-t) & \Gamma_4\,(t_4-t) \\
0 & (\Delta_2 - C_2 / S)\,(t_2-t) & (\Delta_3 - C_3 / S)\,(t_3-t) & (\Delta_4 - C_4 / S)\,(t_4-t)
\end{bmatrix}
\begin{bmatrix}
w_1 \\ w_2 \\ w_3 \\ w_4
\end{bmatrix}
=
\begin{bmatrix}
\Delta \\ \Gamma \\ 0 \\ 0
\end{bmatrix}
$$

Table 8   Delta-Gamma-Rho Hedging

Bond Price Moves from 100 to 110 and the Carrying Cost of the Options Drops 100 bp.

	Initial Value	New Value	Change in Value
Target call	8.44	9.08	6.62
.594 of 3-month call	3.60	63.27	4.95
.204 of bond	20.40	22.44	2.04
-.256 of Eurofuture	-23.74	-24.00	-0.26
Error			-.01

hedge at any point is a function of the asset price, time to expiration and volatility that exists at that time, the total volatility hedging cost cannot be known at the outset of the hedge. And because the cumulative cost of a volatility hedge is uncertain, the risk imposed by variations in volatility cannot be eliminated.

The distinction between hedging delta and gamma and hedging volatility should not be surprising. The Black-Scholes model was developed explicitly with the assumption that volatility is known; so any application of the model to a market with stochastic volatility is asking more of the model than it was designed to do.[18]

---

where the first column presents the characteristics of the underlying asset, and the last three columns present the relevant exposure measures for the options used in the hedge. Rows 1, 2, 3 and 4 address delta, gamma, kappa and rho risk, respectively. The third and fourth rows apply functional relationships to the neutrality conditions to re-express kappa and rho in terms of the other parameters. The options are denoted by subscripts 2, 3 and 4. The target option's characteristics are not subscripted. The time to expiration is denoted by t for the underlying option, with the appropriate subscript added for the hedging options. Note that options of more than one time period must be used in the hedge.

18 It could be argued that because the Black-Scholes model also assumes that interest rates are constant, it is beyond the bounds of the model to create a delta-gamma-rho hedge as well. It is possible, however, with minor modifications, to restate the Black-Scholes model to take into account stochastic interest rates. Merton allows for variable interest rates in his original paper on the subject, "Theory of Rational Option Pricing," by R.C. Merton, Bell Journal of Economics and Management Science 4, pp. 141-183. Allowing for variable interest rate changes the model option prices, and therefore the cost of hedging.

Table 9   Hedge Option Specification

	3-Month Call	6-Month Call
Underlying Bond:	Same as target call	Same as target call
Exercise price:	$95	$100
Time to maturity:	3 months	6 months
Interest rate:	7.25%	7.75%
Price volatility of		
the underlying bond:	18%	18%
Exposure Measurements:		
Price:	6.06	6.06
Delta:	.7111	.7111
Gamma:	.0389	.0389
Kappa:	.0017	.0017
Rho:	.0016	.0016

To illustrate a delta-gamma-kappa-rho hedge, a second option is added to the hedging strategy. While one option is sufficient to hedge the gamma exposure, two options are needed to address simultaneously the gamma and kappa exposure. Furthermore, the relationship between gamma and kappa requires that the options have different times to expiration for an effective hedge.

In this hedging procedure, an option with six months to expiration is added to the three-month option already employed. The characteristics of the two hedging options are summarized in Table 9.[19] With these two options, a hedging procedure similar to that of the delta-gamma-rho hedge can be used. The only difference is that in the first step, the hedger must solve simultaneously to eliminate both the kappa and the gamma exposure. He then can move sequentially through the adjustments for delta and rho exposure, using the underlying asset and the Eurobond futures contract. This procedure is illustrated in Table 10.

---

19 Assume the present value of the coupon payments for the six-mongh option is $3.80, so that the option valuation will be done assuming an initial price for the option of $96.20. In addition following the same convention used for the three-month option, translate half a year into assuming there are 182.5 days to expiration.

Table 10   Steps in Delta-Gamma-Kappa-Rho Hedge

Step 1: Eliminate Gamma and Kappa Exposure

	Delta	Gamma	Kappa	Rho
Target call option	.6264	.0231	.0035	.0049
−.977 of 3-month call option	−.6943	−.0380	−.00163	−.00155
1.878 of 6-month call options	.9867	.0610	.00509	.00429
Remaining exposure	.3340	0	0	.0021

Step 2: Eliminate Delta Exposure

.334 of underlying bond	.3340	0	0	0
Remaining exposure	0	0	0	.0021

Step 3: Eliminate Rho Exposure

−.470 of Eurodollar futures	0	0	0	.0021
Remaining exposure	0	0	0	0

Table 11 compares the results of this hedge with delta hedging and delta-gamma hedging under conditions in which the bond price gaps up from a price of 100 to 110, the interest carrying cost drops by 100 basis points and volatility increases from 18 percent to 22.5 percent. The delta hedge has a tracking error of −1.71. The delta-gamma hedge drops that error by over half, to −.78. Adding the second option to address the kappa exposure drops the hedging error to .33, nearly a five-fold reduction in absolute value from the error of the delta hedge.

It bears repeating that this hedging improvement does not come without a cost. The continual adjustments in the shorter-term options to address the risk of volatility changes leads to an additional hedging cost, and that cost is not determined completely until the hedge is completed.

Table 11 Delta-Gamma-Kappa-Rho Hedging

Scenario: Bond Price moves from 100 to 110, the carrying cost of the options drops by 100 bp and the volatility moves from 18% to 22.5%

A. Delta Hedging

	Initial Value	New Value	Change in Value
Target call	8.44	16.41	7.97
Δ bond	62.64	68.90	6.26
Error			−1.71

B. Delta-Gamma Hedging

	Initial Value	New Value	Change in Value
Target call	8.44	16.41	7.29
.594 of 3-month call	3.60	8.75	5.15
.204 of bond	20.40	22.44	2.04
Error			−.78

C. Delta-Gamma-Kappa-Rho Hedging

	Initial Value	New Value	Change in Value
Target call	8.44	16.41	7.97
−.976 of 3-month call	−5.91	−14.38	−8.47
1.878 of 6-month call	9.16	23.06	13.90
.344 of bond	33.40	36.74	3.34
−.470 of Eurodollar futures	−43.60	−44.07	− .47
Error			.33

(Table continues)

Table 11   Delta-Gamma-Kappa-Rho Hedging (Continued)

D. Delta-Gamma-Rho Hedging with Volatility/Gap Protection

	Initial Value	*New Value*	*Change in Value*
Target call	8.44	16.41	7.97
.315 of 3-month call at 110	.19	1.43	1.24
.489 of 3-month put at 90	.27	.09	– .16
.642 of bond	64.20	70.62	6.42
–.202 of Eurodollar future	–18.74	–18.94	– .20
Error			– .67

A second way to take a hedge position against volatility is to use a straddle, a position that uses both at-the-money puts and calls,—or a strangle, a position that uses both out-of-the-money calls and out-of-the-money puts. Both strangles and straddles give a payoff based on the amount the asset price moves, regardless of the direction in which it moves. These strategies, thus, have a volatility-related payoff.

Table 12 presents the specifications of the options to be used in the strangle: a put option with a $90 strike price and a call option with a $110 strike price. These are selected over the $95 strike price call of the previous examples for two reasons. First, it is postulated that a surge in volatility will be accompanied by a move of approximately 10 percent in the market. Second, options that give the greatest kappa "kick" under such circumstances are more desirable. These out-of-the-money options enjoy a much greater increase in value, per dollar invested, from an increase in volatility and from the change in the market that it is postulated would ac-

Table 12   Strangle Option Specification

	3-Month Put	3-Month Call
Underlying Bond:	Same as target call	Same as target call
Exercise price:	$90	$100
Interest rate:	7.25%	7.25%
Time to maturity:	3 months	3 months
Price volatility of the underlying bond:	18%	18%
Exposure Measurements:		
Price:	.5596	.6126
Delta:	–.1236	.1417
Gamma:	.0232	.0255
Kappa:	.0010	.0011
Rho:	–.0003	.0003

company an increase in volatility, than would be the 95 call option.[20]

Having selected the hedging vehicles, the creation of the hedge follows the same mechanics as the delta-gamma hedge in Case 2. First find the amount of the call and put option to hold to match the gamma of the target call option if the Treasury bond drops to $90 or rises to $110.[21] Second, eliminate the aggregate

---

20 Obviously if the increase in volatility is not accompanied by a large price change, an alternative strategy might perform better. However, unlike the delta, gamma and rho hedges, there is no costless, deterministic way to hedge kappa exposure because no pure volatility hedging instrument exists. In practice, some trading judgment must, therefore, be used in addressing the kappa exposure.

21 This is done by solving the following two equations:
Solve for SC = short call fraction and
SP = short-term put fraction in the following set of equations:

$$SC\ \Gamma_{call\ (90)} + SP\ \Gamma_{put\ (90)} = \Gamma_{(90)}$$
$$SC\ \Gamma_{call\ (110)} + SP\ \Gamma_{put\ (110)} = \Gamma_{(110)}$$

Thus,

$$\text{short call fraction} = \frac{\Gamma_{(90)} \times \Gamma_{put\,(110)} - \Gamma_{(110)} \times \Gamma_{put\,(90)}}{\Gamma_{put\,(110)} \times \Gamma_{call\,(90)} - \Gamma_{put\,(90)} \times \Gamma_{call\,(110)}}$$

delta of this position by taking the appropriate position in the underlying bond.[22] Because the bond has zero gamma, this position has no effect on the gamma hedge already put in place. Third, eliminate the aggregate interest rate exposure from this position by taking the appropriate position in the Eurobond futures.[23] Just as the Treasury bond has no gamma exposure, the Eurobond futures have no delta or gamma exposure, and they can be applied to the hedge without disturbing the dimensions of the hedge that already have been put it place.

Part D of Table 11 presents the hedge results. These results can be compared with the simple delta-neutral hedge, the delta-gamma-rho hedge and the delta-gamma-kappa-rho hedge of that table. Applying the straddle hedge results in the second lowest hedging error, 67 basis points.

What About Theta Hedging?

Those who are familiar with the option lexicon may be wondering why theta is ignored in the treatment of the members of that Greek family. Theta measures the change in the price of an option with a change in the time to expiration, so it is a measure of the time decay of an option position. Theta exposure is closely related

---

22

$$\text{short put fraction} = \frac{\Gamma_{(90)} \times \Gamma_{\text{call (110)}} - \Gamma_{(110)} \times \Gamma_{\text{call (90)}}}{\Gamma_{\text{call (110)}} \times \Gamma_{\text{put (90)}} - \Gamma_{\text{call (90)}} \times \Gamma_{\text{put (110)}}}$$

Eliminate remaining Δ for the bond price equal to 100 by taking a long position of the underlying bond where B is as follows:

$\Delta_{\text{long (100)}} - SC \, \Delta_{\text{short call (100)}} - SP \, \Delta_{\text{short put (100)}}$

23 Step 3: Eliminate the remaining ρ for the bond price equal to 100 by shorting

$$\frac{\rho_{\text{Eurofuture(100)}}}{\rho_{(100)} - SC \, \rho_{\text{call (100)}} - SP \, \rho_{\text{put (100)}}} \quad \text{Eurofutures}$$

to gamma exposure; in hedging the delta and gamma risk theta exposure is hedged as well. That is, a delta-gamma neutral position automatically is also theta-neutral, so theta hedging does not need coverage here. The relationship between delta-gamma and theta neutrality means that, even though these hedges are formed on the basis of the current instantaneous exposures, a well-conceived hedge retains its effectiveness over a long time period. Indeed, in practice the hedges described in this section potentially can be maintained for months without the need for further adjustment.

EXPOSURE MEASUREMENT

Any hedging strategy faces a number of sources of error. The exposure measures can be used to disaggregate the total error of a hedging strategy. In particular, the error can be disaggregated into four categories:

1. Error due to directional bond price movements (Delta Error)

2. Error due to bond price gap movements (Gamma Error)

3. Error due to changes in the option carrying cost (Rho Error)

4. Error due to changes in volatility (Kappa or Vega Error).

For example in the case presented in Table 10 where the bond price moved from 100 to 110, the option carrying cost dropped by 100 basis points and the volatility increased from 18 percent to 22.5 percent, the delta-neutral hedge generated a total tracking error of 171 basis points. This error can be decomposed as follows:

Delta Error:[24]	0
Gamma Error:[25]	95
Rho Error:[26]	–59
Kappa Error:[27]	<u>144</u>
Total Error:	180

The exposure analysis shows a total error of 180 basis points compared with a realized error of 171 basis points, leaving an unexplained error of –9 basis points. Because this example is model-based, the unexplained error is due to the use of linear approximations in doing the calculations. In practice, the unexplained error may be attributable to the approximation methods, errors in volatility or interest rate estimation, or model misspecification. Pinpointing the residual error requires analysis beyond the exposure measures described here.

The time series characteristics of the error can provide insight into hedging performance. Ideally, the unexplained residual should have a zero mean. Improvements in hedging expertise are manifested by the standard deviation of each of the sources of error decreasing over time. Improvements in the option model are manifested by decreases in the standard error of the unexplained residual.

Assessing Disaster Scenarios

Because the greatest risk in option replication strategies comes from price gaps and volatility changes, a useful "what-if" exercise is to look at the potential losses should price gaps or volatility changes occur. Tables 13 and 14 present exposure measurement matrices for the delta-neutral hedge of Case 1 and the delta-

---

24 Because the position is delta neutral, there is no impact from directional bond price movements.

25 Gamma Error $\approx$ ds $(\Delta_{s + dS/2} - \Delta_s)$ = dS $\Gamma_{s + dS/2}$ dS/2
   = [(dS) 2/2] $\Gamma_{s + dS/2}$ = (10 + 10/2) Γ_{105} = 50 .019 = 95 basis points

26 Rho Error $\approx$ $\rho_{s + dS/2}$ d (interest rate) = ρ_{105} (–100b.p.) = .0059 (–100) = –.59 basis points

27 Kappa Error $\approx$ $K_{s + dS/2}$ d (volatility) = K_{105} (22.5% – 18%) = .0032 (450b.p.) = 144 basis points

Table 13   Exposure Matrix

Delta Hedging

Error in Basis Points
(Initial Volatility = 18%)

Bond Price	Ending Volatility		
	13.5%	*18%*	*22.5%*
110	6.84	−102.02	−231.21
109	30.88	−83.80	−216.85
108	53.26	−67.12	−203.86
107	73.84	−52.08	−192.29
106	92.45	−38.76	−182.21
105	108.95	−27.26	−173.67
104	123.16	−17.66	−166.73
103	134.93	−10.05	−161.44
102	144.12	−4.52	−157.85
101	150.55	−1.14	−156.03
100	154.10	0.00	−156.02
99	154.64	−1.17	−157.87
98	152.03	−4.71	−161.63
97	146.19	−10.69	−167.33
96	137.02	−19.15	−175.02
95	124.47	−30.16	−184.74
94	108.49	−43.73	−196.52
93	89.08	−59.91	−210.37
92	66.23	−78.69	−226.33
91	39.99	−100.10	−244.41
90	10.42	−124.11	−264.61

Table 14   Exposure Matrix

Delta-Gamma Hedging

Error in Basis Points
(Initial Volatility = 18%)

Bond Price		Ending Volatility	
	13.5%	18%	22.5%
110	81.78	−16.89	−126.61
109	89.75	−12.49	−123.56
108	96.49	−8.87	−120.97
107	102.00	−5.99	−118.80
106	106.28	−3.79	−116.98
105	109.38	−2.19	−115.47
104	111.40	−1.12	−114.20
103	112.44	−0.47	−113.11
102	112.66	−0.14	−112.13
101	112.23	−0.02	−111.19
100	111.37	0.00	−110.23
99	110.26	0.02	−109.21
98	109.12	0.12	−108.06
97	108.10	0.40	−106.74
96	107.35	0.91	−105.23
95	106.93	1.67	−103.50
94	106.86	2.70	−101.56
93	107.07	3.97	−99.42
92	107.44	5.42	−97.10
91	107.78	6.96	−94.66
90	107.85	8.49	−92.15

gamma neutral hedge of Case 2 in the previous section. These tables measure the exposure for bond prices ranging from $90 to
$110, and for volatility values of 13.5 percent, 18 percent and 22.5
percent. The matrix form of the table is especially useful because
large gaps in price generally are accompanied by at least short-
term changes in volatility.

By looking at the exhibits, the risk of various size gaps and
changes in volatility can be assessed. For example if the underlying Treasury bond were to gap up in price 5 percent to $105 and
volatility were to simultaneously increase from 18 percent to 22.5
percent, the delta hedge would realize a mistracking of –173.67
basis points.[28] Under the same circumstances, the delta-gamma
neutral hedge would realize a loss of –115.47 basis points. The
error potential is not one-sided; a drop in volatility would lead to
unexpected gains.

---

28 The increase in volatility is assumed to be a one-time jump that will continue for the remaining
life of the option.

Chapter 21

Rolling Down the Vol Curve

Stan Jonas
Shearson Lehman Hutton

Perhaps, the most persistent empirical relationship in the options marketplace is beginning to exert its influence once again. The relationship in question is the spread between the implied volatility of the first option on Eurodollar futures and that on the second future contract. Today that spread is between the September '89 Euro's and the options on the December, 1989 contract. While this relationship has almost run its course with the nearby expiration of the September Euro on September 18th, 1989, the pattern is beginning to repeat itself with the December/March contracts.

The accompanying chart plots the average difference between the implied volatility[1] of the at-the-money option on the nearby Eurodollar futures contract versus the implied volatility of a similar at-the-money option on the second or deferred Eurodollar futures. This relationship is plotted against days to expiration of the first option (futures); the data is the average of the experience of each expiration cycle since the inception of Eurodollar option trad-

---

1 Volatility based on current option prices and a option pricing model is called implied volatility.

ing. So the relationship shows the typical spread with 100 days to maturity, and following 75, 50 and eventually 1 day to expiration.

The chart also tracks the difference between the realized[2] volatility of the first contract versus the second, scaled again, against days to expiration.

As is seen from approximately 100 days to expiration, there is a persistent collapse of the nearby volatility relative to the deffered. While at three months to expiration the two series of options are trading at equal implied volatilities, within weeks the spread widens to over two percentage points in implied volatility terms. This difference eventually tends to widen to nearly 5 percent in "vol" terms.

REALIZED VERSUS IMPLIED

Perhaps more interesting relationship is between the realized volatilities of the two contracts. This relationship appears to follow the same pattern as the implied. As time progresses toward expiration, the nearby contract experiences less volatility than the second contract. This relationship lends more credence to that between the implied volatilities. Eurodollar traders have long known of the nearby contracts "suction to cash" and its resulting decline in volatility. Contrary to academic speculation, the nearby Eurodollar contract tends to be less volatile than the second, just as cash—with its increments of 1/16th's rather than ticks—is less volatile than futures.

THE GREEK ALPHABET

While Implied volatility is an interesting intellectual concept, it takes some manipulation to actually capture the difference in implied vols. Such trading depends on the underlying parameters of

---

2 Historical or realized volatility is generally expressed as the annualized standard deviation of the percentage daily change of a series of price, yields, or returns, historical volatility can be based on 20 days of data or 5,000 days. Historical volatility is a moving average.

the option as well as broad faith in the standard option pricing model.

The delta of a derivative security, Δ is defined as the rate of price change with respect to the price of the underlying asset. It is the slope of the curve that relates the option price to the price of the underlier. Suppose that the delta of a call option on a future is 0.6. This means that when the futures price changes by a small amount, the option price changes by about 60 percent of that amount.

The gamma, Γ of a portfolio of options on an underlying asset is the rate of portfolio delta change with respect to the price of the underlying asset. A position in the underlying futures contract has zero gamma. For hedging purposes, making a delta-neutral portfolio gamma neutral can be regarded as a first correction because the position in the underlying asset cannot be changed continuously when delta hedging is used.

The vega of a portfolio of derivative securities, Δ is the rate of portfolio value change with respect to the implied volatility of the option. Up to now, it has been implicitly assumed that the volatility of the asset underlying the option is constant. In practice, implied volatilities change over time. This means that the value of an option is liable to change because of movements in implied volatility as well as changes in the asset price and the passage of time.

A volatility forecast is an implicit projection of the distribution of prices (yields) over time. For example, a yield volatility forecast of 10 percent in an 8 percent interest rate environment implies that the distribution of possible yield levels in one year has a standard deviation of 80 basis points. (10% × 8%). Furthermore, this suggests that there is roughly a 67 percent probability that rates in one year will fall within one standard deviation of the mean (8 percent).

IMPLIED VOLATILITY IS LIKE KEYNES' BEAUTY CONTEST

Implied vol is merely a consensus of what people today think of the market's probability of movement. It is subject to supply/demand, option pricing inconsisitiencies and metaphysical constructions. Keynes likened the stock market to a beauty contest in which it was not important to pick who is thought was the winner, nor even who is thought the judges will pick as the winner; rather it is who investors in general think the judges will pick as the winner. This type of regress most closely characterizes implied volatility trading.

VEGA NEUTRAL AND ALL THAT

The key to a vega-neutral position is to establish a trade that isolates only the relative difference in implied volatilities. In other words, the bet is only on the difference between the two implied vols. It is important to mold the trade in such a fashion that investors are indifferent to shifts in any of the other parameters. Such a trade is referred to as "vega-neutral" in which quantities of each option are chosen so that they are equally sensitive to a change in implied volatility. As seen from Table 1, this means a smaller position in the longer-date options, which by definition are more sensitive to changes in implied vol, i.e., they have greater vega.

Once the position's size is chosen, sufficient futures must be taken to ensure delta neutrality.

This position utilizes at-the-money straddles in both the December '89 and the March '90 option series. As can be seen, 25 percent more of the nearby options are utilized to achieve "vega-neutrality." The additional futures in each month are necessary to delta-neutralize as well as to immunize against spread-risk between the underlying contract months themselves. *The position is then delta-neutral, vega-neutral, and negative gamma.*

The negative gamma is effectively the price paid for entry into such an attractive trade. Positive gamma means that the inability to hedge an instantaneous change in the price of the underlying results in a gain and not in a loss. Negative gamma, unfortunately, has the exact opposite connotation. At any time, the cost of this

Table 1

	F	STRIKE	NET POSITION	DELTA	WT. GAMMA[1]	WT. VEGA	WT. THETA
-13	F		-13.00	1.00	0.00	0.00	0.00
-125	Dec-89	91.5 C	-55.33	0.443	-60.25	-2.2	0.19
-125	Dec-89	91.5 P	67.59	0.541	-62.13	-2.20	0.18
		SUB-TOTAL	-0.74		-122.38	-4.40	0.37

	F	STRIKE	NET POSITION	DELTA	WT. GAMMA	WT. VEGA	WT. THETA
16	F		16.00	1.00	0.00	0.00	0.00
100	Mar-89	91.75 C	40.59	0.406	32.84	2.31	-0.11
100	Mar-89	91.75 P	-56.65	0.566	35.42	2.30	-0.10
		SUB-TOTAL	-0.06		68.26	4.61	-0.21

	NET POSITION	DELTA	WT. GAMMA	WT. VEGA	WT. THETA
TOTAL	-0.80		-54.12	0.21	0.16

[1] Weighted Gamma: the Gamma of each option multiplied by its quantity.

negative gamma can be estimated through a simple approxima-tion:[3]

$$\frac{1}{2} \times [\text{Change in Futures Price}]^2 \times \text{Gamma}$$

So if this position is continually rebalanced, a move of, say, nine basis points per day in theory produces a loss of:

$$\frac{1}{2} \times [(.09)^2 \times \$2500] \times [-54.12] = -\$547.00$$

This loss is offset by the positive time decay of the position, which is approximately $400 per day. A yield volatility of 17 per-cent implies approximately nine basis points per day of move-ment. Note that a relatively quick shift of two percentage points in volatility differential equals $9,500[4], not considering the impart of positive time decay. This "positive volatility decay" can more than offset the risk of negative gamma.

RIDING DOWN THE VOL CURVE

The regularity of this differential between the first and the second option presents attractive arbitrage and hedging strategies.

---

3 This result can be shown mathematically by taking the Taylor expansion of the option value around its present price. If $U(f,t)$ represents the price of the option where f is the futures price and t is the calendar time, it is approximately correct that for an instantaneous change, h, in the futures price, the new value of the option will be equal to:

$$U(f+h,t) = U(f,t) = h \times Delta + .5 \times h \times h \times Gamma$$

This relationship shows that the change in the value of the traded option $(U(f+h,t) - U(f,t))$ is not exactly equal to the change in the value of the synthetic option $(h \times Delta)$. The difference is equal to the amount $(.5 \times h \times h \times Gamma)$ derived in the text.

4 Obviously, the profitability of the volatility differential depends on when the movement occurs. As time progresses a given change in volatility has less dollar impact on both options. In the extreme, implied volatility may be less than the bid and offer spread in a very short dated option.

- A trader can sell vol in the *second* option and buy vol in the *third*, realizing that eventually the second contract becomes the first. This type of arbitrage is similar to rolling down the yield curve in the government securities marketplace. In effect, he is warehousing positions until they enter the decay cycle.

- Cap market participants may find this relationship an integral part of their hedging strategy. The nearby option provides an attractive area to sell volatility either against existing cap positions, or against deferred contracts. The risk of negative gamma is more than offset by the relative decline in volatility.

- Volatility/gamma players must be cautious: in the latter part of the decay cycle, it is difficult to capture profits from traditional positive gamma calendar spread tactics. At some point, however, the vol differential may be so wide that on a *forward/forward* volatility basis the nearby option looks attractive. The accompanying figures (Figure 1 and 2) show the volatility spread and the inferred *forward/forward volatility* inferred by that differential.

WHY IS IT THERE?

There is no relationship that occurs with such regularity in any listed option market place. Why should Eurodollar futures display such a phenomenon? It is believed that Eurodollar futures are, indeed, different. They represent an option on a policy variable of the United States Central Bank, the Federal Reserve. Though its power is wide-reaching in the financial marketplace, the Fed only has tight control on short-term rates or Fed Funds and—through arbitrage pressure—three-month-Eurodollar rates. Bonds, currencies, stocks, although influenced by Fed policy, are driven by a multitude of other factors that can often swamp purely domestic monetary policy considerations. Put in the vernacular, Allan Greenspan controls Euros but not very much else.

As maturity draws closer, market participants feel they can more closely estimate near term moves in Central Bank policy and, thus, they implicitly truncate the potential distribution of possible terminal values for the Eurodollar futures contract. As a result, implied volatility of the nearby option drops as maturity approaches. In this regard, the Eurodollar futures option is like an option on an agricultural commodity with a crop support program; part of the distribution is impossible to achieve, and so the value of the option must be diminished.

Futures traders have long considered the spread between the first Eurodollar future and the second as an implied option as delivery draws closer. The key premise is that whatever happens, "it will happen more to the second contract than the first." This "suction to cash" has been carried over into the option market place. Its existence, while obviously inconsistent with any option pricing model, can be ignored only at the financial peril of the trader.

Figure 1   3 Month Forward Implied Volatility Average (12/87-06/89)

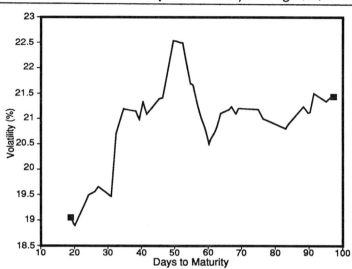

**Figure 2   2nd-1st Eurodollar Implied vs. 20 Day Historical Volatility
Historical Average (06/88-03/88 thru 09/89-06/89)**

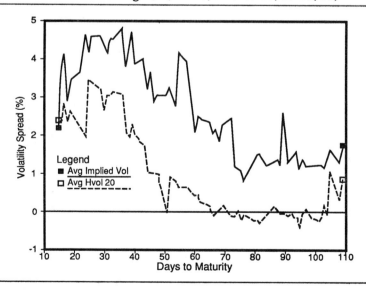

Chapter 22

How to Use the Holes in Black-Scholes[*]

Fischer Black
Goldman, Sachs & Co.

The Black-Scholes formula is still around, even though it depends on at least 10 unrealistic assumptions. Making the assumptions more realistic hasn't produced a formula that works better across a wide range of circumstances.

In special cases, though, we can improve the formula. If you think investors are making an unrealistic assumption like one of those we used in deriving the formula, there is a strategy you may want to follow that focuses on that assumption.

The same unrealistic assumptions that led to the Black-Scholes formula are behind some versions of "portfolio insurance." As people have shifted to more realistic assumptions, they have changed the way they use portfolio insurance. Some people have dropped it entirely, or have switched to the opposite strategy.

People using incorrect assumptions about market conditions may even have caused the rise and sudden fall in stocks during 1987. One theory of the crash relies on incorrect beliefs, held be-

---

[*] This article appeared in *Journal of Applied Corporate Finance* 4 (Winter, 1989).

509

fore the crash, about the extent to which investors were using portfolio insurance, and about how changes in stock prices cause changes in expected returns.

THE FORMULA

The Black-Scholes formula looks like this:

$$w\,(x,t) = xN(d_1) - ce^{-r(t^*-t)}N(d_2)$$

where

$$d_1 = \frac{\ln(x/c) + (r + 1/2v^2)\,(t^*-t)}{v\,\sqrt{t^*-t}}$$

and

$$d_2 = \frac{\ln(x/c) + (r - 1/2v^2)\,(t^*-t)}{v\,\sqrt{t^*-t}}$$

In this expression, w is the value of a call option or warrant on the stock, t is today's date, x is the stock price, c is the strike price, r is the interest rate, t^* is the maturity date, v is the standard deviation of the stock's return and N is something called the "cumulative normal density function." (You can approximate N using a simple algebraic expression.)

The value of the option increases with increases in the stock's price, the interest rate, the time remaining until the option expires, and the stock's volatility. Except for volatility, which can be estimated several ways, we can observe all of the factors the Black-Scholes formula requires for valuing options.

Note that the stock's expected return doesn't appear in the formula. If you are bullish on the stock, you may buy shares or call options, but you won't change your estimate of the option's value. A higher expected return on the stock means a higher expected return on the option, but it doesn't affect the option's value for a given stock price.

This feature of the formula is very general. I don't know of any variation of the formula where the stock's expected return affects the option's value for a given stock price.

HOW TO IMPROVE THE ASSUMPTIONS

In our original derivation of the formula, Myron Scholes and I made the following unrealistic assumptions:

- The stock's volatility is known, and doesn't change over the life of the option.
- The stock price changes smoothly: it never jumps up or down a large amount in a short time.
- The short-term interest rate never changes.
- Anyone can borrow or lend as much as he wants at a single rate.
- An investor who sells the stock or the option short will have the use of all the proceeds of the sale and receive any returns from investing these proceeds.
- There are no trading costs for either the stock or the option.
- An investor's trades do not affect the taxes he pays.
- The stock pays no dividends.
- An investor can exercise the option only at expiration.
- There are no takeovers or other events that can end the option's life early.

Since these assumptions are mostly false, we know the formula must be wrong. But we may not be able to find any other formula that gives better results in a wide range of circumstances. Here we look at each of these 10 assumptions and describe how we might change them to improve the formula. We also look at strategies that make sense if investors continue to make unrealistic assumptions.

Volatility Changes

The volatility of a stock is not constant. Changes in the volatility of a stock may have a major impact on the values of certain options, especially far-out-of-the-money options. For example, if we use a volatility estimate of 0.20 for the annual standard deviation of the stock, and if we take the interest rate to be zero, we get a value of $0.00884 for a six-month call option with a $40 strike price written on a $28 stock. Keeping everything else the same, but doubling the volatility to 0.40, we get a value of $0.465.

For this out-of-the-money option, doubling the volatility estimate multiplies the value by a factor of 53.

Since the volatility can change, we should really include the ways it can change in the formula. The option value will depend on the entire future path that we expect the volatility to take, and on the uncertainty about what the volatility will be at each point in the future. One measure of that uncertainty is the "volatility of the volatility."

A formula that takes account of changes in volatility will include both current and expected future levels of volatility. Though the expected return on the stock will not affect option values, expected changes in volatility will affect them. And the volatility of volatility will affect them too.

Another measure of the uncertainty about the future volatility is the relation between the future stock price and its volatility. A decline in the stock price implies a substantial increase in volatility, while an increase in the stock price implies a substantial decrease in volatility. The effect is so strong that it is even possible that a stock with a price of $20 and a typical daily move of $0.50 will start having a typical daily move of only $0.375 if the stock price doubles to $40.

John Cox and Stephen Ross have come up with two formulas that take account of the relation between the future stock price and its volatility.[1] To see the effects of using one of their formulas on the pattern of option values for at-the-money and out-of-the

---

[1] See John Cox and Stephen Ross, *Journal of Financial Economics* (January/March 1976).

money options, let's look at the values using both Black-Scholes and Cox-Ross formulas for a six-month call option on a $40 stock, taking the interest rate as zero and the volatility as 0.20 per year. For three exercise prices, the values are as follows:

Exercise Price	Black Scholes	Cox-Ross
40.00	2.2600	2.2600
50.00	0.1550	0.0880
57.10	0.0126	0.0020

The Cox-Ross formula implies lower values for out-of-the-money call options than the Black-Scholes formula. But putting in uncertainty about the future volatility will often imply higher values for these same options. We can't tell how the option values will change when we put in both effects.

What should you do if you think a stock's volatility will change in ways that other people do not yet understand? Also suppose that you feel the market values options correctly in all other respects.

You should "buy volatility" if you think volatility will rise, and "sell volatility" if you think it will fall. To buy volatility, buy options; to sell volatility, sell options. Instead of buying stock, you can buy calls or buy stock and sell calls. Or you can take the strongest position on volatility by adding a long or short position in straddles to your existing position. To buy pure volatility, buy both puts and calls in a ratio that gives you no added exposure to the stock; to sell pure volatility, sell both puts and calls in the same ratio.

Jumps

In addition to showing changes in volatility in general and changes in volatility related to changes in stock price, a stock may have jumps. A major news development may cause a sudden large change in the stock price, often accompanied by a temporary suspension of trading in the stock.

When the big news is just as likely to be good as bad, a jump will look a lot like a temporary large increase in volatility. When the big news, if it comes, is sure to be good, or is sure to be bad, the resulting jump is not like a change in volatility. Up jumps and down jumps have different effects on option values than symmetric jumps, where there is an equal chance of an up jump or a down jump.

Robert Merton has a formula that reflects possible symmetric jumps.[2] Compared to the Black-Scholes formula, his formula gives higher values for both in-the-money and out-of-the-money options and lower values for at-the-money options. The differences are especially large for short-term options.

Short-term options also show strikingly different effects for up jumps and down jumps. An increase in the probability of an up jump will cause out-of-the-money calls to go way up in value relative to out-of-the-money puts. An increase in the probability of a down jump will do the reverse. After the crash, people were afraid of another down jump, and out-of-the-money puts were priced very high relative to their Black-Scholes values, while out-of-the-money calls were priced very low.

More than a year after the crash, this fear continues to affect option values.

What should you do if you think jumps are more likely to occur than the market thinks? If you expect a symmetric jump, buy short-term out-of-the-money options. Instead of stock, you can hold call options or more stock plus put options. Or you can sell at-the-money options. Instead of stock, you can hold more stock and sell call options. For a pure play on symmetric jumps, buy out-of-the-money calls and puts, and sell at-the-money calls and puts.

For up jumps, use similar strategies that involve buying short-term out-of-the-money calls, or selling short-term out-of-the-money puts, or both. For down jumps, do the opposite.

---

2 See John Cox, Robert Merton, and Stephen Ross, *Journal of Financial Economics* (January/March 1976).

Interest Rate Changes

The Black-Scholes formula assumes a constant interest rate, but the yields on bonds with different maturities tell us that the market expects the rate to change. If future changes in the interest rate are known, we can just replace the short-term rate with the yield on a zero-coupon bond that matures when the option expires.

But, of course, future changes in the interest rate are uncertain. When the stock's volatility is known, Robert Merton has shown that the zero-coupon bond yield will still work, even when both short-term and long-term interest rates are shifting.[3] At a given point in time, we can find the option value by using the zero-coupon bond yield at that moment for the short-term rate. When both the volatility and the interest rate are shifting, we will need a more complex adjustment.

In general, the effects of interest rate changes on option values do not seem nearly as great as the effects of volatility changes. If you have an opinion on which way interest rates are going, you may be better off with direct positions in fixed-income securities rather than in options.

But your opinion may affect your decisions to buy or sell options. Higher interest rates mean higher call values and lower put values. If you think interest rates will rise more than the market thinks, you should be more inclined to buy calls, and more inclined to buy more stocks and sell puts, as a substitute for a straight stock position. If you think interest rates will fall more than the market thinks, these preferences should be reversed.

Borrowing Penalties

The rate at which an individual can borrow, even with securities as collateral, is higher than the rate at which he can lend. Sometimes his borrowing rate is substantially higher than his lending

---

3 Robert Merton, *Bell Journal of Economics and Management Science* (1977).

rate. Also, margin requirements or restrictions put on by lenders may limit the amount he can borrow.

High rates and limits on borrowing may cause a general increase in call option values, since calls provide leverage that can substitute for borrowing. The interest rates implied by option values may be higher than lending rates. If this happens and you have borrowing limits but no limits on option investments, you may still want to buy calls. But if you can borrow freely at a rate close to the lending rate, you may want to get leverage by borrowing rather than by buying calls.

When implied interest rates are high, conservative investors might buy puts or sell calls to protect a portfolio instead of selling stock. Fixed-income investors might even choose to buy stocks and puts, and sell calls, to create a synthetic fixed-income position with a yield higher than market yields.

Short-Selling Penalties

Short-selling penalties are generally even worse than borrowing penalties. On U.S. exchanges, an investor can sell a stock short only on or after an uptick. He must go to the expense of borrowing stock if he wants to sell it short. Part of his expense involves putting up cash collateral with the person who lends the stock; he generally gets no interest, or interest well below market rates, on this collateral. Also, he may have to put up margin with his broker in cash, and may not receive interest on cash balances with his broker.

For options, the penalties tend to be much less severe. An investor need not borrow an option to sell it short. There is no uptick rule for options. And an investor loses much less interest income in selling an option short than in selling a stock short.

Penalties on short selling that apply to all investors will affect option values. When even professional investors have trouble selling a stock short, we will want to include an element in the option formula to reflect the strength of these penalties. Sometimes we approximate this by assuming an extra dividend yield on the stock, in an amount up to the cost of maintaining a short position as part of a hedge.

Suppose you want to short a stock but you face penalties if you sell the stock short directly. Perhaps you're not even allowed to short the stock directly. You can short it indirectly by holding put options, or by taking a naked short position in call options. (Though most investors who can't short stock directly also can't take naked short positions.)

When you face penalties in selling short, you often face rewards for lending stock to those who want to short it. In this situation, strategies that involve holding the stock and lending it out may dominate other strategies. For example, you might create a position with a limited downside by holding a stock and a put on the stock, and by lending the stock to those who want to short it.

Trading Costs

Trading costs can make it hard for an investor to create an option-like payoff by trading in the underlying stock. They can also make it hard to create a stock-like payoff by trading in the option. Sometimes they can increase an option's value, and sometimes they can decrease it.

We can't tell how trading costs will affect an option's value, so we can think of them as creating a "band" of possible values. Within this band, it will be impractical for most investors to take advantage of mispricing by selling the option and buying the stock, or by selling the stock and buying the option.

The bigger the stock's trading costs are, the more important it is for you to choose a strategy that creates the payoffs you want with little trading. Trading costs can make options especially useful if you want to shift exposure to the stock after it goes up or down.

If you want to shift your exposure to the market as a whole, rather than to a stock, you will find options even more useful. It is often more costly to trade in a basket of stocks than in a single stock. But you can use index options to reduce your trading in the underlying stocks or futures.

Taxes

Some investors pay no taxes; some are taxed as individuals, paying taxes on dividends, interest, and capital gains; and some are taxed as corporations, also paying taxes on dividends, interest, and capital gains, but at different rates.

The very existence of taxes will affect option values. A hedged position that should give the same return as lending may have a tax that differs from the tax on interest. So if all investors faced the same tax rate, we would use a modified interest rate in the option formula.

The fact that investor tax rates differ will affect values too. Without rules to restrict tax arbitrage, investors could use large hedged positions involving options to cut their taxes sharply or to alter them indefinitely. Thus tax authorities adopt a variety of rules to restrict tax arbitrage. There may be rules to limit interest deductions or capital loss deductions, or rules to tax gains and losses before a position is closed out. For example, most U.S. index option positions are now taxed each year—partly as short-term capital gains and partly as long-term capital gains—whether or not the taxpayer has closed out his positions.

If you can use capital losses to offset gains, you may act roughly the same way whether your tax rate is high or low. If your tax rate stays the same from year to year, you may act about the same whether you are forced to realize gains and losses or are able to choose the year you realize them.

But if you pay taxes on gains and cannot deduct losses, you may want to limit the volatility of your positions and have the freedom to control the timing of gains and losses. This will affect how you use options, and may affect option values as well. I find it hard to predict, though, whether it will increase or decrease option values.

Investors who buy a put option will have a capital gain or loss at the end of the year, or when the option expires. Investors who simulate the put option by trading in the underlying stock will sell after a decline, and buy after a rise. By choosing which lots of stock to buy and which lots to sell, they will be able to generate a series of realized capital losses and unrealized gains. The tax advantages of this strategy may reduce put values for many taxable investors. By a similar argument, the tax advantages of a simulated call option may reduce call values for most taxable investors.

Dividends and Early Exercise

The original Black-Scholes formula does not take account of dividends. But dividends reduce call option values and increase put option values, at least when there are no offsetting adjustments in the terms of the options. Dividends make early exercise of a call option more likely, and early exercise of a put option less likely.

We now have several ways to change the formula to account for dividends. One way assumes that the dividend yield is constant for all possible stock price levels and at all future times. Another assumes that the issuer has money set aside to pay the dollar dividends due before the option expires. Yet another assumes that the dividend depends in a known way on the stock price at each ex-dividend date.

John Cox, Stephen Ross, and Mark Rubinstein have shown how to figure option values using a "tree" of possible future stock prices.[4] The tree gives the same values as the formula when we use the same assumptions. But the tree is more flexible, and lets us relax some of the assumptions. For example, we can put on the tree the dividend that the firm will pay for each possible future stock price at each future time. We can also test, at each node of the tree, whether an investor will exercise the option early for that stock price at that time.

Option values reflect the market's belief about the stock's future dividends and the likelihood of early exercise. When you think that dividends will be higher than the market thinks, you will want to buy puts or sell calls, other things equal. When you think that option holders will exercise too early or too late, you

---

4 John Cox, Mark Rubinstein, and Stephen Ross, "Option Pricing: A Simplified Approach," *Journal of Financial Economics* Vol. 7 (1979), 229-263.

will want to sell options to take advantage of the opportunities the holders create.

Takeovers

The original formula assumes the underlying stock will continue trading for the life of the option. Takeovers can make this assumption false.

If firm A takes over firm B through an exchange of stock, options on firm B's stock will normally become options on firm A's stock. We will use A's volatility rather than B's in valuing the option.

If firm A takes over firm B through a cash tender offer, there are two effects. First, outstanding options on B will expire early. This will tend to reduce values for both puts and calls. Second, B's stock price will rise through the tender offer premium. This will increase call values and decrease put values.

But when the market knows of a possible tender offer from firm A, B's stock price will be higher than it might otherwise be. It will be between its normal level and its normal level increased by the tender offer. Then if A fails to make an offer, the price will fall, or will show a smaller-than-normal rise.

All these factors work together to influence option values. The chance of a takeover will make an option's value sometimes higher and sometimes lower. For a short-term out-of-the-money call option, the chance of a takeover will generally increase the option value. For a short-term out-of-the-money put option, the chance of a takeover will generally reduce the option value.

The effects of takeover probability on values can be dramatic for these short-term out-of-the-money options. If you think your opinion of the chance of a takeover is more accurate than the market's, you can express your views clearly with options like these.

The October 19 crash is the opposite of a takeover as far as option values go. Option values then, and since then, have reflected the fear of another crash. Out-of-the-money puts have been selling for high values, and out-of-the-money calls have been selling for low values. If you think another crash is unlikely, you may want to buy out-of-the-money calls, or sell out-of-the-money puts, or do both.

Now that we've looked at the 10 assumptions in the Black-Scholes formula, let's see what role, if any, they play in portfolio insurance strategies.

PORTFOLIO INSURANCE

In the months before the crash, people in the U.S. and elsewhere became more and more interested in portfolio insurance. As I define it, portfolio insurance is any strategy where you reduce your stock positions when prices fall, and increase them when prices rise.

Some investors use option formulas to figure how much to increase or reduce their positions as prices change. They trade in stocks or futures or short-term options to create the effect of having a long-term put against stock, or a long-term call plus T-bills.

You don't need synthetic options or option formulas for portfolio insurance. You can do the same thing with a variety of systems for changing your positions as prices change. However, the assumptions behind the Black-Scholes formula also affect portfolio insurance strategies that don't use the formula.

The higher your trading costs, the less likely you are to create synthetic options or any other adjustment strategy that involves a lot of trading. On October 19, the costs of trading in futures and stocks became much higher than they had been earlier, partly because the futures were priced against the portfolio insurers. The futures were at a discount when portfolio insurers wanted to sell. This made all portfolio insurance strategies less attractive.

Portfolio insurance using synthetic strategies wins when the market makes big jumps, but without much volatility. It loses when market volatility is high, because an investor will sell after a fall, and buy after a rise. He loses money on each cycle.

But the true cost of portfolio insurance, in my view, is a factor that doesn't even affect option values. It is the mean reversion in the market: the rate at which the expected return on the market falls as the market rises.[5]

Mean reversion is what balances supply and demand for portfolio insurance. High mean reversion will discourage portfolio insurers because it will mean they are selling when expected return is higher and buying when expected return is lower. For the same reason, high mean reversion will attract "value investors" or "tactical asset allocators," who buy after a decline and sell after a rise. Value investors use indicators like price-earnings ratios and dividend yields to decide when to buy and sell. They act as sellers of portfolio insurance.

If mean reversion were zero, I think that more investors would want to buy portfolio insurance than to sell it. People have a natural desire to try to limit their losses. But, on balance, there must be as many sellers as buyers of insurance. What makes this happen is a positive normal level of mean reversion.

THE CRASH

During 1987, investors shifted toward wanting more portfolio insurance. This increased the market's mean reversion. But mean reversion is hard to see; it takes years to detect a change in it. So investors did not understand that mean reversion was rising. Since rising mean reversion should restrain an increase in portfolio insurance demand, this misunderstanding caused a further increase in demand.

Because of mean reversion, the market rise during 1987 caused a sharper-than-usual fall in expected return. But investors didn't see this at first. They continued to buy, as their portfolio insurance strategies suggested. Eventually, though, they came to understand the effects of portfolio insurance on mean reversion,

---

5 For evidence of mean reversion, see Eugene Fama and Kenneth French, "Permanent and Temporary Components of Stock Prices," *Journal of Political Economy* Vol. 96 No. 2 (April 1988), 246-273; and James Poterba and Lawrence Summers, "Mean Reversion in Stock Prices: Evidence and Implications," *Journal of Financial Economics* Vol. 22 No. 1 (October 1988), 27-60.

partly by observing the large orders that price changes brought into the market.

Around October 19, the full truth of what was happening hit investors. They saw that at existing levels of the market, the expected return was much lower than they had assumed. They sold at those levels. The market fell, and expected return rose, until equilibrium was restored.

MEAN REVERSION AND STOCK VOLATILITY

Now that we've explained mean reversion, how can you use your view of it in your investments?

If you have a good estimate of a stock's volatility, the stock's expected return won't affect option values. Since the expected return won't affect values, neither will mean reversion.

But mean reversion may influence your estimate of the stock's volatility. With mean reversion, day-to-day volatility will be higher than month-to-month volatility, which will be higher than year-to-year volatility. Your volatility estimates for options with several years of life should be generally lower than your volatility estimates for options with several days or several months of life.

If your view of mean reversion is higher than the market's, you can buy short-term options and sell long-term options. If you think mean reversion is lower, you can do the reverse. If you are a buyer of options, you will favor short-term options when you think mean reversion is high, and long-term options when you think it is low. If you are a seller of options, you will favor long-term options when you think mean reversion is high, and short-term options when you think it's low.

These effects will be most striking in stock index options. But they will also show up in individual stock options, through the effects of market moves on individual stocks and through the influence of "trend followers." Trend followers act like portfolio insurers, but they trade individual stocks rather than portfolios. When the stock rises, they buy; and when it falls, they sell. They act as if the past trend in a stock's price is likely to continue.

In individual stocks, as in portfolios, mean reversion should normally make implied volatilities higher for short-term options than for long-term options. (An option's implied volatility is the volatility that makes its Black-Scholes value equal to its price.) If your views differ from the market's, you may have a chance for a profitable trade.

Chapter 23

Applications of Interest Rate Swaps

George C. Eliopoulos
Credit Suisse Financial Products

Strong credit companies have a comparitive advantage over lesser credits in the fixed rate debt markets. Swap structures were devised to exploit this credit arbitrage. A strong credit company with floating funding requirements can issue fixed, and a lesser credit with fixed funding needs can issue floating. Then, they can swap cash flows to achieve better levels of the required funding than they would get going directly to the respective markets.

Today there is no need for an institution to find another counterparty with different funding requirements. In the mature swap market, market makers can intermediate and execute a swap with an institution, without having an offsetting swap at the other end. Swap positions are hedged in the Treasury and futures markets until offsetting swap counterparties are found. Meanwhile, swap uses have expanded widely in all aspects of asset/liability management, as well as in yield enhancement structures and investment strategies.

Asset/Liability Management Tool

Swaps are used widely as a tool to alter portfolio price characteristics and interest rate sensitivity effectively. Modern portfolio theories described in *Section A* use duration and convexity to quantify portfolio exposure to interest rate movements.

Swap price sensitivity is very similar to bond sensitivity. The impact of a swap on portfolio price characteristics is analyzed in *Section B*, where it is demonstrated that swaps, by adding price volatility to a portfolio without altering its size, have a proportionally incremental effect on portfolio duration and convexity.

Swaptions

A swaption gives the buyer the option to enter into a certain swap transaction at a specified future time. This is a new market that has grown rapidly in the last couple of years. The primary use of swaptions is to arbitrage the difference between the premium for a callable loan and the price of a swaption, as discussed in *Section C*.

Other Applications

Three different structures are shown in the *Appendix*. The first strategy is designed to result in gains from a *curve steepening*; it is more applicable for relatively flat yield curve environments when the chances of a curve steepening are increased.

The second application, the *super floater swap*, is designed for institutions expecting low LIBOR volatility. An institution can sell caps to reduce its cost of fixing. If there is not substantial upward rate movement, the cost of fixing is reduced by the premium from the cap sales.

In the last application, the exploitation of the difference in steepness between the corporate yield curve and the swap curve is shown. The swap curve is flatter because the risk exposure in a swap is limited only to fixed-floating rate differentials, while a bond has principal repayment risk in addition to the coupon payment risk. This makes swaps more *efficient liability lengtheners and asset duration shorteners*.

SECTION A
PORTFOLIO MANAGEMENT & IMMUNIZATION

Introduction

Cash-matching and duration-matching are techniques used to immunize a portfolio against interest rate changes. The objective is to finance a liability stream with a specifically-selected asset portfolio. Portfolio managers want to invest an amount of money today to meet the liabilities by withdrawing the scheduled amounts from the asset portfolio at specified dates. The goal is to minimize the cost of the asset portfolio, or maximize its yield.

In cash-matching, the cash-flows of the asset portfolio and the cash-flows of the liability side are matched in timing and size. This is also known as a "dedicated portfolio." While this method is viewed as the safest, it is generally more costly. In duration-matching, the durations of the assets and liabilities are matched. This is far more flexible than cash-matching and often allows investors to obtain lower cost portfolios. There is a greater risk, however, associated with certain types of movements of the yield curve which might result in a lower return compared to the return of a cash-matched portfolio.

Cash-Matching

By this method, the asset portfolio cash-flows equal the liabilities stream in both timing and amount. Portfolio managers have to decide on the eligible securities for use in the portfolio, or the "universe" of securities, stratified by maturity, coupon, credit quality, industry sector and other factors. It may not be possible to match assets and liabilities perfectly in timing. Therefore, the borrowing and lending rates also are major parameters to be considered. In order to minimize the cost of the immunized portfolio, managers should have the greatest possible latitude of selection.

Normally, there is a wide range of coupon bonds of different credit levels and, consequently, different prices. A computerized optimization technique called "linear programming" is used to select the least-cost portfolio that satisfies the constraints. The selection process is often time-consuming because the obtained computer results require modification as recommended types of bonds may not be available or prices may have to be revised. Cash-matched portfolios are the simplest and safest form of immunization. However, cash-matched portfolios have two major disadvantages. First, they normally have higher initial costs and, second, they are more difficult to manage over time.

Higher initial costs result from the fact that the method selects securities according to maturities, rather than investment characteristics. For example, a certain maturity range of bonds may have relatively lower yields due to excess supply and yet, cash-matching may require the investor to select these bonds.

Because changes take place constantly in the bond market, it is desirable to have the flexibility to adjust the portfolio and take advantage of new opportunities such as new issuance, changes in industry attractiveness, special opportunities in individual securities and the maturing of the portfolio itself (so that distant cashflows that were originally at one credit level can be adjusted). Cash-matched portfolios are tightly constructed, which makes them more difficult to capitalize on new opportunities. What usually happens using dedicated portfolios is that the whole portfolio is reanalyzed on a periodic basis, and large blocks of securities are bought or sold to benefit from the cumulative changes in the bond market since the last rebalancing.

Cash-matching, while safer than certain duration-matching techniques, usually creates portfolios which are more costly and more difficult to manage over time.

Duration-Matching

In duration-matching, the cash flows of assets and liabilities are not necessarily matched. Instead, some measure of maturity is matched, usually duration. This allows much greater flexibility in the selection of securities because the constraint is not the maturity of the securities; instead, it is a certain duration target for the whole portfolio, which can be achieved by many combinations of different securities. A lower cost portfolio normally is possible, with a greater flexibility to add value through portfolio management (swaps etc.). This method has a risk associated with certain types of "adverse" yield curve shifts that may cause the portfolio to underperform relative to the return of a cash-matched portfolio.

Duration

Duration (or Macaulay duration) of a security is a measure of the price sensitivity of this security to yield changes. Higher duration indicates higher price sensitivity to yield changes. If all other characteristics are kept constant, longer maturity securities have greater duration and price sensitivity. A higher coupon rate results in lower duration. Figure 1 depicts graphically the concept of duration. A portfolio of a number of securities has a duration equal to the weighted-average of the durations of its securities. This is the indication of the whole portfolio's sensitivity to yield changes.

An Interpretation of Duration

In general, investors face two kinds of risk: (1) price risk, when they are forced to sell a bond prior to maturity, and (2) reinvestment risk, when the bond matures prior to the investor's horizon. In the first case if rates have gone up since purchase, the investor receives a lower price than anticipated. In the second case when the investor is forced to reinvest the proceeds until the horizon, the investor earns a lower return over the remaining years if yields declined over the period he held the bond.

Duration represents the point in time of the life of a bond at which price risk exactly offsets reinvestment risk for a single parallel shift in the yield curve. Consequently if an investor's asset portfolio has a duration equal to the liability time horizon, he is protected (immunized) against a single parallel shift in yields.

Figure 1   The Concept of Duration (Example: 10 Year Bond with 10% Coupon)

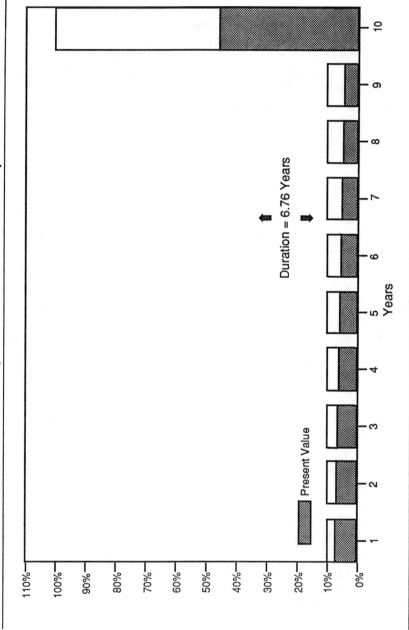

Convexity

Assume two portfolios: Portfolio A, consisting of four-year zero-coupon bonds and Portfolio B, consisting of 50 percent cash and 50 percent eight-year zero-coupon bonds. Both portfolios have the same duration of four years. If yields change immediately after purchase, the impact on the two portfolios is exactly the same even though their durations were initially equal. While the duration of Portfolio A remains constant, the duration of Portfolio B increases when rates decrease and decreases when rates increase—both beneficial effects which put Portfolio B at an advantage over Portfolio A. The cause of this benefit is convexity. Portfolio B is more convex (its price-yield curve is more convex).

To understand this better, assume that rates rise by 1 percent and view this as a two-step process. In the first step, rates rise by 0.5 percent and both portfolios depreciate by the same amount because their initial durations are equal. In the second step with another 0.5 percent rise in rates, the two portfolios behave differently because their durations are no longer the same. While the duration of Portfolio A remains constant, the duration of Portfolio B declines as rates rise (the relative weight of the present value of the eight-year zeros drops below 50 percent of the portfolio value). Therefore, Portfolio B—entering the second step with a shorter duration—declines in value by a lesser amount.

Figure 2 shows two portfolios with different convexities. Convexity is the rate of change of duration as yield changes and is defined as the second derivative of price with respect to yield. More convex portfolios perform relatively better as a result of either a parallel rate increase or decrease. If two bonds have the same risk (or duration), convexity must trade-off with yield in order to realize the same return.

Interest Rate Swaps & The Comparative Advantage Theory

The interest rate swap market has grown impressively; at the end of 1988 the size of the market was estimated at $1.3 trillion of swaps outstanding. Since its inception in the late 1970s, the interest

Figure 2   Convexity

Portfolio A is more convex than portfolio B. Although both portfolios have the same value at current yield levels Y_0, portfolio A outperforms portfolio B if rates move in either direction. A's value appreciates faster when rates decline and depreciates slower when rates rise.

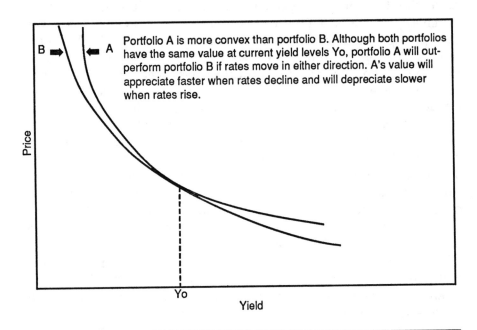

rate swap has grown in popularity among portfolio managers who have found several effective uses for this flexible interest rate risk management product.

Swaps were developed to arbitrage different credit levels. Higher credit institutions can lower the cost of floating rate funding, while lower credit corporations effectively can reduce their fixed rate borrowing cost. Here is how the comparative advantage theory works with different credit level swap counterparties.[1]

---

1   In international trade, this theory explains why more and lesser developed countries have mutual interest in trading with each other.

Assume that an AAA Japanese bank on LIBOR floating funding requirement has five-year fixed rate cost of funds 10 percent and floating rate funding cost LIBOR flat. On the other end, assume that a BBB corporate with 12 percent fixed borrowing cost in five years and LIBOR +3/4 percent floating funding cost has decided to issue five-year debt.

The AAA bank has a significant advantage over the BBB corporate in both the fixed and the floating rate markets. The AAA bank's comparative advantage in the fixed rate market, 2 percent, is substantially stronger than its 0.75 percent advantage in the floating rate market:

		Fixed Rate	Floating Rate
AAA:		10%	LIBOR Flat
BBB:		12%	LIBOR + 3/4%
	Net:	2%	0.75%
	Arbitrage:		2%–0.75% = 1.25%

The bank and the corporate can pick up the 1.25 percent arbitrage and reduce their cost of funds by entering into a swap agreement. The bank can create sub-LIBOR funding and the corporate can reduce its borrowing cost significantly. Here is how the comparative advantage strategy can be implemented.

The AAA bank, which needs floating funds, issues fixed at 10 percent. The corporate, with fixed funding needs, issues floating at LIBOR +3/4 percent. The bank and the corporate enter into a swap agreement exchanging fixed and floating cash flows:

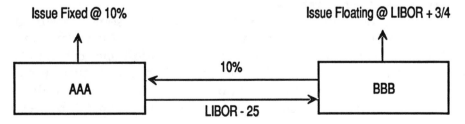

Fixed rate paid to AAA:	10%
– Floating rate received from AAA:	LIBOR – 25bp
+ Floating rate borrowing cost:	LIBOR + 75bp
	11%

With this swap, AAA bank can raise LIBOR–25 floating rate funds instead of LIBOR flat, and the corporate can raise fixed debt effectively at 11 percent, instead of 12 percent.

Current Practice of Portfolio Immunization

Originally, the basic idea of duration-matching was comprised of three steps:

Step 1:   To set the value of assets equal to the present value of the liabilities.

Step 2:   To set the duration of assets equal to the duration of the liabilities to eliminate risk.

Step 3:   To set the convexity of the asset portfolio to be greater than or equal to the convexity of the liabilities.
  The third step is required to guarantee that the value of the assets increases more than the liabilities when rates go down, and decreases less when rates rise. A shift in the yield curve may cause a duration mismatch between assets and liabilities due to a convexity difference. The investor has to actively manage the portfolio and rebalance it after each shock to restore duration equality between assets and liabilities, using either the cash markets or derivatives, like interest rate swaps.
  The most common approach is to maximize some measure of portfolio yield subject to the restriction that the Macaulay durations of assets and liabilities be matched. Additional constraints, such as credit and diversification constraints, are frequently employed. The most common additional constraint, other than duration, is convexity, which requires a convexity mismatch between

Table 1   Duration and Convexity Calculations Table

Discount rate = 10.02% (annualized s.a. yield)

(1) Period	(2) Cash Flows	(3) PVs	(4) CF weights	(1)×(4) Duration	(4)×((1)²+(1)) Convexity
0.50	6.065	5.78	0.05	0.03	0.04
1.00	6.065	5.50	0.05	0.05	0.10
1.50	6.065	5.24	0.05	0.07	0.17
2.00	6.065	4.99	0.04	0.09	0.26
2.50	6.065	4.75	0.04	0.10	0.37
3.00	6.065	4.52	0.04	0.12	0.48
3.50	6.065	4.31	0.04	0.13	0.60
4.00	6.065	4.10	0.04	0.15	0.73
4.50	6.065	3.91	0.03	0.16	0.85
5.00	6.065	3.72	0.03	0.16	0.99
5.50	6.065	3.54	0.03	0.17	1.12
6.00	6.065	3.37	0.03	0.18	1.25
6.50	6.065	3.21	0.03	0.18	1.38
7.00	6.065	3.06	0.03	0.19	1.51
7.50	6.065	2.91	0.03	0.19	1.64
8.00	6.065	2.77	0.02	0.20	1.77
8.50	6.065	2.64	0.02	0.20	1.89
9.00	6.065	2.52	0.02	0.20	2.00
9.50	6.065	2.40	0.02	0.20	2.11
10.00	106.065	39.90	0.35	3.53	38.79
10.50	0	0.00	0.00	0.00	0.00
11.00	0	0.00	0.00	0.00	0.00
11.50	0	0.00	0.00	0.00	0.00
12.00	0	0.00	0.00	0.00	0.00
12.50	0	0.00	0.00	0.00	0.00
13.00	0	0.00	0.00	0.00	0.00
13.50	0	0.00	0.00	0.00	0.00
14.00	0	0.00	0.00	0.00	0.00
14.50	0	0.00	0.00	0.00	0.00
15.00	0	0.00	0.00	0.00	0.00
		113.1365	*Macaulay Duration:*	6.30 years	58.06
			Modified Duration:	5.99	
			Convexity:	0.24	

assets and liabilities with asset convexity exceeding the convexity of the liabilities.

Other types of constraints also are employed, such as a measure of risk due to a twist in the yield curve, or a change in spread between long and short maturities. These risks can be addressed through a multivariable duration analysis using more variables and introducing relative duration measures. In this analysis, variable for curve steepening and also for a twist of the curve are added to the variable for parallel rate movement, which is the only variable employed in a traditional duration method.

The most common yield measure to maximize are the duration-weighted yield and the weighted average yield. Portfolio average yield is the average yield of the securities weighted

Price Change Due To Yield Change Table

$$dP = -(mod.\ DUR) \times Price \times dYa + 1/2 \times CONVEX \times Price \times (dYa)^2$$

dYa = –1.00%
dP = **$70,538.20**

due to Duration:	$67,825.06	95.89% of actual change
due to Convexity:	$ 2,713.14	3.84% of actual change
	$70,538.20	
actual change:	**$70,733.34**	

NEW PRICE = ORIGINAL + PRICE CHANGE

New Price =	$1,201,903.11
Original Price =	$1,131,364.91
Price Change =	$70,538.20
Actual New Price =	$1,202,098.25
Actual Price Change =	$70,733.34
Residual Price Change =	$195.15 0.28%

according to their present values; duration weighted yield is the average yield further weighted according to the duration of each security. The duration weighted yield has been proven superior for certain purposes.

The goal is to achieve the optimal combination of constraints and optimization criteria that lead to the best performing programs. Duration-matching works quite well in practice, even though the yield curve may shift in ways not protected by certain duration and convexity constraints. In general, the duration constraint plus some relative convexity constraint combined with a duration-weighted yield optimization criterion result in a better performing portfolio than a cash-matched portfolio.

SECTION B
SWAP APPLICATIONS IN PORTFOLIO MANAGEMENT

Bond-Swap Combined Volatility

The price volatility of a bond-swap synthetic structure is calculated in this section for 1 percent rate movement. In the following section, duration approach is employed to calculate the combined duration of the bond-swap structure.

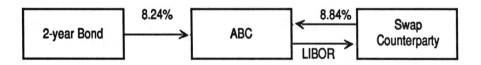

Assume $100 portfolio of two-year bonds that pay an 8.24% semi-annual coupon and are priced at par. The addition of a $100 swap in which the bond-holder receives a fixed rate of 8.84% and pays six-month LIBOR creates the following semi-annual cash flow stream:

Table 2

	Period 1		Period 2		Period 3		Period 4	
Bond	4.12	+	4.12	+	4.12	+	104.12	+
Swap-Fixed	4.42	+	4.42	+	4.42	+	4.42	+
Swap-Floating	-L1/2	-	L2/2	-	L3/2	ꞏ	L4/2	
	8.54-L1/2		8.54-L2/2		8.54-L3/2		108.54-L4/2	

when 4.12 = 8.24/2,   4.42 = 8.84/2

and L1, L2, L3 and L4 are LIBOR levels for the four periods.

Then add and subtract \$100 at the end of period 4:

Table 3

	Period 1		Period 2		Period 3		Period 4	
Bond	4.12	+	4.12	+	4.12	+	104.12	+
Swap-Fixed	4.42	+	4.42	+	4.42	+	4.42+**100**	-
Swap-Floating	-L1/2	-	L2/2	ꞏ	L3/2	-	L4/2-**100**	
	8.54-L1/2		8.54-L2/2		8.54-L3/2		108.54-L4/2	

    The swap fixed cash flows plus \$100 at the end look like the cash flows of a two-year bond; the LIBOR outflows minus \$100 at the end are identical to a floating rate note (FRN).

    An FRN with a six-month LIBOR index has the same price sensitivity as a six-month zero; the rate resets every six months at the prevailing market level and, therefore, the price returns to par every six months.

    To calculate the price sensitivity of the bond-swap structure, calculate the price change of this synthetic asset, as shown in Table 2, for a 1 percent change in rates. To calculate the price change of the first two lines, the bond and the swap-fixed side, discount the relative cash flows at 1 percent lower (or higher) discount rates; for the third line, simply discount a six-month zero at 1 percent lower rate.

$$\text{PV of portfolio: } = \frac{4.12}{(1.0362)^1} + \frac{4.12}{(1.0362)^2} + \frac{4.12}{(1.0362)^3} + \frac{104.12}{(1.0362)^4} +$$

$$+ \frac{4.42}{(1.0392)^1} + \frac{4.42}{(1.0392)^2} + \frac{4.42}{(1.0392)^3} + \frac{104.42}{(1.0392)^4} -$$

$$- \frac{104.3125}{(1+0.038125)^1}$$

$$= 101.81 + 101.80 - 100.48$$

$$= \$103.13$$

$$\text{when } 1.0362 \quad = 1 + \frac{8.24\% - 1\%}{2}$$

$$\text{and } 1.0392 \quad = 1 + \frac{8.84\% - 1\%}{2}$$

$$104.3125 = 100 + \frac{\text{LIBOR}}{2} = 100 + \frac{8.625}{2}, \quad 0.038125 = \frac{8.625\% - 1\%}{2}$$

This shows that the value of the portfolio, with both the bond and the swap, increases by 3.13 percent, from \$100 to \$103.13.

Bond-Swap Combined Duration: Duration Approach

Duration reflects the percentage points of price change for a one percent rate movement and is calculated as the present value-weighted average time to the payment of the cash flows. Therefore, examine whether the duration of the bond-swap structure is 3.13, which is the previously-calculated percentage price change for 1 percent rates movement.

The duration of the swap floating side in Table 2 is 0.5, equal to the duration of a six-month zero, with a modified duration of 0.48:

$$[= 0.5 / \frac{(1 + 0.08625)}{2}]$$

The size of the bond-swap portfolio is $100 (the addition of the swap does not change the market value of the portfolio because it does not involve any cash outlays).

The duration of the bond is:

$$\frac{1}{100} \times \frac{4.12}{(1.0412)^1} \times (0.5) + \frac{1}{100} \times \frac{4.12}{(1.0412)^2} \times (1.0) +$$

$$\frac{1}{100} \times \frac{4.12}{(1.0412)^3} \times (1.5) + \frac{1}{100} \times \frac{104.1}{(1.0412)^4} \times (2.0)$$

$$= 1.88 \text{ years}$$

$$\text{Modified Duration} = \frac{1.88}{1 + 4.12\%} = 1.81$$

The duration of the fixed side of the swap is:

$$\frac{1}{100} \times \frac{4.42}{(1.0442)^1} \times (0.5) + \frac{1}{100} \times \frac{4.42}{(1.0442)^2} \times (1.0) +$$

$$\frac{1}{100} \times \frac{4.42}{(1.0442)^3} \times (1.5) + \frac{1}{100} \times \frac{104}{(1.04442)^4} \times (2.0) +$$

$$= 1.88 \text{ years}$$

$$\text{Modified Duration} = \frac{1.88}{1 + 4.42\%} = 1.80$$

The net modified duration is:

$$
\begin{array}{ll}
1.81 & \text{- Bond} \\
+1.80 & \text{- Fixed side of swap as in Table 3} \\
\underline{-(0.48)} & \text{- Floating side of swap as in Table 3} \\
3.13 &
\end{array}
$$

The duration of a swap is equal to the duration of a bond with the same maturity and coupon (1.80), minus the duration of a FRN with the same resetting frequency (0.48).

Swap Effect Vs. Bond Effect on Portfolio

Adding an 8.84 percent coupon bond at par to the original portfolio, instead of a swap, affects the portfolio duration much differently. The price of the two-bond portfolio changes as follows for 1 percent rates drop:

$$\text{PV of portfolio:} = \frac{4.12}{(1.0362)^1} + \frac{4.12}{(1.0362)^2} + \frac{4.12}{(1.0362)^3} + \frac{104.12}{(1.0362)^4} + $$

$$+ \frac{4.42}{(1.0392)^1} + \frac{4.42}{(1.0392)^2} + \frac{4.42}{(1.0392)^3} + \frac{104.42}{(1.0392)^4}$$

$$= 101.81 + 101.80 = \$203.61$$

The original two-bond portfolio value of $200 increases by $3.61, which is 1.805 percentage points change (1.805 = 3.61/200).

The duration, therefore, of the two-bond portfolio is 1.805, significantly different from the 3.13 duration of the bond-swap portfolio. While durations are quite different, the dollar value changes of the two portfolios for 1 percent rates change are pretty close:

Bond Swap: Price change = $100 × 3.13%   = $3.13
Two Bonds: Price change = $200 × 1.805% = $3.61

	Two Bond Portfolio (size: $200)	Bond-Swap Portfolio (size: $100)
Duration	1.805	3.13
Dollar Exposure (1% rate change)	$3.61	$3.13

Proportionally Incremental Effect of Swaps on Portfolio Duration

When the notional amount of the swap is different from the size of the bond portfolio, the impact of the swap is incremental proportionally to the swap notional amount.

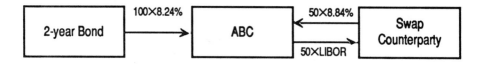

Assume again that a $100 bond portfolio is comprised of two-year bonds at par paying 8.24% on a semi-annual basis. The addition of a $50 swap (instead of $100 previously), where the bondholder the fixed rate of 8.84%, creates the following cash flow stream:

Table 4

	Period 1		Period 2		Period 3		Period 4	
Bond	8.24%×100/2 =+4.12	+	4.12	+	4.12	+	104.12	+
Swap-Fixed	8.84%×50/2 2.21	+	2.21	+	2.21	+	2.21	+
Swap-Floating	L1%×50 -L1/4	-	L2/4	-	L3/4	-	L4/4	

Again, add and subtract $50 at the end of period 4:

Table 5

	Period 1		Period 2		Period 3		Period 4	
Bond	8.24%×100/2 =+4.12	+	4.12	+	4.12	+	4.12	
Swap-Fixed	8.84%×50/2 2.21	+	2.21	+	2.21	+	2.21+50	+
Swap-Floating	L1%×50 -L1/4	-	L2/4	-	L3/4	-	L4/4-50	

A rate decline of 1 percent causes the following present value change of the bond-swap portfolio [as in Table ?].

$$\text{PV of portfolio:} = \frac{4.12}{(1.0362)^1} + \frac{4.12}{(1.0362)^2} + \frac{4.12}{(1.0362)^3} + \frac{104.12}{(1.0362)^4} +$$

$$+ \frac{2.21}{(1.0442)^1} + \frac{2.21}{(1.0442)^2} + \frac{2.21}{(1.0442)^3} + \frac{52.21}{(1.0442)^4} -$$

$$- \frac{52.1563}{(1+0.038125)^1}$$

$$= 101.81 + 50.90 - 50.24$$

$$= \$102.47$$

when $52.1563 = 50 + 50 \times \dfrac{\text{LIBOR}}{2} = 50 + 8.625\% \times 50/2$

This shows that the portfolio value increases by 2.47% from $100 to 102.47

Duration approach: Again, it is shown that the modified duration of the bond-swap structure has to be 2.47. So examine which combination of the bond duration (1.81) and the swap duration (1.80-0.48) gives the calculated combined duration of the bond-swap structure. The answer is:

$$1.81 + 50\% \times (1.80 - 0.48) = 2.47$$

When 50 percent of the swap duration is added to the bond duration, the 50 percent portion is the ratio of the swap notional amount ($50) over the size of the bond portfolio ($100).

Summary

Swaps are a flexible tool in portfolio management for gap reduction and duration shortening; using swaps is a superior strategy to selling long-term assets and investing in shorter maturities. This is because the swap curve is flatter than the bond yield curve; therefore, swaps involve a smaller yield give-up to ride down the curve, and reduce maturities and duration to close the gap.

The duration of a swap is nearly equal to the duration of a comparable bond. The impact of swaps on portfolios can be quantified as follows: the combined duration of a bond-swap portfolio, D_p, is equal to the duration of the bond portfolio, D_b, plus a fraction, k, of the duration of the swap, D_s:

$$Dp = Db + k \times Ds$$

The fraction, k, is the ratio of the swap notional amount divided by the size of the bond portfolio. The factor k is negative when swap fixed cash flows and bond cash flows are opposite in direction; swaps subtract duration and reduce price volatility in this case.

Swaps, therefore, have a porportionally incremental effect on portfolio duration and price volatility. They are a flexible tool in portfolio gap management and in synthetic asset creation to enhance yield.

SECTION C
SWAPTIONS

Monetization of Debt Call Options

Callable debt gives the borrower the right to prepay should rates decline. This strategy to benefit from a rate decline clearly has value. Traditionally this value has been greater than the cost of acquiring it. This strategy shows how borrowers can pick up this arbitrage to reduce their cost of borrowing. It involves the issuance of callable debt and, simultaneously, the sale of a swaption.

Example

An institution with AAA credit rating can issue five-year non-callable debt at a spread of 45 basis points over the five-year Treasury rate. Swapping this fixed rate debt to floating, the institution can create LIBOR-30 funding rate.

Alternative Strategy:

- Issue five-year debt callable in three years. (Issue is called if rates decline in three years; borrower reissues at a lower rate).

- Enter into a five-year swap to create floating rate funding (receive fixed, pay floating).
- Sell the right to terminate the swap in 3 years. (The swap counterparty has the right to terminate the swap should rates decline.)

If rates rise in three years, the borrower, paying below market rate, does not prepay his debt. The swap counterparty, paying a lower than market swap fixed rate in such a scenario, does not exercise its swaption to terminate the swap.

If rates decline in three years, the borrower calls his debt and reissues at the prevailing lower rates. Similarly, the swap counterparty paying a higher fixed swap rate in a declining rate environment, exercises its swaption to terminate the swap.

The additional cost to the borrower for such a callable issue is estimated at 15 basis points, resulting in a borrowing rate of 60 basis points over the Treasury. The borrower, on the other hand, receives a premium from the counterparty from the sale of the swaption. This premium, amortized over the life of the swap, results in an annual income of about 25 basis points. The net result for the borrower is a reduction of the cost of borrowing by 10 basis points. (25 bps income from the swaption, minus 15 bps additional cost for the callable issue.)

Issue Non-Callable Debt

Issue five-year Fixed Non-Callable Debt:

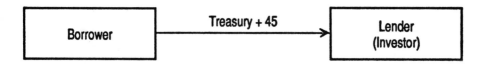

Enter into a five-year swap to create floating rate funding:

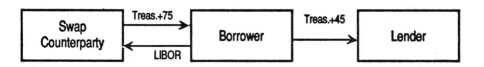

Resulting LIBOR-30 floating rate funding:

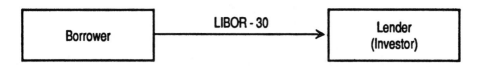

Alternative Strategy: Issue Callable Debt-Sell Swaption

Issue Fixed Debt Callable in 3 years:
(15 bps additional premium: Treas. + 45 + 15 = Treas. + 60)

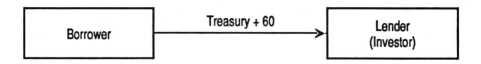

Enter into a five-year swap to create floating rate funding. Sell a swaption to a buyer who has the right to terminate the swap in three years should rates decline.

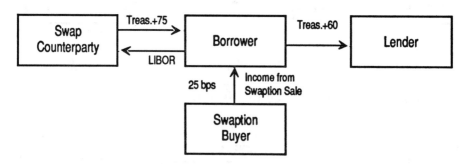

Resulting LIBOR-40 floating rate funding:

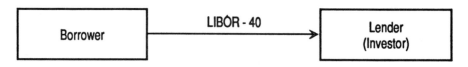

Scenario I:
Rates Rise in 3 Years

The borrower, paying a lower rate, does not call the issue.

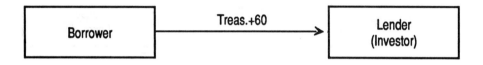

Similarly the swap counterparty, paying a lower rate in the swap, does not exercise its option to terminate the swap.

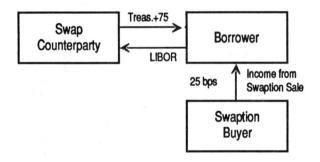

Resulting LIBOR-40 floating rate funding:

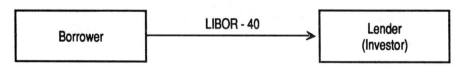

Scenario II:
Rates Decline In 3 Years

The borrower calls the debt and reissues at a lower rate:

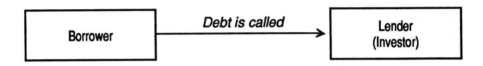

Similarly the swap counterparty, paying the fixed rate in a lower rate environment, exercises its option to terminate the out-of-the-money swap.

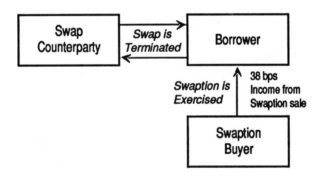

Resulting LIBOR-53* three-year floating rate funding:

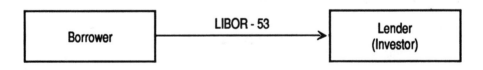

---

*The swaption premium amortized over three years gives an annual income of 38 bps, resulting in LIBOR-53 cost of funding. (Amortized over five years, the swaption premium creates an annual income of 25 bps, as shown on page 549).

APPENDIX
OTHER SWAP APPLICATIONS

Strategies to benefit from:

A. Curve Steepening

B. Low LIBOR Volatility

C. The Flatter Swap Curve

A: Strategy to Benefit from a Curve Steepening

Pay the fixed rate in a long-term swap and receive in the short term on duration-balanced amounts (to immunize against parallel rate movements).

For example, the swap rate curve was relatively flat during the second half of 1989. In that environment the following strategy was developed to exploit this rate environment and yield gains from a curve steepening:

- Pay fixed on $55 million for four years starting one year later (forward swap rate: 9.08%).

- Receive fixed on $100 million for two years starting one year later (forward swap rate: 8.92%).

- Reverse out of both tranches within the next year whenever the curve steepens.

Forward swaps were chosen over straight spot start swaps to avoid the negative carry that results from such a structure because of relatively high short-term rates at the time. The principal amounts of the two swaps were selected to immunize a client against parallel rate movements if the position were unwound in one year.

This strategy results in gains from a steepening of the swap rate curve, which can result from a Treasury yield curve—at the time inverted between two and four years, or from the volatility of the swap spreads—especially the two-year swap spreads, which closely track the volatile Eurodollar futures.

Analysis Under Different Rate Scenarios

Assume the rates as follows:

	Treasury Yield	Swap Spread	All-in Swap Rate	Difference
3 year	8.25	T + 0.72	8.97	
5 year	8.18	T + 0.84	9.02	.05

A four-year swap one year forward, when the client pays the fixed, is structured as (1) a combination of a spot five-year swap in which the client pays the fixed and (2) a one-year swap, in which the client receives the fixed:

Five-year Swap rate (client pays fixed)	9.02%
One-year Swap rate (client receives fixed)	8.81%
	0.19%

The forward swap rate is calculated by amortizing the 0.19% first-year carryover the subsequent four years of the swap (0.057% per annum):

1 × 5 Forward Swap Rate (client pays fixed)
$$9.02 + 0.057 = 9.08\%$$

Similarly, a two-year swap one year forward in which the client receives the fixed rate is structured as a combination of a spot three year swap in which the client receives the fixed, and a one year swap in which the client pays fixed:

Three-year swap rate (client receives fixed)	8.90%
One-year swap rate (client pays fixed)	8.87%
	0.03%

0.03% amortized over two years is 0.017% per annum:

1 × 3 Forward Swap Rate (client receives fixed)
$$8.90 + 0.017 = 8.92\%$$

In the following analysis, spread scenarios are compared between four-year and two-year Treasury rates in a year when the position is designed to be terminated. The structure can be reversed whenever the rate environment is favorable. By duration matching the exposures a year later, the structure is immunized against parallel rate movements if unwound at that point. This one-year time horizon can be modified to match the client's rate outlook.

The average spread between four and two years averages 40 b.p. over the last five years, with a standard deviation of about 15 b.p. In the analysis, today's two-year swap rate (offer side) of 8.94% (8.31 + 0.63) is kept constant, and the four-year rate (bid side) to create the different spread scenarios is changed. Today, the four-year bid swap rate is 8.89% (8.23 + 0.66).

In scenario 1, assume that the four-year bid-two-year offer swap rate differential increases from the current -5 bp (8.89-8.94) to the average of 43 b.p., resulting in a gain of $486,168 when the position is reversed out in a year. Keeping today's swap spreads the same, this means that the four-year-two-year Treasury spread returns to the average 40 b.p. level.

Scenario 2 examines a more favorable development, in which the four-year bid-two-year offer swap rate spread increases to 58 b.p., which creates a gain of $753,792. This corresponds to a four-year-two-year Treasury spread of 55 b.p., one standard deviation above the average.

In scenario 3, assume that the curve is flatter than the average in a year, with a four-year bid-two-year offer swap rate spread of 28 b.p. The corresponding four-year-two-year Treasury spread is 25 b.p., one standard deviation below the average. In this case the gain is $216,904.

The break-even spread between four-year bid and two-year offer swap rates is 16 b.p., which corresponds to a four-year-two-year Treasury spread of 13 b.p., as shown in scenario 4. This means that if the transaction is terminated in a year, a greater spread results in gains, while a narrower spread results in losses. Because this spread is more than two standard deviations from the mean four-year-two-year spread, the historical probability of a loss is about 2 percent; the probability of gains is 98 percent.

The risk inherent in this strategy is a further inversion of the swap rate curve; current swap spreads were used in all spread scenario analyses. The average differential between the four-year bid spread and the two-year offer averaged about 10 b.p. over the last five years, significantly higher than the current 3 b.p. (66 vs. 63 b.p.). The two-year swap spreads (which track quite closely the Eurodollar futures) are far more volatile than the four-five year spreads. A client can unwind the position at any time over the next three-12 months, profiting from a curve steepening that can result solely from the two-year swap spread volatility.

Scenario Analysis

Scenario 1: 4yr-2yr Spread rises to 40 b.p. in a year
2yr Treas. = 8.31%,
  2yr Swap rate = 8.31 + 0.63 = 8.94%
4yr Treas. = 8.71%,
  4yr Swap rate = 8.71 + 0.66 = 9.37%
Position terminated in one year

Customer pays fixed on $100 million 2 year at	8.94%
Customer receives fixed on $55 million 4 year at	9.37%

PV of loss on original 1× 3 year position	($35,900)
PV of gain on original 1× 5 year position	$522,069
Net Gain:	$486,168

Scenario 2: 4yr-2yr Spread rises to 55 b.p. in a year
2yr Treas. = 8.31%, 2yr
  Swap rate = 8.31 + 0.63 = 8.94%
4yr Treas. = 8.86%,
  4yr Swap rate = 8.86 + 0.66 = 9.52%
Position terminated in one year

Customer pays fixed on $100 million 2 year at   8.94%
Customer receives fixed on $55 million 4 year at   9.52%

PV of loss on original 1× 3 year position	($35,900)
PV of gain on original 1× 5 year position	$789,792
Net Gain:	$753,792

Scenario 3:   4yr-2yr Spread is 25 b.p. in a year
               2yr Treas. = 8.31%,
                 2yr Swap rate = 8.31 + 0.63 = 8.94%
               4yr Treas. = 8.56%,
                 4yr Swap rate = 8.56 + 0.66 = 9.22%
               Position terminated in one year

Customer pays fixed on $100 million 2 year at   8.87%
Customer receives fixed on $55 million 4 year at   9.22%

PV of loss on original 1× 3 year position	($35,900)
PV of gain on original 1× 5 year position	$252,804
Net Gain/Loss:	$216,904

Scenario 4:   4yr-2yr Spread is 13 b.p. in a year. (Break-even)
               2yr Treas. = 8.31%,
                 2yr Swap rate = 8.31 + 0.63 = 8.94%
               4yr Treas. = 8.44%,
                 4yr Swap rate = 8.44 + 0.66 = 9.10%
               Position terminated in one year

Customer pays fixed on $100 million 2 year at   8.94%
Customer receives fixed on $55 million 4 year at   9.10%

PV of loss on original 1× 3 year position	($35,900)
PV of gain on original 1× 5 year position	$36,203
Net Gain:	$303

Cumulative Distribution of 4 Year — 2 Year Treasury Spreads

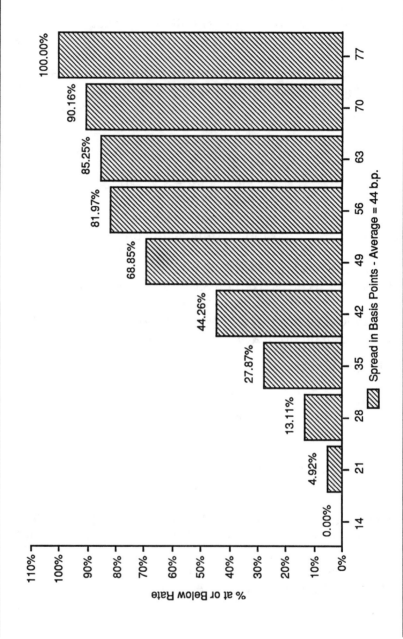

B: Super Floater Swaps

A super floater swap is a standard interest rate swap combined with the sale of interest rate caps, which is designed to reduce the cost of fixing. This structure is suitable for institutions expecting low LIBOR volatility

Example: Assume the five-year swap rate is 9.45% (offer side). In order to fix in a five-year liability, an institution pays 9.45% and receives LIBOR in a standard five-year swap. The net payments for different LIBOR levels are shown on page ?2. In a super floater swap, in addition to the swap, the institution sells two interest rate caps with a strike level of, say, 10 percent. These caps trading at 285 basis points each, allow a reduction in the cost of fixing from 9.45% to 7.98%.

The net payments of a super floater swap are shown on page ? for different LIBOR scenarios. For LIBOR levels below 10.73%, a super floater swap outperforms a standard swap; at higher levels, a standard swap creates greater earnings. If LIBOR rises above 12.02%, the super floater swap results in negative net payments.

Variations of SFS

The strike prices of the two caps may be different. In the previous example, both were at 10 percent. The institution can sell one cap at 10 percent strike (upfront fee = 285 bp) and another at 11 percent strike (upfront fee = 200 bp). This reduces the cost of fixing by 1.25% (versus 1.47% in the previous example), but the super floater swap outperforms a standard swap for LIBOR levels up to 11.125% (versus 10.73% in the previous example). This super floater swap results in negative net payments when LIBOR exceeds 12.80%, versus 12.02% in the previous example. The graph on page ? illustrates this structure, which is designed to elongate the range of LIBOR levels with positive net payments.

Floor purchases can be part of a super floater swap structure. In this case, the cost of fixing still can be reduced because the proceeds from selling the caps exceed the cost of the floors.

Super Floater Swaps vs. Standard Swaps

Super Floater Swaps vs. Standard Swaps

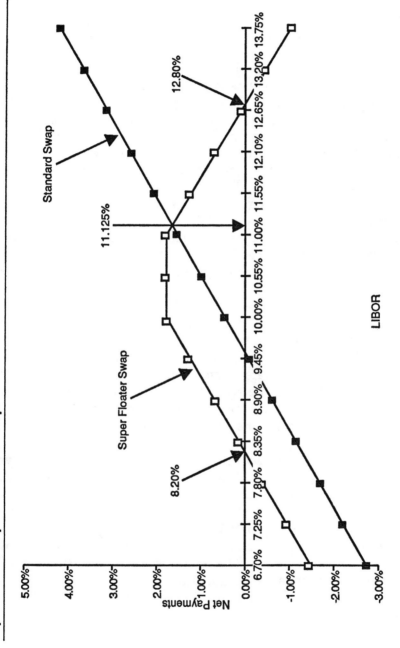

C: Swaps: Efficient Asset Shorteners and Liability Lengtheners

When faced with gap problems, financial institutions sell long-term fixed assets and invest the proceeds in shorter maturity assets to bring down the asset/liability gap. Often, though, portfolio managers prefer to keep these long-term assets in their books for a number of reasons. For example, in years with high income, they prefer not to sell premium assets (and recognize additional gains); in years with losses, they prefer not to sell discount assets and recognize further losses.

An alternative strategy is to use swaps to "defease" long-term assets and bring the gap down. Assume that a portfolio manager feels that he can resolve a gap imbalance by selling 10-year bonds and investing the proceeds in two-year investments. He can achieve the same gap reduction by entering into the following two swaps:

1. A 10-year swap paying fixed to "defease" the 10-year bonds. The swap cash flows are identical to the bond cash flows and opposite in direction. This structure is virtually insensitive to rate movements: if rates rise, for example, the gain from the swap is offset by the loss in the bond's value. The only remaining exposure is the differential between the bond and the swap rate.

2. Add a 2-year swap receiving fixed to convert the 10-year bond's price volatility to a 2-year bond's volatility effectively.

In fact, this strategy of riding down the swap rate curve has a significant advantage over the traditional approach of riding down the bond yield curve: the swap curve is flatter and, therefore, the yield give-up to shorten maturities is smaller. This means that swaps are a more efficient tool for gap reduction and duration shortening.

Swaps: Efficient Duration-Shorteners

Example: Shorten the duration of a 10-year bond to that of a 2-year bond.

Selling 10-year bonds and investing in two-year bonds to shorten duration involves a 37 bp yield give-up, as shown on the following page.* The alternative strategy results in the same duration-shortening effect with only a 28 bp yield give-up to ride down the curve:

1. Pay fixed in 10-Year swap to "defease" the 10-year bonds.

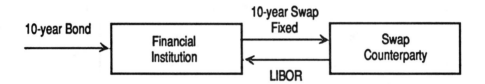

2. Add a two-year swap receiving fixed to effectively convert the 10-year bond's price volatility to a two-year bond's volatility.

The graph on page 562 represents specific market conditions at a certain time. For market conditions with different rate environment, the swap curve will always be flatter than the A corporate bond yield curve. Extending swap maturities entails only net fixed-floating payments risk and there is no principal repayment risk as in the case of bonds. For this reason, it is less likely to extend a swap than to extend the tenor of a bond issue; therefore, the required additional spread is smaller for swap.

Swaps: Efficient Duration-Shorteners

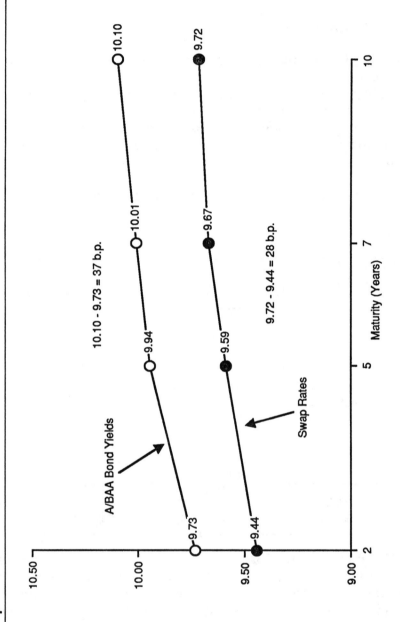

The swap rate curve is flatter than the bond yield curve. Therefore, riding down the swap curve to shorten durations is more efficient than riding down the bond yield curve.

Extending Liabilities

The flatter swap curve makes swaps a more efficient tool to extend liabilities, since it involves a smaller increment in the cost of funds. In the previous graph, using swaps to extend two-year liabilities to ten years would save 9 basis points (37 − 28 = 9 b.p.).

REFERENCES TO SECTION A

John C. Cox, Jonathan E. Ingersoll, Jr. and Stephen A. Ross, "A Theory of the Term Structure of Interest Rates," *Econometrica*, 1985.

Stanley Diller, "Parametric Analysis of Fixed Income Securities," Chapter 4, *Fixed Income Analytics: State-of-the-Art Debt Analysis and Valuation Modeling*, Ravi E. Dattatreya, ed., Probus Publishing Company, 1991.

Kenneth D. Garbade, "Bond Convexity and Its Implications for Immunization," Bankers Trust Company-Money Market Center, March 1985.

Michael Granito, Jane Buchan, David Jacob, Annette Kraus, Daniel Nevins, "Bond Immunization," J.P. Morgan Investment Management Inc., November 1986.

Stephen M. Schaefer, "Immunization and Duration: A Review of Theory, Performance and Applications" London Business School, November 1984.

Chapter 24

Spread Trading in Financial Futures

Eileen Baecher
Goldman, Sachs & Co.

Not all trading decisions are made by answering that fundamentai question, "Is the market going up or down?" In fact, the question many portfolio managers must ask is, "Which securities are the best performers regardless of the market's direction?" For arbitrageurs this question is extended to, "How can positions be held in better performing securities while minimizing market risk?"

In the cash markets, trading yield spreads between securities can be made difficult by delivery requirements, financing costs and accounting restrictions. Particularly for short time horizons, the cost of establishing spread positions may be prohibitive. The futures markets provide an efficient, low-cost environment for trading yield spreads. Following is a description of the techniques used for establishing and monitoring several of the most active futures spread trades.

TRADING PRACTICES

Spread trades take many different forms but all are designed to profit from relative market movements rather than absolute market movements. There are two basic spread trades, *intermarket* and *intramarket*, each with its own objective and accompanying basis risk. Both types require a long position in the market (or security) expected to perform well with a risk-equivalent[1] short position in the underperforming market. Intermarket spreads are designed to profit from changes in the yield spreads of two different types of securities such as corporate bond yields versus Treasury bond yields. Intramarket spreads are structured to profit from changes in yield spreads between securities of the same type but with different maturities or settlement dates. An intramarket Treasury spread might be a long position in 3-month Treasury bills versus a short position in 1-year Treasury bills.

The most active futures spread markets are associated with contracts that combine the following features: one of the contracts has a very liquid market of its own and both contracts trade in close physical proximity to the other. For example on the Chicago Board of Trade, the 30-year Treasury bond contract is the most liquid financial contract, trading an average of 300,000 contracts daily.

Trading is conducted in a ring or "pit" through an open outcry of bids and offers. The bond pit is located adjacent to the pit where 5- and 10-year Treasury notes and the Bond Buyer Municipal Index contracts are traded. Spread traders are able to stand between the two pits, monitoring the price movements of all these contracts and executing orders in each pit virtually simultaneously.

The spreads traded between the bond and note pits are referred to by acronyms such as the "MOB," denoting Municipal over Bond. These intermarket spreads and a few others are described in detail below.

---

1 Equivalent risk positions are defined here as those with the same price exposure to a given yield change. Risk is measured by the position's duration estimate.

THE NOB SPREAD

The Note-over-Bond, or NOB spread, is an intramarket spread between 10-year Treasury notes and 30-year Treasury bonds; specifically, it is the yield spread between the cheapest-to-deliver securities in each of these sectors. The first step in establishing a NOB spread is to identify the expected yield curve movement. To take advantage of a steepening yield curve, the shorter maturity security is purchased and the longer maturity security is simultaneously sold. Conversely if the curve is expected to flatten, the shorter maturity security is sold and the longer maturity security is purchased.

The second step in establishing a NOB spread is to determine the proper weighting or hedge ratio between the note and bond contracts. The objective of the NOB trade is to profit from changes in yield spreads between two term sectors of the treasury market. Therefore, the absolute movement of interest rates is of no concern and should be protected against.

In order to minimize or eliminate the interest rate level risk, the dollar duration of the long and short positions must be equated. Dollar duration is defined as the expected price change of a security for a given change in its yield. If the dollar durations are equal in the long and short positions, any parallel shift in the yield curve creates no gain or loss because the price movements offset. Only if there is a change in the yield curve is there an unequal change in the contracts' prices. Because the bond contract always has a greater duration estimate than the note contract, a weighted NOB requires more note than bond contracts. Appendix I outlines the procedure for determining the positions used in a duration neutral or Weighted NOB.

Unweighted NOB spreads are commonly traded but carry an element of market risk that many traders do not accurately estimate. An unweighted spread uses equal numbers of each contract, for example, long 10-note contracts and short 10-bond contracts. Because the price sensitivities of the contracts to changes in yields are not the same, this spread position has, in fact, the risk of a short bond position.

Figures 1 & 2 illustrate the difference in movement of un-weighted and weighted NOB spreads.

Clearly, the unweighted NOB is much more sensitive to changes in the level of interest rates than is the weighted NOB spread. A weighted spread is not necessarily better than an un-weighted spread, however, the difference in their risk profiles must be acknowledged.

Spread levels generally are quoted as the absolute number of thirty-seconds between the prices of the two contracts. For exam-ple if the note contract is trading at 92 26/32s and the bond con-tract at 90 30/32s, the spread is quoted at "60." The bid and offer are usually 2- to 4/32s apart and a market might be quoted at "59 bid, at 61." The execution of weighted NOB spreads on the ex-change actually is handled in two parts: an unweighted, par-for-par spread, and a limit or market[2] order for the additional note contracts. A buy order is used to buy note contracts and sell bond contracts; a sell order is used to sell notes and buy bonds.

THE MOB SPREAD

The Municipal over Bond, or MOB, spread is an intermarket spread that sets the performance of long-term, tax-exempt bonds against the long-term treasury market. Municipal futures began trading on the Chicago Board of Trade in June 1985 and have de-veloped a consistent, though relatively low level of volume and open interest.[3] Establishing a MOB spread position is similar to establishing the NOB spread; the first step is to identify which market is expected to outperform and then to determine a hedge ratio that removes the exposure to absolute movements in interest rates.

The instrument underlying the minicipal contract is actually an index of 40 long-term municipal revenue and general obligation

---

2 A limit order is an order to buy or sell at a specific price; a market order is an order to buy or sell at whatever price is available at the time the order is given.

3 Open interest is the number of open agreements to exchange the underlying instrument; one long position (buyer) and one short position (seller) combined create one unit of open interest.

Figure 1

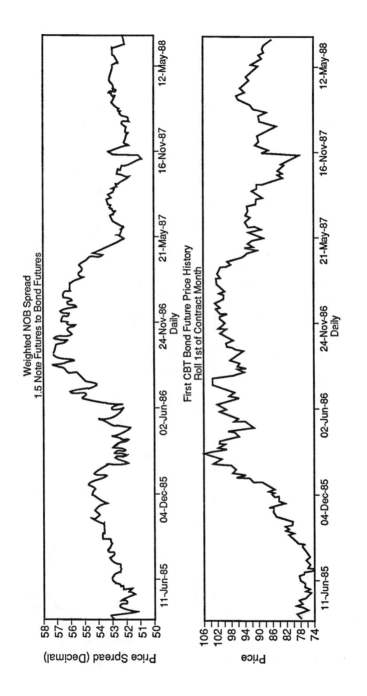

Weighted NOB Spread
1.5 Note Futures to Bond Futures

First CBT Bond Future Price History
Roll 1st of Contract Month

Figure 2

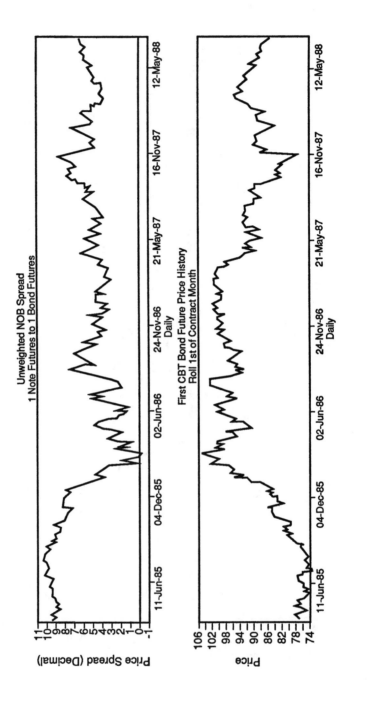

Unweighted NOB Spread
1 Note Futures to 1 Bond Futures

First CBT Bond Future Price History
Roll 1st of Contract Month

bonds. The index is updated biweekly to maintain a current sampling of bonds and the futures price reflects the averaging of the factor adjusted forward prices of these issues.[4] As bonds are replaced in the index, a coefficient is used to eliminate any arbitrary change in the futures price. However, the impact of bond substitution on the dollar duration of the index is not smoothed and this adds a level of complexity to maintaining municipal futures hedge ratios.

Trading municipal futures spreads differs from trading municipal cash spreads in the tax treatment accorded the long position in municipal bonds. Long cash positions receive tax-exempt interest over the holding period. Additionally, the cost of carrying a short treasury position is deductible as interest expense. However, there is no differential tax treatment for the municipal contract vis-a-vis the Treasury contract despite the fact that a portion of a long futures position's change in price over a holding period is an implicit recognition of the value of interest income.

All gains and losses from *nonhedge related* futures trading are designated as 60 percent long-term, 40 percent short-term *capital gains* regardless of the actual holding periods. Additionally, all open positions are marked-to-market at year end, and the unrealized gains or losses netted with gains and losses from positions that were closed during the year.[5] Although the 1986 tax ruling has minimized much of the importance of capital gain distinctions,[6] investors should note the way in which profits are treated, particularly that the tax status of the underlying security is irrelevant when determining futures hedge ratios.

As illustrated in Figure 3, the municipal and Treasury markets have had a volatile yield spread history over the past three years.

---

4 For a complete discussion of the pricing and construction of the Municipal index please refer to "The Municipal Bond Contract" by Eileen Baecher, Goldman Sachs & Co.

5 The 60/40 mark-to-market rules apply to Section 1256 contracts and may be elected out of through a hedging designation that applies when the futures position substantially diminished the risk of holding one or more other positions. More information can be found in FASB 80 and from your tax counsel.

6 The capital distinction is significant to the extent that capital losses can offset only capital gains and not ordinary income.

Figure 3

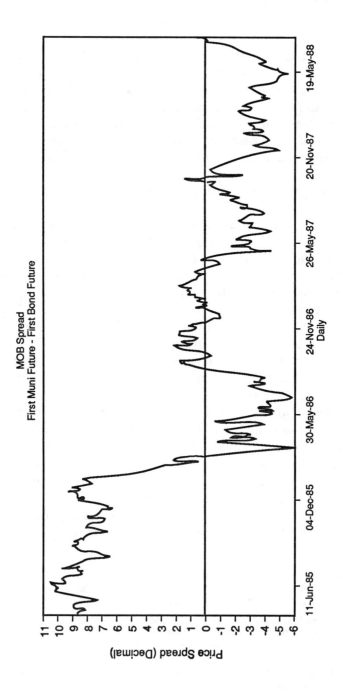

MOB Spread
First Muni Future - First Bond Future

This alone makes the MOB spread interesting to trade, but the additional volatility of the relative value of the municipal contract to its cash index, as illustrated in Figure 4, is an added incentive to trading this spread.

Figure 4 highlights the fact that whenever futures spreads are being considered the value of the contract relative to its index or deliverable issue must be considered. If a spread trade is initiated when a future is either rich or cheap to cash, the price change as it returns to fair value easily can offset any profit from a change in the spread. Alternatively, the divergence from fair value is an opportunity, in itself, for the spread trade to become a vehicle for profiting from the mispricing.

Another consideration when establishing duration weighted spread trades is that duration calculations are not static; they are influenced by yield levels and the characteristics of whichever securities are most likely to be delivered. Hedge ratios must, therefore, be monitored and adjusted in order to maintain a position that is sensitive only to relative yield spreads.

THE TED SPREAD

The Treasury over Eurodollar or TED spread provides an opportunity to trade the rate on 91-day U.S. Treasury bills versus the rate on 3-month LIBOR.[7] These contracts are traded in adjacent pits on the Chicago Mercantile Exchange. The Eurodollar contract is the more liquid of the two, although this was not always the case. When the contracts began trading in the early 1980's, the Treasury bill contract was the more active. At that time the TED spread traded primarily as a credit spread between the "risk-free" rate of U.S. Treasuries and the rates on short-term bank notes. Shocks and nervousness in the banking system caused the spread to widen, often quite dramatically.

As the Eurodollar contract replaced the Treasury bill contract as the most liquid short-term future, its price increasingly reflected

---

7 London Interbank Offering Rate.

Figure 4

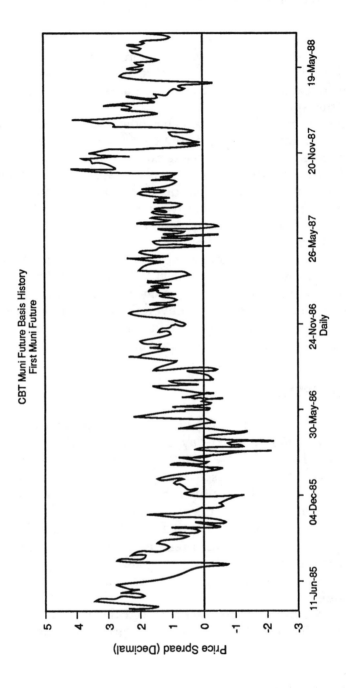

CBT Muni Future Basis History
First Muni Future

the market's perception of short-term rates in general rather than just the credit quality of the banking system. Today, the level of the TED is affected by technical aspects of supply in the T-bill market (because the contract requires the delivery of a specific Treasury bill) and swap market activity—in addition to market sentiment regarding the direction of rates and an occasional flight to the safety of Treasury bills.

The price of both these contracts is determined by subtracting the interest rate from 100. For example, a Treasury bill contract price of 92.25 implies a discount rate of 7.75 percent. The TED is quoted as the price difference, in basis points, of the Treasury bill contract less the Eurodollar contract. If the Treasury contract is trading at 93.25 and the Eurodollar contract at 91.80, the TED is quoted at 145 basis points. A normal bid-offer spread is one or two basis points. Figure 5 illustrates the range of the TED spread over the past two years, based on the prices of the lead contracts at the time.

Unlike the NOB and MOB spreads, the TED is traded using equal numbers of each contract. Both the Treasury Bill and the Eurodollar are three-month investments with one million dollar face values and, consequently, they have comparable price sensitivities to changes in yields. Therefore if Treasury bill rather than LIBOR rates are expected to decrease, an order to buy the TED is entered for a particular amount, i.e., "buy 100 June TEDs at 145." The position becomes long 100 million face value of Treasury bills for delivery in June and short 100 million face value of Eurodollar deposits[8] to be settled in cash, not the delivery of a security, in June as well.

A TED spread that uses contracts of different months, such as a June Treasury contract and a September Eurodollar contract, is called a TANDEM. In addition to trading two different rates, this creates an exposure to changes in each of their yield curves. Tandems are attractive alternatives to TED's if there are significant differences between the shapes of the bill and LIBOR curves or if the

---

8 The Eurodollar contract does not require the delivery of a security. Its final settlement is made in cash at a price level determined by a consensus among dealer banks on the current 3-month LIBOR

Figure 5

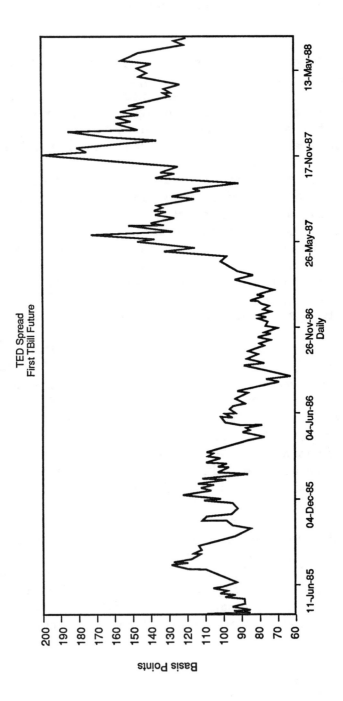

TED Spread
First TBill Future

futures in one contract month are valued differently (versus the cash market) than they are in another contract month.

CONCLUSION

Spread trading is really an art in the increasingly scientific world of fixed-income portfolio management. It allows a manager to separate the systematic risk of fixed-income investments from the returns of relative price performance. The futures markets provide the manager with an efficient, liquid method for executing many types of spreads.

Index